A New History
of the
English Public Library

A NEW HISTORY
OF THE
ENGLISH PUBLIC LIBRARY

Social and Intellectual Contexts,
1850–1914

Alistair Black

Leicester University Press
London and New York

Leicester University Press
A Cassell Imprint
Wellington House, 125 Strand, London WC2R 0BB, England
215 Park Avenue South, New York, NY 10003, USA

First published in 1996

British Library Cataloguing-in-Publication Data
A catalogue record for this book is available from The British Library.

ISBN 0-7185-0015-6

Library of Congress Cataloging-in-Publication Data
Black, Alistair.
    A new history of the English public library: social and intellectual contexts, 1850-1914 / Alistair Black.
        p.   cm.
    Includes bibliographical references and index.
    ISBN 0-7185-0015-6
    1. Public libraries—Social aspects—England—History—19th century.   2. Public libraries—Social aspects—England—History—20th century.   I. Title.
Z791.E5B58   1996
027.442—dc20   95-41411
                                                                                         CIP

Typeset by BookEns Ltd, Royston, Herts
Printed and bound in Great Britain by Redwood Books, Trowbridge, Wiltshire

CONTENTS

ACKNOWLEDGEMENTS

There are a great many institutions I need to thank for helping me to access the evidence of early public library development. Most of these, the great majority public libraries, are noted in the sources. However, I reserve special thanks for the British Library Information Science Service. Also, I am grateful for the 'haven' environments of those libraries where much of the text of this book was written. In this respect I make particular note of the library of Bradford and Ilkley Community College, Ilkley Public Library and the public libraries in Calpe and Morella in Spain.

Regarding individuals it pleases me to acknowledge the following: Dr Pat Thane, Dr Kevin McGarry, Dr Nigel Webber, Dr David Blackbourne, Dr Keith Manley, Dr William Munford, Dr P. J. Corfield, Dr Simon Pepper, Marian Bartlett, Polly Penrose, Michael Dewe, Peter Cadogan, William Ewart, Sylvia Bugg and Gita Lund. With the exception of the first four, the order in which these names appear is not determined – to invoke the philosophical leanings of the discussion – by any teleological assessment of guidance received; rather, it is based on an idealist conception (perhaps the fundamental driving force of the public library also) that the contribution of each has been valuable and cannot be measured in any vulgar utilitarian fashion.

This study began life as a doctoral thesis (my thanks here go, therefore, to the former Polytechnic of North London and to the Economic and Social Research Council for its funding through a competition award). It is thus incumbent on me to list the institutions and individuals that have helped me transform thesis into book. Hence, I express my gratitude to Leeds Metropolitan University, and to Professor Wayne Wiegand, Dr Paul Sturges, Dr Simon Gunn, Peter Hoare, Dave Muddiman, Mike Pearce, Elizabeth Anderson, Thierry Masserot, Chris Murphy and Chris Oxlade. I also very much appreciate the encouragement afforded me by the Library History Group of the Library Association (UK).

*For Teresa, Yolanda
and my parents*

THE 'EPIPHYTE' INSTITUTION

Nearly a century and a half after its inception, the municipal public library remains a common feature on the British urban and cultural landscapes. Its civic presence was also visible by the time of the First World War, which brought to a close the formative period of public library development. However, assertion of the public library's visibility, then and now, requires qualification. For the vast majority, the public library is today viewed superficially, as an uncontroversial cultural institution, without a history, meaning all things to all people and commanding a ready acceptance which verges on the taken-for-granted. Its social neutrality and impartiality are almost mythical, reflecting, as it were – leaving aside for the moment images of stuffy condescension and class superiority – characteristics of moderation, gradualism, reserve, tolerance, fair play, reflective investigation, seriousness, respectability, quaintness, rational leisure, mild eccentricity, and respect for tradition associated with a clichéd British way of life. Yet the true story of the public library, certainly in its early years, does not read so simply. Fictitious narrative, which constitutes the essence of myth, is the defining factor in popular attitudes – generally revolving around an innocuous dissemination of 'sweetness and light' – towards the public library's past development and, indeed, present purpose.

It behoves cultural investigation in search of reality to challenge, wherever possible, accepted cultural 'truths' and myths. In fact, the more 'accepted' an institution or mode of behaviour, the more likely it is to be the product of powerful, dynamic cultural forces (although some, it should be recognized, consider the cultural decoding of any social institution or activity as potentially pretentious and thus obtuse). Obviously, such hidden and complex cultural forces need to be revealed, if only because, by virtue of their clandestine nature, they make for intriguing analysis. More importantly, however, disclosing profound cultural forms is the appropriate method for challenging apparently unchallengeable cultural entities and assumptions – whether that might be, in the British context, a monarchy which is nothing but harmless and benevolent, or the notion that egalitarianism among trade unionists is ubiquitous, or the cliché that Anglo-Saxons are energetic and inventive, while 'Latins' are innately sleepy and inefficient!

To continue this line of analysis, questions might also be asked of the proposition that ostensibly 'innocent' and 'plain' cultural institutions like public libraries evolve essentially, to employ a botanical analogy, like epiphytes – otherwise known as air-plants because they have no attachment to the ground, deriving their nourishment instead, in the case of certain tropical orchids, from atmospheric moisture and from the debris that collects on the plants from which they hang. In the popular mind, public libraries appear similarly rootless or, at the very most, as the visible manifestation of a simple system of anchoring roots. The public library is said, stereotypically, to have no social or political axe to grind. It is regularly awarded the simplistic, tripartite, platitudinous purpose of 'information, education and recreation'. The public library is 'accepted'; it is merely 'there'.

There is, perhaps, one immediate exception to this depiction of cultural neutrality and shallowness, in that the public library sometimes offers a symbolic reminder of society's past intellectual achievements and – to use a modern and contentious word – heritage. This historic, 'retro' image is conveyed not just by the public library's fundamental purpose as a repository of accumulated knowledge, but also by the symbolic coding, in many instances, of its pre-modern architectural style – either inherited or even recently adopted. In many ways, the public library is seen as a 'history' institution, offering as it does a window to the culture and cultures of the past.

The desire of society to look backwards – a noticeable tendency of British culture, at any rate – is multi-motivated. One crucial factor is the reluctance of societies experiencing tension or crisis to look forward, for fear of observing worsening social circumstances. Fear of the future blunts social vision. In this context, the much-publicized discourse of post-modernism should be noted. If postmodernism stands for anything – for its meaning is, to say the least, varied and intricate – it stands for a poverty of social vision. Any authentic social vision (for example, any of the grand 'isms' of the past, whether radical or authoritarian) addresses itself to the social whole. It entails the formulation of over-arching theories of social change: in other words, an ideology (system of ideas) which can be applied to society's disparate problems and conditions. It is the evolution of social ambition, anticipation and – dare it be said in the age of the market – planning, which characterizes the 'modern' condition, and which the pragmatic 'postmodern' condition claims to have made redundant.

The public library before the First World War (even now to an extent, despite the claimed dominance of the postmodern perspective in the cultural sphere) was an intrinsically modern institution. It was but one ingredient in the social vision of Victorian and Edwardian liberalism – this being, at its most basic, the ideology of unbounded social progress, of emancipation and of self-realization. The early public library was an institution with a mission, which, in contrast to late-twentieth-century interventionist and messianic proposals and appeals (like community librarianship and the role of the public library as an agency of the dawning information age), displayed resilience, transmitted a simple message and commanded widespread support across urban communities. The public library, unmistakably, had a social purpose. In an era of unprecedented commercial activity the public library was as eager as any enterprise to distribute its wares. The goods it purveyed were cultural goods, both spiritual-aesthetic and material-practical in fabric. The public library acted as an enabling institution, providing individuals and society with cultural enrichment, for the purpose of civilized development. It was an institution which might have been said to be 'going somewhere'. It was a 'progressive' phenomenon. Its anchorage was that of an earnest, ethical social vision of universal betterment. Such a view not only shames today's poverty of political vision in respect of public libraries; it also turns on its head the belief that late-twentieth-century public library theorists and practitioners have nothing to learn from their distant progenitors. In fact, the realization that the past holds crucial lessons in terms of integrating objectives, of presenting a convincing, cogent purpose and of generally illuminating current models of provision, is something which the 'establishment' of the late-welfare-state public library should continually acknowledge.

But, one hears the counter-claim, what about that conservative aspect of the public library ethos which, from the outset, and in the tradition of social criticism, praised the integrity of past culture and stressed the imperative of warehousing wisdom? Surely this important aspect of purpose negates the notion of the early public library as aggressively visionary? The simple answer is that this perspective too can be embraced by the 'public library as progress' thesis: for there existed in the period under consideration a strong common-sense (essentially modernist) view that development and improvement were only possible if founded, to some degree at least, on the intellectual experience of the past; even if that experience's credibility, in terms of critically investigating custom and superstition, was questionable. The public library promoted the idea of looking forward by, in part, referring back. It exhibited an impulse for reform based on retrospection as well as on pure visionary inspiration and intellectual originality.

The culture of progress which the public library evinced incorporated both material and spiritual concerns. This study aims to integrate these concerns. It seeks to establish a theory of early public library motivation and provision by proposing that those who encouraged free access to knowledge in municipal libraries did so for both practical and aesthetic social ends. Pursued independently, these ends aimed to help stabilize industrial society. But an even greater contribution to social stability could be made, or so public library enthusiasts appeared to believe, from the existence and exploration of a symbiotic relationship between the two. It is imperative to stress, however, that the civilizing project that this symbiotic axis was constructed to pursue is not to be viewed as unproblematically progressive. The modernism and progress in which the public library was saturated were defined by the new market society and the political economy that justified it; they were not premised on the 'liberation' agenda of an emergent working class. The latter's radical social aims, to be delivered ideally through their autonomous educational development, were more feared than shared by public library protagonists seeking a preservation of industrial capitalism.

This study is located in the field of cultural history; not simply because of the public library's status as a cultural institution, but also by virtue of the fact that the discipline of cultural history can (for there are other interpretations) be construed as the manufacturing of a type of 'total' history – based methodologically on the exploitation of the wide range of history fields that nowadays present themselves. To make this claim in the now changed climate of historical research is far from fashionable. Whereas mapping the interlocking forces of history with a view to producing universal explanations of historical development was once attractive, the current trend is, arguably, towards a more eclectic and idiosyncratic, and less deductive, treatment of subjects. While this study is not premised, consciously at any rate, on any grand historical theory, it nevertheless attempts to illuminate the public library's past by addressing fundamental issues in, among other things, intellectual history: specifically, the utilitarian and idealist dimensions of classical liberalism. In the pursuit of a holistic explanation a conscious effort has been made to approach the subject of the public library by drawing on a variety of historical subsets: whether urban, social, political, economic, architectural or intellectual history. It is hoped that the author's interest in these various historical enclaves can be reciprocated by a heightened interest in library history among 'other' historians, to date largely (meaning by no means universally) neglectful of the public library's past – an oversight which becomes even more perplexing in view of the value now ascribed to the serious historical research of familiar, commonplace institutions. By the same token, it is anticipated that the study's broad historical base will speak to library historians who, generally, have thus far been more attracted to the production of well-populated chronologies than to the formulation of theory and to the benefits arising from an inter-disciplinary perspective.

No apologies are offered here for presenting a heavyweight treatment of the subject, especially in terms of providing the deductive *contexts* of broader history, especially *social* and *intellectual*, into which the relatively narrow story of the public library can be inserted. This study is not meant to be a textbook, in the tradition of Thomas Kelly's exhaustive though mostly descriptive *History of Public Libraries in Great Britain 1845–1965* (1973); it is, rather, an interpretation, thereby justifying the word 'new' in the book's title. The approach taken has been conceived, in part, as a rebuff to the relatively narrow 'new vocationalist' slant of much research and education in the library and information studies field, and elsewhere. In accordance with the need to broaden the canvas of library history, the discussion which follows is extensively referenced. The public library has never been a self-contained institution. As argued above, its numerous cultural roots spread far and wide. The complexity of these roots is reflected in notes which feed into the discussion from a variety of directions, and which, on occasion, serve as signposts to further deliberation in subject areas impinging on the public library's development. It is hoped that the variety of sources and perspectives employed has not undermined the formulation of a cohesive explanation of the early public library's ethos. The intention has been to weave a common thread – namely, that of utilitarian–idealist tension – through each chapter. However, this is not to say that most chapters cannot be read as separate essays in their own right.

A word at this point about scope and sources. The book's focus is the *English* public library. There are two reasons for limiting the study in this regard. First, the backdrop is essentially English culture, which can surely – although this is not the place – be defined differently from the culture of the Irish, Welsh or Scots (witness, for example, the divergent educational and legal tradition of Scotland). Second, the logistics and restrictions of the field research which underpins the study dictated that the source-base be kept at a manageable level. This meant that mainly English repositories, yielding, naturally, mostly English evidence, were consulted. This is not to say that no evidence outside the English experience has been considered. It would make little sense, for example, to focus solely on English as opposed to British economic decline as a contextual input to the public library's evolution: for it is in national, generic terms that economic malaise is primarily discussed. Nor would it have made sense to have dismissed, say, the pioneering work in children's librarianship undertaken by John Ballinger in South Wales; or to have ignored the irrepressible fact that the other great public library narrative of the nineteenth century, which occurred in the United States, has much to offer the historian of the English scene, not least in terms of the occasional transfer of pathfinding techniques and ethos from the American experience.

The deductive base – containing a discussion of culture, the issue of social stability and library history methodology – on to which sources are fitted is explained in Chapter 1. The communication of theoretical stances is enhanced when the reader knows something of the raw data used as the basis of theory formulation. Consequently, Chapter 1 also contains various factual details of public library development. Public libraries did not materialize overnight: thus, the record of 'spade-work' initiatives is set out in Chapter 2, along with a detailed (owing to its neglect by most library historians) discussion of the crucial contextual area of class; for despite the recent decline in interest in social class as an essentialist explanation of nineteenth-century social development it remains a vitally important lens through which modern history can be viewed, and was certainly to the fore in the public library debate throughout the period under consideration. A key element in this study is the direct relevance of intellectual thought to the public library's evolution. Chapter 3 essentially addresses a perennial question: 'Do esoteric philosophies precipitate social change or merely follow and reflect on it?' In linking utilitarianism with the promotion of public libraries 'on the ground', a case is made for the practical relevance and determinism (of social forms) of intellectualism, accepting that abstract reflection endures as a feature of philosophical thought. The material pertinence of philosophy is further exposed in Chapter 4, where the utilitarianism of the twin founders of the public library, William Ewart and Edward Edwards, is explained. These pioneers, dismayed by society's persistent instability, were at once men of culture and supportive of scientific materialism. This symbiosis is discernible in the parliamentary investigation leading to the first public library legislation in 1850, especially in the investigation's concern for the material advantages of culture through art education, a discussion of which forms the core of Chapter 5. An extensive analysis of material concerns follows in Chapter 6, where strong emphasis is placed – as has not been the case previously – on the public library's role as an engine of economic advance and an agency of dominant economic thought. A return to the philosophical theme is made in Chapter 7. Idealism is assessed as a possible successor to utilitarianism as the intellectual flywheel of development in the half-century before the First World War. This discussion paves the way for an investigation in Chapter 8 of cultural and aesthetic concerns, including themes of social control and negotiation, and the emergence of middle-class consciousness through cultural advance. The study's enquiry into the utilitarian–idealist, material–aesthetic dichotomy continues in the final two chapters. It is argued that the library profession (Chapter 9) and library architecture (Chapter 10) are similarly defined by tensions between liberal and scientific education, in the case of librarians, and between a desire for cultural recognition and a demand for function, in the case of the built-form.

CHAPTER 1

IN SEARCH OF AN ANALYTICAL MODEL

Given that library history, rather than being founded on abstract knowledge, is by definition a subject that deals with the activities of an institution, it is imperative that theoretical models be formulated to help analyse and interpret past library provision. Municipal public libraries originated and developed in the period from about 1850 to 1914 as a means of helping to secure social stability. They were intended by their promoters to help spread 'civilization', as defined by the *Oxford English Dictionary* (1893) in the sense of making 'civil', of having 'proper public or social order', of ensuring a 'well-ordered, orderly, well-governed society ... to bring out of a state of barbarism, to instruct in the arts of life, and thus elevate in the scale of humanity; to enlighten, refine and polish'.[1] In the first half of the nineteenth century the word which most closely matched the meaning conveyed by 'civilization' was 'civility'. After about 1850, however, the word 'culture' gradually replaced, in academic parlance, the use of 'civility' as a synonym for what was considered to be a civilized existence;[2] although by the twentieth century, if not earlier, an important body of social criticism had established a doubt over the interchageability of the words 'culture' and 'civilization', in that modern, complex, industrial society might be considered to have attained a sophisticated level of civilization without necessarily displaying a sensitivity for culture.

Defining culture

A chief concern of power-holders and reformers in the nineteenth century was the improvement of society's precepts. Standards of moral conduct would be improved, it was hoped, through cultural elevation. The word culture is first employed here in its humanistic sense of the 'art of improvement and melioration', as Dr Johnson defined it.[3] In this sense, culture possesses connotations of urbanity and respectability concomitant with a civilized life, and alien to so-called primitive society. This view of culture as civilized living – the 'culture and civilization' tradition – has sought to idealize the 'organic' culture (characterized by 'élitist', 'communal' and 'folk' social dimensions) of the pre-industrial age. The 'culture and civilization' tradition has been consistent in its condemnation of both the demise of pre-industrial social forms and the 'deficient' popular or mass culture that replaced them.[4]

In the nineteenth century, the most strident exponent of the thesis of cultural degeneration was Matthew Arnold, whose *Culture and Anarchy* (1869) warned that, aesthetically, the culture of democracy was becoming increasingly impotent. Arnold's panacea for this malaise was the resurrection of society's hunger for culture, which he defined in a much-cited statement as:

> a pursuit of our total perfection by means of getting to know, on all matters which most concern us, the best which has been thought or said in the world; and through this knowledge, turning a stream of fresh and free thought upon our stock notions and habits.[5]

It is widely accepted, however, that Arnold's phrase 'the best which has been thought or said in the world' was derived from a narrow and lofty view of culture: in effect, the protection and reinforcement of élite, 'high', minority-taste cultural pursuits, which the popular use of the word 'culture' would explain as sophisticated literature, art, music (above all, perhaps, in the nineteenth century) and learning generally – pursuits synonymous, moreover, with high social position.

Arnold saw 'high' culture as the antidote to the blinkered existence which industrialism engendered. His opinion of the new industrial world was that it had, as one historian has put it:

> no sense of contact, no sense of direction, little in fact, but the worship of Mammon and machinery supported by a faith in 'doing-as-one-likes' and a complacent belief in material progress.[6]

Mass society, said Arnold, produced chaos in terms of social order and mediocrity in both intellectual and material production. In the twentieth century, with the continuing massification of society – as seen in the explosion of cheap (mostly paperback) novels, mass circulation magazines, the popular press, cinema, radio, popular music and television (the arch-enemy) – the 'culture–civilization' baton has been taken up, among others sensing the death of cultural integrity, by the literary critic F. R. Leavis and the cultural theorists Richard Hoggart and (to an extent) Raymond Williams.

In the context of explaining that 'the English people did once have a culture' but had lost 'the organic community with the living culture it embodied', Leavis in 1933 denigrated mass society, which mostly entailed:

> the competing exploitation of the cheapest emotional responses; films, newspapers, publicity in all its forms, commercially-catered fiction – all offer satisfaction at the basest level, and inculcate the choosing of the most immediate pleasures, got with the least effort.[7]

Williams, in 1961, wrote of the:

indignation and despair at the cultural condition of the mas᠁es ... Our cultural institutions are in the hands of speculators, interested not in the health and growth of society, but in the quick profit that can be made by exploiting experience.[8]

In similar vein, in 1958, Hoggart attacked the influences of mass society which invited people to live lives which were 'restless and shallow', and commented on:

> the danger of reducing the larger part of the population to a condition of obediently receptive passivity, their eyes glued to television sets, pin-ups, and cinema screens.[9]

Such tirades against the march of the machine and its cultural fall-out have led some to perceive a divorce between culture and civilization; that the two have become, as F. R. Leavis asserted in *Mass Civilization and Minority Culture* (1930), 'antithetical terms', whereas once they were seen as synonymous. Current British public library theorists and practitioners will recognize immediately the intersection of the 'declining standards' intellectual tradition with the stereotypical exclusive, stuffy image of public library service. Indeed, the origin of the public library cannot be understood without reference to the notion of 'culture as civilization' and to the driving force behind that notion, namely the continuing adulteration of culture and a so-called civilized existence. Historically, public libraries have often been viewed as defences against a rising tide of vulgarity. In the last quarter of the twentieth century, however, it appears to some that the institution itself is in danger of being swamped by the coarseness of commercial, marketing and populist ethics. It is thus no coincidence that, in addition to other cultural practices, Hoggart has chosen to comment on the state of public library provision, and to do so in the same context of cultural decline.[10]

Throughout its history the public library has served as an arena where intense cultural battles have been fought out (this accords with the Marxist interpretation of culture as conflict, as opposed to the functionalist analysis of culture as an instrument of consensus and harmony). It is, therefore, to the advantage of those seeking to construct theories concerning the institution's social role that, in keeping with the chameleon-like nature of the concept of culture,[11] not one, but several, meanings of the concept have been explored. Clearly, it is neither useful nor imaginative to conceptualize culture solely in terms of Arnoldian 'sweetness and light', as the image of the public library is often perceived. A second meaning of culture, one which is also relevant to the evolution of the public library, is the anthropological view of it as a 'whole way of life'; this being one of Raymond William's four definitions of culture given at the beginning of his seminal *Culture and Society 1780–1950* (1958).[12] According to this definition culture includes everything created by humankind in society: everything 'human-made' to include attitudes, values, beliefs, ideologies and behaviour patterns, as well as physical artefacts and structures; and the skills required to make these, including communication skills. As T. S. Eliot wrote in 1948, culture is:

> all the characteristic activities and interests of people ... Derby day, Henley Regatta, Cowes, the twelfth of August, a cup final, the dog races, the pin table, the dartboard, Wensleydale cheese, boiled cabbage cut into sections, beetroot in vinegar, nineteenth century Gothic churches, and the music of Elgar.[13]

At first glance, this pluralistic, 'collective' conceptualization of culture differs markedly from the cerebral, narrow and élitist 'culture–civilization' perspective outlined above. Yet, in respect of nineteenth-century English industrial society, the two are closer than a cursory inspection would suggest. Social critics (Arnold, Carlyle, Ruskin and Morris among them), uneasy with the changing and fractured society which industrialism had created, set out to rediscover the sense of organic community which science and material progress had diminished.[14] The organic view of society prescribed that social and political institutions evolved best as a result of a gradual accumulation of practice, custom and tradition: in other words, the piecemeal construction of a structure of rules and precedents, whether in the field of law, political institutions or social relations.[15] The chief means of restoring society's organic harmony, social critics argued, was to invoke the efficacy of past institutions, social organization and norms of behaviour.

The point to stress here, with a view to synthesizing the two notions of culture discussed thus far, is that humanistic culture – the quest for civilizing improvement – was akin to the suggested resurrection of a 'surrendered' way of life or 'lost' culture. This overlapping of perceptions of culture occurred by virtue of the fact that 'higher' cultural pursuits, in the Arnoldian sense, were in essence the product of past endeavour; tapping, as it were, into the stock of human knowledge created by a process of historical growth. In the context of nineteenth-century social criticism, it was thus possible for the culture of perfection and the culture of organic community to coalesce.

The public library served as a site for the mixing of these cultural imperatives. It spoke the language of improvement and excellence, while at the same time proclaiming its status as a 'heritage' institution preserving the knowledge which was both the basis of society's proclaimed élitism (in the sense of the pursuit of humanistic excellence) and the symbol of a glorious past culture. It is directly relevant, indeed, to traditional perspectives of British public library service that in 1992 government responsibility for the institution passed to a newly formed Ministry of Heritage.

But the early public library stood for more than a mere combination of 'sweetness and light' and organic views of culture. The exploration of culture, which, in the author's opinion has come closest to combining the anthropological and 'culture as civilization' positions – but in doing so goes beyond the narrow Arnoldian preoccupation with élitist activities in the direction of a scientific and investigatory view of learning and social affairs – is that stated by the early anthropologist E. B. Tylor in his *Primitive Culture*

(1871). Tylor's thesis was proximate to the nineteenth-century German perception of culture: the essence of *Kultur* being excellence and outstanding human achievement.[16] It argued that modern industrial society was accelerating away from a primitive existence towards a highly civilized arrangement of its affairs. This was manifest in the persistent refinement of ideas and modes of behaviour.

Tylor asserted that:

> Culture or civilization, taken in its wide ethnographic sense, is that complex whole which includes knowledge, belief, art, morals, law, custom, and any other capabilities and habits acquired by man as a member of society.[17]

Tylor added a qualitative dimension by explaining that 'the phenomenon of culture may be classified and arranged, stage by stage, in a probable order of evolution'.[18] Tylor believed that culture, far from being relative, could be graded against an absolute measurement of civilization. 'The principal criteria of classification', he declared:

> are the absence or presence, high or low development, of the industrial arts, especially metal-working, manufacture of implements and vessels, agriculture, architecture, etc., the extent of scientific knowledge, the definiteness of moral principles, the condition of religious belief and ceremony, the degree of social and political organization, and so forth.[19]

In accordance with this formula he asserted (in a way which mirrored, incidentally, the hierarchial class structure of the day) that:

> Few would dispute that the following races are arranged rightly in order of culture: Australian, Tahitian, Aztec, Chinese, Italian.[20]

This scale of civilization, he believed, represented 'the extremes of savage and cultured life'.[21]

Tylor's view of culture was closely tied to the Enlightenment idea of civilization as 'development'.[22] Culture was something to be achieved in varying degrees (and that which was achieved could also, of course, be lost or 'degraded').[23] By the second half of the nineteenth century this was no revolutionary concept. The idea of improvement permeated Victorian society. For example, the *New Oxford English Dictionary* (1893) stated that culture was: 'The cultivation or development (of mind, faculties, manners, etc.); improvement or refinement by education and training'. However, the key element to extract from Tylor's observations is his insistence that the pursuit of material prosperity, and the means of achieving material objectives – including the 'industrial arts' and 'scientific knowledge' – contributed significantly to what he termed culture. Tylor argued that culture incorporated excellence and progress in scientific materialism and, indeed, the social and political organization required to deliver it. This was an interpretation of culture which fused Arnoldian perfectionism (shorn of its emphasis on 'high' culture) and the 'whole way of life', anthropological perspective.[24] Such a view echoed the contemporary opinion that society's progress was surely based on material as well as moral development.

The civilized society which, by the time public libraries began to be discussed, the Victorians were used to celebrating was, in part, the product of progressive, scientific investigation (including, of course, the natural sciences but also discovery and deliberation in politics, social science, moral philosophy and economics). 'Civilization' was not simply the result of assimilating past precedent and practice. Champions of science argued that their intellectual domain was not just practical but should become part of general education; part, indeed, of the humane, liberal culture which had paved the way to the civilized society. To some a plague, the pursuit of scientific materialism was to others a blessing in terms of both its intellectual rigour and its value to the material prosperity which promised to reduce work and increase the opportunities for aesthetic culture and learning. Here again, the public library can be seen to have met the diverse cultural criteria demanded of it. The public library offered, in the context of excellence, the means of pursuing empirical discovery alongside traditional learning and the assimilation of past wisdom. Its reputation as an institution of culture was based to a considerable degree on its image as a storehouse of wisdom (past culture) *and* as a reforming, scientific, questioning mechanism (culture as progress or improvement).

To summarize the discussion thus far, the idea of 'culture as civilization', as discussed by nineteenth-century conservative social theorists, encapsulated the proposition that mass society required persistent readjustment in order to bring it closer to an organic, traditional culture characterized by social harmony and by improvement in exemplary 'higher' intellectual and leisure pursuits. This view of culture, by virtue of its retrospective assessment of the social processes and organization which had produced 'excellence', not least in terms of organic harmony, incorporated the notion of culture as 'a whole way of life'. Those sympathetic to progress through science and investigation rejected both the self-proclaimed superiority of 'high' culture and its reliance on organic growth as the major source of knowledge, but did not disassociate themselves from that aspect of the 'culture as civilization' thesis which acclaimed the doctrine of improvement and perfectionism. In this respect, the Tylorian, Whiggish version of culture – that which facilitates progression from a primitive to a civilized society in all its aspects, including activities of 'sweetness and light' – offers a workable theory for understanding the motives of those who promoted the Victorian and Edwardian public library. Tylor's 'culture as progress' assessment satisfies at once both the organic and the progressive perception of a cultured existence. In accommodating the full range of interpretations of culture, from the spiritual-idealist to the practical-utilitarian, the public library endorsed in the widest sense the 'retreat from barbarism' – which should be acknowledged as the core element of that definition of civilization given above at the outset. In short, aesthetic-innate and experience-worldly interpretations of the source of knowledge were coterminous in the context of the early public library's social agenda. They were also coterminous in respect of the stable society each interpretation sought, the one through the universal dissemination of culture, the other through the universal acceptance of materialism; social stability being an objective, crucially, of the public library also.

Social stability

According to the definition given at the start of this chapter a fully civilized society was one which had achieved stability: that is to say, having 'proper public or social order ... well ordered, orderly, well-governed'. Social stability has not been a constant feature of English society. However, this is not to say that efforts to manufacture an ordered society have not been strenuous. In the period under consideration stability was pursued in two ways – one moral, the other economic. Moralizing the masses was by no means the only guarantor of a civilized society. Historically, social stability has been tightly intertwined with economic equilibrium. As one historian has written:

> there is a sense in which the ruling classes in all European countries over the last three hundred years have assumed 'No wealth, no stability; no stability, no wealth' as a motto to justify and explain their direction of affairs.[25]

Charles Babbage wrote in 1835 that 'it is only in countries which have attained a high degree of civilization ... that the most perfect system of the division of labour is to be observed.'[26] Clearly, contemporary opinion viewed a stable, civilized society and economic advance as inextricably linked.

The idea that anarchy is only three square meals away might be a cliché, but it is a message which authority has in the past well understood. In pre-industrial society sharp price rises had often led to riots calling for the restoration of normal levels in accordance with Tudor law; it was not uncommon for magistrates to intervene in the market to stabilize prices and reduce social tension.[27] It has been pointed out that on numerous occasions in the eighteenth century popular disturbance coincided with a poor harvest.[28] This awareness of the relationship between prosperity and stability continued into the industrial era. It has been argued that stability in the nineteenth century rested on two pillars: 'the Constitution and the ability of the economy to produce a satisfactory standard of living'.[29] The political economist Samuel Fothergill wrote that:

> Food, clothing, and shelter are the first condition of man's being ... the cravings of hunger are so powerful and all absorbing that, when long continued or frequently occurring, they destroy all sense of responsibility, and all fellow-feeling, except in rarely balanced and highly virtuous minds, and give rise to crimes of violence against person and property which, in proportion as they prevail, demoralise the perpetrators and all whose similar suffering leads them to sympathise with all acts of lawlessness. At the same time the community is further impoverished, and that confidence is destroyed which is an essential requisite for the free and beneficial exercise of productive industry. Hunger and revolution are in very intimate relationship.[30]

It is debatable whether economically motivated social unrest is produced by 'absolute' or 'relative' deprivation.[31] Certainly, once society began to 'move' in the late eighteenth century the heightening expectation of both reform and better conditions made for a 'less stable social world'.[32] But with regard to the nineteenth century, economic deprivation *per se* has been seen as conducive to the formation of social protest movements, including trade unionism and political militancy.[33] Deprivation was closely linked to the violent trade fluctuations which characterized early industrialism. Initiatives which promised to reduce trade fluctuations and deliver economic stability, and which did not breach the prevailing faith in *laissez-faire*, were thus warmly welcomed. To quote Fothergill again:

> Whatever tends to facilitate and cheapen production is a direct gain to society, and whatever renders production more costly and more difficult is correspondingly injurious.[34]

The public library was one such 'material' initiative. It aimed to supply, as far as was in its power, economic prosperity. Thus, in 1890, in West Ham, a public library was proposed:

> Because there is no rate from which there is so *immediate and tangible benefit* [italics added] as out of the penny rate for support of a free library.[35]

There is indeed a case for arguing that libraries are essential 'instrumentalities' of an economy and that 'a well-developed prosperous economy rests upon a sophisticated record-keeping system'.[36] Those who promoted public libraries in West Ham and elsewhere sensed this. But it should be stressed that a library in West Ham was also proposed:

> Because they are educational institutions, and education deepens the sense of the *duties and privileges of citizenship* [italics added].[37]

Municipal libraries thus accommodated both aesthetic-spiritual and materialist-practical concerns. They aimed to facilitate national and individual economic advance, while the literary knowledge they dispensed emphasized the importance of humanistic culture, which was but the result of human progress through epochs supposedly organic in their culture and harmonious in their nature. Public libraries stood for *well-being*, in terms of their economic dimension. They also encouraged *well-doing*, in the sense of pursuing cultural perfection within a communal, societal context.

That the public library combined aesthetic-spiritual and material-practical aspirations bestows upon the institution a degree of dynamism which is worthy. Since the inception of urbanized, industrial society a tension has been evident, no more so than in the nineteenth century, between humanistic culture and materialism; between aesthetic appreciation and scientific progress; between nativist and empirical assessments of the source of knowledge; between the vocational and the liberal curriculum; between the tranquil country and the turbulent city.[38] It is to the credit of the early public library that it negotiated these tensions and, for the most part, represented both spiritual and material impulses.

A major means by which culture as 'improvement' or 'progress' (both material and spiritual) was pursued in the nineteenth century was education – this being the public library's main province. This study argues that material and spiritual culture, sought through the public library as an educational force, each aimed to deliver social stability. The means (education) and the aim (social stability) were thus shared by the divergent notions (material and spiritual) of culture described. Moreover, education (a means to culture) possessed, like culture itself, a social stability dynamic. The social pacification, which both practical and moralizing education could provide, was explained by the Glasgow weekly, *The Commonwealth*, in its first issue in 1853:

> The laws of life, of health, of economy, of self respect; the development of the nobler faculties and instincts of human nature – these, in their clear appreciation and power, can never come but through the medium of cultivated minds bearing educationally on the minds of others ... [Education] growingly takes its place as of the highest and momentous import in regard to the permanence of our liberties and the safety and stability of our institutions.[39]

The sharing by material and spiritual culture of the pursuit of stability through education and training cannot hide the deep rift which exists between idealist (or rationalist) and utilitarian (or empiricist) perceptions of human existence. The utilitarian-empiricist position asserts the priority of being, of existence, of matter, of environment, of observation, of sense-based experience over the idealist-rationalist emphasis on spirit, on inward thought, on mind and on pure reason as a source of knowledge. On the surface there would appear to be no synthesis possible between these divergent utilitarian and idealist conceptions of the world.[40] But the history of the public library shows that such a negative relationship is perhaps an oversimplification. It is not simply that to view utilitarianism as wholly arid and devoid of humanistic culture and aesthetic sensitivity is dangerous[41] – the evidence on Ewart and Edwards presented in this study can hopefully quash that stereotype. More to the point, was it surely not the case that in the Victorian and Edwardian eras the striving for cultural uplift (improvement and excellence in all social activity, but especially in terms of the evocation of high moral standards and a cohesive, civilized society) provided a rationale for industrial capitalism? The pursuit of humanistic culture was justified to a large extent by its value, albeit non-quantifiable, as an investment for the material advance from which social stability would, it was hoped, flow. Humanistic culture and materialism enjoyed a symbiotic relationship: humanistic culture provide economic benefits *external* to it.

The history of the public library is explored in this study by way of testing the evidence of the institution's past against a model of pre-1914 utilitarian–idealist symbiosis. (Without a model, research runs the risk of floundering in a mass of individual observations which command no apparent link. Testing evidence against a model facilitates linkage of data, and renders data more relevant; thereby allowing the model's validity to be assessed.[42]) It is a model – a theoretical framework – into which the early history, if not the current practice, of the public library fits extremely well. The institution's conception and early life were utilitarian inspired; later development became mostly an idealist responsibility. Yet elements of the two philosophical stances coalesced in the public library context throughout the period. For example, utilitarians and idealists supported the establishment of public libraries out of respect for their social harmonizing effect: idealists in search of a communal, organic past; utilitarians peering into a future of unbounded progress shared by all. Further, both utilitarian and idealist motivation focused on the public library's material role, as is evident in the institution's persistent concern to produce, in the context of the quest for social stability, better educated, more efficient workers; a confident, enterprising middle class; and individual and national economic success.

Library history

The approach to library history adopted in this study diverges from the characteristic methodology of past research and writing in the field. Not only is a non-library theoretical model employed, the methodology is located outside library history. While a great deal of the evidence presented here relates specifically to the public library, this evidence is discussed in the *context* of recent theoretical debates in historical fields which impinge upon the institution's experience. This *deductive* approach involves discussions on economic decline, class conflict, technical education, cultural 'failure', social control, the social foundations of architecture and, most importantly, philosophical thought – matters which are of direct relevance to the formulation of a theory of early public library development.

To produce such a theory is not easy. This is not simply because of the difficulty of choosing a model for analysis appropriate to the diverse evidence and varied aspects of the public library experience. Theoretical assessments are problematic essentially because of the poverty of theory which has afflicted library history. The research and writing of library history, as a discipline in its own right, is relatively new; though isolated interest in the subject can certainly be traced back as far as Edward Edwards's *Memoirs of Libraries* (1859), if not further. Formal academic recognition of the subject in Britain was given only as recently as 1962, with the formation of the Library Association's Library History Group.[43] Despite its short pedigree library history has attracted an extensive and varied literature. However, the value and the quality of the literature are unquestionably uneven, the major criticism being that too little attention has been paid to wider social, economic and political developments. With a few exceptions library history has been myopic (though this charge applies more, perhaps, to British than to American and German research).[44] Too frequently researchers have taken the documents relating to a library, or group of libraries, and examined them with a view to producing a mere chronicle, bereft of references to non-library influences. Such an approach misses the central purpose of library history, which should not be pursued for its own sake, or for the glorification of individuals and institutions, but for the comprehension of social processes, historical and contemporary.

This is not to say that the shallowness of library historiography, which the simplistic, factual approach has engendered, has not been improved upon. For example, studies of individuals who influenced library development become highly valuable when they verge on psycho-history, and avoid a congratulatory approach.[45] A biographical approach offers one way of penetrating the inaccessible reaches of embryonic library culture. In addition, analysis has occurred in relation to the library's 'coeval social milieu'. The device of 'context' has been adopted in an effort to break the hermetic seal of descriptive library history.[46] A typical contextual contribution can be quoted from the publication celebrating the history of the Bolton Public Library:

> From its opening, the use made of Bolton's public library was closely linked to prevailing social and economic conditions, as it still is today. War and peace, boom and slump, the spread of education, the impact of radio and television, the increase in leisure time, increasing affluence, the emancipation of women – all these have had their effect on the service.[47]

A classic statement of contextual library history analysis is Jesse Shera's *Foundations of the Public Library: the Origins of the Public Library in New England 1629–1855* (1949), which begins with the assertion of the general principle that:

> the origins of any social agency must be sought in the internal constitution of the social milieu ... We are concerned with those elements in American life which contributed directly or indirectly to the growth of the public library as a social agency and the character of the environment from which it emerged.[48]

Shera's contextual approach has been influential, certainly in the United States.

Context, however, does not alone provide the answer. The contextual approach to public library history has been too narrow in terms of the social, economic and political developments against which library development can be tested. For example, the question of class – to be discussed below – has been strangely under-represented in comparison to its treatment in social and cultural history generally. Further, contextual analysis of a general kind cannot alone root out a theory. Merely to paint the broad backcloth against which library activity took place is not enough. Such an approach might explain very superficially 'how' libraries came to be. It does not necessarily explain the fundamental 'why' of development and practice. Ideally, in addition to it being given sufficient depth, context should not simply be described but interpreted, in an effort to pin-point the social functions and micro-worlds of libraries, and their professionals providers, and patrons.[49] Interpretation of context, allied to the assembly of models, can result in the evolution of several schools of thought (and indeed methodologies) – which is the hallmark of a mature discipline.[50]

The aetiology of library development requires more qualitative attention. Yet the contextual approach has not been wasted: it can be diversified and exploited. First, it can and should be emphasized that libraries are not only 'of' but 'making of' society. (Interestingly, although Shera argued that the public library followed social change he did not appear to believe – mistakenly, it can be argued – that to any great extent it created it.[51]) Second, library history can benefit from historical research and debate of those contextual areas which impinge upon library development. Altick has written of the nineteenth-century public library that:

> the issue of public subsidisation of reading was entangled with the far broader issues of social reform and *laissez-faire*; and the whole subsequent history of the public library movement offers an instructive cross section of English opinion on such matters as taxation for the general benefit, the problem of drink, poverty, and crime, and the relation of the inferior classes to the ruling one. What seems to us in the perspective of a century, a fairly simple question – shall, or shall not, government provide the people with free reading facilities? – involved all sort of peripheral, if not actually irrelevant, considerations.[52]

There is no reason why libraries should not be examined with reference to the history of leisure, or urbanization, or ideas, or class, or social policy, or the economy, or culture, or central–local government tension, or social space, or professional-expert discourses, or any other issue. In such cases valuable concepts and methods can be borrowed from research in those areas. Third, contextual explanations can be linked to help to provide a meaningful 'why' of development. Disparate aspects of library provision are enriched by being juxtaposed (as this study attempts to do, for example, in respect of utilitarian and idealist prescriptions), thereby helping to create theoretical perspectives.

Theories and coherent themes of public library history have been slow to develop. This is surprising considering, as Sturges points out, the supposed homogeneity of the rate-supported libraries.[53] A theoretical culture within library history might have emerged sooner with the assistance of historians working in broader fields. The eschewing of library history by professional historians is indeed curious in view of 'how much time they must, or ought to, spend in libraries'![54] It is also regrettable. As Davis, from an American perspective, argues:

> Since library history is part of the larger concern of social and cultural history, it is unfortunate that historians frequently fail to touch upon libraries, collections, reading habits or literacy at all. If they do the treatment tends to be marginal. Library historians, as well as cultural historians, need to call these omissions to the attention of one another and thereby attempt to correct a deficiency which impoverishes both.[55]

The same observations are applicable to British professional and mainstream historians. For example, historians of local government have ignored the cultural domain of the public library, opting instead to concentrate on the larger, practical, 'life' issues of gas, water, transport, the poor law, education and administration.[56]

Failure to lift the public library into any mainstream of historical research has partly been due to the institution's low status as a public service. The public library's relatively low political profile is as real today as it was before the First World War, when the librarian W. C. B. Sayers presented it as 'one of the least understood [politically] of municipal institutions'.[57] In 1924, in urging a new library building, the *Doncaster Gazette* asked if it had ever happened that in any town 'a member of the Town Council has had the fear of losing his seat put into him because of his lack of support to the provision or extension of a Free Library'.[58] The public library has never interested politicians, demagogues and reformers to the extent of interest shown in other areas of social policy, such as education, public health, housing and social welfare.[59] Why is this?

With regard to the pre-1919 period the question of low funding is crucial. Between 1850 and 1919 public libraries were subject to a statutory rate limitation of one half penny in the pound under the Public Libraries Act (1850) and of one penny in the pound under amending legislation of 1855. Other local services such as education, water supply, tramways, electricity and gas were not rate-capped. Given the low level of spending on public libraries it is not surprising that they attracted little political attention. Library committees remained 'Cinderella' bodies. Usually of an executive nature and reporting to the parent organization once a year, committees were essentially non-political entities, with a high proportion of co-opted members, and with relatively small budgets – although it should be noted that by 1914 about sixty library authorities had obtained parliamentary sanction, through local legislation, to charge more than the statutory penny in the pound rate.[60] Attempts to give local libraries financial assistance from central government were easily thwarted. Both William Ewart (the parliamentary pioneer of public libraries and mover of the inaugural legislation in 1850) and Edward Edwards (the British Museum cataloguer who provided a substantial part of the evidence to the Select Committee on Public Libraries in 1849) were sympathetic, certainly initially, to the idea of central funding, along lines similar to the assistance given to education, which received its first public grants in 1833. Ewart and Edwards encountered strong 'non-interventionist' opposition. The Public Libraries Act (1850) was thus severely restricted: it was merely permissive; was confined to boroughs of populations exceeding 10,000; required a poll of ratepayers; and included a rate-cap.[61] Throughout the period under consideration attitudes to public library central funding hardly shifted. In 1891, at the opening of the St Martin-in-the-Fields Public Library, Gladstone poured scorn on the idea that even a small dose of central government help – which some in the public library movement were continuing to advocate – was 'a sure and infallible specific, supplying all deficiencies, surmounting all difficulties, and curing all social evils'.[62]

However, to argue that public libraries were placed low on the political agenda because of low funding is, to an extent, putting the chicken before the egg. Arguably, the low financial priority was less a cause of non-politicization than a result of the public library's lack of popularity. In 1906, the librarian James Duff Brown estimated that just 6 per cent of those in a position to use public libraries did so.[63] It is difficult to detect what can be called a 'public opinion' with regard to library provision; we can speak of a public library movement, but only just.[64] The loudest opinions were often of the negative sort.[65] There was considerable ratepayer opposition to culture on the rates. In support of its local library the *Islington Daily Gazette*, in 1906, attacked narrow-minded citizens who objected to the financial burden of enlightening the community:

> They demur at the imposition – however small – of additional rates. They are so selfish that they will not trouble to inquire if the benefits that accrue from the outlay are commensurate with the money expended ... They are blind to all improvement. They shout against progress. They complain bitterly, that their pockets are touched by the necessities of civilization. These are they who may be described as social misers. They are communal Scrooges. They are, in a civic sense, whatever they may be personally, hard fisted Gradgrinds.[66]

The most vehement criticism of the library rate came from the social localism of a petty bourgeoisie whose income depended, in part, on property and on the low wages of its small workforces, kept low by negligible taxation. As Crossick argues, this explains both the petty bourgeoisie's not insignificant involvement in local government in attempting to disrupt the grandiose plans of the expenditure-oriented bourgeoisie, and its participation in *ad hoc* pressure groups acting on specific issues like the library rate.[67] The latter was not large, in many places being less than one penny in the pound. The fear was, however, that once the principle was breached, library expenditure would rise inexorably. An anti-library handbill in York, in 1881, argued:

> It is said that the Rate will not exceed 1d in the £ per annum, but what security have you that Parliament will not grant a rate of 3d or 4d in the future?[68]

Such arguments influenced working-class ratepayers too. In 1884, when the Trades Union Congress discussed public libraries for the first time, it was argued by one delegate that it was not just the well-to-do who thwarted education via the public library: 'Many of the working classes were unwilling to pay any rate for the adoption of the [Public Libraries] Act.'[69] In 1902, the town clerk of Shoreditch wrote to Andrew Carnegie for financial support for the district's library movement, arguing that:

> Owing to Shoreditch being one of the poorest districts in London, the complaints of the people at the high rates they now have to pay, make it practically impossible to increase them.[70]

Even those working-class tenants who did not pay rates directly would not have relished the prospect of seeing their rents – in which rates were compounded – increased owing to the erection of a new library.[71] Pelling has argued that the working class was generally hostile to state welfare and social schemes (like public libraries), arising out of a suspicion of an 'intrusive' state,[72] though this general assessment requires refinement.[73]

Whether of working-class or middle-class origin, ratepayers often opposed library expenditure, while perhaps saying less about expenditure in other areas. In 1886, at a meeting of the Gosport and Alverstoke Ratepayer's Association, it was argued 'that a district whose sanitary arrangements are still in a primitive condition will act wisely in attending to necessities first and luxuries [a public library] afterwards'.[74] Clearly, culture dispensed by the public library was not considered as immediately important as the more recognizably tangible aspects of life. Hence, public library development was slow.[75] Just 27 library authorities had been founded in Great Britain by 1868; and only 125 by 1886. Thereafter the rate increased markedly, so that by 1918 there were 566 library authorities in existence. The rapid increase in the thirty years before the First World War was facilitated by a myriad of minor benefactions and a vast programme of financial assistance given by the Scottish-American steel baron Andrew Carnegie, mostly in the period after 1899.[76] In addition, an 1893 amendment to the Public Libraries Act of the previous year permitted the adoption of enabling library legislation on the decision of councillors, without them having to gain the specific approval of their ratepayers in a referendum on the issue. This removed a significant obstacle to public library development.

It is interesting to consider that adoptions escalated, towards the end of the nineteenth century, at the very time when rate charges were increasing. Whereas between 1868 and 1890–1 average rates in the pound increased nationally by 10 per cent, in the period 1890–1 to 1898–9 they increased by 31.8 per cent.[77] Clearly, therefore, rates were not the only factor influencing library development. If they had been then one would have expected to see a marked slowing of library development in the 1890s, whereas the total number of adoptions of the public library acts increased from 169 by 1890 to 348 by 1900.[78]

Other general factors which determined development were the spread of education after the inauguration of state elementary schools in 1870, the improvement in literacy and the growth of civic pride. With regard to the latter, London suffered severely from a lack of public libraries partly because of an absence of civic feeling. The first municipal library in London was established jointly in 1856 by the parishes of St Margaret and St John, Westminster. No further libraries appeared until 1883 when Wandsworth began a service – this being followed by a spate of adoptions in London, many in 1887 and 1888 to mark Queen Victoria's jubilee. In explaining the slow pace of development in London, the librarian J. Y. W. MacAlister referred to the 'congeries of village communities'.[79] In 1909 the magazine *Sunday Strand* explained how the vestries of pre-1899 London were 'not distinguished by public-spirit, enterprise or thought of public well-being,' and were thus slow to recognize the importance of libraries. The magazine noted the 'absence of a strong municipal spirit among the ratepayers [of London], such as marks the life of a big provincial town, and the difficulty in creating such as a spirit, especially when it means an increase in the rates'.[80] Much earlier, in 1840, Francis Place had explained to Richard Cobden that London:

> has no local or particular interest as a town, not even as to politics. Its several boroughs in this respect are like so many very populous places at a distance from one another, and the inhabitants of any of them know nothing, or next to nothing, of the proceedings in any other, and not much indeed of those of their own.[81]

Paradoxically, evidence of the deficient civic pride of London's districts comes from the ceremonial ostentation of local authority events like public library openings, which were, arguably, more contrived than those elsewhere.[82]

Issues such as local taxation and deficient civic pride (in London) might not explain wholly why municipal libraries developed slowly; they do illustrate, however, that the public did not clamour for free literature. There is little evidence to explain why people did not use public libraries. Any evidence that exists is supplied by providers. This is similarly the problem in ascertaining why people did use libraries, for the evidence is essentially élitist and administrative in nature.[83] Identifying motives of use falls short of an exercise in divination; basic reasons such as the desire for self-help and improvement are plainly evident. However, it is clearly not possible to reach firm conclusions in respect of detailed motives owing to the sparse testimony of the users themselves, and to the dangers of relying on providers' perceptions of why people used libraries – which would naturally distort the true picture by saying more about the motives of supply than of consumption. Thus, more is justifiably said in this study about the impressions of promoters and managers as to why people entered public libraries, or ought to have done so.

Although the 'why' of public library use is elusive it is possible to say much about who used libraries, and what was used – though not precisely who used what. Librarians were meticulous in recording their readership's occupation, age, gender and taste. They have bequeathed to the historian a vast archive of statistics in annual reports and periodic Parliamentary Returns.[84] However, processing these statistics is problematic. Statistics were compiled according to varying criteria and terminology, and must therefore be interpreted with caution. Quantitative evidence must be complemented by qualitative, contemporary views concerning the issue of use. As the librarian E. A. Savage wrote: 'Indulged in, statistics are dope; let us never forget their distortions, limitations and reticence.'[85]

Librarians were anxious to produce tables of readers' occupations which illustrated a wide social class use, thereby emphasizing the public library's democratic purpose as a 'non-exclusive aristocracy'.[86] Two suitable representative examples can be found in the Portsmouth Free Public Library *Annual Report* (1887–8) and the Leyton Public Library *Annual Report* (1902–3), which are reproduced here in Appendix 1 and Appendix 2, respectively. These occupational lists show that the majority of public library users in Portsmouth and Leyton were working class. This is true of other towns and of other eras. There was also a significant presence of white-collar and professional occupations – the clerk, for example, begins to make a significant impact on late-nineteenth-century library statistics. It has been argued that both the professional and non-manual element of public library patronage was considerably over-represented in comparison with their proportion in the population at large.[87] The social width of the readership was noted by Thomas Greenwood in 1886 when he wrote that:

> A glance at the published statistics of any of the Free Libraries of the country as to the occupations of the readers shows how widely they are used by every trade and profession ... To all sections alike they are accessible, and to say that the 'great unwashed' alone use them is saying what would not be true.[88]

Opponents of the public library attempted to portray the institution as existing only for the lower classes, yet paid for unfairly by the better-off. This helped to deepen the mark of charity which, owing to the frequent choice of the prefix 'free', to a degree stigmatized the municipal library for much of its early life.[89] No doubt the 'soup kitchen' image kept some middle-class readers away.[90] But this should not detract from the fact that a large number of middle-class readers did frequent public libraries – because it made economic sense to do so. Thus, in R. N. Carey's *Doctor Luttrell's First Patient* (1897), a struggling young physician was described as someone who was:

> devoted to the works of Thackeray and thirsted for a complete set of his works, but at present only 'Vanity Fair' and 'The Newcomers' were on his modest bookshelves. Neither the husband nor the wife thought it right to spend those few shillings on the purchase of books when they could make use of the Free Library.

Ostensibly, the public library was for all in society – although it has been argued that at its inception, purpose was very much oriented towards a working-class patronage.[91] In advocating a library for York in 1881, J. S. Rowntree proclaimed that:

> Free libraries are used by every class of the population; male and female, rich and poor, learned and unlearned, boys and girls, the blind, the deaf and the maimed, all resort to a good free library.[92]

The rhetoric did not reflect reality as far as women were concerned. In 1876 at South Shields Public Library only 25 per cent of lending library borrowers and just 7 per cent of reference users were female.[93] Little is known of the occupations of women users. The occupational breakdown given by South Shields Public Library to Parliament in 1876 – reproduced in Appendix 3 – is extremely rare.

The public library was not simply the preserve of males, but of young males. Early this century the librarian James Duff Brown estimated that 16 per cent of the users were under the age of 14; 32 per cent were aged 14–19; 34 per cent were aged 20–39; and 8 per cent were over the age of 40 (the ages of 10 per cent of users were not ascertained).[94] Heavy use by the young is a pattern which is applicable throughout the period under consideration, though to an increasing extent from the 1880s onwards, when children's libraries began to proliferate.

Librarians also recorded what their socially diffuse readership was demanding. The evidence of what was read is extensive. The Leicester Public Library *Annual Report* (1889–90) offers representative evidence – the classification of issues in lending and reference departments is given in Appendix 4. At Leicester, as elsewhere, fiction was the staple diet of the library borrower. This fact lent considerable ammunition to the public library's critics. The debate over usefulness was a consistent characteristic of early public library development. But the debate's often heated nature has perhaps allocated a disproportionate importance to fiction in historians' assessments of the overall literature demands of public library users. There is evidence to suggest that the use made of non-fictional works – including such materials as magazines, newspapers, directories, timetables and patents, as well as 'serious' literature – should not be under-estimated.[95] The desire for self-improvement through knowledge was manifest in all classes; its appeal would have been sensed across the whole range of public library users. Albert Blakemore, a railway clerk, recorded in his autobiography how:

> When the [Shrewsbury] Free Library opened, and I was allowed to borrow books, it was a feast of feasts, of which I never grew tired. But the time came when I turned to more serious books, learned something of astronomy, geology, biology, and the natural sciences generally. I began to get answers to questions I had long been seeking.[96]

Librarians occasionally (for it would have been a time-consuming exercise) produced tables to show that serious literature was consumed by all types of public library user (see Appendices 5 and 6).

The statistics of public library use are subject to the strictest qualifications. The statistics are not easily synthesized – this is especially true of occupational data. It is safer to analyse the statistics of different public libraries in isolation, with reference to a town's social, economic and political make-up. The diversity of locality should be emphasized. Urbanization did not create a single type of town; each evolved as a complex entity with variations in economic activity, political interests and social formation. This realization is particularly relevant to the study of public library development, which was essentially parochial. As the *Westminster Review* reported in 1872, in looking back over two decades of public library activity:

> It is interesting to find that these libraries have been established among different

kinds of population, and in almost every sort of town; in large manufacturing and separate towns; in smaller manufacturing places, in metropolitan, university, cathedral and agricultural towns.[97]

Studies of individual library authorities are thus a crucial aspect of public research and writing. This is particularly true with regard to assessing the motives of major promoters and benefactors. Victorian and Edwardian urban élites were not homogeneous.[98] Precise reasons for providing a public library would have differed, inevitably, from one town to the next. However, general motives can, and indeed must, be identified. It is thus possible to take issue with Kelly's belief that the 'heart of library history ... is not to be found in its more general aspects ... [but] in the often highly individual history of the hundreds of individual libraries which together make up the library service'.[99] Of course, local evidence remains the prerequisite of building general trends and theories. But it is these generalities – especially the theoretical models – which should provide the impetus in library history, not the idea of case studies as ends in themselves. Indeed, the case study approach is at its most effective when general theories exist for local, specific evidence to work against. This study does not include in-depth investigations of individual public library experiences. Rather, it aims to establish – through the examination of extensive local public library evidence, the attitudes of leading promoters and recent key debates in wider history – a theory of provision which can be applied, to a greater or lesser extent, to diverse early public library development.

CHAPTER 2

FOUNDATIONS OF THE PUBLIC LIBRARY IDEAL

The provision of libraries freely open to the public was not in 1850 a novel idea. The Public Libraries Act of 1850 (and the work of the Select Committee which preceded it) should not be seen as the great watershed it is so often described to be.[1] The idea of local public libraries had been raised a number of times in the 1820s, 1830s and 1840s: the events of 1849–50, to be discussed below, were as much a culmination as a beginning.[2] Proposals for a truly free library service did not appear overnight: they emerged on the back of a healthy tradition of independent library provision made by a diverse range of social, political and educational institutions – whether mechanics' institutes or coffee houses, commercial circulating libraries or Chartist reading rooms – for their members and patrons.[3]

Forerunners and early suggestions

Despite the vitality of this independent provision, however, there existed in the first half of the nineteenth century a strong, unsatisfied demand for free literature, of both the conventional and alternative kind. The absence of adequate supplies of free literature was especially detrimental to the poorer classes. Libraries for use by the poor did exist, but were rarely free.[4] Even those libraries which were ostensibly open to all – such as the Reading Room of the British Museum – were often, in reality, not so.[5] Relative to continental Europe, Britain was said to be woefully deficient in truly public libraries.[6] As Altick has asserted: 'Nowhere [before the municipal library], in short, was any considerable collection of books available to all the people, without charge, and completely detached from social, political and religious prejudices.'[7]

Before 1850, to be sure, some quasi-public libraries had developed. Sometimes ecclesiastical bodies, like the Religious Tract Society, freely distributed small libraries, mostly to schools and churches.[8] Collections of books in Sunday Schools were not uncommon.[9] Free literature was often available in pubs and coffee houses.[10] Some employers (including those who established alternative, utopian communities) provided factory or workshop libraries for their employees.[11] However, none of these libraries can be termed wholly public: first, because they were not funded from the public purse; and, second, although material might have been free at the point of use, restrictions operated in the form of individuals being 'attached' to an institution as an employee, worshipper, student, consumer, political activist or otherwise. Early-nineteenth-century library nomenclature is thus problematic. Many libraries before 1850 claimed the description 'public' – subscription, national, cathedral and small shop libraries among them – because they were accessible to the public in the same way that the market place was, theoretically, an open public sphere. For this reason municipal libraries frequently assumed the prefix 'free', in the hope that in the library context this would distinguish them from the common usage of the word 'public'.[12]

An early proposal for public libraries (though not rate-aided) came from the reformer Robert Slaney, whose *Essay on the Beneficial Effects of Rural Expenditure* (1824) urged generous bequests for the purpose from the well-to-do; this, he argued, was how the great collections of Europe had mostly been assembled. Slaney expressed blatant utilitarian beliefs (more of this in Chapter 3) in advocating free libraries. They would shield the ignorant and vulnerable, by encouraging 'reflection', from 'temptation'; confront bigotry, superstition and ignorance; and develop 'latent genius and ability'. The first concrete proposal for free, rate-aided libraries came, as Kelly notes, from the lawyer C. H. B. Ker, who approached the educationist and mechanics' institute enthusiast Henry Brougham on the matter. Both were members of the Society for the Diffusion of Useful Knowledge (SDUK), which Brougham founded in 1826. In that year the issue of 'free' libraries was raised with the SDUK's General Committee, with the intention of introducing into Parliament a Bill for towns or districts of a given population to tax themselves for establishing a library open to all local inhabitants. The scheme appears not to have reached beyond the confines of SDUK business.[13]

The SDUK's creed of improvement was echoed in the work of the Select Committee on Inquiry into Drunkenness (1834) – colloquially named the 'Drunken Committee'. In its report, the Committee called for both legislative and moral endeavour to stamp out the intemperance which was said to be so 'destructive of the general welfare of the community';[14] so responsible for the 'retardation of all Improvement, inventive or industrial, civil or political, moral or religious';[15] and so vital to the continuance of disorder.[16] As a possible legislative remedy to these problems the establishment of local public libraries was suggested – in addition to the removal of taxes on knowledge,[17] restrictions on drink in the armed forces[18] and control of imported distilled spirits.[19] Item '37' of the report called for:

> The establishment, by the joint aid of the government and the local authorities, and residents on the spot, of public walks and gardens, or open spaces for athletic and healthy exercises in the open air, in the immediate vicinity of every

town, of an extent and character adapted to its population, and of district and parish libraries, museums and reading-rooms, accessible at the lowest rate of charge; so as to admit of one or the other being visited in all weather, at any time; with the rigid exclusion of all Intoxicating Drinks from such places, whether in the open air, or closed.[20]

This recommendation was strongly influenced by the evidence of the utilitarian Francis Place. Government action on drunkenness in the eighteenth century (the Gin Acts and increased duties) was seen to have failed.[21] Place none the less believed that legislation could still help to abate the evils of drink.[22] He observed that working people had become less intemperate since the Napoleonic Wars.[23] (This was not true in the case of beer drinking where the trend had been upward.[24]) This he put down to improved instruction. Evidence from the Committee's proceedings illustrates Place's enthusiasm for public library education as a means of moral uplift:[25]

> Q. 2079 [To Francis Place]. The Committee understand that the chief remedy you recommend is, increased facilities for the diffusion of information among the people, and institutions of an entertaining and instructive nature? – Yes, these must inevitably raise their character.

> Q. 2032 [To Francis Place]. Do you think the establishment of parish libraries and district reading-rooms, and popular lectures on subjects both entertaining and instructive to the community, might draw off a number of those who now frequent public-houses for the sole enjoyment they afford? – Certainly.

The chairman of the Drunken Committee, James Silk Buckingham (MP for Sheffield), was the first to present a Parliamentary Bill for the provision of public libraries. His Public Institutions Bill (1835) proposed the establishment of public institutions to diffuse literary and scientific knowledge, including libraries and museums. This Bill was introduced in tandem with another to secure public walks and open air places of recreation.[26] The wording of the Bill regarding libraries was virtually identical to the statement on the need for public libraries which had been made in the report of the Drunken Committee. Buckingham abhorred intemperance. In introducing his Bill he quoted the Drunken Committee report at length in order to demonstrate what he believed to be the evil effects and negative utility of drink. He advocated libraries because he sincerely believed workers went to pubs not for love of drink but for 'cheerful and friendly intercourse'.[27] Indeed, to a large degree it was this very social intercourse – the prospect of working people exchanging and developing ideas – more than the effects of alcohol, that middle-class reformers perceived as the main threat to public order. (In this respect, those who have seen the origin of the public library as essentially a temperance issue have largely missed the point.) Buckingham was so immersed in the temperance issue that he had financed, with no prospect of profit, the production of a cheap edition of the minutes and evidence of the Drunken Committee. Several thousand copies were sold. In addition, more than a million broadsheets containing an abstract of the report were circulated.[28] Having reached the Committee stage before being abandoned, the Public Institutions Bill was reintroduced in 1836 (again in tandem with a Bill on public walks), only to fail at its first reading. The same fate befell a further Bill introduced by Buckingham in 1837 which integrated the public walks and institutions Bills of the previous two years.[29]

It is not certain why these Bills failed, but with regard to the Public Institutions Bill (1835) it is interesting to note that its introduction preceded the Municipal Corporations Act, which would perhaps have offered a more acceptable vehicle for adminstration. Ewart, for instance, supported the Bill in principle but argued that 'its provisions would be better administered by the local Councils under the Municipal Bill'.[30] In short, legislating for something which forthcoming changes to municipal affairs might encompass made little sense. However, possibly the chief reason for the failure of the Public Institutions Bill (1835), and its later versions, was the issue of local taxation. It was envisaged that councils would be empowered to levy a rate for repaying loans secured in establishing institutions, if a public meeting of ratepayers agreed by a two-thirds majority. In opposing the Bill Lord John Russell argued that although public education was a national issue, it could only thrive if left to voluntary effort. He believed the public would not be interested in electing the officials who would have to run institutions of public education (whether schools or libraries) and that only voluntary action would ensure enthusiastic management.[31] Another member asserted that 'the House would stultify itself if it passed this Bill through the present stage with the Clause relative to the compulsory rate'.[32] In fact, the *House of Commons Journal* records that the chamber only found itself able to divide, albeit to the detriment of the Bill, once the rating clause had been dropped.[33] This parliamentary episode is significant in that it highlights the issue of funding from local taxation – an issue which was to plague public library provision for decades after 1850.

Buckingham's Bill had one further implication for the future objectives of the public library, in that the Bill articulated the link between moral and material uplift. Libraries were viewed as moralizing agencies which, at the same time, would seek to help eradicate universally damaging secondary poverty; where income spent unwisely not only inflicted unnecessary and avoidable hardship on the individual, but also strained the resources society had allocated for welfare protection and the containment of crime. In supporting the moral motive, the public library enthusiast, Joseph Brotherton, told the House of Commons at the time:

> Anything that tended to promote the comfort and improve the morals of the lower classes deserved the most favourable consideration ... in as much as the country owed much of its prosperity to the labouring classes.[34]

The desire to improve both 'comfort' and 'morals' resulted from the widely accepted ugliness of industrialism and the consequent desire to improve the quality of life. It is no coincidence that Buckingham's library proposals were linked with those for the establishment of public open spaces. The latter were seen as an antidote to industrialization's darker side. In his evidence to the Select Committee on Public Walks (1833) Brotherton had agreed that in his home town of Salford workers were shut up in manufacturing employment 'for a considerable part of the day' and thus required 'open spaces for their health and comfort'.[35] The same potential for dissolving squalor was attributed to public libraries. For example, in 1885 the public library promoter Janetta Manners wished that where possible there should be 'a recreation-ground in connection with every reading room'.[36]

If bringing people out of a demoralizing physical environment, whether it be the public house or insanitary housing, was one means of social engineering, then the civilizing influence of social interaction in a controlled public space was another.[37] It was argued that the corralling of the recreational masses into designated, purpose-built public areas would reduce the nuisance of leisure trespass on private property.[38] Further, it was hoped that public perambulation would promote self-respect and good conduct.[39] In short, people would be socialized (or self-policed) into dressing, behaving and interacting in an orderly fashion. Similar social engineering objectives were formulated by public library enthusiasts, who viewed the public space which their institutions provided as a site for the class mixing deemed so essential to maintaining social order and improving moral standards.

A further parliamentary discussion of the public library issue occurred in the proceedings of the Select Committee on Arts and their Connection with Manufactures (1835–6) chaired by Ewart.[40] In the 1830s, despite the nation's economic advance over the previous half-century, some manufacturers, traders and their political representatives began to express concern over the declining competitiveness of certain British products, most notably in the 'fancy trade' (more about this in Chapter 5). The Committee's report stressed the importance to a trading nation like Britain of the connection between art and manufacturing, but questioned the strength of the bond between them in the birthplace of industrialization.[41] The report lamented the 'want of instruction in design among our industrious population', and called for an improvement in artistic taste through the opening of public museums and art galleries funded by local and central government jointly.[42] It also called for schools of design to be set up along the lines of those found in Germany and France.[43]

The report did not call specifically for the establishment of public libraries, but a desire for them was inferred by reference to their accessibility elsewhere. It was noted, for example, that:

The free, open and popular system of instruction ... and the extreme accessibility of their museums, libraries and exhibitions, have greatly tended to the diffusion of a love of art, as well as of literature, among the poorer classes of the French.[44]

However, the minutes of evidence, as distinct from the report, contain specific pleas for the setting up of public libraries to help extend a knowledge of the arts, particularly in their industrial application. For example, Ewart put the following questions to Philip Barnes, an architect from Norwich:

Q. 1353. Do you think that the institution of schools and places of instruction in art would be a great advantage to the manufacturing population of Norwich? – Undoubtedly [answered Barnes].

Q. 1354. Do you think that the opening of galleries where they might see the most beautiful works of art, and opening libraries where probably such works might also be exhibited, together with books, would not also be a very great advantage to the manufacturers? – I would, decidedly [answered Barnes].[45]

One institution which had begun to address the question of design education for industry was the mechanics' institute. In this, as in other ways, the mechanics' institute served as the progenitor of public library purpose. The proliferation of mechanics' institutes in the first half of the nineteenth century helped to further the public library ideal, even if the library facilities which they provided were not 'public' in the true sense of the word. Munford has correctly described them as the 'pioneer ancestors'.[46] Not only did they set the example of a socially widening use of libraries, they also anticipated, in their internal workings, issues such as managerial control and popularization of stock, which were also to feature in the debate over the early public library's purpose.

The link between the public library and the mechanics' institute is more obvious in terms of the former's physical inheritance from the latter. Public libraries were often formed, or fed, from the decaying remnants of previously thriving mechanics' institute libraries (as in Wolverhampton in 1869[47]) which had fallen on bad times as a result of increased competition from the subsidized municipal library, or from a cheaper literary market-place, or because of the pursuit by middle-class promoters of policies and programmes alien to a working-class clientele. This latter cause of decline possessed important implications for the public library in terms of both its financial justification and its social purpose. Voluntary bodies like mechanics' institutes, while attracting philanthropic support, especially in their formative stages, were none the less expected to work within a market framework. As befitted the values of their promoters, mechanics' institutes functioned in accordance with the market mechanism – in other words, they were expected to pay their way.[48] In order to do this institutes were forced to make cultural concessions: their libraries, for example, became notorious for their stocks of fiction, something which conflicted with the purity of pioneer statements concerning the dissemination of useful knowledge. Arguably, public libraries were subjected to the same market pressures. Despite being sheltered from the market by virtue of their municipal funding, public libraries never escaped the scrutiny of the marketeers and anti-collectivists. Financial latitude, as determined by the rate-cap on library spending, was in any case narrow. Thus, even though they could never make a profit in cash terms, they were under constant pressure to be successful in terms of numbers of users. At the behest of the market ethos, attracting patrons through the door – 'bums on seats' in the modern vernacular – became a priority objective. To meet this objective public libraries therefore followed, eventually, in the footsteps of the mechanics' institutes and evolved a popular, 'responsive' image which contrasted with the higher intentions of the free library's purist pioneers. The abandonment of the policy of providing only 'solid' literature (more about this in Chapter 8) was part of this concessionary, market-led process.

Such was the similarity between the ethos of the mechanics' institute and that of the public library that the former's guiding hand, the SDUK, itself proposed the establishment of free collections of literature. In 1839, the SDUK published its *Manual for Mechanics' Institutions*. This pamphlet aimed to assist those intending to found mechanics' institutes, and offered advice to those in existence. A chapter on libraries dealt with aspects of provision in the institutes' repositories, but also called for the cooperation of all types of town library in pooling resources and making them accessible to the public. To encourage this, it was suggested that government grants, supplemented by a local rate, could be made for both buildings and core collections. This funding principle, the manual suggested, might be extended to the establishment and maintenance of small village libraries, possibly located in schools.[49]

The 1840s witnessed an intensification of the pressure to establish free municipal libraries. A decade after the Select Committee on Arts and Manufactures, Ewart succeeded in securing one of its key recommendations – an Act for 'encouraging the establishment of Museums in large towns'.[50] The link between the good design of industrial products, on the one hand, and the viewing in public museums of man-made artefacts or objects of natural history, on the other, had been established by the Committee on Arts and Manufactures. The Museums Act (1845) was partly the result of the Committee's deliberations in this aesthetic area of political economy. Ewart's enabling Bill passed without opposition. This is surprising considering that its provisions were to be virtually replicated in the Public Libraries Act (1850), which, far from passing through Parliament quietly, sparked vibrant debate in the Commons. Books and reading were perhaps seen as more threatening than the passive viewing of museum artefacts.

The Museums Act contained the following provisions: first, municipal boroughs with a population of not less than 10,000 were empowered to establish 'museums of art and science'; second, money, for buildings only, could be raised through borrowing funded from the borough's general rate account; third, a rate limit for maintenance spending (for example, on salaries, lighting, cleaning and other running costs) was set at one half penny in the pound; and fourth, admission charges were not to exceed one penny per visit. Three councils – Canterbury (1847), Warrington (1848) and Salford (1849) – took advantage of the ambiguities of the Act (allowing provision of 'Specimens of Art or Science, and Articles of every description', interpreted by some to include books) to establish libraries within their public museums. These were thus the country's first rate-aided libraries; though it should be noted that at the Canterbury and Warrington institutions the penny admission charge to the museum was payable before the library could be used.[51]

The pre-1850 proposals and developments outlined above rehearsed the intellectual debates on cultural control and economic utility which were to dominate the public library issue in its formative decades. Keynote issues, such as the inducement of high moral values, the tendency towards collectivism, the pursuit of economic prosperity by cultural means and the tension between a quest for excellence (in the Arnoldian and Tylorian sense) and a popular or marketable image, resonated through the free library question throughout the pre-1914 period, having first been struck in the socially unstable 1820s, 1830s and 1840s. Early suggestions for public libraries, and the first tentative steps taken towards their creation, occurred against a backdrop of cultural and economic crisis which, if the essence of the early public library movement is to be understood, requires careful analysis. It is particularly important to focus attention on the question of class, in which the development of modern English society, including the phenomenon of the municipal public library, is firmly rooted.

The class catalyst

The social, economic and political tensions of proto-industrialism manifested themselves most obviously in the issue of class, the cultural ramifications of which were clearly visible in the debate on public libraries. Socio-economic context has been of keen interest to recent library historians seeking to broaden their historical canvas.[52] The early history of the public library movement has been examined against a backcloth of both social and economic development.[53] However, relatively little has been written about class conflict as a determinant of the public library's origin.[54] Yet early public libraries were conceived in a world riven with social strife and disaffection; their aim being to help rid industrial society of the division which threatened its existence.

The emergence of the public library ideal was, in part, a reflex to the unprecedented level of protest which characterized the turbulent years between the close of the Napoleonic Wars and the climax of the Chartist movement; though more particularly, perhaps, to the 'radical' 1830s and the 'hungry' 1840s, the 1820s, according to Thompson, being a relatively quiet and 'mildly prosperous plateau of social peace'.[55] These were years of increasing agitation against the worst aspects of the new industrial order, and the monopoly of political power which went hand in hand with economic exploitation. In the first half of the nineteenth century waves of social unrest broke time and again; most notably in 1811-13, 1815-17, 1819, 1829, 1829-35, 1838-42, 1843-4 and 1847-8.[56] In rural areas unrest was, perhaps, more due to economic hardship. In industrial and urban areas, however, the economic impetus was invariably linked with some sort of political dynamic, the latter even taking prominence in 1815-19, 1829-32 and above all in the Chartist era. There emerged, therefore, a volatile mixture of economic deprivation and political suppression which fashioned a widespread discontent among working people, who 'felt themselves hungry in a society reeking with wealth, enslaved in a country which prided itself on its freedom, seeking bread and hope, and receiving in return stones and despair', as Hobsbawm has forcefully described.[57]

By the 1840s British capitalism had entered its first secular crisis, the trough arriving in the catastrophic economic depression of 1841-2. The post-Napoleonic era had been one of rapid capital accumulation in which vast fortunes were made. But it was also marked by violent fluctuations in the trade cycle caused by falling prices.[58] The latter resulted from technological change and over-production. Industrial capitalism was proving inherently unstable; essentially because the accumulation of capital was tending to race ahead of the conditions that could sustain it.[59] This was a major economic feature of the 1820s, 1830s and 1840s when supply frequently outstripped demand, causing both downward pressure on wages and rising unemployment.

So severe was the economic depression of the early 1840s that, at the time, it would not have been entirely unrealistic to think of the period as 'the final agony of capitalism and the prelude to revolution'.[60] Some contemporary observers, such as Engels, sensed an impending conflagration. In his *Condition of the Working Class in England* (1845), written just five years before the first public library legislation, Engels forecast that 'the revolution must come; it is already too late to bring about a peaceful solution'. He went on:

> The war of the poor against the rich now carried on in detail and indirectly will become direct and universal ... The classes are divided more and more sharply, the spirit of resistance penetrates the workers, the bitterness intensifies, the guerilla skirmishes become concentrated in more important battles, and soon a slight impulse will suffice to set the avalanche in motion. then, indeed, will the war cry resound through the land: 'War to the palaces, peace to the cottages!' – but then it will be too late for the rich to beware.[61]

Revolutionary insurrection would be the culmination of what Marx and Engels saw as the irrevocable movement in capitalist society towards an urban-based class system polarized between a mushrooming and increasingly impoverished proletariat on the one hand, and a contracting bourgeoisie controlling ever increasing concentrations of capital on the other. The resultant dichotomy of class interests, perhaps with the catalyst of intensifying economic competition from abroad, would galvanize the workers into seizing power.

But what was the prospect of revolution in Britain before 1850? Firm conclusions concerning the existence of a *truly* threatening working-class consciousness are elusive. It is not appropriate in the context of this discussion to explore extensively the debate concerning the emergence of such a consciousness: this has been done elsewhere.[62] However, a brief analysis of the working-class aspect of the 'social question' is required if the motivation behind the early public library ideal is to be fully appreciated. Divorced from the context of class the aims of protagonists like Ewart and Edwards, and the work of the 1849 Select Committee, are colourless.

In his seminal work *The Making of the English Working Class* (1963) E. P. Thompson explained that 'class happens when some men, as a result of common experiences (inherited or shared), feel and articulate the identity of their interests as between themselves, and as against other men whose interests are different from (and usually opposed to) theirs.'[63] In other words, Thompson saw class less as a question of homogeneity than of shared differences with others. He further argued that the class experience 'is largely determined by the productive relations into which men are born – or enter voluntarily'.[64] That is to say, it is an individual's *economic* function which determines his or her social relations.

It was the Industrial Revolution, says Thompson, which combined these constituent elements in the definition of class and gave rise to an embryonic class consciousness among not just factory workers but working people generally (Thompson's analysis includes farm labourers, artisans and domestic workers). As he writes: 'In the years between 1780 and 1832 most English working people came to feel an identity of interests as between themselves, and as against their rulers and employers.'[65] Thus, by 1832 the working-class presence was 'the most significant factor in British political life'.[66] However, in challenging this assertion it should be stressed that the birth of a working-class consciousness was 'a complex, syncopated process, operating at different speeds in different areas'.[67] It is true that in the early nineteenth century the folk culture of pre-industrial England was undermined, slowly but surely, by a vibrant urban folk culture; but this process of change would not have been uniform. Nor could it have been entirely revolutionary: patterns of pre-industrial culture inevitably informed the new urban consciousness. Some commentators have argued against the idea of evolutionary change by taking the line that something very special was *lost* in the decline of England's culture of *Gemeinschaft*. They have painted a black and white picture of wholesale transition from a healthy to an ailing culture.[68] This depiction surely ignores the tendency of 'whole ways of life' not to transmute but evolve. Moreover, as the thrust of Thompson's argument indicates, urban folk culture was no less vibrant or less worthy than the rural folk culture it eclipsed. The new urban consciousness, including its working-class dynamic, cannot be construed crudely as either 'damaged' or 'diseased'.

Thompson's assertion that a widely sensed working-class consciousness appeared during proto-industrialization has been supported by Perkin and Foster.[69] Unlike Thompson, who stressed the economic basis of class formation, Perkin primarily discusses social causes, in particular 'the abdication on the part of the governors': the rising middle-class entrepreneurial ideal rejected the paternalistic sense of duty to the lower order which pre-industrial ruling élites had recognized and practised as a means of control. It was this rejection, ultimately enshrined in the Poor Law Amendment Act (1834) but evolving in the generation before it, which brought a working-class consciousness to fruition during the radical protest of 1815–20. Foster follows Perkin in similarly considering social causes, but combines these with economic inputs in an assessment of class which is tangible: class being measured in terms of income, occupation, relationship to the means of production, area of residence and marriage patterns. In a quantitative analysis of the textile town of Oldham he identifies a period of labour consciousness (a marked trade union solidarity) lasting from about 1770 to 1830, followed by a full-blown revolutionary consciousness from 1830 to 1850. Foster is nearer to Thompson (who sees 1832 as a crucial year) than to Perkin in his timing of a working-class consciousness. None the less, all three believe that such a consciousness was in place by the time the public library idea came to be discussed in earnest.

The work of other commentators, such as Hobsbawm and Briggs, finds this conclusion to be premature. Hobsbawm views the pre-1850 period as crucial to the eventual emergence of a fully fledged working class: he too stressed the importance of working-class consciousness. However, in his opinion the final 'crystallization' of a working-class self-awareness does not occur until after 1870. Briggs has pointed out that although the term 'working class', inferring unity, can generally be said to have been a nineteenth-century linguistic construction, the description 'working classes' endured alongside it, even as, towards the end of the century, the singular became commonplace, thereby casting doubt on an early-century formation of working-class solidarity. The literature of the public library, to be sure, contained numerous references to the plural, even as late as the 1890s. Apparently in support of these views, another commentator has described the last quarter of the nineteenth century as 'the period in which the tentacles of class became all-embracing'.[70]

Despite arguments over the dating of working-class consciousness it is clear that the upheavals which accompanied the Industrial Revolution, and – it would not be an exaggeration to say – tore apart the social landscape of Britain, radically affected the stratification of society and the allegiances held by men and women to the various social groups that constituted it. Small, stable, vertically integrated communities began to be replaced by large, unplanned, urban environments, inherently unstable because of the dehumanizing and alienating working and living conditions in lower-class ghettos. To state that the first half of the nineteenth century witnessed the creation of a widespread revolutionary working-class consciousness might be an exaggeration. However, the existence of a proletariat (albeit fragmented) growing in self-awareness, and with a propensity to self-organize and associate to further its interests, is undeniable.

For the respectable classes in the nineteenth century the emergence of a proletariat took on sinister overtones, conjuring up as it did images of volcanic social eruption reflecting the revolutionary chaos and mob rule experienced in late-eighteenth-century France. Proletarian protest constituted much more than the sporadic crowd turbulence of the past. The phenomenon of 'the riot' had long existed as the 'characteristic and ever-recurring form of popular protest, which, on occasion, turned into rebellion or revolution'.[71] Workers had for centuries past combined to dispense a 'rough-and-ready' kind of 'natural justice',[72] whether in the form of industrial arson, rick-burning, the looting of grain stores, vandalism or violence against persons – these in response to such traditional popular grievances as rack-renting, usury, legal abuses, enclosure, taxation, rising prices, or cuts in wages. In the pre-industrial age such actions were the stock-in-trade of rioters, who were dismissed by contemporaries as 'banditti', 'desperados', 'convicts', 'the mob' or 'rabble'.[73]

With increasing working-class solidarity, however, riotous assembly – or, more poignantly, the prospect of it as anticipated by dominant social groups – presented the establishment with control problems of an entirely different order. In the first half of the nineteenth century the fear of the mob coalesced with workers beginning to display a sense of 'sustained commitment to a movement of their own class objectives, and a confidence which enabled them to stand up against the physical and moral resources of their opponents'.[74] Local social protest was supplemented by the rise of the social movement (defined as a sustained public demand, backed by demonstration, that power-holders redistribute power and wealth) which could manifest itself nationally.[75] As stated above, the existence of a single, confident working class by the middle years of the nineteenth century has been doubted. Both the failure of general unionism in the 1830s and the subdued nature of class relations in the mid-Victorian period (though this was by no means free of social division and conflict) support this view. Nevertheless, the degree of consciousness which did exist before 1850 was 'felt by a considerable proportion of working people'; above all, 'it was institutionalized, and [as such] the authority of the ruling class was under challenge'.[76]

In the minds of the propertied classes the institutionalization of class (illustrated most clearly in the establishment of independent working-class organizations) was at its most menacing in the era of Chartism, the first avowedly independent working-class political movement. This was a movement largely free from the fetters of middle-class leadership or aristocratic patronage. Moreover, although its aims were not out of keeping with those of previous reform campaigns, its methods were sometimes new; at times little different from those insurrectionary movements which in recent generations the British ruling classes had observed sweeping through Europe, in particular France. This was certainly true with regard to the peak of Chartist agitation between 1839 and 1842, this being the time of 'mass meetings and torchlight processions, secret drillings, clashes with police and soldiers, and talk of revolution'.[77] Rumours of arming, drilling and other paramilitary operations spread alarm in the minds of the ruling classes. Indeed, that the opponents of Chartism endeavoured to split the movement and discredit the underlying constitutional legitimacy of the Chartist protest, by encouraging a distinction between 'moral' and 'physical' force, is clear evidence that they took meaningful account of the intimidating aspects of the agitation.

But is there a danger of overestimating the fears which the middle and upper classes displayed towards Chartism? It has been argued that in any given era of modern history, but particularly at times of marked social unrest, society has tended to exaggerate its own susceptibility to violence by referring back to some fictitious 'golden age' of law and order – this in an attempt to deplore the excesses of any current wave of turbulent behaviour, thereby winning support for the control mechanisms that authority wishes to apply.[78] However, as far as modern British history is concerned, no such 'golden age' has ever existed, except in the imagination of those troubled by the prospect of moral decline and social disintegration. This was true of early Victorian respectable opinion, which located the golden age of respect for the law and public order in pre-industrial 'Merrie England', and which consequently overestimated the odds of social cataclysm.

Historians can judge from hindsight that during the Chartist era the ruling classes retained a monopoly on the instruments of control (army, police, special constables, magistrates, the spy network, the railway and telegraph system) it required to prevent serious social conflict.[79] Moreover, not until 1848 did there exist an external threat (in the form of unrest on the Continent) which might have sapped military strength. The chance of revolution in the years approaching the first Public Libraries Act were slim. Although Chartist violence did occur, talk of violent social upheaval was in the main mere bluster. Ministers were not preoccupied with revolution.[80] Chartism was itself divided and unable to call on a mature working-class consciousness owing to the continuing occupational fragmentation of the lower orders. True, it was a movement which embraced a substantial minority of workers; but, as one historian has put it, 'a minority is still less than half'.[81] That revolution did not occur in the Chartist era can be attributed not to any sudden upturn in living standards – often perceived, though perhaps mistakenly, to have occurred in the late 1840s and 1850s[82] – or to the undeniable strength of authority; but primarily to 'the absence of any popular desire for revolution'.[83] As such, it must be concluded that, notwithstanding the hazards of retrospective analysis, there existed little chance of revolution at the time that public libraries appeared on the socio-political agenda.

This is not to say that fears of serious social conflict were not genuine. Strong and persistent, indeed, was respectable opinion's social anxiety. On the evening of the Chartist's Kennington demonstration in April 1848 Gladstone exclaimed in relief that 'our hearts feel profoundly the mercies of this remarkable day'.[84] Fears were perhaps even greater in the early days of Chartism when a Manchester poster urged: 'Be ready to nourish the tree of liberty with the blood of tyrants.'[85] The schoolgirl daughter of a respectable Manchester tailor and draper recalled, in 1875, the fears of Chartist disturbance she had experienced in 1841:

> in going from Cheetham Hill to Broughton each day, often terrified out of my wits almost, seeing the processions going to Kersal Moor where their great meetings were held ... How the riots commenced I do no know, but a mob got infuriated and set fire to one of the mills. This was followed by a general plunder of provision shops and loaves were taken from bakers' counters and thrown amongst the people. Then special constables were sworn in by hundreds ... Roughs for miles around flocked into town to join in the plunder ... One day a party of ruffians came rushing up to the Cheetham Hill Road carrying with them sacks filled with stones, which they had taken from the sides of the roads where they had been placed in heaps for repairing. These fellows rushed to the doors of the houses threatening to smash both the doors and windows unless something was given them, so some gave money, others bread, everyone had to give in one kind or another. Each day some dreadful outrage or other was committed. The factories had to be guarded by soldiers. Valuable machinery was smashed and many shops plundered of everything which could be laid hold of. This state of affairs continued for many weeks.[86]

Despite the increasing temperature of class conflict indicated by this and other contemporary observations, supporters of the public library lobby in Manchester hoped that the institution they were promoting could overcome social differences. A flavour of class consciousness pervades their mid-century utterances.[87] The opening ceremony of the Manchester Public Library took place in 1852. The building itself was symbolic of the desire to sweep away the class threat. Its previous role was as an Owenite Hall of Science, one of the institutions which were seen by their supporters as 'new churches of the people' and 'centres for the dissemination of society',[88] but by their opponents as evil socialist halls disgraced, according to one later source, by orgies and dancing parties.[89] 'I think it is fortunate', said a less propagandist speaker at the ceremony, 'that in future we shall never see in these halls a Chartist meeting.' Speaker after speaker at the ceremony couched comments in the context of class war and the consequential need for reconciliation. Charles Dickens was confident that libraries would teach 'that capital and labour are not opposed, but are mutually dependent and mutually supporting'.[90] The Salford library promoter Joseph Brotherton hoped that all classes 'would learn how necessary they were to each other – how labour and capital were bound together by a link, and how the interests of all the classes, rich and poor were intertwined, like the ivy with the oak.'[91]

A decade later social relations in Manchester were seen to have calmed. Whether the town's public library provision had been instrumental in dissolving tension is difficult to say. However, at a branch opening ceremony in 1866 the chairman of the Manchester Free Libraries Committee was adamant that libraries: 'had already been of great use in making the social position of masters and workmen better understood. The principle was being admitted that capital and labour were not opposed but were beginning to see that there was not necessarily anything antagonistic in the relative position of master and workman.' About the same time, in Doncaster, a similar tone of reconciliation was in evidence. At the library's inaugural ceremony a working man stated that the new library would have 'a great effect in making the working classes feel more contented in the position in which they were placed'.[92]

The class threat, as expressed in the early debate on public libraries, was bound up with respectable apprehensions of the perceived criminal tendencies of the labouring poor. Anti-social consequences flowed, in part, from the economic conditions of the working classes. But poverty was viewed by much of contemporary respectable opinion to be the result not of the economic system but of ignorance and immorality. Crime, too, which Engels reported had increased sevenfold between 1805 and 1842,[93] was considered to originate in cultural, not economic, deficiency. The crime which perplexed respectable opinion was twofold. First was that committed by the 'dangerous' classes (defined not as 'revolutionary' or 'ragged', but as the professionally 'criminal' or 'predatorial' classes).[94] Second, there was the crime which contained a political dynamic: a lawlessness which was believed to foreshadow the possibility of political insurrection among the lower orders.[95] The 'dangerous' classes were not seen as a potent threat to existing social arrangements: Marx regarded them as 'scum' who were prone more to reactionary than revolutionary activity (Marx distinguished the lumpenproletariat from the 'dangerous' classes, even though translators have confused the two).[96] On the other hand, an emergent working class, thirsting for liberation via education, yet retaining a propensity for violence, was much more menacing.

In this respect too fears were perhaps exaggerated: the utility of violence being eclipsed in some working-class minds by that of piecemeal advance. As Christopher Thomson (a skilled worker who had established an artisans' library) wrote in 1847:

> The thinking man knows, that although he may lack a bread-loaf, he shall not procure one by burning a farmer's corn stacks. Though the thinking man writhes beneath the curse of indirect taxation, he does not expect to cheapen his bread and wine by pulling down a grocer's shop, or breaking into a warehouse ... Until education shall teach a majority of the toiling artisans of England to become calm, sober, thinking, and self-dependent men, uniting themselves in a deliberate league for the emancipation of labour, they will continue to be at the mercy of the mammon-lovers, who thrive by their ignorance and division.[97]

The radicalism of reading, the counter–attack of culture

The reasoning of workers like Christopher Thomson represented the voice of an increasingly influential 'respectable' element of working-class opinion which stood for social advance not through irrational and counter-productive direct action, but through culture, education and literacy. The latter was a key ingredient in the class struggle. As class rivalry intensified, the controversy over the need to improve literacy grew more fierce. Working-class radicals viewed improved literacy as a means to liberation. Conservative die-hards recognized the danger it posed to social stability and the established social order, arguing that ignorance was beneficial in preventing imagination, independent thought and social ambition.[98] The propertied classes were divided on the issue. Industrialists might be more inclined than those drawing their income from traditional and landed sources to obtain for the benefit of their workers, and for the benefit of their profit margins, the literary and other skills commensurate with an economy growing ever more technical and complex. It is equally true, however, that some industrialists would have viewed education 'for the hand' as highly desirable, but education 'for the whole person' as potentially dangerous and thus best kept within limits – this despite the inherent capability of a 'rounded' education to mould intelligent, flexible workers.

That emergent industrialism and improved literacy were causally linked is by no means certain. The statistics on literacy reveal little improvement during the period of proto-industrialism. In 1754, 60 per cent of men and 40 per cent of women could reproduce their names in the marriage register. By 1840 these proportions had changed little in the case of men (66 per cent) and not at all in the case of women.[99] (However, it should be recognized that marriage register analysis is not an entirely reliable method of establishing rates of literacy: many probably did not sign lest they embarrassed their partner, a phenomenon perhaps more true of women than of men.[100]) Moreover, the pace of improvement in literacy was geographically diverse.[101] None the less, the fact that more people could read than could write – a tradition which stretched back certainly into the eighteenth century – meant that any increase in literary output would not fall on stony ground.[102] Indeed, a marked increase did occur. Commentators have stressed the vitality of reading in the area of early-nineteenth-century street and popular literature.[103] Contemporary evidence can be employed to illustrate the growth of reading. For example, *Seymour's Humorous Sketches* (1836) – described as a light-hearted look at contemporary social life – stated that: 'Literature has become the favourite pursuit of all classes ... Even the vanity of servant-maids has undergone a change, they now study Cocker [the seventeenth-century mathematician], and neglect their figures.'[104] More widespread reading was naturally crucial to an industrializing society. However, even more fundamental, especially to the *maturing* of industrialism, was the growth of *serious* reading, including practical information. Whether it be a scientific treatise or a railway timetable, serious and practical reading complemented the age of progress. The growth of interest in serious literature and raw, pertinent information was reflected in increased library activity.[105] Public library protagonists among the middle classes pointed to the beneficial effect which a free provision of wholesome, serious literature would have in assisting the move towards a more productive and open society, but without – and this requires emphasis – upsetting the fundamental laws of property and enterprise. Such cultural control desires were understood by working-class leaders like William Lovett, who sought a self-motivated moral and social regeneration of the people. Lovett saw that authority had a role to play in encouraging the education which would deliver a more sober and moral culture, but rejected centralized, overbearing schemes (he called, for example, for considerable control to be invested in teachers and locally elected school committees).[106] With regard to middle-class reformers he stated that 'those who stand in the list of education-promoters, are but state-stickers, seeking to make it an instrument of party or faction'.[107] The middle classes sought to influence, in a conservative direction, the thirst for reading displayed by the early-nineteenth-century working class.[108] In this respect, middle-class founded libraries were indeed, as one commentator has put it, 'centres of power'.[109]

Public libraries originated, in part, as a counter-attack against that aspect of working-class literacy and self-organization which threatened public order; their most potent weapon in this counter-radicalism strategy was 'safe', conventional literary culture. However, middle-class promoters of culture were divided on the question of the precise objective of their mission. To begin with, utilitarians and idealists disagreed about what constituted culture, its precise purpose and how it could be used to address the class question. To illustrate this it is appropriate to quote the Tory-inclined newspaper, *Newcastle Courant*, which in August 1839 condemned Chartism and warned:

> Should the movement be not effectively checked now, [it] cannot fail to destroy the glory of England as a nation. Their aim is to overthrow the structures, and uptear the foundations of civilized society.[110]

It is unlikely that the opponents of Chartism who read this would have been able to agree on a definition of the term 'civilized society'. Traditionalists such as Samuel Taylor Coleridge believed civil society to be under threat from *laissez-faire* industrialism. As an antidote to the latter Coleridge proposed an increased espousal of culture by society. His conception of culture was two-pronged. First, he viewed it in the conservative-anthropological sense of respect for experience and custom (as opposed to reason) as informers of character and conduct; he believed that industrial society had dissolved the social bonds of a previously responsible, integrated society, and had instigated vicious, destabilizing trade cycles. Second, he saw culture as high achievement in terms of intellectual excellence, the fine arts and a refined and liberal style of thinking and behaviour – matters which, in his eyes, little interested the champions of 'progress'. In answer to the corrosive action of industrial society on human expression and the 'inner life' he advocated, in the tradition of Kant, a renaissance in aesthetics.

Coleridge's cultural critique of commercial society stands at the beginning of an idealist tradition embracing Carlyle, Ruskin, Arnold, Morris, Green, Tawney and others.[111] This tradition exhibited unease with industrialism, especially its alienating and brutalizing effect on the masses and its creation of a class society. A society injected with an appreciation for culture, on the other hand, would be less likely to tear itself apart in pursuit of a materialism which left ignorance – a prime source of instability – unscathed. Thus, for nineteenth-century social critics, politics and culture were closely intertwined.

Conversely, utilitarians believed that civilization was enriched by industrialism. They were aware of the squalor and class disaffection which accompanied industrialism, but believed progress would eventually eradicate these problems. A maturing economy required attention to be paid to 'useful' education and scientific culture, which was in itself, the utilitarians believed, a cultural pursuit of high worth. Education for material advance would secure social stability; not just because its result would 'buy off' discontent, but because it taught the self-reliance and social atomism which negated radical cooperation.

These views on the role which education and culture might play in solving the class problem of industrial society are divergent. Yet both utilitarian and idealist perspectives – though, initially, more so the former – nourished the public library movement from its inception. Some explanations of public library development have placed the institution alongside other liberal reforms of the nineteenth century which aimed to stifle workers' discontent by facilitating a measured rise in the standard of living of the labouring classes.[112] This kind of socio-economic analysis is valid and worthy: too little has been written about the public library's materialist and class origins. But it does not offer a complete theory of development. The ingredient which needs to be added, as will be argued below, is the idea of the pursuit of culture through the public library, as a means of enriching the quality of life in all its aspects, the aesthetic included, thereby helping to preserve social order.

However convincing the Dickensian image of a new breed of culturally vacant social masters might be, even utilitarians, the public library pioneers Ewart and Edwards among them, did not reject aesthetic culture. It is simply that the utilitarian view of culture frequently differed from that associated with idealism, most obviously in the former's loathing of both exclusivity and the acceptance of unscientific custom, or the love of tradition for its own sake. Utilitarians reached for an open and efficient society based on social and scientific empiricism. In such a society, the pervasive question of class, whose critical importance to the emergence of the public library ideal this chapter has attempted to stress, would cease to be a problem. It was the mission of utilitarian cultural agencies like the public library to give effect to the social vision of a new age, at once meritocratic, progressive and free of class antagonism. While idealist traditionalists tended to view the emergent industrial society as 'diseased', and advocated a romantic return to the culture of the past in order to lessen the pain of social transformation, utilitarians diagnosed no serious problem apart from the cultural growing pains of a revolutionary epoch. Utilitarians intended that public libraries should help to smooth cultural transition – in terms of both refining an emergent but, as yet crude, antagonistic, popular urban culture and strengthening the high values of an increasingly dominant (in its eyes) middle class. It is wholly apparent that the issue of class, as expressed through the increasing consciousness of both a middle-ranking and a popular culture, served as the catalyst for a free library ideal which utilitarians, preoccupied with the phenomenon of class, found no difficulty in propagating.

The genesis of the public library can to a significant extent be located in the reaction – both practical (in terms of legislative repression like the imposition of stamp duty) and intellectual (through utilitarian and idealist thought) – to the radical threat presented by the emergence of an autonomous, self-organizing working-class culture, including the reading of 'anti-social' literature. This view, most convincingly argued in a (unfortunately) widely ignored discussion by Corrigan and Gillespie,[113] cannot be restated enough. However, the control thesis requires refinement; and not merely in respect of the failure of control. Those seeking to control working-class radicalism and reading through social policy initiatives like public libraries approached the task from different directions. Idealist thought aimed at an aesthetic reform of industrial capitalism; while utilitarianism, to which attention is now turned owing to its pre-eminence in intellectual thought at the time public libraries first came to be advocated, sought its rigorous prosecution.

CHAPTER 3

THE UTILITARIAN FLYWHEEL

Utilitarianism dominated British thought in the first half of the nineteenth century. It came to the forefront of theoretical discussion in the 1820s, and in its practical applications had its maximum impact in the reforms of the 1830s and 1840s. The fact that the philosophy was at its height when free literary provision began to be discussed, allied to the proposition that the outlooks of Ewart and Edwards were close to the philosophy, dictates that any analysis of early public library development should pay detailed attention to Benthamite-inspired utilitarianism and, crucially, to its later modification under John Stuart Mill (whose name, interestingly, was often invoked in the rhetoric of the early public library ideal). An exploration of utilitarianism will illuminate the origins of public libraries, as well as the discussion in the chapter which follows on the the motives of their principal pioneers. Moreover, although the influence of utilitarians waned in the second half of the nineteenth century, much of what they said was echoed in the public library debate up to 1914, if not beyond that date to the present day. A discussion of the relationship between utilitarianism and the public library requires that close attention be paid to the meaning and place given to education (inclusive of broad epistemological and ethical considerations) in the philosophy. Education was a key constituent of utilitarianism: 'Scratch a Benthamite or a political economist and one quickly uncovers an educationalist'.[1]

Empiricism and reason

The philosophy of utilitarianism has been influential, to the extent that 'there is scarcely a writer on moral and political theory who is free from every taint of utilitarianism'.[2] The utilitarianism of the Victorian age meant something more than a close adherence to the teachings of Jeremy Bentham or John Stuart Mill, for: 'What may be called a utilitarian ethos was pervasive and can be found in representative figures who would not have called themselves utilitarian.'[3] The philosophy can none the less be analysed with fair precision, even though it came to mean different things to different people.

The evolution of a utilitarian theory of education was firmly rooted in the Enlightenment. 'What is known as Utilitarianism, or Philosophic Radicalism', Halevy wrote, 'can be defined as nothing but an attempt to apply the principles of Newton to the affairs of politics and morals'.[4] The belief emerged that just as in the world of scientific discovery, where there existed fundamental laws disclosed by empiricism, so also in society there were laws which controlled human behaviour, verifiable by observation and experience. The utilitarians sought to evolve 'a science of morals on the model of the laws of physical science';[5] in essence, the application of scientific investigation to the worlds of morals and politics. Moreover, the proposition arose that if the laws of nature could be harnessed by men and women to facilitate understanding through controlled and predictable experiment, then so also could fundamental social laws be devised to change society itself. As the secularist Holyoake explained, it was possible to 'see the element of improvability which is in every human nature ... for there is no condition so bad which may not be improved'.[6]

Enlightenment thinkers and writers came to believe that human behaviour, and society itself, could be improved by rational thought. They were optimistic about the limits and powers of rationalism: the human capacity for reason which can be defined as 'the mental attitude which unreservedly accepts the supremacy of reason and aims at establishing a system of philosophy and ethics verifiable by experience and independent of all arbitrary assumption of authority'.[7] The power of criticism, cultivated through educational endeavour, was considered sacred. Armed with reason and critical observation, individuals were consequently in a position to challenge all preconceived ideas, exactly because 'the rational man would observe society, see what was good, and do it because it was rational'.[8]

The empiricist view of society conformed with the concept of utility. According to the early utilitarians all people acted in relation to the dictate of self-interest, the objective being to maximize personal happiness (defined as pleasure) by maximizing utility (although it should be noted that even orthodox utilitarians did not advocate blatant, unfettered egoism; believing as they did that benevolent philanthropic action often served an individual's own long-term interests).[9] To achieve this goal correct choices had to be made, restraint having to be exercised upon decisions and actions based solely on impulse and passion. Consequently it was to reason and critical observation that individuals should look to improve judgement of what was in the individual's best long-term interest. Powers of reason and criticism would be strengthened through educational pursuit; and 'through their increase in intelligence, men would begin to act rationally, give the long-term priority over the short-term and recognize their interdependence with other men'.[10] Individuals would act rationally when they calculated 'the balance of hedonistic consequences'.[11] Self-interest in this context would take on an added dimension and emerge as enlightened self-interest. From the cradle to the grave, therefore, men and women should strive to be regulated by the empiricism of experience and observation related to their personal well-being but, crucially, to be guided by reason. The latter, cultivated through education, was the means of increasing personal utility, or maximizing self-interest. Thus, in terms of raw utilitarianism, education could be considered primarily to be a function of egoism and not a means of self-culture for an ultimate social good – the latter being, in the utilitarian construct, essentially a by-product of the self-interested desire for educational advance motivating the individual.

Utilitarian orthodoxy on education has been referred to as 'mechanical materialism' (by political theorists) or 'passive sensationalism' (by psychologists). The latter term is more illustrative of how utilitarians viewed the essence of education and learning, and the source of knowledge. In opposition to the idealist conception of reason as a pre-programmed, categorizing action of the mind working on reality, utilitarians conceived of the reasoning process as originating with sense data. The mind was accorded a passive, receptive and quiescent role, allegorically pictured as an empty cabinet or bucket, a dark room or a blank sheet.[12] This conception was first convincingly purveyed by John Locke in the eighteenth century (see Chapter 7), and was taken up by French philosophers of the period.[13] The vacant mind – a *tabula rasa* – would register knowledge through the sensation of experience. The emphasis was on external stimuli: 'the mind was acted upon passively, receiving and making up impressions from the outside'.[14] Contrary to idealist thought, utilitarianism held that very little of an individual's character was innately determined; heredity was not a key factor. Character was made for, not by, the individual. The bedrock of utilitarianism was the hypothesis that all knowledge consists of generalizations from experience; that there existed 'no knowledge a priori ... no truths cognizable by the mind's inward light, and grounded on intuitive evidence'.[15] According to this proposition, the richer the environment the more complex would be the association of ideas (these being formed by sense experience) which made up the reasoning process. All learning depended on what we experienced and in what order. This explains the utilitarian interest not only in education – 'Properly directed, it [education] could determine the thoughts and so the character and disposition of man',[16] explained James Mill – but in material circumstances too. Thus, taking on board eighteenth-century theories of existentialism, and combining these with notions of enlightened self-interest as the basis of morality, early utilitarians came to believe that all ideas and actions were linked to sensations of pain and pleasure caused by external stimuli. To this mechanical learning process was added reasoned judgement, a capacity which existed beyond the ability merely to receive external stimuli.[17] With the intervention of reason, refined by education, individuals could construct agendas of preference conducive to utility (or happiness). It was a philosophy, therefore, which envisaged the perfectibility of the human being, contrary to the traditional Christian notion of human beings as both wayward and blemished by innate 'original sin'. Individuals could be improved by social engineering because not innate influences, but external stimuli, which could be controlled, were the determinants of the character which produced actions.

Bentham

Conceptualizing the mind as subordinate to the 'external' was a revolutionary doctrine which challenged organic society's foundation in divine revelation. The organic view of society, based on the idea of progress through piecemeal adjustment, is opposed to abrupt, radical change derived from doctrinal, ideological sources. One such source was the teachings of Jeremy Bentham – teachings which are central to any exploration of utilitarianism and which are seen as the origin of the utility thesis. Yet Bentham was not the creator of the concept of utility. In the eighteenth century David Hume discussed the utility of personal traits; Francis Hutcheson also pursued the concept in examining how pleasure and pain determined moral sense (it was also Hutcheson who initiated the 'greatest happiness of the greatest number' principle).[18] Moreover, as discussed above, Bentham had borrowed much from earlier existentialism; this being in keeping with the general prerequisite that 'Every consistent scheme of philosophy requires as its starting-point, a theory respecting the sources of human knowledge, and the objects which the human faculties are capable of taking cognizance of.'[19] Similarly, Bentham was able to look upon past conceptualisations of utility – specifically, the individual's mechanistic and egotistic striving for pleasure which lay at the root of his philosophy – as a first principle which he could receive as self-evident.[20]

Notwithstanding Bentham's inheritance of the concept of utility, he was the thinker who did most to develop and popularize it, although it was the publications of the students he inspired rather than his own literary output which made the most impact. His views on the self-interested pursuit of pleasure as the key determinant of morality struck a cord with prevailing ideas of *laissez-faire* as the touchstone of economic progress. For Bentham, the world of morality was fundamentally equivalent to that of commerce: 'a collection of persons pursuing each his separate interests or pleasure'.[21] In keeping with the spirit of the age, his 'felific calculus' brought the concept of utility, derived from self-interested reason, into the realms of precise (or so he thought) science.

Bentham's contribution to reform was based not simply on the radical content of his thinking, nor on his skill or reputation both as the 'great questioner of things established' and 'the great subversive'.[22] For his thinking was, above all, ideological, in that he attempted to transform a system of ideas into reality. Though detached from much of the real world – John Stuart Mill accused him of being a closeted student who knew little of 'the most natural and strongest feelings of human nature'[23] – Bentham none the less turned his philosophical thought to concrete schemes of reform. His was 'an essentially practical mind'.[24] However, it was a mind viewed by authority (for much of the time and especially during the Napoleonic Wars) as the focal point of an eccentric sect worthy of abuse.[25]

Given the contemporary view that originally the Benthamites stood outside mainstream society and politics, it is therefore curious that Bentham has been labelled as an authoritarian. This assessment of him requires careful revision. While Bentham cannot be described as a modern democrat, his advocacy of positive liberty (as opposed to the negative liberty associated with his shallow view of morality engineered by spurs and checks) should be noted. His conception of liberty was founded on the idea of security – the establishment of 'a framework within which each person could realise his or her own happiness'.[26] It was the duty of the legislator to provide security against the pain which prevented self-development. Government and the law should promote a 'security of expectation' by securing property rights, by securing the individual against crime, by securing people against misrule, by securing the poor against deprivation and by securing the masses against ignorance.[27] It was security, said Bentham, that underscored the 'moral rules which forbid mankind to hurt one another'.[28]

In view of this 'security' agenda, and despite the professed adherence of Benthamites to *laissez-faire*, it is difficult to view Bentham as the champion of minimal government.[29] The 1830s witnessed transforming legislation widely attributed to utilitarian thought. The Poor Law Amendment Act (1834) was not only a watershed in the provision of social welfare, it also made the (utilitarian) statement that the pursuit of the 'material' was the primary human value and motivation. Further, the Municipal Corporations Act (1835), though narrower in scope than utilitarians had wished, provided the framework for the development of local state services aimed at securing increased social utility. Practical utilitarian influence might have been even more extensive had it not been eclipsed on the political stage by a Free Trade movement which attracted much of the intellectual energy of the middle classes. By the 1840s, the parliamentary agents of utilitarianism – the philosophic radicals – had lost their influence.[30]

The perception of Benthamism as the major ingredient in the reform movement of the second quarter of the nineteenth century has been challenged.[31] This perception was first effectively propagated by A. V. Dicey, who, in his *Law and Public Opinion in England during the Nineteenth Century* (1905), pointed to the period 1825–70 as an age characterized by legislation for individualism, in stark contrast to the era of collectivism which was initiated by Gladstone's first administration (1868–74). Benthamism was portrayed as a coherent creed armed with a sense of purpose and a capability of transforming ideas into legislative reality. (This is also the line traditionally taken by Marxist commentators conceiving of utilitarians as the conspiratorial ideologues of emergent industrial capitalism.) However, it is possible that this forthright perception of Benthamite influence was an exaggeration born of an anguish sensed by contemporary liberals (Dicey was a liberal turned conservative) over widening divisions in late-nineteenth-century liberalism: hence, the inclination to resurrect examples of past unity among economic and social liberals.[32]

Whether or not a unified creed known as Benthamism was the guiding force behind reform in the second quarter of the nineteenth century is a question which should not at this point delay the discussion. Suffice it to say that it would be strange if Benthamite utilitarianism was the sole determinant of reform. Clearly, many advocates of reform were not Benthamites. However, it would be equally curious if, while conceding the opinion that reforms in public health, in the factories, on the railways and elsewhere would have probably occurred without utilitarianism, the latter's influence was insignificant.[33] This is certainly the case, as will be argued, if the evidence of the evolution of the reformist public library ideal is taken into account. On the other hand, what is required before the discussion can proceed is a clarification of the word utilitarian in terms of its meaning in relation to Benthamism. For although the words Benthamism and utilitarianism are usually uttered in the same breath, it is far from being the case that they now stand to mean the same thing. It is true that in common intellectual usage utilitarianism and Benthamism were, by the mid-nineteenth century, seen as synonymous, and were generally applied to 'any outlook which was militantly liberal, logically coherent and indifferent to the historic past'.[34] From hindsight, however, it is apparent that what Bentham understood as utilitarianism was very different from the variant which evolved, under John Stuart Mill, into the classical set of tenets we today comprehend, or try to comprehend, as Victorian utilitarianism.

John Stuart Mill

There are two distinct phases to the utilitarian movement of the nineteenth century, the second of which owed less to Bentham than the first. The dividing line was roughly the year 1824. Until that date Bentham and James Mill had been the undisputed leaders of the utilitarian sect, attracting the loyalty and attention of, among others, Francis Place. After 1824, John Stuart Mill and a group of younger utilitarians began to form the nucleus of the movement, using as their mouthpiece the *Westminster Review*, established in that year. This publication was of a high literary standard (though some might say turgid in style). Esoteric books and articles became the hallmark of the new generation of utilitarian thinkers, in contrast to the more digestible, practical newspaper and encyclopaedia writing (as produced by James Mill) of the earlier generation.[35]

It was not, however, merely a question of style of presentation which differentiated Mill's approach to utilitarianism from that of Bentham. It was also, crucially, a matter of substance. Under John Stuart Mill, utilitarianism was shaped into a popular philosophy relevant to the realities of life in a complex industrial society. In practical areas such as state intervention and democracy, and in philosophical matters of epistemology and ethics, utilitarianism developed a strong anti-Benthamite dimension. To trace this 'intellectually strenuous modification'[36] is interesting in its own right; but more than this it enhances an understanding of the public library ideal which, arguably, coincides more with the pertinent philosophy of Mill than with the utopian thinking of Bentham.

Mill's starkest contradiction of Bentham was epistemological. His revision of the source and nature of human knowledge propelled him in the direction of the Romantics, though without him jettisoning his faith in the power of environment.[37] The important development was his recognition of the 'innate'. This stemmed from a reaction to, first, the strict regime of systematic rational learning to which he was subjected at an early age; and, second, the crisis of mind he suffered in young adulthood. Following his rigorous upbringing and his consequent period of introspection he turned for mental rejuvenation to those intellectuals who appealed to the emotions rather than to logic: writers such as Wordsworth, Carlyle and Coleridge. Mill wrote to Carlyle in 1833 of 'the dogmatic disputatiousness of my former narrow and mechanical state', and subsequently recommended a non-vulgar utilitarianism which took into account 'the whole of human nature not the ratiocinative [reasoning] faculty only'.[38] In assessing positively the thinking of Coleridge, Mill criticized 'that cold, mechanical and ungenial air which characterises the popular idea of a Benthamite'.[39] Human nature was not a machine, said Mill, but like a tree, 'which requires to grow and develop itself on all sides, according to the tendency of the *inward* [italics added] forces which make it a living thing'.[40] His defence of Wordsworth at the London Debating Society in 1829 made public his epistemological divorce from Bentham. He became convinced, as were the Romantics, of the existence of innate human characteristics; thereby dissenting from the view of the undeveloped human mind as a *tabula rasa* or 'empty slate'. For Mill, the basis of morality was clearly not the self-interested quest for happiness measured in levels of utility (or pleasure). This, for him, was 'much too complex and indefinite an end to be sought'.[41] In any case, to think of happiness all the time would, if anything, make an individual unhappy. Rather, the human mind possessed deep intuitive powers which coloured moral judgement. For example, he looked at his father's laborious life and concluded that he had scarcely any conception of pleasure. Surely, Mill asked himself, there had been powerful innate forces and desires driving his father on.

Benthamism, argued Mill, 'had no profound knowledge of the human heart',[42] and overlooked 'the existence of about half the whole number of mental feelings which human beings are capable of'.[43] Mill pointed out that as far as morality was concerned Benthamism taught 'the means of organising and regulating the merely "business" part of the social arrangements'.[44] Mill saw that Benthamism made no allowance for humane impulses. He could not accept that the promptings of innate conscience – whether generosity, mercy, compassion, self-sacrifice or love – made no contribution to human motivation. Further, while he accepted that circumstances, to an extent, determined character, he observed that those with a strong enough innate 'will of purpose' could defy determinism and place themselves 'under the influence of other circumstances'.[45]

Mill's epistemological conversion to the fundamental importance of emotion had implications for the ethical teachings of Bentham. Feeling, Mill argued, was a natural dimension of the social nature of a humanity which clearly exhibited a capacity for fellow-feeling. Not only did this imply an innate awareness of the need for self-development which others obviously shared; it also conflicted with Bentham's atomistic hedonism, in that it impressed upon the individual the need for self-culture and self-improvement for the common as well as for the individual good. Mill's analysis challenged Bentham's atomistic hedonism in two ways. First, Mill stressed the moral obligation of duty in place of egoism. Second, while not denying the human quest for pleasure, he redefined pleasure in a way wholly different from that perceived by early utilitarianism.

Mill addressed Bentham's failure fully to reconcile egoism with social harmony. Bentham had argued that an individual's first priority was to act in a way which produced the greatest pleasure for himself or herself. This might include, as stated above, helping others to achieve happiness: adding to the general happiness – the greatest happiness of the greatest number – was potentially beneficial to the individual who would share in the aggregate good. However, helping others was not morally correct if our own self-interest was thus damaged. It was argued that what was best in our own interest was usually best for society – for example, refraining from the giving of charity was something which saved the giver money and the recipient from demoralization.

Mill disagreed with this negative liberalism; that is to say, the drawing of a circle around each individual to deter outside interference and to defend the pursuit of individual happiness as the foundation of morality.[46] In opposition to this raw utilitarianism he offered a variant that was more in keeping with the need to construct social harmony at a time of rapid and unsettling social change. Mill could not accept – as his recognition of the 'innate' demonstrated – that morals were merely an extension of trade, in which the welfare of the individual was central, and that of the community, though related, was secondary. He proposed that the foundation of morality was *general*, not *individual*, happiness. His interpretation of the 'greatest happiness' principle was that we are morally obliged to act in a way which maximizes the happiness of the aggregate; to maximize pleasure in each individual is valid, but only as much as is compatible with the maximum general happiness.[47] Mill wrote of 'an indissoluble link between his [the individual's] own happiness and the good of the whole'.[48] As the antithesis of Benthamite thought he stated that:

> the happiness which forms the utilitarian standard of what is right in conduct, is not the agent's own happiness, but that of all concerned.[49]

In a fashion which resurrected the Tory-aristocratic ideal of the protection and direction of the poor by the rich, Mill proposed an altruistic utilitarianism in which individuals considered communal happiness to be the prime objective; not because individuals might accrue happiness from that obtained by the aggregate, or win approbation for charitable acts, but because duty was a non-negotiable attribute of innate social human nature.

Mill's rejection of the primacy of self-interest might be construed as a condemnation of the doctrine of self-help. On the contrary, self-help was transformed by Mill into a value system – a religion almost – which underpinned his conception of communal utilitarianism, thereby destroying Bentham's belief that all self-help endeavour was born of self-interest. Utilitarians had always stood four-square behind the doctrine of self-help, especially in the context of education. Francis Place, for example, was unequivocal in his advocacy of education – the assimilation of 'information' as he put it – as a means of self-improvement:

> As a man's understanding is directed to some laudable pursuit, his desire for information will increase; he will become decent in his conduct and language, sober, discreet, taking reasonable pride in his own person and in that of those who are dependent on him. Such a man will frequently rise as the uninformed man sinks; his prospects will not be so invariably hopeless of attaining to a somewhat better condition; he will seldom be without some money, some small property; the Benefit Club will maintain him in sickness, and save his family from immediate distress when he dies.[50]

Self-help, as constituted by such endeavour as the acquisition of information to make correct choices, was the corollary to the utilitarian distaste for the privileged society. Utilitarians believed that power, social position and wealth should be achieved by merit, talent and industriousness, and not bestowed by influence (though inheritance was only occasionally denounced). Education, it is worth emphasizing, would be the cornerstone of this meritocracy. Education would bring increased pleasure not only in terms of direct tangible results, but also by way of the very act of achieving those results: self-motivation, perseverance and other attributes represented positive utility.

But self-help was clearly not a doctrine confined to utilitarians alone. Other radical movements, such as Owenite cooperation and Chartism, also espoused calls to individual improvement. Owen, like Bentham, believed that self-motivation in education would enhance materialist society and improve individual character. However, Owen looked upon education as a function of community interest, and not of self-interest, which he considered an evil. Chartists too believed in the beneficial effects of self-improvement through education. Lovett viewed education – based on local organization as opposed to Prussian-style centralization – as an individual social right from which would flow liberation.[51] The point of departure between idealist stances like those of Owenism and Chartism, on the one hand, and Benthamism, on the other, was that self-improvement for the latter was equated primarily with egoism. In other words, individuals would welcome education not for the communal good it bestowed but for personal benefit, in keeping with the felific calculus philosophy that all decisions were to be reduced to a crude calculation on a balance sheet of personal utility. Bentham was confident in the belief that self-interest, whether pursued through educational endeavour or otherwise, was the foundation of ethics.

Mill's eventual conception of self-help drew more on idealism than on Benthamite hedonism. The ultimate purpose of self-help, Mill argued, was the improvement of society as a whole. Yet he did not abandon his belief in the psyche as a consumer of pleasure. He argued that the pursuit of communal happiness, which could only be made if individuals sought improvement and independence, constituted the highest of pleasures. To overcome instantaneous satisfaction of desires and temptations damaging of character, and to concentrate instead on the feelings of others, was commendable in the extreme. This emphasis on self-denial and empathy for the general good raises the question of how Mill perceived the notion of pleasure. For if Mill's dream was of a society in which individuals had no higher desire than to act socially – to act in a way which was not harmful, and perhaps even beneficial, to the common good – he would, in effect, be shifting pleasure into a wholly different dimension.

This is precisely what Mill did. Drawing on his father's gradation of human desires, Mill differentiated, where Bentham had not, quality and quantity of pleasure.[52] (It should be noted, however, that at least one commentator has argued that Bentham was aware of the higher–lower pleasure distinction.[53]) Like Bentham, Mill equated happiness with pleasure. But whereas Bentham largely theorized pleasure in terms of equal units, the various accumulation of which produced greater or lesser happiness, Mill identified a quality to pleasure. For example, the maximization of utility by an animal could not begin to be compared with even the skimpiest accumulation of utility by a human being; hence Mill's assertion that he would 'rather be Socrates dissatisfied than a pig satisfied'.[54] This qualitative interpretation of pleasure enabled Mill to perceive what constituted happiness on its highest plane. He proposed that complete happiness was the perfection of the human nature. As one historian has written:

> The ideal happiness was that experienced by individuals who had fully developed their faculties, who had complete mastery of their wants, especially their animal desires, and could recognise and realise their individual and collective interests.[55]

The idea of the fullest development of human potential was a communal goal, yet one to which individuals contributed by striving to fulfil their own potential.

The culture of self-improvement thus coalesced with that of collective betterment. The logic of this relationship was that to improve oneself was, in effect, an altruistic act – because the community extracted utility from the moral advance of its individual members. In this sense happiness was obtained indirectly, not at first hand through changes in external circumstances. The ultimate source of happiness was the long-term development of ennobling mental culture - personal affection, social feeling, the arts, and senses of duty, sacrifice, truth and beauty - which was intrinsically communal.[56]

The teleological growth towards human perfection which Mill envisaged repudiated Bentham's atomistic hedonism. Atomism was rejected in favour of altruistic moral conduct. Hedonism was revised to give happiness, in its highest form, an outward-looking dimension. Furthermore, Mill's progress towards altruism as the basis of action has been construed, in terms of political economy, as an endorsement of socialistic principles. As such, what he saw as the responsibility of government went far beyond that advised by Bentham.

It is a myth that there ever existed in the industrial age an epoch of pure *laissez-faire*. Not even the classical economists called for complete non-intervention. State intervention in education, for example, was advocated by both Adam Smith and Malthus. James Mill, too, saw no harm in government assisting in the education of the people: where social utility was increased, he and others argued, government action was justified. This relationship was founded on the teleological nature of utilitarianism: that is to say, an action should be judged according to its consequences. If an action resulted in a positive accumulation of utility then that action was justified. Thus, in the field of government, intervention could be condoned if society's happiness was increased; having taken into account, of course, such negative consequences as loss of individual independence.

Thus, the Select Committee on Inquiry into Drunkenness (1834), driven by a strong utilitarian influence concerned with the eradication of drink-related disorderly conduct, stated: 'That the right to exercise legislative interference for the correction of any evil which affects the public weal, cannot be questioned, without dissolving society into its primitive elements.'[57] Even the Poor Law Amendment Act (1834), which stood as the epitome of *laissez-faire* economics - its aim being to disengage as much public money as possible from the provision of welfare - included in its provisions the imposition of central administration and a system of inspection, both of which were deemed necessary to ensure that the positive social utility obtained was not lost by inefficient management. It is argued that in accepting the efficacy of state action in certain economic and social fields, utilitarians originated the theme of the 'coercive welfare state'. This was certainly the opinion, for example, of the Victorian thinker Herbert Spencer.[58] In making this accusation he distinguished between early and later generations of utilitarians only by degree. However, to denigrate Mill's outlook more than that of Bentham, merely because the former widened the constituency of government control, was to misread the refinement of Mill's philosophy.

It is true that Mill appears to evolve a more interventionist stance than earlier utilitarians. In this, as in other respects, he was influenced by

Coleridge. Mill recognized that Coleridge was 'at issue with the "let alone" doctrine, or the theory that governments can do no better than to do nothing'. Though conceding that governments should not 'chain up the free agency of individuals', Coleridge claimed that it did not follow from this stance that:

> government cannot exercise a free agency of its own – that it cannot beneficially employ its powers, its means of information and its pecuniary resources (so far surpassing those of any other association, or of any individual), in promoting the public welfare in a thousand means which individuals would never think of, would have no sufficient motives to attempt, or no sufficient powers to accomplish.[59]

Thus, Mill found himself able to adopt an almost socialist perspective:

> While we repudiated with the greatest energy that tyranny of society over the individual which most socialist systems are supposed to involve, we yet look forward to a time when ... it will no longer either be, or thought to be, impossible for human beings to exert themselves strenuously in producing benefits which are not to be exclusively their own, but to be shared with the society they belong to.[60]

These sentiments, from Mill's autobiography, were echoed by economic liberals after his death. Thomas Mackay (who entertained libertarian arguments against the provision of public libraries[61]) explained that the final philosophy of Mill was 'consciously or unconsciously affected by the socialist aspirations which were then only beginning to exercise an influence on modern politics'.[62]

It is emphasized by one historian that:

> Mill's list of what a government may legitimately facilitate if it considered the market product to be unsatisfactory covers almost the entire output of twentieth-century welfare states.[63]

Yet Mill's apparent commitment to welfarism should be qualified by his enthusiasm for voluntary action, which he considered preferable to government action.[64] However, to pursue the authenticity of Mill's conversion to the economics of the aggregate simply in terms of degrees of intervention advocated is to be deflected from uncovering the motive underpinning his recommendation of state action in certain circumstances. It is important to stress that Mill advocated state action in those circumstances where hindrances to fuller self-development could be removed and where basic citizen rights – for example, minimum levels of subsistence and equality of opportunity – could be protected. (State sponsored education was a case in point: it would help to teach individuals how not to infringe the freedom of others, while providing for all the basic equipment for self-development.) The object of state action, said Mill, was to pull down as many obstacles as possible standing in the way of improvement by individuals. His statism was not derived from any vision of the economic efficiency of shared resources or from any disgust of private ownership; it was fashioned by his belief in self-culture as ultimately an altruistic pursuit. In short, the state could serve to encourage the self-culture which engendered the altruistic spirit.

The assistance of the state in providing a fertile environment for the development of culture – both humanistic and communal – echoed Bentham's theory of security guaranteed by law (in this respect, if not perhaps in others, it is clear that Mill did not move away from Bentham to the extent that is commonly described and was, in fact, indebted to him[65]). However, it can be argued that Bentham's main concern was with the aggregate social utility this produced: as long as the 'greatest happiness of the greatest number' was secured it did not matter that the personal happiness of some individuals was not maximized. Mill, on the other hand, challenged early utilitarianism as the philosophy of the majority: he argued in favour of individual claims to justice in contrast to the ruthless application of *laissez-faire* principles.[66] Mill stressed the importance of the individual and his or her self-development as the key to the development of the whole. The provision of social conditions appropriate to self-development thus became a social right. This argument pulls Mill closer to the type of idealism expounded by T. H. Green (see Chapter 7).

An important instrument of self-improvement for Mill's generation of utilitarians was local government. The Municipal Corporations Act (1835) is a prime example of utilitarian interventionism for egalitarian improvement. The legislation won support for four basic reasons: first, to provide towns with effective policing; second, to reflect more truthfully the changing balance in society towards the entrepreneurial classes; third, to extend representation, and lessen corruption and privilege; finally, as a corollary to the franchise reform of 1832,[67] utilitarians saw Municipal Reform in 1835 (and, more importantly, amending legislation in 1837 enabling non-chartered towns to be brought under the provisions of the Act) as a blow against the rights of privilege and as a move towards that representative system of government which would precipitate enlightened middle-class rule and, consequently, social harmony. Moreover, democratically elected corporations (though in some cases property restrictions reduced the local authority electorate below that of the parliamentary) would enhance the bid for social utility. Utilitarians such as Francis Place and J. A. Roebuck 'glimpsed a municipal future which might indeed lead to a form of local socialism'.[68] In urging municipal reform Roebuck, for example, argued that the new corporations should be endowed with extensive administrative powers in such areas of social policy as gas, lighting, police, public charities and public markets.[69] Place, in his prospectus for town corporations, hoped that:

> the powers of the council were to include the control of the magistrates, police, and gaols, of paving, lighting, water, markets, bridges, docks, harbours, sewers, etc., the making of bye-laws, and the adminstration of all town property and trusts for hospitals, schools and charities.[70]

Administrative powers of the intensity advocated by utilitarians were not included in the Municipal Corporations Act – something which was to have implications for the origins of the public library. The utilitarian dream of effective local government was slow to materialize: for the idea of locally evolved social policy raised the vexed question of taxation. Despite the fact that by modern standards local taxes in the early nineteenth century were minimal and increased only slowly, economy remained the order of the day. The petty bourgeoisie, although much of it had been politically radical in the early nineteenth century, became in the wake of its enfranchisement in 1832 depoliticized relative to its previous commitment. However, the role of the petty bourgeoisie in local as opposed to national affairs and politics remained strong after 1832. The line usually adopted by the petty bourgeoisie was that of retrenchment to protect their own ratepaying position.[71] The thought of the local council spending large sums 'filled the brewer, the baker and the candlestick maker with alarm', for the unprogressive tradesman class was, generally speaking, 'not accustomed to dealing with big transactions and high figures'.[72] Not that hostility to spending was a trait only of the petty bourgeoisie. Members of the substantial bourgeoisie only adopted a pro-spending position later in the century, while working-class ratepayers, whose numbers increased in the second half of the nineteenth century, 'were by no means always committed to doctrines of higher spending and higher rates for public purposes'.[73] Ratepayers found hard to swallow the fact that their taxes were for a communal good from which they (indirectly) benefited. None the less, utilitarian reformers battled away in the attempt to establish the principle of justifiable public spending which, providing it was not wasteful, would enhance individual and social utility.

Empowering the citizen

The corollary of public spending was political accountability. Later utilitarians, unlike most Whigs, believed that political reform in 1832 had not gone far enough. Those, like John Mill, who argued for a further extension of the franchise, did so for three reasons. First, they were convinced that good government – one which was efficient and free from corruption – could only be secured by the granting of meaningful political representation to as wide a section of society as possible. John Mill was more liberal on the franchise issue than either his father or Bentham, each of whom believed that people did not need to participate in their own government if their governors ruled wisely. John Mill disassociated himself from the view that participation in 'wise' government was immaterial, arguing that the variety of public opinion which democracy entailed acted as a check against misgovernment. In this respect Mill was more closely associated than were early utilitarians with mainstream nineteenth-century liberalism.[74] Mill's democratic prescription was qualified, however, by his suggested denial of the franchise to non-taxpayers and non-ratepayers, to those who depended on relief and to those who had turned to crime.[75]

Some utilitarians continued to advocate a property qualification and the exclusion of women.

The second reason for the espousal of democracy was the conviction that history was on the side of the masses, in that a wider distribution of political power was deemed inevitable. Utilitarians observed that power was passing from influential individuals to the masses, and considered this trend to be beneficial 'in principle': for the crucial additional ingredient was education. The argument was summed up by the philosophic radical J. A. Roebuck, who, writing in the wake of municipal reform in 1835, stated:

> Day by day we see the people gaining power – day by day therefore the necessity increases for the possession of information by the people. We do not suppose indeed, that the mass of mankind can become legislators – or even acquire the knowledge which a legislator ought to posses. But we do hope and confidently trust, that the people generally may be so far instructed as to be able to judge accurately of the intellectual and moral worth of those whom they select as their representatives.[76]

Utilitarians stressed that electoral reform could only proceed if attention was paid to educational provision. Whereas Tories saw education as a destabilizing force because it gave the masses ideas above their station and an understanding of anti-social teachings – *Blackwood's* proclaimed in 1825 that 'whenever the lower orders of any great state have obtained a smattering of knowledge they have generally used it to produce national ruin'[77] – utilitarians believed that education was the prerequisite of emergent democracy, of the forthcoming popularization of politics and of social calm. An educated electorate would 'bestow the necessary degree of attention on the information provided, and arrive at correct conclusions on the questions of the day'.[78] To further the assimilation of information, utilitarians were strenuous in their advocacy of a free press, and fought alongside working-class radicals for the abolition of the taxes on knowledge. A free press was likened to the Newtonian conception of the universe – a free flow of ideas, or forces, out of which would arise a perfect balance of reasoned argument leading to correct decisions and action. (However, it is worth adding that when stamp duty was repealed in 1855 it was done so less in the interests of a truly liberal press than of mainstream publications which had been held back by taxes from both investing in new machinery and attracting new readers.[79])

In the context of electoral reform the eradication of ignorance became a familiar battle cry. Speaking in favour of Buckingham's Public Institutions Bill (1835), one MP was of the opinion that 'the public mind was in a state of most melancholy ... mystification'. He related to the House of Commons an interview he had conducted with some farmers on a recent trip to Devon. 'Would not you prefer coming in an independent way to vote, and not being brought in your landlord's train?', he asked. One farmer replied: 'Can't zay, I generally comes a horseback.' He asked another farmer: 'Would you not like to go to poll by way of the ballot my friend?' To which he received the reply: 'Don't know sir; I've been always used to go by way of Daalish [Dawlish].'[80]

Such ignorance, it was feared, placed individuals under the evil sway of political demagogues and agitators. As Henry Brougham wrote: 'The more widely science is diffused, the better will the Author of all things be known, and the less the people be "tossed to and fro by the sleight of men, and cunning craftiness, whereby they lie in wait to deceive".'[81] Ignorance was seen as a contributory factor in social unrest. Place, in 1831, expressed the opinion that had there been a free press, the agricultural disturbances of the previous year would not have occurred.[82] Moreover, a free press, he believed, would have induced the establishment of other educational agencies, including libraries, fighting to eradicate ignorance:

> Had there been an unshackled press knowledge would have been spread in so many ways, and in so many directions, so numerous would have been the schools, the reading clubs, the local libraries, so multifarious the cheap publications, so accurate the knowledge and so extensively would it have been spread, that not one of the terrible evils we deplore, the consequences of ignorance, would have been inflicted on the community.[83]

Education was also central to the third reason why utilitarians promoted democracy. It was intended that democracy would strike a blow at the traditional, corrupt society which thinkers like Bentham and John Mill so despised. Bentham aimed his thinking at 'an assault on ancient institutions'.[84] He unrelentingly attacked the British monarchy and aristocracy.[85] Privilege and exclusivity were seen as particularly distasteful aspects of the old order, and were to be replaced by meritocracy and openness – Mill's toleration of the 'eccentric' and of diverse culture should be noted in this respect. However, in the absence of a traditional aristocratic rule, a working-class hegemony was not envisaged as the inevitable outcome of a more liberal society. Rather, utilitarians predicted that the middle classes would emerge as the dominant social formation. This would be by virtue of two factors. First, the middle classes would enhance their power by reforming existing educational institutions (grammar and public schools and the universities) and establishing new ones (like public libraries) in which they could participate. It was argued that the middle rank in society, in touch as it was with the rigours and requirements of the industrial age, would use its newly won educational standing to provide leadership and exert influence over other social groups. Clearly, this was an élitist scenario founded on a concern for high achievement; it might also be construed as a control impulse involving the dissemination of values. The natural working of the educational system would inject into society, said John Mill, 'the insights and aspirations of gifted individuals, by diffusing into the mass of the population the elevated standards of a highly educated elite, and at the same time raise the economic, intellectual and cultural levels of the labouring classes'.[86] At issue here, therefore, are the notions of culture as improvement and as ideology discussed in Chapter 1.

The second factor given by utilitarians in predicting the middle-class triumph was the arrogant belief that, empowered with the vote, the masses would without hesitation invest power in superior middle-class political representatives. An alliance would then be formed between the middle and the working classes in opposition to aristocratic oligarchy. Potentially disruptive working-class aims would be undermined by the natural supremacy of middle-class cultural and political leadership; established interests in land and church, blind to social change and the urgent need for precautionary reform, would also be weakened by a confident, advancing middle class drawing support from the masses.

Materialism, reason and the 'useful' curriculum

Political accountability, the utilitarians stressed, was essential to the social aspects of *laissez-faire* and the practicalities of industrialization. Closed societies, argued utilitarians, were not appropriate to the pursuit of prosperity based on the culture of improvement and the fulfilment of latent talent. As the utilitarian philosophy developed it became increasingly enthusiastic, in contrast to early utilitarianism, about the prospects of an economic advance towards a utopian millennium in which rationalism provided the material environment necessary for the fullest development of human nature. To an extent, the economic theory of early utilitarianism – as was the case with economics generally – incorporated Malthusian ideas on the relationship between population and prosperity. To thinkers like Bentham, despite the teleology of his ethics, the concept of the 'stationary state' – the theory that the growth of production and the accumulation of capital could not outrun population increase – would have been familiar. It is possible, indeed, that John Mill's attack on atomistic hedonism was partly informed by the need for an altruistic redistribution of wealth and for the protection of individual liberty at a time when the prospects of near infinite material happiness were as yet unproven. This said, utilitarians were both aware and supportive – much more than others – of the industrial and economic changes that were taking place.

Despite John Mill's acceptance of pleasure derived from imagination, utilitarians never decoupled materialism from happiness. The relevance of materialism to the utilitarian philosophy is illustrated by the fact that by the early twentieth century the two were sometimes seen as synonymous. At the jubilee celebrations for Manchester Public Libraries, the Chairman of the Public Libraries Committee spoke of how the provision of literature could help to balance the greed of day-to-day living. Manchester, he believed, was essentially 'a city whose chief characteristic has been the deification and pursuit of material achievement'. This 'sole aim and end of life', he continued, was popularly called utilitarianism.[87]

For the utilitarians the pursuit of materialism resulted not only from a conviction in the benefits to be derived from the free play of economic forces, but also from the notion that a confident and advancing capitalist society contributed to social stability. As James Mill put it in 1818, 'When the people are wretchedly poor, all classes are vicious, all are hateful, and all are unhappy.'[88] The crisis which befell capitalism in the generation after 1815 appeared to redouble the efforts of those who hoped to bring about social stability through a bolstering of capitalism. At a time when confidence in many sectors of manufacturing (such as cotton) was being undermined by the acceleration of cost-cutting investment, the introduction of new technology and the resultant downward pressure on wages and employment; when it was becoming more apparent that, despite economic advance, oscillation between bouts of depression and recovery were growing ever more violent; when, indeed, the very survival of industrial capitalism itself was perceived by some as without guarantee, utilitarians stood firmly behind the belief that industrial capitalism would endure, that it was ordained by natural laws of economic behaviour, and that it could be managed successfully to ensure social tranquillity.

To deliver the materialism which was to underscore social harmony, utilitarians turned to the transforming power of education. They viewed education as a crucial factor in the strengthening of industrial capitalism. This explains, to a significant extent, why they became so deeply involved in the formulation of educational policies, in the work of educational movements and in the parliamentary promotion of measures for a more educated society.[89]

Utilitarians sought to use education for economic purposes in two ways. First, it was obvious that a dissemination of the facts of the 'blessings of machinery ... of mechanics, metallurgy and hydraulics'[90] would multiply production. Utilitarianism championed the creation of a scientific culture through an expansion of technical education – the Society for the Diffusion of Useful Knowledge and the mechanics' institutes being prime examples of the pursuit of this objective. Until the nineteenth century 'useful' education (aside from apprenticeship) had been the preserve of a middle-class scientific sub-culture. It was not just that early industrialism's need for scientific knowledge and technical education was far from critical, the Industrial Revolution being based, to a large degree, on the exploitation of long-standing skills. It was also the case, arguably, that there was simply little money for educational investment. Interest in materialist-oriented education advanced when, after about 1810, the economy moved into a position of abundance in terms of investment resources.[91] Even then, in the absence of state sponsorship, the opportunity cost of education – elementary, let alone higher technical – for individuals was high.[92]

Utilitarians enthused about the value and prospect of scientific advance. The latter was praised as wholly relevant to the now progressive world. Utilitarians pointed out that an expansion in scientific knowledge could not be brought about by a closed, privileged, élitist society addicted to traditional learning, and unsympathetic to the exploitation of hidden talent and new knowledge. As Bentham wrote in respect of the arts and the sciences:

There is no method more calculated to accelerate their advancement, than their general diffusion: the greater the number of those by whom they are calculated, the greater the probability that they will be enriched by new discoveries. Fewer opportunities will be lost, and greater emulation will be excited in their cultivation.[93]

Such explanations of the benefits of openness and equal opportunity depict utilitarianism in its liberal aspect. However, the second of the two ways in which utilitarians viewed education as economically relevant might be considered controlling in nature. The diffusion of a practical education (and this would include basic literacy) was crucial to the health of industrial capitalism. In addition to this, a knowledge of the workings of capitalism, said utilitarians, constituted an ingredient in educational endeavour. It was argued that through an assimilation of powers of reason, fostered by education, the masses would come to accept capitalist principles as truth. Utilitarians believed that capitalism was morally correct and would be proved as such by an increased understanding of its intricacies; not just through direct education in political economy – though this was not unimportant[94] – but by educating individuals to become more intelligent and more receptive to theoretical propositions.

Utilitarians hoped that reason would reveal the laws of economics. Bentham believed that men should be swayed by reason: that they should 'scrutinise political and social institutions through the eyes of reason'.[95] Failure to adhere to reason, he argued, was a consequence of the man-made world of politics where, unlike in the natural, physical world, no fundamental laws operated; and so in keeping with this analysis utilitarians set out to create laws and institutions which did have a scientific basis.

In the economic sphere, by contrast, utilitarians thought they could see the existence of fundamental iron laws, with which governments should not interfere: 'There was an iron law of wages and of rents, a law that determined price according to the supply of and demand for a commodity, and a law, of evil portent, that showed that population rose faster than the means of feeding it.'[96] And at the root of this market society was the perceived freedom of the private ownership of property, which since the seventeenth century had 'become for more and more men the critically important relation determining their actual freedom'.[97] It was further argued that because economic laws were fundamental they could be harnessed by men and women to make reality of one of Bentham's own guiding tenets – 'profit maximised, expense minimised'[98] – in the same way that science could bring about progress and prosperity by subjugating the forces of nature to the human will. Education was seen as a materialist emancipator because it taught men and women through observation, judgement and reason to make use of the laws of economic behaviour. It taught them how to buy in the cheapest market and sell in the most expensive, whether the commodity be goods, capital or labour; in effect, how to be 'at one' with the acquisitive nature of capitalist society.

Education for the utilitarians was, in part, moral and principled – in that, in an era of unprecedented economic activity, values corresponding to the free market society and possessive individualism were considered non-negotiable. After all, the laws governing economic activity were themselves unbending. The educational content of utilitarianism added to its role as a justificatory theory of market society. All that was required was for individuals to be inculcated with the reason and knowledge which would make the existence, nature and operation of economic laws self-evident. Reason, through education, would enable the minds of individuals to absorb the external stimuli of practical economic behaviour and capitalize on their realizations, thereby contributing to their personal utility. For most people, as Simon has argued, this meant that they:

> must come to understand that their interests coincided with those of the industrial capitalist; that their prosperity, like that of the middle class, was dependent on the institution of private property, and the free play of capital. Such appreciation of the harmony of interests would be the inevitable outcome of the spread of 'enlightenment'.[99]

The utilitarian prescription for educating the lower orders was to tie them in with the dominant tenets of middle-class political philosophy. Above all, 'it was necessary to control and direct the thoughts and actions of the workers – to win them as allies in the task of establishing a capitalist order'.[100] This could best be achieved by appealing to workers' powers of reason by which means they 'would understand that it was in their best interests to become calm, orderly and acquiescent'.[101]

When they had become familiar with the mechanics of capitalist society, it was believed that workers would be able to participate in the capitalist game, instead of calling for its abandonment from the terraces. Utilitarians made a direct association between the assimilation of 'useful' knowledge and the opportunity for acquiring the higher material existence which capitalism appeared to offer. As Francis Place put it: 'the best-paid classes are the best informed'.[102] This does not mean, of course, that other schools of thought were excluded from supporting either materialism or the knowledge of the market required to pursue it. Traditional élites, even those closer to the land than to commerce, were hardly likely to relinquish the opportunity of participating in the fruits of industrial expansion; Whigs, emulating utilitarians in proclaiming the propagandist potential of education, came to see by the end of proto-industrialization that 'educated labourers would be brought more easily to understand the infallibility of McCullochian economics'.[103] Faith in the power of reason to reveal economic truths and to acquire material goods was clearly not exclusive to utilitarianism. However, unlike other schools of thought, it did represent a core element: utilitarians were entranced by the prospect of infinite happiness derived from a practical education pertinent to the laws of supply and demand and to industrial progress. The masses were 'bad calculators', said Mill, because they lacked 'practical good sense'.[104] Utilitarians believed they could deliver the education required to produce 'good calculators'.

Providing the means of 'getting on' in capitalist society was central to the utilitarian concept of education. Bentham taught that all subjects should be considered with reference to their practical utility in normal day-to-day life – 'knowledge in his view must serve a social function'[105] – which in the industrial age meant the application of science and technology. Utilitarians therefore emphasized, as none had before, the vocational principle in education: that is to say, the utility-bearing capacity of skills training which fitted pupils for the division of labour that characterized industrial society. Even popular elementary education was seen to possess a materialist end. As Altick has written:

> A reasonable bit of elementary schooling made better workers: it increased production, reduced waste, assured more intelligent handling of machinery, even increased the possibility of a workman's hitting upon some money-saving short cut.[106]

In their enthusiasm for 'useful' education utilitarians attacked the received wisdom of traditional education; for example, theology, the Classics and 'dead' languages. The latter were considered useful only in so far as they improved logical thinking or grammar. Bentham wrote that to prefer the study of dead languages

> to the study of those useful truths which the more mature industry of the moderns has placed in their stead, is to make a dwelling-house of a scaffolding, instead of employing it in the erection of a building.[107]

Similarly, the Classics were admitted into the utilitarian curriculum not as a preliminary for studying the life and thought of ancient civilizations (though James Mill's extensive study of the Greeks, especially Plato, should be noted as a contradiction here) but for their practical worth in teaching the construction of good English: texts were thus often studied in isolated chunks, not as a whole.[108] Traditional learning might be of use to traditional professions, said utilitarians; but medicine, the church and the law were not as important – though not, of course, irrelevant – to the dynamism and acquisitiveness of industrial capitalism or to the materialist ambitions of society as they had been to pre-industrial society. Utilitarians prescribed that the nation's education curriculum should suit the culture of scientific materialism which was emerging.

Utilitarianism never surrendered this mechanistic interpretation of educational need; the philosophy did, however, juxtapose it with a toleration of aesthetic, liberal learning. As argued above, John Mill became more aware than did early utilitarians of the non-rational factors shaping society. He related in his autobiography that, following his nervous breakdown, he

> never turned recreant to intellectual culture, or ceased to consider the power and practice of analysis as an essential condition both of individual and of social improvement. But I thought that it had consequences which required to be corrected, by joining other kinds of cultivation with it. The maintenance of a due balance among the faculties now seemed to me of primary importance. The

cultivation of the feelings became one of the cardinal points in my ethical and philosophical creed ... I now began to find meanings in the things which I had read or heard about, the importance of poetry and art as instruments of human culture.[109]

Whereas his father had seen the arts – poetry, for example – as largely a vehicle for refining the sensibilities and sharpening observation, John Mill was more convinced of their inherent joyfulness.[110] He questioned the 'nurture' his father had given him, where non-scientific culture was said to have no connection with political philosophy. He turned instead to the 'nature' content of Wordsworth's poetry and other literature which addressed itself to the non-material fundamentals of life.[111] In sympathy with liberal culture he advised that individuals should 'know something of everything', not simply 'everything of something', as pure utilitarianism taught.[112] He defended the study of the classics as a contribution to the culture of improvement which industrialism espoused.[113]

Good citizenship

The combination of useful and liberal learning which John Mill's philosophy came to enshrine similarly characterized the notion of 'good citizenship'. The ethics of citizenship which idealists were to promote later in the century were also an aspect of utilitarianism. Utilitarians sought to engineer 'good citizens'. The term is an amorphous one. It has been suggested that it originated in the Enlightenment: that it was a hangover from the 'social darkness' that had gone before.[114] During the Enlightenment history had been seen as 'a saga of rudeness and barbarity tempered by despotism', the English Civil War being the nadir in this respect. Consequently, the Enlightenment

> sought to replace militancy with a civil and political order. These required civility and politeness ... Rudeness has to yield to a new moral order of refinement'.[115]

As urbanization threw people together in close proximity, in an anonymous environment where informal social controls were significantly weakened, the pressure on citizens to become more 'sociable' increased. People became more 'clubbable', to borrow Dr Johnson's phrase.[116] The first half of the nineteenth century was an era when people came together as never before for mutual material benefit, amusement and intellectual stimulation; whether in the masonic lodge, the tavern meeting, the coffee house, the friendly society, the book club, the subscription library or the mechanics' institute. The ethos of such organizations incorporated consensus and cooperation: they flourished as 'free republics of rational society'.[117] 'Good citizens' were educated and could display tolerance to others in social affairs and the transactions of daily existence; they were politically sophisticated, sound in practical judgement, cultivated in common sense, loyal, reliable, responsible and dutiful. Utilitarians were party to these exalted manifestations of rationality.

Such qualities were said to enhance the dynamism of industrial capitalism. The market society was also deemed conducive to harmonious citizenship. Division of labour produced a harmony of interests in that the principle underlying it was a mutually beneficial trading of acquired skills. The acquisitiveness at which the division of labour was aimed was not, according to early political economists, anti-social but socially stabilizing: there existed an intimate link with others who, not in direct competition, sought the same material rewards. As such, an extensive division of labour was thought to coincide with a civilized society enjoying social peace. Individuals were to be civilized and controlled by the 'collision' (the increasingly complex interplay between individuals) which the dynamism of industrialization wrought. Individuals were like parts of a machine: they had to work together smoothly and harmoniously if the greater entity of which they were a part was to operate efficiently.

Beyond this economic sphere utilitarians also sought a harmony of interest in political and civic matters. 'Good citizenship' was bound up with the presentation of the municipality as the dominant institution of town life: the council was the focus of citizenship. A representative system of local government afforded a channel down which the political energies of townspeople could be drawn. The process of electing a council constituted a safety valve for more dangerous forms of political agitation. A 'good citizen' expressed political opinions through the narrow confines of established political institutions, unlike the bad citizen who sought a redress of grievances via uncontrolled, perhaps extra-legal, methods.[118] Finally, the 'good citizen' was of good character. Whereas in the early nineteenth century good character was pursued for reasons of egoistic piety, for personal redemption, after about 1870 – coinciding, interestingly, with the increasing momentum in the public library movement – the term came to be conceptualized as descriptive of someone displaying an altruistic, dutiful attitude towards society.[119]

The intersection of utilitarian and public library philosophies

The archetypal 'good citizen' corresponded to the version of utilitarianism which developed under the direction of John Mill. In keeping with Mill's epistemological conversion, the 'good citizen' was refined in liberal culture as well as in the culture of science; and was sensitive to the importance of both progress and tradition, 'to a future which', as Mill anticipated, 'unite the best qualities of the critical with the best qualities of the organic periods'.[120] Ethically, he or she had adopted an altruistic perception of the self-improvement of the individual. This self-culture was founded not on atomistic hedonism, but on an innately sensed teleological growth towards human perfection. Yet, without surrendering the intrinsic good of their individuality, 'good citizens' also conformed to the Benthamite idea of individuals as mechanistic units activated by social conditions. On a more practical plane, the 'good citizen' participated in a political democracy (though certain immoral and dependent groups were to remain dis-enfranchised); and was open-minded and tolerant of a diversity of cultures, providing they did not threaten the fundamental right of property. He or she shared in the quest for infinite happiness in terms of the communal nature of 'enabling' state intervention (especially the local kind), which aimed to establish the conditions appropriate to the self-realization of the individual and of the whole, not least in the sphere of material progress.

This description of mid-nineteenth-century utilitarianism might equally be applied to the arguments offered in support of the early public library movement. The public library, like utilitarianism, aimed to manufacture 'good citizens'. Utilitarians found the ideal of the public library ideally suited to their enthusiasm for the self-attainment of the knowledge and reason conducive to the struggle for perfect citizenship. 'Good citizenship' is a recurrent theme in the writings and utterances of promoters: the term is commonly found in the vocabulary of the early public library movement. Each constituent element of utilitarian 'good citizenship' – whether it be the justification of materialism or the condoning of interventionism, the pursuit of higher pleasures or the negation of exclusivity – was to be found in the theory and practice of the free library, most strongly in the early Victorian era, but also throughout the period under consideration in this study.

Materialism was central to the public library ethos. The utilitarian association of materialism and 'useful' education is exemplified in a plea by Bentham himself for better library facilities. He proposed the establish-ment of district libraries to provide books on the 'art of legislation, history in all its branches, moral philosophy and logic, comprehending metaphysics, grammar, and rhetoric', as well as materials in support of advised lectures on medicine, surgery, midwifery, the veterinary art, chemistry, botany, natural history, agriculture and branches of trade. He suggested that to aid all these subject areas the government 'might establish in each district [certainly where lectures had been arranged] ... an increasing library appropriate to these studies. This would be at once to bestow upon students the instruments of study, and upon authors their most appropriate reward.'[121] Later, in 1861, in support of 'materialist' education, it was said in relation to the Liverpool Public Library that 'the man who desires to pursue the part of trade and commerce will there find the history of the trades and commerce of the world; and the man whose taste and genius lead him to mechanical pursuits will find every known treatise on mechanism'.[122]

To be sure, the spirit of materialism, as manifest in proposals for 'useful' libraries, was not the preserve of utilitarians. For example, at the opening of the Tamworth Library and Reading Room in 1841 Robert Peel, seeking to widen the definition of Toryism, asked his audience not to believe that

the acquisition of knowledge, of such knowledge as we shall offer you, is inconsistent with the success of your worldly pursuits ... society is now in the position that increased intelligence and increased knowledge are absolutely essential in your worldly pursuits.[123]

The Tamworth institution at which Peel was speaking was not funded from the rates. None the less, he might easily have made the same argument in the context of the municipal library. Clearly, the vision of abundance – the satisfaction of worldly pursuits – which utilitarians clung to, was becoming widely disseminated. However, what enabled utilitarianism, rather than less questioning schools of thought, to give extensive support to educational endeavours like public libraries was, first, an unreserved faith in scientific industrialism, the faltering of which in the 1830s and 1840s appeared to invite stabilization strategies; and, second, a hatred of exclusivity.

Utilitarian resentment of exclusivity was expressed, in addition to other contexts, in relation to public access to libraries. An article in the utilitarian *Westminster Review* in 1827 stated that it could not

> believe that any nation under the canopy of heaven can equal, much less surpass us in locking readers out of libraries: we are unrivalled in all exclusions ... The principle of exclusion is unhappily most prevalent and it is the sure mode speedily to render everything worthless.[124]

In the wake of the Select Committee on Public Libraries (1849) the utilitarian Society for the Diffusion of Useful Knowledge published its thoughts on exclusivity. The Society identified the key problem of library provision in the country as one of access: although Britain possessed more literature than most others it was less well distributed. The Society lamented that in the British Museum Reading Room there were to be found 'only men of letters and artists, the teachers of the people'. In the National Library in Paris, by contrast, the *people* came to read. There you could see 'groups of students from the civil and military colleges, soldiers of the line in their blue-coats, officers, clerks, shopkeepers, porters, and generally speaking specimens of all classes of the population'. Further, the Society found scandalous the truth (as it saw it) that the 'peasant of Devonshire has fewer books available to him in public collections than the peasant of Poddia ... the citizen of London or Liverpool than the weaver of Catalonia'.[125]

Whether tales of European openness were true or not matters little; in that the discourse can in itself be seen as reflecting a deep desire to banish exclusivity from industrial society, through institutions like public libraries. Public library protagonists decried exclusivity and praised meritocracy and equality of opportunity for the fostering of talent. This utilitarian standpoint emphasized the need for greater democracy, as well as the universal education accompanying that need: 'wherever political power is deposited', John Bright told an early free library gathering, 'there should be wisdom and virtue'.[126] However, it was not intended that in the world of politics the result of enlarged participation would be the unconditional transfer of power to the lower orders. Rather, the free operation of political forces and choices would deliver *middle-class* leadership. Public libraries, for all the talk (then and now) of their establishment primarily for the working classes, were proposed very much as a means of furthering middle-class ambitions in keeping with utilitarian political theory. Success in education was crucial to middle-class aspirations. Utilitarians saw that public money would facilitate stocks of books and other information sources far beyond the resources of voluntary effort in the form of subscription libraries, book clubs and other private repositories. The plan, in essence, was for a series of small, provincial British Museum Reading Rooms providing knowledge to aspiring, middle-ranking citizens. For example, the Select Committee on Public Libraries (1849) announced that: 'A great Public Library ought, above all things, to teach the teachers; to supply with the best implements of education those who educate the people whether in the pulpit, the school, or the press.'[127]

Beyond the resourcing of society's 'teachers' public libraries also enhanced the growth of nineteenth-century middle-class culture by providing the literary and statistical data for the questioning of physical, moral and political structures. The emergence of the public library was part and parcel of the the growing realization that to *reform* and *regulate* a burgeoning population and its connected problems the first step was to accumulate, in an accessible repository, knowledge and data on the norms, habits and conduct of the new society. It is, perhaps, no coincidence that key figures in the foundation of the Manchester Statistical Society – one of the earliest and most famous institutions to expound the science of 'moral statistics' – were also active in efforts to secure a public library for the city.[128]

Plans for a sophisticated information and library service, proposed alongside other service initiatives, required the taxing of the people at a new level. The argument that ratepayers should not tax themselves for services they were not going to use was to prove an awkward stumbling block to public library provision in its first decades. The rejoinder to this argument became as familiar as the argument itself. As early as the debate over institutions like free libraries in the Public Institutions Bill (1835), when opposition arose on this very issue, James Silk Buckingham pointed out that collectivism was already in existence and was, moreover, working efficiently – for example, the utility-generating British Museum (including its library) and similar institutions like the National Gallery were supported by a compulsory assessment levied on the country.[129] It also became fashionable to summon up the teleological basis of utilitarianism as a sweetener to those threatened with higher taxes. In debates on the Public Institutions Bill support was given to the idea of shared institutions like public libraries because:

> They were indispensably necessary as some set off against the multitudinous and enormous barracks, gaols, and workhouses, which in their splendour, were a deep disgrace to the country.[130]

Later, in 1849, Ewart used the platform of the Select Committee on Public Libraries to emphasize this message in arguing that every pound spent on libraries would save many more in expenditure on criminals and poor relief.[131]

The teleological argument for education (more of this in Chapter 6) was neatly summed up by the education reformer James Hole (who among other things pointed to the efficacy of popular libraries in informal education institutions):

> Tested by utilitarian views alone, that expenditure which is wisely devoted to the education of the people, to their moral, physical, and social improvement, is of all outlays the most economical.[132]

Goal-directed utilitarianism explained that free libraries increased social utility; not just in terms of cash saved in not having to provide institutions of correction, but also in the sense of helping to prevent costly anti-social actions in the first place. It was this teleological reasoning which enabled utilitarians to argue that free libraries should be provided in accordance with the first principle of government: to intervene to protect public safety.

The legislative discussion which had promised most to facilitate intervention at the all-important accountable, local level was that which preceded the Municipal Corporations Act (1835). In its final form, however, this legislation did not bestow upon local authorities the range of powers which utilitarians had advocated as ideal. This had implications for public library development. The assumption of powers not awarded in 1835 proceeded in a piecemeal fashion at a pace set by general legislation; thus, public library promoters had to wait a decade and a half after the missed opportunity which the Act represented for the right to establish local libraries. More than this, the inclination not to be too collectivist in planning local services from the centre - a tendency which early public library legislation encapsulated - meant that the ideal utilitarian library service could not be offered. The Public Libraries Acts (1850 and 1855), limited as they were in terms of their *permissive* nature, can be viewed in this context. On the other hand, permissiveness might be seen to have *promoted* intervention by the (local) state, in that, unlike clumsy, uniform, universal legislation, it allowed for local attitudes and conditions, and thus carried greater moral authority: an example of dispersal of responsibility enhancing the power of municipal localism.[133]

With central government taking little interest in conferring strong interventionist powers on local authorities the onus fell on imagination and initiative at the local level to evolve social policy. As far as the public library issue was concerned it was felt that this often acted against the development of a creditable service, or indeed any service at all. As Edward Edwards wrote in 1869:

> In relation to matters intellectual and education there had existed, for a long time, a social prepossession against extending the functions of Local Councils and Parish Vestries, and a social prejudgment that in the hands of town corporations and of parish vestrymen any powers of dealing with such matters would be pretty sure to be abused on the one hand, or to be neglected on the other.[134]

Though Edwards looked back on municipal reform as an important development he was none the less clearly disappointed with the dull-headed, unimaginative approach of councils in general to issues like public library provision. He believed that 'professional men, men of independent social position, and educated men had been as little represented on most councils ... as artisans', with a result clearly observable to all.[135] Little had changed by 1878, according to George Dawson, who believed that the government of towns over the years had sunk into 'the hands of the vulgar, and the self-seeking, and the mean'.[136] The early history of the public library thus illustrates the teething problems experienced by civic society. While utilitarianism and its effects represented one step along the way to a bureaucratized, ethically motivated welfare state, the tension in the philosophy between strict, state direction and inspection and less rigid decentralization and autonomy was very real; and is certainly reflected in the early public library's status as an interventionist agency, yet at once the symbol of local independence and self-help.

Perhaps as a result of this less than full commitment to effective intervention, and despite the utilitarian belief in the efficacy of state interference in areas like culture and education, voluntaryism remained a powerful utilitarian value. In debating the proposal for public libraries in the House of Commons in 1850, Roundell Palmer spoke out against the imposition of public management and compulsory rating because he considered the 'voluntary and self-supporting principle ... to be the life and essence of the cause of utility of such institutions'.[137] Where local government would or could not provide a service like a free library (or provide it sufficiently well) then private action might be called upon to by-pass blocked official channels to offer the service required. Benefaction, which assisted – perhaps more than any other local service – the municipal library, can be viewed in this context. The world of private politics was crucial to public library development.[138] Moreover, private action, or voluntaryism, and state intervention were not incompatible. For example, to highlight once again the Public Institutions Bill (1835), the legislative remedy was in this instance set alongside that to be brought about by private means. In supporting his interventionist proposals Buckingham spoke of the achievement of 'moral ends' by 'private agency and association', in addition to legislation – which could offer financial or enabling assistance. The fact that the Public Libraries Act (1850) did not permit materials to be bought, but only to be donated to institutions, illustrates the continuing faith in the value of voluntary effort. It was a faith which later benefactors were to inherit with vigour.

Whether promoted through private or public agency, free libraries enshrined the utilitarian advocacy of reducing constraints on self-development. Public libraries were the perfect means of teaching individuals how to teach themselves; how to exploit, in effect, the fertile conditions and education security (from ignorance in the Benthamite sense) which the communal ownership of literature offered at a relatively low cost. Improvement achieved through self-motivation was considered much more valuable than that which was enforced. William Ewart's contention (when bringing in his Public Libraries Bill in 1850) that the education which individuals gave themselves was more important than that which was acquired from a teacher, suited the relatively liberal – compared with school – regime of the public library.[139] It was a utilitarian tenet which echoed down the years. When a public library was promoted in York in 1881 Ewart's plea was resurrected; it was suggested that: 'There are two educations which a man receives, one is that which others give him, and the second is that which he gives himself – the second is far better than the first.'[140] Other pioneers of the public library movement were similarly linked to the self-help ethic. Samuel Smile's *Self-help* (1859) contains glowing references to the Salford manufacturer and radical politician Joseph Brotherton (who did more work than most on the Select Committee on Public Libraries, in 1849).

Attempting to fulfil one's potential without coercion constituted a quality of happiness of a high order. Understandably, by virtue of the squalor of urbanization, a great deal of leisure in the early Victorian age appealed to the satisfaction of basic human sensations. Utilitarians considered such sensual pleasures to be more appropriate to animals, and thus of a lower quality than those of the intellect and imagination. Rational recreation, on the other hand, as dispensed in public libraries, constituted happiness on a high plane – which partly explains the enduring temperance ingredient in public library promotion. Utilitarians recognized that education, unlike sensual happiness brought by say drink or sexual pleasure, was not depleted once consumed. To quote again the public library campaign in York in 1881:

> Education is everyday proving itself to be the truest thrift of all. Give a child that education and give him the opportunity of completing it for himself, and you give him the only fortune that a man can never run through.[141]

The 'fortune' which education bestowed was not just personal but communal. The highest happiness, said utilitarians, was the realization (considered to have a common-sense, innate foundation according to John Mill) that self-development should assist the development of society as a whole. To develop oneself for the good of the whole, however, required that the individual planned actions in the long term and made judgements based on intelligent assessments of the general good (which was more difficult a task than assessing one's own interests). Public libraries aimed to teach individuals to empathize; to identify the general happiness. They also exhibited the language of independence – to learn not to be dependent on others was for the good of all, not simply of the individual.

At a time of social unrest appeals to work for the common good were highly appropriate. Utilitarians hoped that increased education provision would lessen anti-social behaviour. It is no coincidence that during the Chartist era interest in education noticeably quickened, 'for ignorance as well as poverty were considered essential for it [Chartist unrest] to flourish'.[142] This was the very time, it should be emphasized, that intense interest in the idea of free libraries came to be expressed by utilitarians and others seeking to block the more revolutionary ideas of the day. The importance of good reading as a protection against demagogues was a feature of the Select Committee on Public Libraries (1849).[143] At the opening of Manchester Public Library in 1852 Richard Milnes, who had served on the Select Committee three years earlier, spoke of reading as an instrument for undermining the irrationality, the 'confusion and destruction', of socialism. In a library, he claimed, the individual in danger of socialist indoctrination would:

> be guided to books which show him how people have thought before him ... he begins to understand himself, is made better of course, and arises an enlightened, sensible, clear-minded philanthropist, instead of being a blind furious fanatic.[144]

The most appropriate reading for the politically 'wayward' was, of course, the literature of political economy. In this regard, the reported words of the Liberal MP Henry Austin Bruce at a Manchester branch library opening ceremony in 1866 are worth quoting at length:

> He could not conceive at this present time a more important thing than that all classes of society should be thoroughly instructed in the sound principles of political economy ... [for] in every town in England there were difficult questions to be settled between employer and employed, which required forebearance, discretion and a sound knowledge of political economy. He had himself, on several occasions, acted as the mediator between master and men during the prevalence of strikes, which inflicted incalculable misery upon the population ... Fifty or sixty years ago there were few writers on political economy and the greatest errors were committed, otherwise they would not have had such imposts as the corn laws, the timber duties, and the navigation laws. All these things until within a very recent period were believed in as necessary to our national existence - believed in, too, by the better-educated and higher classes. Well, if there were so much ignorance of the true principles of political economy among the educated and higher classes, it was not to be wondered at if such ignorance even still prevailed among the uneducated and working classes. Now, however, even the working classes need not be ignorant of the great and *true* [italics added] principles of political economy, since there were brought within their reach by such institutions as free libraries the ... admirable works of John Stuart Mill and other eminent political economists, in which they would ... find the soundest knowledge of all the great principles which governed their labour.[145]

Echoing these sentiments at the same ceremony another speaker explained that:

> the principle of political economy rests for its soundness upon the principles of common sense. Hence, if more were known of political economy; of the relations of capital and labour; of the relations between employer and employed, whenever a conflict arose between them, it would be seen that the solution was very simple, and common sense would apply it at once. Capital is one thing and labour is another ... but they were not opposed to each other,

and where the two came apparently into conflict, the true solution of the difference is the application of common sense.[146]

The utilitarian conviction that, once 'informed', citizens would come naturally, by the route of common sense, to see the wisdom of political economy's advocacy of the free market and of the cash nexus was a creed that public library protagonists were to publicize often. The 'political economy' credentials of the early public library are convincing. They stretch back, in fact, to the genesis of the public library idea. Robert Slaney's call for free libraries (see Chapter 2) was derived from a firm belief in the economic teachings of Malthus. Slaney contended that government intervention in the form of the old poor law had the effect of lowering, not raising, wages, by increasing the supply of labourers beyond the demand for their services.[147] He wrote of the 'impossibility of increasing employment [and prosperity] by direct legislative enactments'.[148] State education provision, on the other hand, would serve as 'the greatest economy',[149] because less ignorant citizens would come to understand the laws and issues of sanitation, the importance of moral and industrious habits and of self-help, the foolishness of improvident marriages and the hidden forces of the market.

For the later utilitarians there were two aspects to the strategy of education for social pacification. Despite its empirical, investigatory origins, utilitarianism came to accept some traditional and aesthetic learning as productive of utility. The realization of the value of, and higher pleasures associated with, the imagination and the emotions followed from Mill's philosophical revision. Thus, utilitarians came to recognize the higher novel as 'a useful art'. Many public librarians said that good novels, among other things, taught good manners.[150] The reading of 'acceptable' literature, it was said, reduced society's barbaric tendencies, which were believed to contribute considerably to disaffection. Utilitarians hoped that good books in good libraries would help to disseminate taste through the population; a motive referred to a number of times in the deliberations of the Select Committee on Public Libraries.[151] It was hoped that through libraries 'people might be taught ... a taste for something better than mere animal enjoyment'.[152]

The public library was said by one of its early historians to have originated primarily as a 'means of improving public taste'.[153] Taste here should not be conceptualized merely in the narrow sense of knowledge of 'high' culture. Rather, in keeping with the utilitarian notion of all actions commanding a measurable utility, taste stood for the ability to make choices which would deliver higher pleasures (those with lasting utility) and which would thus provide a higher quality of life. To make tasteful choices, to be tasteful and successful in one's preferences, required inputs of information, the importance of which to leading a 'useful' existence was stressed, as noted above, by utilitarians like Place and Roebuck (an analysis that bears remarkable resemblance to our perceived modern, choice-abundant 'information society'). As Disraeli once declared: 'As a general rule the most successful man in life is the man with the best information.'[154] Ideally, however, inputs of information, from libraries and elsewhere, would be used to help secure the general happiness rather than simply the happiness of individuals. The theory of 'the greatest happiness of the greatest number', as John Stuart Mill came to see it, meant promoting as much pleasure in each individual as was compatible with the general happiness. Thus, in the use of information and knowledge to facilitate 'good choice' – to become tasteful and cultured, in essence – the happiness of others should feature as prominently as personal happiness. Indeed, being dutiful to others, a lesson in social stability which the public library movement was keen to disseminate, was the highest pleasure conducive to personal happiness.

The second means of pacification, to return to a materialist theme, was the everyday education which came from earning one's living and from experiencing a social existence. Utilitarians, including those who promoted public libraries, were never deflected from their faith in the power of external stimuli and in the possibilities of social engineering. There was no richer environment than the public library for the confirmation of this faith. It was intended that public libraries should provide the information complementary to a successful material existence. More than this, it was believed that the physical micro-environment of the public library could encourage virtuous behaviour. Enlightenment psychological theory, upon which raw utilitarianism was based, emphasized a link between physical environment and sensation on the one hand, and perception and behaviour on the other. This associationist psychology induced an enthusiasm for theory concerning the regulation of space. Moral reformation and the built-form environment became linked. Design was attributed a moral power – by engineers, administrators and architects (including, interestingly, a friend of Edward Edwards, the architect George Godwin).[155] The clearest and best known example of the 'architecture of morality' in the early industrial period is the work of Bentham, whose plans in the 1790s for a pauper industry-house (the blueprint for the post-1834 workhouse) and a panopticon prison (more about this in Chapter 10) depicted a form of design in which every act of misconduct could be observed, catalogued and thus deterred.[156]

Similar 'social engineering' considerations appear to have informed ideas on early public library architecture. At the opening ceremony of the Hulme branch library in Manchester in 1866 one speaker equated parks with libraries in terms of the beneficial external stimuli they generated: both were stimulating 'fields of pleasure', social space from which 'we come away refined and polished, having our minds stored with many a pleasant thought, and our imagination raised from sensual and sordid things to things high, and pure, and lovely'.[157] Further, one of the earliest commentaries on public library design, *Museums, Libraries and Picture Galleries* (1853), by J. W. Papworth and W. Papworth, is dominated by the concern to allocate space for operational efficiency derived from the tight regulation of both readers and library staff. In a stridently utilitarian tone this blueprint declared that: 'Libraries are not storehouses merely, but should be the "fittest" places of study, in which the overawing abundance of literary resources and of applicants for them, must secure ... precision of working and attention to the public.' In keeping with this utilitarian message an ideal type of public library design was suggested: a 'dodecagonal building' housing a central reading room with a 'polygonal form', similar to both Bentham's panopticon and the plan for the British Museum's new reading room announced in 1852.[158] Manifest in the architectural ideas put forward by the Papworths was the power of the built environment to shape and regulate the chaos of multitudinous atoms of people and books.

The inherent ability – continually stressed by utilitarians – of environment to mould the good character conducive to a successful life was expressed by the leading public library promoter of the early Victorian period, William Ewart. In recognizing the external influence on the individual of inter-personal and intellectual friction wrought by a dynamic urban, industrial society, Ewart wrote in one of his personal notebooks that:

> Minds of manufacturers and mechanics who live 'in society' in towns become 'acuter by collision'.[159]

Ewart's apparent emphasis here on experience and mechanical-practical learning should not cloud the breadth of his intellectual and cultural interests. His awareness of the importance of 'practicalities' was supplemented, in a way which mirrored the ethos of the early public library movement, by a love of aesthetic culture. Ewart, and his associate Edwards, like the public library phenomenon they created, were dually motivated in the mixture of technical and humane education they advocated in the cause of social tranquillity.

CHAPTER 4

THE PRINCIPAL PIONEERS: EWART AND EDWARDS

In the second part of the epilogue of *War and Peace*, Tolstoy asks the question: 'What is the force that moves nations?' Two possible answers are set before the reader. On the one hand, biographical historians and historians of individual peoples understand the force that moves nations as 'a power inherent in heroes and rulers'. Universal historians, on the other hand, 'do not recognise it as a power pertaining to heroes and rulers but regard it', says Tolstoy, 'as the resultant of a multiplicity of variously directed forces.' With the advent of the the 'new history' in the post-war era, and its emphasis on 'history from below' in particular, the 'great man' thesis of history – the first of Tolstoy's answers – has been forcefully denigrated. The influence of mechanistic explanations of historical development, most notably the Marxist materialist, determinist interpretation, has subordinated the history of individuals to that of society, its groups and its ideologies. While this process has been of paramount importance in encouraging a now vibrant, eclectic and democratized (in its production and sources) history discipline, the historical importance of individuals in shaping key events and developments of the past should not be ignored.

In keeping with the notion that history, traditionally, concerned itself with telling the story of 'winners' – the story being mostly written by 'winners', moreover – historians of the public library movement have focused on the individual as the prime mover of history. In particular, attention has been lavished on the movement's heroic pioneers: Ewart, Edwards and others. Thus the coverage of determining social factors has been less than adequate. Yet, however important it might be to improve that coverage, as this study attempts to do, a move towards 'wider' interpretations should not be at the expense of biographical, especially psycho-historical, analysis of the contribution of individuals to the shaping of the past. Consequently, this chapter examines the role of the key 'players' in the story of the early public library; although emphasis is placed on their social – especially their ideological – motivation.

The contribution of William Ewart and Edward Edwards to the public library movement should be placed in the context of the climate of reform which characterized the second quarter of the nineteenth century and which utilitarians, among others, induced. The Benthamite process of reform has been defined as consisting of three stages: first, the development and discussion of ideas in Benthamite cliques, and the transmission of those ideas to 'second-degree' Benthamites; second, public pressure for reform through the press and the manipulation of enquiries; third, the securing of official employment for the reform's supporters to oversee its implementation and possible extension.[1] To these should be added the very particular process of promoting and guiding a Bill through Parliament.[2] The efforts of Ewart and Edwards in obtaining the inaugural public library legislation of 1850 match the framework outlined above. Edwards's contribution was his enthusiastic agitation for reform, including his evidence to the Select Committee and his pamphleteering. He was also influential in implementing and reinforcing utilitarian prescriptions for free libraries by filling public librarianship's top job at the time. Librarians have understandably lauded one of their own, the librarian Edwards, as the key variable in the genesis of public libraries. Taking a more objective view, however, it is clear that the ideal would have come to nothing but for the political contribution and influence of Ewart, especially in respect of the second stage of the reform process described above.

William Ewart

It should be remembered that there was no popular agitation leading to the establishment of a Select Committee on Public Libraries in 1849 or the subsequent free library legislation: public libraries were imposed from above rather than demanded from below. Ewart was the leading figure in this esoteric agitation. He enrolled Edwards in the small knot of public library enthusiasts drawn from public life. Most importantly, he complemented ideally the detailed propaganda supplied by Edwards by translating theory and argument into legislative reality: he controlled the work of the Select Committee and guided its proposals through Parliament.

Thus, it is with reference to Ewart's dual role as public library spokesman and practical politician that any investigation of the pioneers of the early public library movement should proceed. Light can be thrown upon the public library debate of the 1840s by examining in detail the political philosophy of the man who, more than anyone, rendered substance and reality to the free library ideal. Specifically, Ewart's thoughts on education and reform can be analysed in an attempt to establish his links with utilitarianism. This approach will prove advantageous in that ideological input, largely ignored in the past, is crucial to any comprehensive explanation of early public library ideas. The ideology of key individuals is as important as the wider social influences which brought reform. As Ewart himself observed: 'The historian who wishes to judge accurately of the times which he describes should endeavour to descend into the station of the politicians who lived within their sphere.'[3]

The nature of early Victorian political representation means that the importance of Ewart's personal role in the campaign for public libraries should not be underestimated. The early Victorian age was an era of embryonic social reform. Yet it was also a time when the necessities of electoral popularity, as manifest in the formulation of party programme and attention to social policy, played little part in the evolution of social reform. The period 1832-67 was indeed the 'golden age' of the private Member and, consequently, we should not devalue the efforts (motives are of course another matter) of individual parliamentarians in creating the social legislation of the day. The parliamentary impetus behind the reform initiatives of the period between the Reform Bill of 1832 and the next great reform of Parliament in 1867 were nothing if not the result of unstinting personal effort – even though, as Ewart's biographer has pointed out, time has tended to 'depersonalize' this phenomenon.[4]

In a satirical poster released by their opponents in Liverpool, in the election campaign of 1835, Ewart and his running partner are depicted as a pair of broken-down 'hacks' ready to be sold off to the highest bidder. Ewart himself is described as a 'nonentity ... being of no use for any other purpose' than appearing at auction.[5] However, 'nonentity' is emphatically not an apt description of the public life of this radical reformer and parliamentarian, despite the fact that after his death 'William Ewart was soon forgotten nearly everywhere'.[6] It is true that he was no political heavyweight, and that it is only relatively recently that he has attracted the attention of a serious biographer.[7] Nevertheless, to contemporary opinion he was by no means obscure, as Edwards noted in assessing the 1849 Select Committee: 'To him the country is already under deep obligation for untiring efforts to amend the laws, to diffuse education and culture, and to promote in various ways the social and economical well-being of people.'[8] Ewart has faded in the memory because he concentrated less than many of his more illustrious radical colleagues in Parliament on the great issues of the day, even though his political interests were wide ranging and included topical issues.[9] Ewart turned his attention mostly to minor (by early Victorian standards) measures, particularly the intellectual well-being of society.[10] Public library provision was one such educational issue. Ewart's contribution in this relatively unimportant area of social policy was recognized only gradually. Thus, late in his life Gladstone (whose Christian names, William and Ewart, were taken in honour of his godfather, William Ewart senior, father of the public library pioneer) spoke of the younger Ewart as: 'a cultivated man, a scholar, highly respected in every relation of life ... his name deserves to be recorded in that he was upon more subjects than one a pioneer, working his way forward doing the rough introductory work in his country's interest, in the interest of the nation, upon subjects which at the time very few had begun to appreciate. The appreciation of his work in regard to libraries, which produced the Act of 1850, has been an appreciation gradually progressing.'[11]

Ewart never held office or sat in Parliament as a member of any great party. But this is not to say that his ideological allegiances were weak and imprecise. He was certainly not a 'wavering Willie', as an election opponent's propaganda once labelled him. On the contrary, he was closely associated with utilitarian principles and worked alongside those who aimed to make a reality of the philosophy. Munford, in his authoritative biography of the reformer, has concluded that 'Ewart's vote in the House of Commons Division was almost but not quite invariably given in true radical fashion and, on innumerable occasions, as one of a gallant but hopeless minority'.[12] An edition of the *Spectator* in 1837 included Ewart in a hypothetical radical cabinet,[13] and Harriet Martineau cited him as being in alliance with the radical utilitarians Grote, Molesworth and Roebuck.[14] He was also in contact with Francis Place.[15] Although Ewart, like many backbenchers of his day, displayed much independence of thought in his political career, his reformism inevitably linked him to philosophic radicalism (the parliamentary affiliation, named by John Mill, whose aim was the rallying of those radicals both disappointed by the limited franchise extension of 1832 and anxious for further reform, social as well as political).[16]

Philosophic radicalism, as the term implies, consists of dual but interlocking roles – a link, in essence, between philosophy and political practice. The philosophy in question was essentially that of Benthamite-inspired utilitarianism (although philosophic radicalism has been described in a more complex way as 'an amalgam of three related strands of ideological consciousness, Malthusian population theories, utilitarian jurisprudence and political philosophy and the economic doctrines of classical political economy'[17]). In terms of practical politics, it is important to recognize that Bentham's lasting contribution was to transform a system of ideas into a living ideology; for he was above all 'a practical thinker concerned not simply with the development of theory but with detailed reform'.[18] Bentham's inspiration did not exist in an intellectual vacuum; many of his associates occupied positions of influence in the worlds of politics, administration, law and culture[19] (this corresponds to the final stage of the Benthamite reform process outlined above). Consequently, the way was open for serious theorizing to be combined with political ambition; and combined it was through philosophic radicalism, providing us with perhaps 'the most striking example in the nineteenth century of a group of intellectuals active in politics, of the attempt to link theory with practice'.[20] In assessing the ideology of the philosophical radicals it is important to avoid the idea that each individual was directly and strongly influenced by utilitarianism. Philosophic radicalism was not identical to utilitarianism: it embraced, as noted above, a variety of opinion and a membership of widely differing social background (industry, commerce and even the country gentry).[21] However, each philosophic radical displayed the utilitarian trait of aiming to give realistic expression, through Parliament, to its theoretical criticisms and plans for reform. Attention to organization for the sake of carrying theory into effect marks the difference between philosophy and ideology. It is in this context that we must view the work of William Ewart; eager as he was for a radical, thorough transformation of society, and involved as he was with the 'nuts and bolts' of reform and with the business of simply getting things done. In terms of the practicalities of the political and legislative process his connection with the 'doer' element in philosophic radicalism is obvious: 'His struggles, achievements and failures appeared to be wholly in the translation of ideas into practical forms and in persuading his fellow members [of Parliament] to accept them', wrote an early biographer.[22]

But to what extent can we associate Ewart with philosophic radicalism's utilitarian theorizing? At a time when party cohesion and loyalty were at best elusive, attaching labels to political figures of the first half of the nineteenth century can be a precarious exercise, no more so than with references to those described as 'radical'. As one historian has pointed out:

> The boundary lines between middle class radicalism and orthodox Whig attitudes are not easy to draw, and men like Place and Brougham moved effortlessly across them. Within the Whig-radical-utilitarian range of attitudes it was easy to be more or less moderate, seek one or another combination of limited reforms, and act within a changing network of alliances.[23]

Notwithstanding the danger of camouflaging 'the individuality of men who are too often merged into an "ism"',[24] it is possible to make a fairly precise assessment of Ewart's political commitment. As stated earlier, on many issues he found himself consistently in the radical camp, both intellectually and physically, in terms of the division lobby. On major issues such as suffrage extension, religious equality and commercial freedom this was clearly the case.[25] His economic liberalism should be emphasized. He was intimately conversant with commercial questions[26] and took copious notes on political economy.[27] However, Ewart was concerned with less sweeping political issues which, by way of establishing his utilitarianism, can be divided into three categories: reform of the criminal law; the freedom of administration from corruption; and education.

Munford has argued that the greater part of Ewart's drive for criminal law reform was derived from his study of the humanitarian aspects of Blackstone's *Commentaries on the Laws of England* and the work of Cesare Beccaria.[28] That Ewart possessed humanitarian traits there appears little doubt. Maccoby referred to him as 'that active wealthy and experienced Parliamentarian, the humanitarian Ewart'.[29] Hamburger relates Macaulay's assessment of the 'effeminate mawkish philanthropy' of men such as Ewart.[30] Nevertheless, although Beccaria's ideas on punishment contained humanitarian impulses they were also born of reason and logic, which attracted Ewart to the thoughts of Bentham, whose own brand of utilitarianism set out a comprehensive plan for criminal law reform. Bentham believed that capital punishment, for instance, had no justification since it was efficient in one of the aims of the criminal law, incapation, but not in the other three: deterrence, reformation and compensation. Quite simply, victims were not compensated, the perpetrator of the crime was obviously denied the chance of reform, and deterrence was seen to depend less on the certainty of being apprehended than on the severity of the punishment. Armed with the logic of these Benthamite arguments, Ewart succeeded in promoting Acts to abolish the death penalty for horse stealing, cattle stealing and stealing in dwelling-houses (1832); and for letter stealing, sacrilege and returning from transportation (1834). Further, his dogged determination to see through the abolition of capital punishment for all crimes secured, for the first time, an official investigation, in the form of a Royal Commission in 1864. Other reforms in the criminal law promoted by Ewart included an Act of 1834 to abolish the practice of exposing dead bodies of prisoners in chains, and his Act of 1836 providing prisoners with a right to legal defence. These were perhaps as much the result of intuitive and humanitarian thinking as of utilitarian rationalism.

Ewart's efforts to free administration from corruption, however, were utilitarian to the core. Utilitarians displayed a deep distrust of government power as traditionally constituted, believing the rule of the old aristocratic order to be open to corruption; for 'Just as in the individual the self-regarding interest is predominant, so too in government.'[31] Moreover, whereas in respect of economics it was believed that fundamental laws existed to control human behaviour, in the world of politics no such controls pertained and, consequently, the practice of government was subject to human error and self-interest. Concurring with these arguments, Ewart, in 1845, moved that Civil Servant appointments be subject to examination. He later proposed, in 1849 and 1852, that exams also be instituted for prospective army officers and candidates to the Diplomatic Service. For Ewart this ethical and efficiency-procuring approach held true for other institutions: hence his insistence on university entrance exams, and distaste for the monopoly of the Royal Academy. Similarly, his enthusiasm for public libraries was based in part on his desire to see increased equality of opportunity.

But it is in the field of education that we can identify most clearly Ewart's links with utilitarianism. Ewart himself once described education as 'the most important of all subjects'.[32] This conviction was based not simply on a humanitarian impulse which sought to diffuse education for its own sake. For Ewart, education possessed a concrete political dynamic. As Munford has written: 'His interest in that cause was well established and his whole political philosophy was securely based upon it.'[33] It is perhaps for this reason that we find in the field of education Ewart's 'most ambitious, provocative and far-reaching efforts'.[34] Certainly, 'by the middle of the 1840s [if not earlier] he had thought out a full programme of educational reform which he pressed on mostly unreceptive Whig and Tory governments'.[35] As was the case with his other political and parliamentary crusades he consistently eschewed the dictate of party: 'Mr Ewart and his colleagues', proclaimed the *Illustrated London News* in a 'Parliamentary Portrait' of the radical reformer in 1848, 'have gone beyond the comparatively narrow ground of party politics, and given social wants something of their study.'[36] However, this is not to say that Ewart's philosophy of education, particularly in terms of the social role he discerned for it, was unique; it will become clear that his basic motivation bears close resemblance to that of the utilitarians.

Throughout his political career Ewart championed the extension of educational opportunity to all classes. His enthusiasm was unequivocal – the adoption of a system of national education, he promised in a Commons debate of June 1839, would be 'the glory of the age'.[37] Moreover, it was his belief that those who opposed him on this issue wished 'to restore society to a state of savage barbarity'.[38] Ewart's relentless engagement in education issues (including public libraries) is commendable. But it is not enough to praise his contribution without relating it to some kind of socio-political dynamic. In a practical politician and social reformer it would be surprising if such a dynamic could not be traced. In fact, he promoted the value of education not only for its own sake in respect of its role in developing the mind and the spirit, but also for reasons of control aimed at the preservation of a social order based on private property, possessive individualism and the workings of the free market.

Ewart believed that education was an important means of stabilizing and strengthening industrial capitalism. He was aware of education's potential as a means of counter-attraction; that is to say, the subtle process of drawing elements in the lower orders away from their indulgence in irrational, socially immoral pastimes. 'If the poor were deprived of innocent sports', he argued, 'they would be driven to what was bad.'[39] In 1854 he informed his sister that public libraries had done much to turn people from 'Alehouses and Socialism' (a likely inference here being that places of working-class intoxication were fertile ground for the growth of radical and threatening ideas).[40] However, notwithstanding his belief in the diversionary powers inherent in rational recreation, it would be wrong to view Ewart simply as a social controller introducing, on behalf of those in positions of power, overt propaganda into a system of popular education. Such an assessment would belie his adherence to certain forms of self-help and voluntary effort. He did not desire, for example, an extension of education in the form of overbearing central government control. He urged that government should rather 'aid and support the tendencies of the people in favour of education, than force it on them'. Further, government 'should not attempt to interfere with opinion, least of all with religious opinions'.[41] In respect of the provision of popular educational provision in the 1840s, he aimed not to destroy the voluntary system but to supplement and encourage it through central government action: 'My object is to develop, not control.'[42] He viewed the German popular education model – a 'colossal Continental system' in his words – as unsuitable for Britain. 'Do not impose uniformity', he argued, 'but give an opportunity of freely adopting voluntary uniformity ... I think we may induce and persuade where we cannot force.'[43] Ewart's stance on education, then, does not tally with the classical description of the social controller employing on behalf of those in positions of power overtly propagandist measures as an integral part of a programme of popular education. Such direct methods were absent from his political make-up. He urged that institutions and political procedures should 'recognise the government as the instrument of the people, not the people as the instrument of government'.[44] Similarly, Ewart's belief in voluntary effort (though not necessarily all forms, particularly that of the politicized worker) must be set against any tendency to view his idea of education as simply a counter-attractive force.

This is not to say that he rejected any link between education and strong government, though he realized that it could not be forged by coercion or overt control. Rather, he believed that good government would be all the stronger for 'having enlisted in its favour the affections of the people';[45] and in keeping with the utilitarian optimism in the power of reason he ventured to suggest that such affection would be forthcoming, as a matter of course, once rationality had itself been spread by an extension of educational opportunity. His faith in the powers of reason are perhaps best illustrated in his prescription for reduced criminality. The criminal law, he surmised, tended to give people only a 'horror of punishment'. What was required was to give people, 'through the agency of education, a horror of the crime'.[46] That is to say, individuals should obey the criminal law not out of fear of punishment, but out of an application of reasoned thought encouraged through education. Thus, like his philosophic radical peers and many other thinkers of the period, Ewart saw order as naturally flowing from the reason which intellectual development and education nurtured. The development of reason pointed the way to good government and, above all, Ewart would have argued, to the considered, gradual reform of society, as opposed to a radical, perhaps violent, transformation in its fundamental socio-economic base.

For Ewart this gradualist approach was the key to preserving social harmony. Time and again, in addressing the great social and political problems of the day, he can be found referring to the desirability of 'prevention' and 'precaution' rather than 'cure'. For example, in March 1832, on the occasion of a Commons debate on a petition calling for an enquiry into the Peterloo Massacre of 1819, Ewart commended the strategy of prevention, arguing that 'if they met the question openly and at once the agitation of it would be at an end ... instead of permitting it, at some further period to explode, when its explosion might occasion danger and detriment to the country.'[47] Some might see such advocacy as political adroitness, or simply good common sense. However, when one examines further Ewart's adherence to the strategy of prevention in social affairs it becomes apparent that his motives were not based entirely on the wisdom of expediency in political self-preservation, for either himself or his radical colleagues; but on a deep-rooted belief in the need to defuse trends in society which spelled danger and anarchy to the social arrangements he espoused.

Ewart identified clearly the role of education in the strategy of prevention. His political faith was based on two basic principles:

> I humbly venture to think that the prosperity and safety of the country are mainly based on these two great principles; – first, freedom of trade; and secondly, national education ... To freedom of trade I look as the best source of prosperity; to the extension of education I look as the real source of order and safety, for until the poorest man should be taught by education how much he was interested in maintaining order, in obeying the laws, and extending the general prosperity of the country, there can be no solid defence against occasional turbulence and disquiet.[48]

In a Commons debate on education in April 1841 further evidence can be found of Ewart's conviction that education could help to nullify agitation for a revolution which threatened the existing propertied and ordered nature of society. Although from hindsight we can see that he overestimated the potential for revolutionary tumult in rural areas, his line of thought is nevertheless revealing. Ewart warned that 'a grossly ignorant rural population when once excited, was the most dangerous, because [it was] the blindest slave of tumult and revolution'. That is why in Germany, he pointed out, government paid more attention to the education of the rural population. There was cause for concern, therefore, that 'even within twenty miles of the metropolis' the rural population existed in 'a state of blighted ignorance'. He was also concerned about education standards among the industrial working class: 'Our artisans', he was sorry to say, 'though the most skilful workmen, have been shewn ... to be far less cultivated in their tastes and intellectual in their pursuits ... than the artisans from countries in which the State exercised a vigilant super-intendence over education.' But at least the British artisan, unlike the farm labourer, he continued, 'received daily, in the common intercourse of their lives, a species of practical education. They learnt in the interchange of commerce and the intermingling of society, a knowledge of the value of property and the benefits of order'.[49] The crux of Ewart's message can therefore be described as a perceived necessity to educate the masses in order to remove potential volatility in political agitation. Moreover, education could be geared to the practicalities of daily activity in industrial capitalist society for the purpose of encouraging respect for order, based, in turn, upon a respect for property. The similarity here with the utilitarian philosophy that education meant a growing familiarity with the fundamental laws of economic activity in the free market is indeed striking.

History has shown that Ewart's anxiety over the prospect of radical social change was groundless. Unlike the Continent, Britain experienced 'no Commune, no barricades, no rivers of blood'.[50] However, as stated in Chapter 2, the possibility of serious conflict *was* envisaged. Ewart was no exception in this respect. On the eve of the 1848 Chartist demonstration at Kennington he expressed his anxieties in a letter to his sister Charlotte Rutson:

We are kept in a boiling, or at least a bubbling, state by the threatened procession of the Chartists tomorrow. I believe that they will be perfectly quiet. Policemen, however, and troops abound in all directions, and almost every gentleman, servant and shopkeeper (besides many operatives) in London have been sworn in as Special Constables. I and my servants of course . . . But the Chartists, in their proclamation today, deprecate all intentions of violence.[51]

Notwithstanding Ewart's confidence in the security forces, and his judgement of the Chartists' doubtful will, a sense of disquiet does come through in reading this correspondence: society was not stable in his view but 'bubbling'. Not that Ewart (like Edwards) was wholly unreceptive to Chartist grievances. He believed that there was indeed 'some injustice at the bottom of it all', and that the real cause of discontent was 'the ascendancy of the landed interest'.[52] He had told the Commons in 1834 that 'if any fatal mark characterized the present times, it was a pampering of the landed aristocracy at the cost of a pauperized and uneducated people'.[53] He believed he 'could not approve of everything in this country'.[54] Yet he viewed 'order indispensable' and called for 'tranquilly and cautiously amending what is wrong'.[55] As Greenwood observed: 'The spirit of true and cautious progress governed his soul.'[56]

Ewart regretted that some who had once sought a 'sound and rational reform of society',[57] as he did, had now taken up too radical a position: 'I regret that the middle class of Reformers should be unhappily at variance with the more popular class, who seemed recently to have run wild – severing their connection with those who might have guided them.'[58] But he reserved his sternest criticism for those who had chosen the path of violence: 'I for my part abjure violence, and hope for improvements through the determination and energy of the really liberal part of the community.'[59] Needless to say, the 'liberal part of the community' was in Ewart's opinion also that part most disposed to education, for he trusted that 'the spread of education would teach those who were disposed to violence, that it was not by a sanguinary movement that they could attain their end, but a steady progress founded on claims of substantial justice.'[60]

Ewart clearly believed that an educated people would be less likely to lend support to violent agitation (in this instance, violent Chartism). To him it appeared obvious that a people imbued with reason would be more likely to identify itself with the peaceful and progressive process of representative democracy; and it was to education that Ewart looked as the basis for popular participation in the political system, believing as he did 'that a strong and sound democracy must rest upon an intelligent and well-informed populace'.[61] Ewart was convinced that the passing of a certain amount of political power to the masses was inevitable. At the time of the 1832 Reform Bill's passage through Parliament he had urged that 'the speedy passing of such a measure was absolutely necessary for the salvation of the country'.[62] Yet in the wake of the legislation which followed he grew disappointed when its effects proved so limited. His *Reform of the Reform Bill*, published in 1837, had expressed a clear indignation with the slow pace of political reform to date; but more than this, the pamphlet serves to illustrate emphatically the essence of Ewart's philosophy of education and reform. It is appropriate, therefore, to examine this document in detail.

For Ewart, 'the peace of society, the maintenance of order, must be presupposed to be the objects of every good citizen. The question is, how, in the present times, these objects may be best attained.'[63] The answer, he ventured, lay in the exploitation of virtues inherent in the representative system of government: 'The use of the representative system is, that, by reflecting as it were with clearness and truth the opinions of society, it may prevent or diminish those political shocks which a variance of opinion between the government and the people it governs is always more or less likely to engender.'[64] However, this consensus model based on the flow of opinions from people to government was, in his opinion, stunted unjustly by the continuing influence of the old order. The scattered fragments of the ancient system, he regretted, 'too incautiously left overlying and encumbering the new one ... have constructed a strong-hold of violence and corruption, from which if they be not dislodged, the country and its liberties will be subject to ceaseless and dangerous depredations'.[65] He considered it essential, therefore, to render the country's laws and political institutions 'less feudal and oligarchical'.[66] The Reform Act of 1832 had not gone far enough, and so he called for a simple household suffrage, a just discrimination of the electoral localities and vote by secret ballot.

The results of not reforming the prevailing system, he cautioned, could prove devastating: 'The smothered fire of popular indignation will at length find a vent, – the more dangerous for having been suppressed – and in some moment of severe distress or of violent excitement, the people will extort a Reform of the Reform Bill.'[67] And he viewed the possibility of demands upon government issuing from an aggressive populace as part of a trend stretching back to the French Revolution, which

> was not a solitary, isolated fact. It was part of the comprehensive whole. It was a mighty wave in a troubled sea, – the sea of human opinion, – which has set in, as in the time of the religious reformation, and which will continue, as then to flow uncontrolled and uncontrollable. Such crisis in our social state may unfortunately assume, if they are misconducted, the form of revolution.

Or, he goes on, 'they may silently subside, leaving behind them the blessed effects of simple, but thorough reformation'.[68] Thus, despite the awesome power of opinion emanating from below, Ewart believed that such opinion could be placated by governments which resorted to 'precautionary reform',[69] and so he asserted that:

> To prepare for and give scope to the inevitable tendency of opinions and events at such a period should be the aim and effort of every wise and patriotic government. Such a course of policy is infinitely safer than the falsely deemed conservative, but which may more appropriately be termed 'cumulative of evil'; since it suppresses complaint till it rises into disorder, and withholds the remedy till the disease is at its height.[70]

As far as the aftermath of 1832 was concerned he consequently questioned whether it was not wiser 'to prevent this explosion by doing justice to the principles of the bill'.[71]

The entire direction of Ewart's political outlook, if his thoughts on electoral reform in the 1830s are anything to go by, was apparently aimed towards conciliation and defusing potential crisis. An insurance policy against confrontation could be taken out by the promotion of reform, including social reform, in which field Britain, he regretted, had 'frequently been in arrears of the less liberal (but highly enlightened) governments of the continent'.[72] Education was a weapon which Ewart considered to be a powerful force in the avoidance of damaging social confrontation. Moreover, poor education among those who sought a redress of grievances, combined with government corruption and inefficiency, was a recipe only for conflagration: 'The danger to be apprehended from revolution', he wrote, 'is in a ratio combined of the ignorance of the people who emancipate themselves and the badness of the government under which they previously lived. Education is the enemy of revolution.'[73] That is to say, an educated populace could play its part effectively, without resorting to revolution, in a system of government which was based on openness and representation, not corruption and privilege.

It is appropriate that Ewart's *Reform of the Reform Bill* has led us into a final assessment of Ewart's ideology, for it spells out with precision his guiding political doctrine, which can be summed up in three words: preservation, prevention and precaution. The first of these political priorities he illustrated in a letter to Charlotte Rutson: 'I am sorry to see you call me a Radical, that I am not; except in the reformatory sense. If to amend is to destroy I admit your inference. But to amend in my opinion is to preserve.'[74] Not that he was opposed to all change, for he looked with favour upon the process whereby the 'slow and silent tide of opinion [was allowed] to flow in upon ancient institutions'.[75] He did not, however, countenance change which threatened the fundamental social arrangements of either the industrial capitalism of which he himself was a social product, or 'the inviolable rights of property',[76] which he defended. Ewart argued that in order to preserve these fundamental principles underpinning civilized society the confrontations which precipitated excessive change had to be prevented before they appeared. It was pointless, he argued, to deal with revolutionary agitation at its peak: if possible 'ceaseless and dangerous depredations'[77] had to be nipped in the bud and not allowed to develop. It followed, therefore, that measures had to be implemented which acted as precautions against unwanted social turbulence. In keeping with this requirement, Ewart's political career developed into a 'long record of persistent and tireless service for reform'.[78] He promoted education because he believed in the necessity of insurance against a revolutionary transformation of society. Similarly, he supported reforms in the economic sphere which would increase prosperity and consequently undermine any challenge to capitalism.

It is in the light of these arguments that we should approach any investigation into the establishment of public libraries. Ewart was the key figure in their creation and early history. Indeed, since his death in 1869 'there has been no other parliamentarian who could promote the cause of public libraries with utmost interest and zeal, and to whom we can refer with the same respect and gratitude not only in England but elsewhere too'.[79] Public libraries were for Ewart not simply a hobby, as *The Times* once suggested.[80] On the contrary, they were an essential element in his ideas for a national system of education which would impart that spirit of rationality so essential to the preservation of industrial capitalist society. They would act as a force for social cohesion, not division. As he anticipated:

> I have always thought that one of the good results of such institutions would be the bringing of all classes together.[81]

Edward Edwards

Edward Edwards was a prophet and pioneer of the public library movement, yet 'forgotten even while he lived'.[82] To this day he remains an obscure historical figure, despite the opinion expressed by Munford that 'it was to him more than any other man, that we owe the municipal library in the form in which it has developed'.[83] Without Edwards's investigative and statistical backbone the argument for public libraries would have been significantly weakened, to the extent of delaying public library provision beyond 1850; perhaps even until the agitation for further electoral reform, and the natural corollary to it, the establishment of a national system of education in 1870. Ewart's work in organizing the Select Committee would have counted for little but for the propaganda supplied by Edwards, who 'appears as the leading and moving spirit alike in the proceedings of the committee and its copious appendices'.[84] As Greenwood, Edwards's nineteenth-century biographer, put it, he kept Ewart's arsenal furnished with ammunition.[85] (Edwards's diary entries for the year 1849 reveal extensive correspondence and consultations with Ewart.[86]) However, in concentrating on his commendable efforts in this regard public library historians have paid inadequate attention to the *political philosophy* of a man who, surely out of some kind of ideological confidence, discovered within himself such intense motivation to promote the free provision of literature, without the prospect of any significant personal financial reward. For Edwards, public libraries most definitely possessed a socio-political dynamic. In his eyes they were, primarily, a means of increasing opportunity for self-education. He was a classic example of self-help in this regard.[87] He was aware, moreover, of the role that education could play in maintaining social stability through a diffusion of culture. Thus, in the exploration of his political philosophy, his thoughts on education serve as an appropriate point of departure.

From early in his adult life Edwards interested himself in the question of spreading education. In his twenties he became involved with radical and anti-establishment friends who agitated over questions concerning the diffusion of culture. One such friend was the architect George Godwin, who, as indicated in the previous chapter, sought to improve the morals of the poor by improving the sanitary conditions of their dwellings. Edwards and Godwin were chiefly responsible for the establishment of the *Literary Union*, a monthly magazine intended as a chronicle of literary and scientific institutions.[88] They were also involved in a mutual self-improvement group called the 'Society of Wranglers', whose members were 'full of earnest purpose and zeal for the widening of educational facilities in every direction'.[89] A common designation among the society's members was that of 'soul-squeezers': socially concerned individuals who were willing to render service in the solution of early industrialism's human problems. Theirs was a reforming, not a revolutionary quest. As Greenwood wrote:

> It was not so much a question with them that the world was out of joint and required putting to rights, as it was one of their individual readiness to help in adjusting things that in their eyes needed readjustment.[90]

The fact that Edwards was socially engaged in this way is of critical importance to an understanding of his public library work. It is also relevant to a revision (which appears in Chapter 9) of the traditional image of the detached librarian.

Edwards believed there to be a 'duty incumbent upon the state to promote the universal education of the people by all means within its power'.[91] What explains this preoccupation with the need for improvements in general education? His commitment arose, in part, from his upbringing as a Dissenter: this fostered an aptitude for investigation and criticism of social norms in areas outside religion.[92] Truth would be revealed by educational endeavour. Self-education was thus a companion to him throughout his life. His academic interests were highly diverse.[93] He displayed a genuine respect for scholarship.[94] Had he not been of such humble origins (his father was an East End bricklayer) Edwards can be pictured in a scholarly career. As it was, his achievements were exceptional. He was author of numerous works on bibliography, library history and librarianship. One of his earliest publications was a commentary on the work of the Select Committee of 1835–6 investigating the affairs of the British Museum.[95] After his work had been brought to the committee's attention he was called before it in 1836 at the remarkably young age (for an authoritative witness) of 24. A high point in his life was his appointment as Manchester Free Library's first librarian in 1850. Such achievements confirmed him in the conviction that everyone was entitled to the opportunity of education. This was an essentially Benthamite prescription: he was, as Munford has put it in explaining Edwards's acceptance of economic liberalism, a utilitarian 'who knew his wealth of nations'.[96] He was well connected with other utilitarians.[97]

Of all Edwards's writings, *Metropolitan University* (1836) conveys most clearly his leanings towards utilitarian radicalism. This pamphlet welcomed the government's intention to grant a charter to London University, but criticized its decision not to go ahead with the idea (which initially it appeared to favour) that a central examining board be established. Edwards argued that professors at Oxford and Cambridge (and London, once chartered) had a stake in the number of degrees awarded, whereas such would not be the case with 'a board of examiners entirely independent of the professors of the subordinate colleges, having no pecuniary interest in the number of degrees conferred'.[98] Moreover, he believed that a central university would give greater opportunity to those who, for various reasons, were prevented from attending 'Oxbridge' or who could not travel to London, but who could none the less obtain an education in the provinces even at an unchartered seminary. The central university idea was built on two fundamental principles. First, 'degrees should truly represent what they profess to represent, viz. certain positive requirements or general ability'. Second, 'such degrees should be attainable by all, without exception, possessed of those requirements or that ability, in what way soever obtained'.[99] Edwards chose to support these points by quoting Adam Smith: 'Whatever forces a certain number of students to any College or University, independent of the merit or reputation of the teachers, tends, more or less, to diminish the necessity of that merit or reputation.'[100] He followed this with a classic utilitarian plea for wider opportunity by saying 'that every man ought to have within his reach the means of obtaining a degree, if he have acquired the knowledge a degree professes to represent, whether the place wherein he acquired that knowledge shall have been a cloistered college, a populous city or a secluded village'.[101]

Edwards's proposals were radical, involving as they would have done sweeping and centralizing legislation. Here again is witnessed a utilitarian trait: 'The great curse of this country is bit-by-bit legislation', wrote Edwards in supporting the utilitarian plea for a greater role for the state in certain fields.[102] It was such outspoken argument which, as stated above, forced him to the attention of the Select Committee inquiry into the affairs of the British Museum. Edwards's thirst for self-education led him into frequent use of the Museum's reading room, from which experience he was able to assess the poor condition of the service and, ultimately, the need for extended education opportunities in the form of public libraries. His unease with standards of service for the exploitation of what was, after all, the nation's premier literary collection led him to attack standards of higher education provision generally:

> Whatever may be our other claims to the distinction – we have not the shadow of a pretention to be considered 'the first nation of Europe' in respect to the condition, organisation or management of our literary and scientific establishments.[103]

Regarding the management of the British Museum, he deplored its dismissive attitude to the question of accessibility. 'It is worthy of observation', he wrote, 'that in this instance, precisely as we descend the scale of official authority, we appear to find a more catholic perception of the objects of the Museum. A dread of the inroads of the "vulgar class" [by which he meant the manual-labour classes in general] does not seem to dwell in any breast of less dignity than that of principal librarian.'[104] The latter, in the form of Sir Henry Ellis, had objected to ideas on wider accessibility, for both the reading room and the Museum as a whole. If the Museum was opened in the evening, he told the Select Committee, 'I think the most mischievous portion of the population is abroad, and about at such a time': late opening would attract a 'more vulgar class' merely intent on gazing at the curiosities, and merely rendering the place unwholesome.[105] Ellis also had restrictive ideas on reading room use, believing that evening opening would encourage 'lawyers' clerks, and persons who would read voyages and travels, novels and light literature: a class of person I conceive the Museum library was not intended for, at least, not for their principal accommodation.'[106] Though not wishing to see the doors of the Museum's library flung open to all without safeguard, Edwards was none the less highly critical of the élitist management of the institution in respect of access. He agreed wholeheartedly with Panizzi's words to the committee that the poorest student in the kingdom should have the same means of 'indulging his learned curiosity, of following his rational pursuits, of consulting the same authorities, of fathoming the most intricate enquiry' as the richest.[107] However, Edwards found at the British Museum little evidence of the equality of opportunity which his utilitarian leanings taught him to expect.

In giving evidence to the Select Committee on the British Museum Edwards was steered clear of the question of wider access. Instead, his evidence centred on the best means of improving internal organization and efficiency; matters of cataloguing, book supply and staff organization. None the less, the anti-privilege zeal which characterized his ideology was not dampened. He continued, through his membership of the Art Union of London (see Chapter 5) and in his writings, to challenge the élitist stance of certain educational bodies. He called, for example, for the Royal Academy to be funded by central government.[108] This, he believed, would bring art into the public domain, for art should be of popular benefit, not just catering for élite taste.[109]

These anti-privilege (almost anti-authoritarian) sentiments stayed with Edwards throughout his life. In one of his scrapbooks, for example, he attacks the notion of the 'keeper' librarian, arguing that the 'public stock of learning in book and press' should be made 'useful to all'. An 'exclusive' library was no more than 'a talent digged in the ground' and those who used such a library, wrote Edwards in language which ridiculed the old-fashioned 'gatekeeper' philosophy, 'made it an idol to be respected and worshipped for a raritie by an implicate faith, without anie benefit to those who did esteam of it far off'.[110] Edwards was, therefore, convinced of the need for universal exploitation of education, of which libraries were an integral part. He was concerned, as the librarian Richard Garnett pointed out in 1902, at the 'waste of talent that lay sterile for lack of culture and opportunity'.[111] To exploit this potential for cultural uplift, the accumulators and keepers of literary culture, including librarians, had a duty to oversee its diffusion. Edwards was said to have 'initiated the considerable professional literature of modern librarianship'.[112] He was the first to emphasize the importance of the librarian *reaching out* to readers. He believed in the efficacy of systematic and practical classification, an aspect of librarianship in which he was ahead of his time: 'For a librarian to say that he prefers not to classify his books', he wrote, 'is much as though a cutler were to say he liked steel best when unpolished.'[113] Edwards had little sympathy with the alphabetical arrangement of titles and authors in catalogues: this, he believed, was useless to 90 per cent of the users of a popular library. But a scientific classification system was not all that was required to open the library to its users. He also favoured the idea of staff going among the readers to assist them.[114] His dream was one of maximum accessibility, the ultimate definition of which was the right to use a library without any formal recommendation or even a ticket (a ticket would of course be required for borrowing).[115] He believed the dangers of popular use to be minimal.[116]

His advocacy of accessibility came from his belief, as stated above, that education was not the prerogative of the rich but the birthright of all. It was in the education sphere that he chose to make himself useful to his fellow citizens, an ambition which he held from an early age. Through librarianship he would be able to respond to his anxieties concerning social affairs. In this respect Altick's assessment of Edwards as 'deaf, reclusive, and utterly humourless' is misleading.[117] Deaf and serious he undoubtedly was, but the word 'recluse' does not fit with his obvious social commitment. His utilitarianism was, after all, not abstract theory; it ultimately found practical expression. The eventual arrival of the universal free provision of literature in public libraries, for which Edwards fought, supports this assertion.[118]

Edwards believed that education had a key role to play in the preservation of social order. Education as a means of control was preferable, in his opinion, to the alternative of coercion: 'Truly the masses need guidance ... more than they need repression.'[119] Highlighting his interest in the fine arts he wrote in 1840 that: 'if it be true ... that these arts of design may be employed with such powerful effect in the great work of popular education, it were strange if the wanton neglect of them were altogether to continue, at a time when the preservation of social order itself is loudly threatened by the unhappy combination of ignorance and discontent.'[120] In the same publication, and in the same vein, he chose to quote the Bishop of London on the matter as follows: 'Whatever of necessity affects the moral condition, the usefulness, the well-being of the people at large', said the Bishop in a speech to the House of Lords in 1839, 'in its results the very existence of social order must fall within the State's directing and controlling power ... Education must needs be a State question.'[121] Edwards was thus keenly aware of the social urgency for widespread educational reform.

Edwards believed that education could reduce social strife by removing ignorance. He agreed with the notion that dangerous political agitation was fostered out of ignorance among the masses; that those at the forefront of the fight to overthrow the social system were using their demagogic power to sway the beliefs of those inadequately informed of the true virtues of industrial capitalism or, indeed, of the evil consequences that would flow from social revolution. As argued above, respectable opinion viewed that, in place of ignorance, the uneducated lower orders could be inculcated with reason, through an educational process geared to establishment views. Certainly Edwards's belief in the power of reason to combat social turbulence was unshakable: 'What can be more likely to defeat turbulent passion than calm appeals to reason? What can be better adapted to make men attached to what is good in existing institutions, and contented to seek by peaceful means the improvement of what they may chance to be defective?'[122]

For Edwards, public libraries were an indispensable weapon in education's armoury: 'If libraries are not educators they have no claim whatever to legislative attention, howsoever serviceable in other respects.'[123] Because education had the potential to bring about public peace, so also did the educative agency of the public library: 'The artisan who delights in visiting a Public Museum on his rare holiday, or in spending some portion of his scanty leisure in a Public Reading Room ... will repress crime in the very heat of insurrection, and practise moderation even amidst the excitement of victory', he wrote at a time of social upheaval, in 1848.[124]

Edwards was aware of the squalor of industrial society. He himself reacted to it by developing an enthusiasm for the countryside.[125] He was depressed by the urban environments's effect on human existence:

> No one can have walked through the more crowded and obscure parts of London on a Sunday, with an observant eye, without shuddering at the dreadful amount of utter idleness, degradation, and consequent drunkenness, and almost every other vice, then so particularly observable.[126]

How, he asked, could such evils be lessened? Edwards told the Select Committee on public libraries that

> the want of some provision, from the public resources, of amusements of a rational and improving character, has led to the introduction, to a large extent in our towns, of brutalising and demoralising amusements.[127]

Edwards believed that rational recreation, for which public libraries stood, would dispel the idleness, listlessness and drunkenness which afflicted society (the danger inherent in non-work, idle time was, of course, that worker could associate and communicate with worker). It would also serve as a social healer. Edwards saw class division as a pressing issue:

The great problem of the age is the diminution, by gradual and peaceful means, of the glaring disparities between the refinement, the luxury, and the splendour which exist at the summit of society, and the destitution and brutishness which grovel at its base. If this can be effected, not by the depression of the lofty, but by the elevation of the lowly society will have safely bridged over the great gulf which, in more countries than one, is now fearfully yawning at its feet.[128]

Divisions could be overcome, he proposed, by instigating 'a high order of mental culture'.[129] Referring to rational recreation, and echoing Mill's distinction between higher and lower pleasures, Edwards wrote that:

Everything which extends a man's sympathies, which makes him a social rather than a selfish being, and which leads him to seek pleasures beyond mere sensual gratification, is a good, just in proportion to the contrary influences which ordinarily act upon him.[130]

His confidence in the intrinsically 'social' nature of humanity thus coalesced with his enthusiasm for education as an elevating force. Education would help to 'dispel that ignorance which lends to social disparity its most alarming aspect'.[131]

Yet the culturally malnourished, said Edwards, could not elevate themselves. They required both administrative and intellectual assistance. He wrote: 'If Prussia can pervert the benign influences of education to the support of arbitrary power, we can employ them for the support and perpetuation of free institutions [i.e. public libraries].'[132] Edwards advised not indoctrination but intellectual guidance from above. He believed that society's reading habits could be modified by enticing people with 'good' reading:

Those who can read will never be without reading of some sort ... to place good literature within everybody's reach is certainly the best way to counteract the empty frivolity, the crude scepticism and the low morality of a portion ... of the current literature of the day ... To make books of the highest order freely and easily accessible throughout the length and breadth of the land, were surely to give no mean furtherance to the efforts of the schoolmaster, and of the Christian minister, to produce under God's blessing a tranquil, cultivated and a religious people.[133]

Edwards initially hoped that public libraries would engineer higher reading tastes. He thus thought it 'a matter of some regret' that borrowers at his Manchester Public Library chiefly demanded 'books of amusement'.[134] His dream had been one of duplicating the reading room of the British Museum (albeit on a smaller scale) in the provinces and in various London districts. A public library for Edwards was an institution of education (not, it should be noted, solely for esoteric research) at the disposal of any person seeking elevation. He never wavered from the belief that public libraries should, in essence, be 'town' libraries belonging to the entire community.[135] In this sense it is unwise to view him as the archetypal social controller, despite his concern that the lower orders required most educational attention.[136]

His desire to diffuse culture for the purpose of assuring social stability was based on no reactionary political stance. Of the revolution in France in 1848, for example, he recorded in his diary that 'news came of insurrectionary movements in Paris to which I earnestly wish success'.[137] Two days later he praised 'a glorious day ... for the downfall of the delusive, corrupt and retrogressive government of Louis Philippe in France'.[138] In the areas of social order, therefore, Edwards was not a conservative (though he did, of course, defect to Toryism later in life).[139] Rather, his sympathies during the 1840s, when he was agitating for the establishment of public libraries, rested with utilitarian reformism. 'We look indeed for no fool's Paradise as conceived by a St Simon or an Owen', he wrote in 1848, but for a world in which

> every man, however, may by patient exertion be enabled to earn honest bread, to cultivate the faculties within him, both for his life and for the life to come, and to acquire some direct and legitimate influence upon that legislation which affects his interests the more powerfully, the poorer and humbler may be his sphere of labour; all authority shall be limited and responsible, and that in king and magistrate, as in peasant or servant, it shall be everywhere made visible that what a man soweth, that shall he also reap.[140]

Accordingly, in order that the individual be given 'some direct and legitimate influence upon that legislation which affects his interests' he supported Chartism in its 'moral' manifestation. At the climax of the Chartist agitation in 1848 he refused to be sworn in as a special constable to help defend the property of the British Museum.[141] He also signed the Charter.[142] His diary entry for the day of the Kennington demonstration recorded that he found himself in 'a minority in condemning the course taken by the government and strongly advocating a wide extension of the electoral franchise'.[143]

Thus, Edwards's view on the general political climate of the late 1840s was far from what one might call alarmist, supporting as he did, in broad terms, the demands of the Chartist movement. He certainly did not share the trepidation of one of his colleagues at the British Museum who read in the official organ of the Chartist movement, the *Northern Star*, that 'an organisation existed in Britain to burn down London, Liverpool and the other Babylons of England, and massacre the loyal inhabitants';[144] and who also appeared to attach some credence to the rumours surrounding the Kennington assembly – 'this new Runnymeade' – that 'the morning of the eventful day arrived, and a revolution was prophesied without fail before sunset'.[145] It is perhaps more likely that he would have concurred with this same colleague's more rational and considered comments that in the wake of the 1848 revolutions in Europe 'there were certain indications in the political atmosphere of our own country, that made thoughtful and observant men a little apprehensive';[146] and that as to the cost and inconvenience of such military precautions as were taken in 1848 for the safeguarding of law and order, 'we must seek a cheaper, less troublesome, and more summary way of suppressing and putting down such a nuisance'.[147] In respect of this last assertion, Edwards proposed public libraries as an alternative, effective means of maintaining social order.

Despite his espousal of the Chartist cause, and accepting that he was no alarmist in observing the contemporary socio-political climate, it is difficult to believe that Edwards could not have been troubled, to some extent, by the agitation which caused a significant section of respectable opinion to sense an impending social cataclysm. Edwards was no social revolutionary. Rather, his support for the Charter was derived from the Benthamite belief in the efficacy of representative government to dissolve corruption, inefficiency and privilege.

Given his belief in education as a means of forging social cohesion and maintaining social stability, the avoidance of abrupt social change must be counted as a prime factor in explaining his enthusiasm for the public library idea. As he testified in 1849:

> At this time especially, upon general grounds ... I think there could be no more wise and prudent expenditure of public money than in the promotion of libraries. At a time when we know that there are a great many subversive doctrines afloat about property it would have an excellent effect.[148]

Edwards recognized the march of history and the destiny of increasing power which awaited the lower orders. This he accepted and, as far as can be judged from his utilitarian outlook, welcomed. But he did so reservedly, in the knowledge that serious social conflict could only be avoided if the masses were educated out of their ignorance in advance of their being offered power. Edwards was convinced that there was 'nothing in any State so terrible as a powerful and authorised ignorance'. 'Powerful and authorised the classes that are ignorant must eventually become', he went on, but 'society has yet to decide whether the removal of ignorance shall, or shall not, precede the attainment of power.'[149]

In response to those who doubted that the removal of ignorance, through institutions like the public library, would leave intact the fundamental balance of power, Edwards sang the message of the pursuit of culture as a shared cause which was bound to pacify and harmonize. He predicted that public libraries would never become, as some feared, 'political schools of agitation', precisely *because* they would 'widen that public domain in which all classes have a common interest'.[150] In true utilitarian fashion Edwards argued that public libraries, by strengthening the faculty of independent thought, would help to defeat dangerous demagogues of all political shades, or, as he called them, 'noisy stump-orators'.[151] Edwards envisaged a liberating yet stable social improvement derived from individual self-improvement. His enthusiasm for public libraries rested upon his enduring respect for the acquisition of culture through education.[152] Moreover, the fact that both public libraries and culture occupied a 'public domain' served to enhance, in Edwards's opinion, the prospects for stable social development.

Edwards has sometimes been accused of harbouring an obsession for cloistered scholarship. Greenwood believed that Edwards 'had the spirit of one of the old monks', content with being 'away from public gaze'.[153] While it is true that Edwards praised the 'utility' of past monastic scholarship – 'to monks', he wrote, 'we are, in the matter of Libraries, primarily and permanently indebted'[154] – the metaphor of the reclusive monk is not one which should be considered appropriate to the social epistemology of the early public library, which he helped to fashion. Rather, it is more convincing to adopt the view of the librarian C. W. Sutton, who stated in 1912 that Edwards was not a 'mere machine for the acquisition and private consumption of knowledge. His aspiration was to help in opening the gates of learning to all.'[155]

To emphasize his social commitment to librarianship it is worth quoting once again Richard Garnett's observation that Edwards 'was impressed by the waste of talent that lay sterile for lack of culture and opportunity'.[156] Edwards deplored the deficiency of culture in society, as well as the means to its acquisition. In keeping with the doctrine of utilitarianism he thus advocated and, what is more, *actively* sought an increased opportunity of access to learning (more about the 'engagement' of public librarians in Chapter 9).

Edwards was not, however, doctrinaire in respect of the utilitarianism he embraced – he was too much of a scholar for that. Edwards also drew heavily on the anti-utilitarian, anti-industrial, romantic, spiritual tradition. It is no coincidence that his favourite writer was Carlyle,[157] whose espousal of 'learning in breadth' reflected a growing dissatisfaction with a society bent on increasing specialization, the latter being equated with shifting sand rather than the solid rock of 'rounded' learning as a foundation for building social serenity and stability.

Edwards was also familiar with the intellectual position of Ruskin. In one of his scrapbooks Edwards took the trouble to copy a lengthy paragraph from Ruskin's *Sesame and Lilies* (1865), part of which asked:

> What do we, as a nation, care about books? How much do you think we spend altogether on our libraries, public or private, as compared with what we spend on our horses? If a man spends lavishly on his library, you call him mad – a bibliomaniac. But you never call any one a horsemaniac, though men ruin themselves every day by their horses, and you do not hear of people ruining themselves by their books ... how much do you think the contents of the book-shelves of the United Kingdom, public and private, would fetch, as compared with the contents of its wine-cellars?[158]

Clearly, Edwards was aware of the danger for culture which the acquisitive society presented. As such, he was part of the tradition of social criticism which questioned the value of scientific industrialism. However, this should neither encourage any description of him as a reluctant progressive nor hide the fact that he recognized the inevitability of material progress. Edwards saw that public libraries had a crucial role to play in a maturing technically educated industrial society; and he complemented this with a desire to disseminate aesthetic culture, both scientific and traditional. When combined, these utilitarian and idealist perspectives were potentially potent in helping to deliver a steady and organic development of society; and nowhere was this prescription more clearly expressed than in Edwards's thoughts, shared to a large extent by Ewart, on the value of art in modern industrial society.

CHAPTER 5

CULTURE, MATERIALISM AND THE 1849 SELECT COMMITTEE: THE CULTURAL MATERIALISM OF ART

Ewart and Edwards approached the public library question from a utilitarian standpoint; in addition, as will be argued, a concern for aesthetic culture, not usually associated with utilitarianism, both motivated them and complemented the impulse behind the concept of books on the rates. The utilitarian aims of the two protagonists were supported by equally authentic utilitarian methods. The public library ideal was furthered by a Select Committee on the subject, established in 1849.[1] This parliamentary inquiry resulted from both practical and philosophic considerations.

The Select Committee

The format of a Select Committee was chosen in preference to a Commons resolution; the latter, according to a constitutional rule, would have disallowed requests for a grant of public money. A Select Committee, on the other hand, kept open the option of central funding.[2] It also afforded publicity. Ewart expected that a Select Committee would draw attention to the issue: 'it would awaken interest in the matter, and would undoubtedly lead to efforts being made for the formation of public libraries'.[3] The public library needed all the propaganda it could muster in the face of vehement opposition from non-interventionists.[4] The argument that literature was affordable in the market-place was a potentially serious obstacle for free library protagonists to surmount.

The theory underlying the choice of the Select Committee method was derived from the reforming essence of utilitarianism and the associated notion of 'vigorous research and enquiry prior to legislation so that the full and impartial facts could be exposed'.[5] The quest for scientific, social legislation based on objective research was not unworthy. However, parliamentary investigation was in practice far from impartial. Utilitarians shaped the direction of the Select Committee on Public Libraries in the same fashion as they had orchestrated inquiries on questions like the Poor Law and municipal reform, which attracted Royal Commissions in 1832 and 1833 respectively.[6] Ewart stage-managed the Select Committee's proceedings. As chairman he mapped out with meticulous care the course of the Select Committee's work. He was closely assisted in this task by his chief witness, Edwards. Munford has described how Ewart and Edwards went 'to immense trouble to prepare in advance both Ewart's questions and Edwards's answers; other witnesses, carefully selected, were brought in to support Edwards's arguments'.[7] The proceedings were engineered with precision, to the extent that, 'If it were possible in 1849 "to leave no stone unturned" Ewart and Edwards had done it.'[8] The result was a convincing report, notwithstanding the inclusion of some inaccuracies such as those concerning the extent of alleged public access to libraries on the Continent (Edwards's rhetoric and propaganda being particularly misleading in this regard).

The type of witness called before the Select Committee, and the nature of the evidence submitted, broadly matched the strategy laid down by Ewart in a letter to Edwards immediately prior to the commencement of the proceedings. Ewart called for a wide variety of areas of knowledge and expertise to be tapped. Aside from information on general matters he called for evidence of:

> travellers and frequenters of libraries here and abroad ... persons who can speak on such subjects as Parish Libraries ... persons conversant with the working classes, and literature as connected with them ... parish clergymen ... [itinerant] 'Lecturers' ... members of the Municipal Councils in our large towns ... perhaps some of the working men themselves ... the Librarians of existing libraries ... some of the founders of modern Village Libraries ... the rate at which books could be supplied.[9]

A reading of the report – comprising a short introductory summary of findings but over 200 pages of evidence – shows that all the areas which Ewart set out to investigate were covered. There was a variety of witnesses, but most can be categorized as possessing a knowledge of literary consumption (including libraries) and/or of the social habits of the masses.

The value of the Committee's evidence to the social historian lies not in the brief which Ewart set himself (in his letter to Edwards) but in the detail of contemporary sociological and cultural references which the witnesses provided. The Society for the Diffusion of Useful Knowledge described the committee's report as 'one of the most valuable and interesting documents which Parliament has added to the stock of blue-book literature for many years'.[10] This was, said the Society, partly because, aside from the core public library aspect:

> Other questions of importance arise out of the evidence ... such as the present state of the social habits, the virtues and vices, of the mass of the labouring population, the history and contents of certain rare books and manuscripts, the rise and progress of a new race of itinerant lecturers, and so forth.[11]

Yet the wealth of data on popular culture in the report (a historical document thus far largely ignored, it should be added, by social historians) has resulted in confusion among library historians concerning the Select Committee's motives. The Committee's diverse preoccupations have not been subjected to imaginative analysis. Instead, motives have been expressed in general and vague terms, such as 'educational and moral improvement',[12] 'the appeasement of the masses'[13] or 'the altruistic work of good and great men'.[14]

What explains the failure of library historians to analyse with a wider vision the events of 1849? One possible answer is that, because the data in the report have been ignored by historians with non-library interests, library historians have lacked a helping hand in the development of perspectives and theories surrounding the report, which might otherwise have thrown light on their subject. But this lack of analytical support has been detrimental to library history generally, not just to those investigating the work of the Select Committee. A more specific explanation might be found in the common and constant desire of librarians and library supporters to improve standards of service. The history of efforts to extend library provision has been seen as one of struggle and painful evolution. Using hindsight it has been easy to construe library development as a teleological growth from lowly beginnings. Public library history has been given a Whiggish 'onwards' and 'upwards' interpretation which strongly infers an unimpressive start. Both the Public Libraries Act of 1850 and the work of the Select Committee which gave rise to it – while recognized as important landmarks – have been considered unhelpful to the development of free libraries. The limited nature of the Act is seen to have bestowed a legacy of slow and tortured development. Kelly has written that the legislation

> is sometimes spoken of as though it were a magic wand which brought a national public library service into being overnight. Nothing could be further from the truth. The powers given by the Act were exceedingly limited and inadequate; they were, moreover, permissive not compulsory. It was only after long and bitter struggles, and much supplementary legislation, that the library service as we know it came into existence.[15]

Such accusations of inadequacy and limited vision cannot be levelled at the Select Committee, which in fact called for state assistance in funding municipal libraries.[16] However, the intentions of the early protagonists, which the Select Committee enshrined, have been classed as too vague for a truly effective free library service to develop. As Murison has argued:

> For many reasons ... legislation and administration did not keep pace with ... philanthropic enthusiasm, and the progress of public libraries was painfully slow. Not the least of the reasons were the variety of aims which were set for the libraries.[17]

Confusion over what induced the earliest pioneers to support the public library ideal is unnecessary. The essence of early public library philosophy is not polyglot and vague, but simple and precise. The Select Committee might have traversed a wide variety of issues, but in the final analysis it possessed merely a dual thrust: namely, concerns for cultural elevation and material advance, both of which held implications for social stability.

The literary and intellectual interests of the Select Committee's membership were reflected in the call for improved library facilities. It was noted that one result of Britain's inferiority in respect of public libraries was that 'our own literature (as well as our own people), denied the benefit of such institutions, must have proportionately suffered'.[18] A picture was drawn of great writers and thinkers hindered in their intellectual pursuits by poor library provision.[19] It was argued that free libraries would be particularly relevant to students in the provinces.[20] Further, they would be welcomed by teachers, who 'required the best implements of education';[21] by journalists, who frequently needed to consult 'political, historical and literary works';[22] and by itinerant lecturers, whose work would consequently be rendered 'less superficial'.[23]

Cultural improvement was not to be confined to the educated and to the middle classes. The effects of a wider diffusion of culture were considered by the Select Committee. It was noted that the recent experiment in making culture more widely accessible – that is to say, the establishment of art galleries, museums and schools of design, and the throwing open to the people the doors of the National Gallery and the British Museum – had not been marked by abuse. Rather, it was said that 'much rational enjoyment and much popular enlightenment have distinguished it'.[24] It was believed that the cultural standards of the masses had recently undergone an improvement, one which free libraries could help to sustain:

> Testimony, showing a great improvement in national habits and manners, is abundantly given in the evidence taken by the Committee. That they would be still further improved by the establishment of Public Libraries, it needs not even the high authority and ample evidence of the witnesses who appeared before the Committee to demonstrate.[25]

The perceived 'increased qualifications of the people to appreciate and enjoy' institutions like public libraries appeared to complement the 'vast and increasing number of new popular works, cheap in price, condensed in form, and valuable in substance'.[26] Such developments, it was believed, strongly invited the establishment of free libraries.[27]

The spread of humanistic culture was one of the Select Committee's intentions. It also aimed – in the socialization, anthropological, sense of the word 'culture' – to reinforce cultural norms. It was hoped that wholesome literature, made widely available in free libraries, would attract the public away from immoral pastimes like the tavern and barbaric sports. For example, one witness testified how in Birmingham bull-baiting had disappeared and dog-fighting was dying out, not because of the interference of the authorities, but because the 'taste' of the people had been improved.[28] The Select Committee questioned the wisdom of abandoning 'the people to a low, enfeebling, and often pestilential literature, instead of enabling them to breathe a more pure, elevated and congenial atmosphere'.[29] This did not mean that the masses should be taught to read only classic literature. True, there was an awareness, as John Stuart Mill articulated, that the mass proliferation of literature militated against 'the laborious and learned' and worked in favour of 'crude and ill-informed writers'.[30] But 'light' literature, provided it was morally sound, was to be encouraged for its counter-attracting potential. As Ewart retorted to the clergyman who complained that the availability of Walter Scott novels at the local subscription library had distracted one young mechanic from attending church: 'But is it not better that they should read Walter Scott's novels than they should do something worse?'[31]

It was not just in the social sphere that deviance could be corrected: it was hoped that free libraries might also reduce the influence of politically unacceptable literature. The Select Committee classified unsavoury political writings as immoral. It noted in the same breath – as if to suggest an inseparable link – its distaste for both immoral and politically deviant literature:

> It is also truly observed that the establishment of such depositories [free libraries] of standard literature would lessen or perhaps entirely destroy the influence of frivolous, unsound and dangerous works.[32]

One witness highlighted the depressed area of Spitalfields and expressed concern over the possible inflammatory effect in such an area of 'dangerous' French novels of 'doubtful social character', which promoted 'loose ideas on the subject of society'.[33] It was envisaged that free libraries would negate the influence of seditious and dangerous political ideas, not by performing a positive, propagandist role, but by presenting themselves as agencies purveying uncontroversial political (and religious) material. The public library would underwrite political norms by being apolitical.[34]

Implicit in the work of the Select Committee, therefore, is the question of control. A fuller discussion of the argument that the public library was conceived as an agency of social control will follow in Chapter 8. It is enough to say here that, notwithstanding the nuances and defects in the social control thesis, sufficient evidence can be gleaned from the deliberations of the Select Committee to warrant such a discussion. The question of control – in terms of preserving both social order and 'the' social order – formed part of the public library agenda. While traditional voices were raised against the extension of education which libraries would bring – one MP feared free libraries might become 'normal schools of agitation'[35] – most who debated the issue were of the persuasion of John Bright, who was

> quite sure that nothing would tend more to the preservation of order than the diffusion of the greatest amount of intelligence and the prevalence of the most complete and open discussion, among all classes.[36]

This is not to say that control was successful. Nor is it the case that the public library was simply an instrument of control: the Select Committee closed its report, it should be stressed, by describing a recent spontaneous development in the 'love of literature and reverence for knowledge' – a trend which, it was hoped, the public library would strengthen.[37] Clearly, the quest for cultural uplift possessed a certain autonomy. It was a quest, moreover, in which all social classes were involved. As the envisaged middle-class use of public libraries demonstrated, the cultural sphere was not one from which the middle classes would disengage in deference to a working class undergoing cultural hegemonization.

None the less, the argument that the public library began as a subtle attempt at control is lent some weight by the institution's utilitarian pedigree. The utilitarian faith in the industrial market society was shared by public library protagonists, and is evident in the work of the Select Committee. That utilitarianism was a powerful influence in 1849 is shown by the fact that culture was discussed by the Committee essentially from the perspective of material and character 'improvement'; there was no specific reference to literary culture for recreation. The early public library debate is only occasionally marked by appeals to the value of non-utilitarian recreational reading, such as that made by *The Times* in 1852:

> In the working of public libraries we can expect no other results than what we already obtain from the cheapness and abundance of books in private hands. Most will read merely to pass the time, and if in doing so they can forget a few cares, and go to bed rather calmer and happier, they will be no losers by their books, whatever it may be.[38]

Materialism and art

Despite the preoccupation with 'useful' literature, little attention has been paid to the utilitarian content of the 1849 report, especially its economic dimension. Utilitarianism permeates the report. As stated above, there was no attempt to shy away from intervention. Voluntaryism was not eschewed, but state intervention in assisting the public library to disseminate knowledge was justified on the grounds of the increased social utility which would result.[39] The Select Committee persistently pursued an anti-privilege line.[40] The efficacy of self-help in connection with free libraries was frequently alluded to, as befitted the achievements of the Committee's membership.[41] Much was made of the need to evolve among the masses powers of reason for a better understanding of political and economic matters.[42]

More needs to be said of the Select Committee's materialist concerns. References were made to the need for business libraries, partly for education in political economy. The report highlighted the evidence of the German Dr C. Meyer, secretary to Prince Albert. He had spoken of the famous Commercial Library in Hamburg, which was said to have had 'a most beneficial influence on the character of the merchants' of the city.[43] Similar institutions were considered appropriate to Britain:

> It would seem that in our large commercial and manufacturing towns, as well as in our agricultural districts, such libraries would naturally spring up [as a result

of public library legislation], illustrative of the peculiar trade, manufactures, and agriculture of the place, and greatly favourable to the practical development of the science of political economy.[44]

Topographical libraries (and museums) were also suggested.[45] These would contain not only a record of 'local events, local literature, and local manners', but also collections of science and art materials 'illustrative of the climate, soil, and resources of the surrounding country'.[46]

Free libraries were proposed as educators in economic practicalities: 'The people may be taught many lessons which concern their material (as well as their moral and religious) welfare.'[47] But materially useful information was not to be confined to the improvement of social habits. A more direct form of 'valuable information' (a term used in the report) was literature on emigration. It was proposed that by providing appropriate information to those seeking a more prosperous life overseas the public library would, in advance, 'make the people well acquainted with our different colonies, the mode of reaching them, and all the requisite measures to be adopted by a settler'.[48]

The utilitarian aims of the Select Committee were not pursued in isolation from its cultural concerns. At a general level the public library was viewed as an intrinsically cultural institution which could advance materialism. In one specific area – the provision of art and illustrated books – the public library was the perfect match-maker. Early public library pioneers were concerned with art and design in a way which merits the description *cultural materialism*.

The Select Committee deliberated on the question of collections of illustrative materials for improved manufacturing.[49] In this regard, part of the evidence of the evangelical lecturer George Dawson is worth lengthy consideration:

> Q. 1252. Would it not be desirable that manufacturers, whose business is connected with design, should have ready access to such books as are connected with that design which belongs to that particular department? – Yes, In Birmingham everything depends upon design now [answered Dawson].

> Q. 2387. Would you say that any library professing to be a public one, should contain among its various literary riches collections of works of design as a matter of course? – Yes [answered Dawson].

> Q. 1288. [In Birmingham, said Dawson,] the materials have always been good, but the forms have been formerly rough and course; the continental manufacturers have always excelled in that.

> Q. 1290. Have you found that works on the principles of art have been much read or inquired for? – Yes, in towns where design is used. In Coventry, for example, where ribbon making is much carried on, it is of great importance [answered Dawson].

This evidence reiterated the results of the Select Committee on Arts and Manufactures (1835-6). This is not surprising in view of Ewart's chairmanship of both this Select Committee and that on public libraries. Ewart was keenly aware of the importance of good design to the success of home manufacturers in international competition, and was similarly knowledgeable of Britain's unfavourable standing in this regard. Like many other 'gentlemen' of the time Ewart had undertaken a Grand Tour, on which he would have been able to note the supremacy of much foreign design. Moreover, the wealthy merchant family firm of Ewart, Myers and Co. 'handled too many products of British factories and mills for Ewart to be unaware of contemporary standards'.[50] Ewart's interest in design for manufacturing centred on the textile industry: he 'knew full well that the financial loss to Britain from buying French designs was ten times as great in the textile trades as in the remaining trades put together'.[51] (There was no incentive to produce good British designs for export, as the French had no copyright protection.) But his concern spread to other areas of manufacturing. He was far from isolated in his realization that foreign design was making serious inroads into British trade in a wide range of articles. In looking forward to the Great Exhibition the *Art Journal* warned that Britain had yielded 'the palm of excellence' to those foreign goods with a critical design element, maintaining its dominance chiefly in 'those objects independent of ornamentation'. For example, whereas domestic production excelled in areas such as Manchester cotton (in terms of price and quality), Preston chintz, Yorkshire broadcloths, steam machinery, Leicester cotton stockings, Belfast linens and Staffordshire earthenware, foreign skills had produced significant market leads in silks (especially Lyon), ribbons (especially St Etienne), jewellery, carpets, coloured glass (especially Bohemia), children's toys, musical instruments, braids and marquetry.[52] Nor was Ewart alone in his criticism of the neglect of design education which lay at the root of this failure. For, as Bell has written, when:

> it became clear to the manufacturers of textiles, ribbon, ornamental metal-work, paper hanging, furniture, pottery and many other varieties of fancy goods, that the customer did not want the product of British factories, despite their admitted technical excellence; when it became obvious also that employers were spending large sums on the importation of foreign designs and foreign artisans, the representatives of industry in the House of Commons were painfully interested.[53]

The Select Committee on Arts and Manufactures had given rise to a number of experiments aimed at improving standards of design. These included: a new building for the National Gallery in Trafalgar Square (1838); a revitalized and more accessible British Museum; the establishment of municipal museums and art galleries; and schools of design assisted by central government. These initiatives represented 'an exposure of the masses to works of art, on a scale which had only been previously available to the middle and upper classes'.[54] In the 1830s and 1840s the art education of the working classes was pursued with a 'missionary-like fervour', in the hope of reducing the attachment of art education to 'conservative connoisseurship' and of introducing into society a wider and heightened appreciation.[55]

The improvement and extension of artistic taste had a strong utilitarian dynamic. This assertion, taken at face value, appears to be a contradiction in terms, scientific materialism being the antithesis of aesthetics. But the democratization of art – radicals like Ewart and Edwards hoped to break the monopoly of the Royal Academy, for example[56] – and the anti-privilege aspects of utilitarianism were in truth highly compatible. In the *laissez-faire* tradition, it was argued that a freer circulation of art, a 'universal cultivation' of art, would foster talent.[57] It mattered not that art would become cheaper as a result: cheap art could also be good.[58] The idea that the 'march of improvement' was now quicker, because of the 'collision of mind with mind', was seen as wholly relevant to the sphere of art.[59]

Further, art education's material value in improving product design had implications for the social stability which utilitarianism predicted would flow from greater prosperity. Protectionists argued that free trade was a destabilizing influence. A petition in 1850 stated:

> We humbly and respectfully submit ... that recent legislative measures have driven the industrial classes of our countrymen into an unequal and unjust competition with foreigners in the home market; which has occasioned grievous distress and excited great and general discontent, now rapidly ripening into disaffection ... by the 'Free Importation' of foreign commodities ... multitudes of artisans and labourers in this country, having lost their means of employment ... [are] driven on the Poor Rates – we seriously apprehend that they may, from destitution and despair, be induced to take proceedings dangerous to the existing institutions both in Church and State ... such flagrant injustice and oppression may at length become absolutely intolerable, and may, as we fear, lead to anarchy, and to all the horrors of a social revolution.[60]

The prospect of intensifying competition arising from trade liberalization thus placed a premium on the improvement of British manufactures. It is important to stress, however, that the Great Exhibition (1851), conceived as an advertisement for supposedly superior British goods at the dawn of the free trade era, was not an unqualified success. As Richard Cobden remarked:

> Did any reflecting man walk through the Great Exhibition without feeling that we are apt to be a little under a delusion as to the quality of men in other parts of the world, and their capacity to create these arts of utility of which we are apt to think sometimes we possess a monopoly of production in this country. I don't think we can wait.[61]

Such pleas to guard against commercial complacency were based on the fundamental belief that prosperous industrialism produced a civilized society. In 1848 one art journal predicted that everyone who visited the Great Exhibition:

> would see in its treasures the results of social order and reverence to the majesty of law ... Industry is the child of order, and a country will only prosper when the labourer is as strongly convinced of this fact as the employer.[62]

It is in this context of a conjunction between material success and social stability that the genesis of the public library should also be seen. The Select Committee on Public Libraries, like the Great Exhibition, was characterized, to a degree, by a pessimistic perception of Britain's standing in the world, and the implications this had for domestic order. The Select Committee noted that the country's library provision was 'unworthy of the power ... of the country'.[63] This deficiency included a poor library provision for art education. The public library was presented as an institution which could remedy the narrow diffusion of art education. The latter thus became a recurrent theme in public library development. Not only were public libraries to run art classes,[64] they also provided illustrative material of direct relevance to workers whose trades included a design input. In 1871 it was stated that

> A very large proportion of the persons using both the [Birmingham] Reference Library and the Art Gallery are ... persons who copy from books and works of art for sale and trade purpose.[65]

In the 1840s, and for a long time before, art was seen – perhaps more than now – as pertinent to the practicalities of life. Technical education was essentially art education; the term 'industrial art' was commonplace. (It is interesting to note that the full title of the RSA, founded in 1754, was the Royal Society for the encouragement of Arts, *Manufactures* [italics added] and Commerce.) What was said about art education was of relevance to technical education generally. Although the Select Committee on Public Libraries heard evidence that workers were little interested in trade books,[66] it was also told of the importance of books for trade purposes. Indeed, recent research has noted a demand for technical education, in terms of design knowledge, from workers shorn of technical skills by the specialization which industrialization encouraged.[67]

Edward Edwards, like Ewart, recognized the material value of art. At 26 Edwards produced what was, for his young age, an exhaustive and accomplished examination into 'the state and prospects of painting, sculpture and architecture, in practice and in public appreciation' – *The Administrative Economy of the Fine Arts* (1840).[68] In this book Edwards stressed the necessity of good design in boosting demand for British manufactures. 'The prosperity of the manufacturers of this country', he wrote, 'depends on an improved taste in design characterising our productions and enabling them to compete in the markets with those of our neighbours'.[69] He repeated this message to the Select Committee on Public Libraries, arguing that the excellence of French designs was due to accessibility of books.[70] Yet Edwards also believed in the ennobling influence of art. He urged that every individual should 'minister to the craving intellect as well as the craving appetite, – to cultivate his moral being as well as his physical being'; in this regard, he argued, art appreciation was the 'capacity of receiving cultivation by the perception of beauty in form and in colour'.[71] Elsewhere he wrote:

No augury can be more happy, if it be indeed a truth that the love of the Beautiful in form and fitness which the Arts induce, carrieth its influence into daily life, and teacheth to see preferably the Beautiful and the Fit therein also.[72]

Ewart too looked beyond art's material value. He displayed a keen aesthetic appreciation of fine arts.[73] He was aware of the cultural importance of the arts generally: he once said that he would 'be gratified if, in a sordid age, when nothing but dividends and percentages absorbed men's minds, an opportunity could be given of inviting them to the more ennobling pursuits of literature'.[74] He thought it a 'mistake to think the mechanic's hand was employed more than his head'.[75]

However, Ewart's plea for the exercising of the mind of the mechanic requires careful qualification in respect of his views on art education. Concerning the distinction between education in fine and mechanical art he believed that the former, while clearly the province of all in terms of public consumption and access, was not as relevant to the formal art teaching of the artisan as the latter. In the debate over what constituted the basis of training in fine art Ewart's position is unclear. The dominant view of the Royal Academy – as had been articulated by Sir Joshua Reynolds – was that good artists were produced by the method of imitation, or mannerism: the exhaustive copying of an eclectic range of historic high art. This ornamental drawing approach was criticized, most notably by Benjamin Haydon, as constituting anti-invention: the mechanical method of fine art training was unimaginative and needed replacing by the study of nature, especially the drawing of the nude figure. It was urged that in keeping with the Greeks, ornamental and high art not be separated – because 'the same principle regulated the milk jug and the limb'.[76]

In this pedagogic discourse Ewart's attitude in respect of fine art cannot be determined; but what can be said is that as far as it applied to the artisan he came down on the side of convention. His concept of design training for operatives was mechanistic, preferring teaching in ornament to that of the figure. He was convinced of the need to apply scientific principles to art, believing that the basis of form in art was geometry.[77] Ewart urged that a furtherance of the teaching of mechanical art, not of fine art (and certainly not of fine art through the study of the 'natural') would provide the basis for improved design in manufacturing, especially in the textile trades lately challenged by the ingenuity of French designs.

Significantly, design training for the French artisan in the schools of the Ministry of Public Instruction and Fine Arts included an exposure to fine art; the distinction between high and low art did not exist. In Britain, however, the strategy followed by the Royal Academy (which controlled the schools of design and whose philosophy infused, in the second half of the nineteenth century, the schools of art run by the Department of Science and Art) was to retain fine art for the élite, not diffuse it to the artisan. To open the minds of the lower orders to fine art was conceived as socially dangerous in that it might encourage individuals, if not classes, to rise above their station (self-improvement *within* one's station was, of course, both accepted and expected).[78] Ewart did not concur with this élitist view of art in society. In his leadership of the Select Committee on Arts and Manufactures he had displayed a commitment to increasing, in Ruskinian fashion, the public's knowledge of fine art.[79] Public education in fine art was for him a contribution to the campaign for useful knowledge.[80] The dissemination of an awareness of fine art was to be achieved through exposing the masses to it through public buildings, monuments, museums, galleries and libraries, each of these being cheaper than the provision of formal art education institutions. A growing awareness of fine art would have the economic effect of improving public taste, the poor standard of which had hampered the design-derived competitiveness of many British goods. (It should be stressed, however, that within high art itself there were, of course, high and low levels of tasteful appreciation and moral respectability: the work of non-controversial artists like Edwin Landseer should be set apart from the sensual and, perhaps, less tasteful paintings of artists like Lawrence Alma-Tadema and Frederic Leighton).

Design for manufacturing was considered by the Royal Academy, on the other hand, as inconsequential – the lowest form of art. Yet this was the very institution meant to be taking the lead in developing the relationship between art and industry (promoting the 'arts of design' was part of its founding brief in 1768). Observing the bad taste intrinsic to many British industrial designs, radicals like Ewart, and indeed Edwards, held the Royal Academy directly responsible. Ewart, for example, refused to serve on the governing body of the Normal School for Design, which was dominated by representatives of the Royal Academy.[81] He did this not because he necessarily disagreed with the way fine art was taught, or with its absence from the curriculum in schools of design, but because he recoiled at the Academy's ring-fencing of high art for a social élite. Ewart saw fine art, as publicized by public libraries and other institutions, as essential to the improvement of culture. He believed that good art revealed the better side of human nature.[82] In effect, an acquaintance with art constituted a moral education. He viewed formal art training for the artisan similarly. His advocacy of mechanistic, ornamental drawing based on the exploitation of geometry was closely connected with a prominent precept in the art world: namely, that this method taught habits such as attention, diligence and perseverance as a result of the care, accuracy and piecemeal assembly required for artistic creation.[83]

Because of its potential for moral and material elevation, Edwards and Ewart urged that art be brought within the reach of the masses. Both joined the Art Union of London, established in 1837. Edwards became extremely active in the Union, being for a time its honorary secretary.[84] The Union was a product of the Select Committee on Arts and Manufactures, which had advocated art unions on the German model.[85] The Union's job was to purchase works and distribute them to subscribers. All purchases would later be shown at public exhibitions.[86] The ethos of the Union was that 'every man has an interest in the highest possible prosperity of the Fine Arts'.[87] It was established to

> extend a knowledge and love of art throughout all classes of society, and affect
> the highest interests of the community as well as the arts and manufactures of
> the kingdom. By placing specimens of good art within the reach of all, making
> the eye familiar with forms of beauty, the latter must necessarily be benefited.
> The great end of art, however, is to develop the mind, to refine and exalt it ...
> The elevation of art is but the means; the elevation of the mind is the end. The
> operation of our association is to advance art by the improvement of public
> taste, and to advance civilization by the improvement of art.[88]

This meeting of material and cultural objectives was set in a social stability context when the Union stated that by opening works of art:

> to the contemplation of the people will be found a powerful means of lessening
> such moral and intellectual difference as there may be between the upper and
> lower orders, not by injuring one but by improving the other. An acquaintance
> with works of art gives dignity and self-esteem to the operative, a matter of no
> slight value as regards the stability of society, besides making him a better
> workman; and furnishes him with delight, independence of position, calculated
> to purify and exalt.[89]

Such ideas on the social value of art – its role as a means of material advance juxtaposed with its capacity for ameliorating the social dangers inherent in materialism – can be applied equally to early proposals for public libraries. That Ewart and Edwards should have been involved with an organization like the Art Union of London is not surprising. They were at once men of culture and believers in scientific material progress.[90] This dual nature was reflected in the Select Committee on Public Libraries when it reported:

> The great practical education of an Englishman is derived from the incessant
> intercourse between man and man in trade, and from the interchange and
> collision of opinion by our system of local 'self-government', both teaching him
> the most important of all lessons, the habit of self-control. But it would be wise
> to superadd to these rugged lessons of practical life some of the more softening
> and expanding influences which reading and which thought supply.[91]

Though utilitarianism was highly visible in the work of the Select Committee and in the early public library debate, cultural concerns were not obscured. The public library question showed that utilitarianism was neither purely atomistic nor mechanistic, but was tinged by altruistic social awareness and a desire for aesthetic spiritual uplift. This was evident in the quest to improve standards of taste – a quest in which the public library was avowedly involved.[92] Ewart hoped the public library would 'promote the extension of solid learning and refined taste'.[93]

The issue of taste was closely linked to the search for social stability. On the one hand, taste has been seen as 'intrinsic' and independent of reasoning. Value in this context is of individual not social relevance; the evaluation of beauty and harmony is purely personal.[94] On the other hand, taste had been ascribed a social utility; something which individuals can only be educated into. It also extends beyond the arts and comprehends 'the whole circle of civility and good manners, and regulates life and conduct, as well as theory and speculation'.[95] It has been seen as a civic virtue encompassing intellectual and social self-development including the skill for making socially beneficial, considered choices in one's actions. Taste in this regard is associated with social harmony and order. It was in this sense that early public library promoters tended to speak of taste.

Art has been highlighted in this chapter because artistic taste was in the 1840s part of a larger conception of taste connected with social stability. A discussion of the material and aesthetic aspects of art education has revealed the social stability aims of institutions, like the public library, which sought to further an appreciation of art. They had a rich soil in which to grow. There existed a significant working-class interest in art; even in classical art.[96] The idea that a meagre existence blunts artistic creativity is denied by the extensive production of art by the nineteenth-century working class.[97] In 1849, at the opening of the Salford Museum and Library, one speaker said that 'pictures were the poor man's books'; moreover, he was quite sure that the objects placed in the museum 'would awaken the attention of the working classes, and lead them to use the library'.[98]

Ewart, Edwards and others who promoted literature on the rates regarded the viewing of fine and applied art in public libraries (and in attached institutions like museums and galleries) as partly a form of technical education.[99] They bestowed upon the latter a dual purpose: material but spiritual. Training in skills – in this instance those of design – naturally produced economic benefits. For this aspect of technical education utilitarian methods were deemed appropriate. In terms of technical education for the artisan, Ewart was an advocate of mannerism: the mechanistic copying of the ornamental physical object and of representations in books. This enshrined the utilitarian idea of knowledge acquisition through the power of circumstances and repetition.

But the need for technical education was derived not simply from a desire to increase personal and national prosperity. Ruskinian and Carlylean social criticism taught that industrialism had brought with it alienation, through the imposition of specialized and monotonous work processes conducive to mass production; the effect of this was a popularized, trivialized and impoverished aesthetic.[100] This trend might be countered, it was claimed, by restoring to workers a knowledge of stages – including that of design, which was fundamental – in the production process, other than those in which they worked. Books were a means of doing this. They were also a means of placing before workers examples of beauty in an age of pessimism and of alienating squalor (many books could themselves, of course, be termed objects of beauty, irrespective of their literary or illustrative integrity). This not only would help to build a sense of social optimism, it would also generate a direct economic gain based on the notion that well-designed, tasteful and beautiful objects were both more competitive and more liable to be manufactured to high aesthetic and functional standards by workers imbued with taste, with a sense of beauty and with worthy skills in design.

There is much to be said for the argument that whereas before 1850 industry dominated art, after 1850 strenuous efforts, sometimes successful, were made to reverse this relationship. The early public library movement coincided with this growing appreciation for applied art – and benefited accordingly.[101] The availability of good art in books in public libraries – indeed, of the architecture of the buildings which housed the collections (see Chapter 10) – again stressed the importance which utilitarians attached to the 'moulding' power of environment. But the public provision of beauty for reflective appreciation also echoed idealistic claims that 'spirit', and human qualities which were innate, could be extirpated and exploited by exposure to good example: in other words, the beautiful side of human nature would respond to beauty.

Technical education, as constituted by the teaching of art awareness, contained for reformers like Ewart and Edwards both economic-material and cultural-spiritual dynamics which were not incompatible. This *cultural materialism* is evident in the general deliberations on the public library in the second quarter of the nineteenth century. However, it is wholly appropriate to ask whether it was utilitarianism or idealist thought that provided the *greater* impetus in these formative years. The utilitarianism of Ewart and Edwards points to a materialist interpretation (though this must be qualified by the contention that ideological positions based on a specific philosophy can rarely be protected hermetically). It is thus owing to the early utilitarian heritage of the public library that attention is now turned to the developing economic role of the institution after 1850.

CHAPTER 6

ECONOMIC CONCERNS: 'USEFUL' KNOWLEDGE AND POLITICAL ECONOMY

It has been proposed that the public library ideal was nurtured in its embryonic stage by utilitarian-inspired efforts to build a more open, meritocratic and progressive society. This ambitious utilitarian objective was to be realized, in part, by an evocation of the commercial spirit. Despite recent assessments of British business élites as languid and conservative (more about this in Chapter 8) it is difficult not to picture pre-First World War industrialism as an era when, as one commentator has observed, the commercial spirit 'overbalanced' to the extent of becoming a national preoccupation.[1] This was surely true of the rhetoric of 'business society', even if words outstripped the reality (as some would have it) of economic anxiety and retardation. Certainly, in the public library, commercialism found a highly suitable mouthpiece. Business society – commerce and industry – frequently supported (with words, influence and cash) initiatives to establish and develop public libraries. Worshippers of the goddess of 'getting on'[2] acclaimed public libraries as procurers of wealth for the community and for its citizenry, and of the self-help, enterprising impulse for the individual. As institutions which dispensed 'useful' knowledge, technical education and commercial information they became relevant, from the 1870s onwards, to developing perceptions of economic malfunction and to creeping anxiety over the socio-political consequences of economic inequality. Contrary to their received image as sources of 'sweetness and light', public libraries can boast an equally convincing materialistic past purpose in terms of their addressing the economic concerns of English society. Between 1850 and 1914, if not beyond, the public library defined culture as the pursuit of knowledge not simply in its dilettante aspect, as is traditionally accepted, but also in its practical aspect. As Butler Wood, Bradford's Chief Librarian, put it in 1904, the public (reference) library was ideally 'like a pert servant girl with an answer for everybody'.[3]

'Useful' knowledge

The quest for utility in terms of material gain was an enduring theme strengthening the public library after 1850. Propagandists constantly stressed the tangible benefits and 'useful' knowledge which library use would bestow.[4] During an adoption campaign in Clerkenwell in 1887 a local clergyman declared that a public library for the area would give residents 'something by which they might benefit themselves, materially and morally'.[5] Of these two benefits library historians have said more about the latter: materialist objectives and achievements have been largely ignored. Why? One answer is that the positive notion of material gain has traditionally been eclipsed by the negative view of the public library as a provider of non-utilitarian, merely recreational materials for the *few* from the taxation of the *many*. One of the most vehement attacks on the public library in the nineteenth century was set in this interventionist context. M. D. O'Brien's essay on free libraries in T. Mackay's *A Plea for Liberty: an Argument Against Socialism and Socialist Legislation* (1892) defined them as 'Socialist continuation schools'.[6] They were institutions, he said, where knowledge was at a discount and sensation at a premium: the question was whether ratepayers should subsidize sensation and amusement which people might easily afford from their own pockets.

It is important to note that the introduction to the book in which O'Brien's essay appeared was written by the economic liberal Herbert Spencer, whose widely read treatise *Education* (1861) had posed the question 'What education is most worth?', to which he answered 'Science'.[7] Spencer accepted that all subjects have some value but argued that there had been in the past too much emphasis on things which 'constitute the efflorescence of civilization', and too little on the education which taught individuals their daily business (which invariably had a technical or scientific basis) for self-preservation.[8]

Spencer's *Education* displayed a 'cocksureness about the Victorian gospel of science'.[9] However, his deep-seated belief that 'the value of a subject depended on its real use in life'[10] – that a subject gained in educational value as it rose in practical value – sat uneasily beside his distaste for state intervention. In his social Darwinist *Man versus the State* (1884) he equated collectivism with socialism and the latter, because society became the owner of the individual, with slavery.[11] His plea was simply that of 'don't interfere'; the workings of evolution, not the state, would bring human progress – that is to say, 'the production of the higher animals'.[12] Yet to be propagated effectively – as the German experience had shown – scientific knowledge required a measure of state action. This line of reasoning was pursued in the late nineteenth century by a new generation of economists such as Alfred Marshall and Stanley Jevons (the latter being a supporter of the free library cause), who challenged classical *laissez-faire* doctrine and acknowledged the role of the state as increasing social utility in areas such as housing, public health and education.[13]

In his much-cited essay *The Rationale of Free Public Libraries* (1881), Jevons reiterated the public library's place in a utilitarian tradition by arguing:

> The main raison d'être of the Public Libraries, as indeed of Public Museums, Art Galleries, Parks, Town Halls, Public Clocks, and many other kinds of Public Works, is the enormous increase of public utility which is thereby acquired for the community at a trifling cost.[14]

He applied to free libraries 'the principle of the multiplication of utility': books shared were more useful than books confined to a single owner. Jevons, whose work continued the cross-fertilization of ideas between economics and utilitarianism which Bentham and John Mill had begun, explained that in areas like communal ownership of literature state intervention facilitated a 'multiplication of utility', thereby delivering the utilitarian aim of 'the greatest happiness of the greatest number'. The 'multiplication of utility' principle has been misconstrued by one interpreter of the public library's past as the process whereby an input of resources multiplies production:[15] that is to say, books, like capital and other resources, produce economic activity in a fashion similar to the Keynesian multiplier effect. What Jevons actually meant by the principle was simply an accumulation of utility in society as a result of the *sharing* of books; something which exploited the inherent quality of books as reproducers of knowledge. (In this sense Jevons was ahead of his time in arguing, as 'information society' protagonists do now, that information is the one resource that cannot be depleted, but reproduces itself when used.) To state this distinction is not pedantic. Public libraries were indeed promoted in the 'efficacy of collectivism' sense stated by Jevons. But they were also tied in with embryonic ideas on economic 'pump priming'. Thus, a proponent of a proposed public library for Widnes described in 1885 how:

> Widnes was a town which essentially depended for its prosperity and development upon the growth of knowledge ... In considering this question they should look at it not immediately from a pounds, shillings and pence point of view; for if they wished to see the town grow and prosper it became essential that the residents should have every possible opportunity of extending their knowledge. Literature, both scientific, historic and poetic, should be readily available'.[16]

In addition public libraries were advocated in the context of the opportunity cost of providing agencies and instruments of formal control such as jails and judges.

The free literature lobby argued that this was money wasted when preventive action through the assimilation of culture offered a cheaper alternative. Hence, the public library supporter Sir John Lubbock explained in 1892 that because of the institution's externalities, as 'a mere matter of pounds, shillings and pence ... it was clear that books and education were an investment, not an expense'.[17] Not only was it often said, therefore, that library expenditure would repay itself in generating wealth (an advantage identified by Greenwood in the late nineteenth century),[18] but it became a cliché of the public library movement that money spent on libraries would be money saved 'in the reduction of poor rates and Government expenditure on crime [for example, jails]'.[19] A lecture in favour of a public library in Lambeth in 1886, in the tradition of utilitarian teleological reckoning, was appropriately entitled 'Crime and culture; which costs the most?'[20]

Pre-First World War public library enthusiasts rarely doubted the economic return their institution made. The librarian Stanley Jast could not understand 'pre-eminently "practical" people' who believed that 'the movements of the great world of intellect have little or no practical importance'. They had failed to learn, said Jast, 'one of the great fundamental facts in the history of man ... that the world in which they wholly live, a world of material events, is in truth only the body of the intellectual world'.[21] Jast was correct in going on to argue that the public library purveyed knowledge which was both directly pertinent (for example, technical education and information) and indirectly beneficial (for example, the broad 'value' of a good education) to economic activity. It was an agency which provided 'useful' knowledge for a maturing industrial capitalism.

Economic decline

It is no coincidence that interest in the public library escalated as anxieties over the nation's economic future grew markedly from the 1870s onwards. The high number of adoptions of the legislation for public libraries in the late Victorian and Edwardian periods was to a considerable extent the result of perceived national economic problems. Economic historians have previously described a post-1870 worsening in Britain's economic performance in relation to both its own record and the performance of competitors. The high rate of growth which marked the 1850s and 1860s, it is said, fell away in the 1870s: the year 1873 is seen as a key moment in this regard.[22] Particularly worrying was the progress made by international rivals, as reflected in Britain's weakening position in world trade. Between 1870 and 1913 Britain's share of world trade declined from 31.8 to 14 per cent, while in the same period those of Germany and the United States increased from 13.2 to 15.7 per cent and from 23.3 to 35.8 per cent, respectively.[23]

Such statistics have been taken at face value by some historians to indicate national economic failure.[24] However, this received image has been questioned. Analysis of decline is too often set in the 'might have been' school of history, the perfect 'alternative road' not being clearly delineated.[25] It has also been argued that the notion of a late-nineteenth-century black-spot has arisen partly from the lack of data for earlier periods.[26] Because the performance of early industrialism – even the mid-Victorian economy – cannot be assessed with sufficient accuracy, the benchmark against which the late Victorian economy is measured is unreliable. In this case notions of failure would thus be exaggerations. Moreover, even if expansion in early periods was much more rapid it is perhaps unreasonable to measure late-nineteenth-century performance against what was possibly an unprecedented phenomenon in Britain's economic history. 'In the last resort', explains Saul:

> maybe we ought to rethink the whole nature of Britain's development over the last two centuries. Possibly we must come round to accepting that the upsurge of the first two-thirds of the nineteenth century was the unique feature in Britain's economic development.[27]

The late Victorian and Edwardian economy was certainly no desert. Mechanization is a case in point. The rapid spread of the steam engine after 1870 should be noted.[28] Contemporaries believed that mechanization was high on the industrial agenda:

> In the working out of the greater problems of industrial effort which now present themselves for solution we may, perhaps, achieve the lead, as we have done before, but we should be all the stronger for giving closer attention than we have done to improvements in detail, and to labour-saving contrivances in particular, mechanical or otherwise.[29]

Furthermore, the range of technological advance widened considerably; for example, the development of steam turbines (which revolutionized shipping), the internal combustion engine, improvements on the railways, high precision engineering (of particular relevance to machine-tools), higher grade steel, synthetic dyes and drugs and electrical power. Each of these advances encouraged a spread of machinery and a decay of the hand trades.[30] Some advances, such as electricity, made for a movement away from reliance on staple industries (though these remained dominant). Electricity wrought industrial change. It was also an innovation which engendered optimism. As one source observed:

> In the application of electricity generally Great Britain has lagged behind, but present indications would seem to promise that in the near future this cause of reproach will be removed.[31]

Where new technologies were applied to older industries this often meant a diversification in products.[32] These instances of mechanization and technological advance belie accusations of failure. If entrepreneurs chose not to innovate this did not mean they had failed. Rather they were acting rationally, seeking and perhaps achieving cost minimization in industries which they believed offered adequate rates of return on investment – in some key sectors of the late Victorian economy profits held up well.[33] Thus, though Britain lagged behind Germany and the United States in many areas this should not obscure the fact that significant positive change was occurring in the British economy in the half-century before the First World War, but with variations of pace in different sectors of industry and regions.

The increasing questioning of the thesis that Britain's economy underwent a sudden decline after about 1870 has been summarized in W. D. Rubinstein's *Capitalism, Culture and Decline in Britain 1750–1990* (1993). Rubinstein argues that theories of decline have wrongly centred on the perception of Britain's economy as predominantly industrial and manufacturing. He contends that over the long term the economy's strength has been in commerce, finance and services. As such, late-nineteenth-century industrial retardation is not a historical surprise; Britain's *industrial* record is relatively unimportant. Equally, the notion of decline, because it was essentially an industrial phenomenon, should also be downplayed.

If decline and slowness are not descriptions that we can attach to the late Victorian economy then 'failure' is certainly not a word which describes accurately Britain's economic problems of the period. It is, however, appropriate to speak of anxieties sensed by contemporaries – anxieties which emerged not from any concrete perception of past growth rates but from the challenge being mounted by international competitors. This view is supported by the utterances of the public library movement on the question of economic malfunction. Enthusiasts who saw an economic role for the public library spoke less in terms of relative decline compared with the high rates of growth achieved in the past, and more of examining means of checking disadvantageous foreign competition. As Greenwood wrote in 1887:

> The national need is that we be not placed at any disadvantage in the neck-and-neck race of competition with the Germans and the Americans, which has become inevitable ... National sentiment alone should lead every town and large rural district where a Free Library does not already exist, to at once see about the adoption of the Act.[34]

The foreign trade menace provided a context for many public library developments. Two can be mentioned here.

A public library was proposed in Oldham in 1881 for the specific reason of countering foreign competition in manufactures. The library committee considered that

> Oldham is probably the largest Town in England without its Free Library ... If we are to keep pace with the intellectual progress of other manufacturing Towns on the Continent of Europe and America, we must neglect no means of cultivation or improvement, nor must we complain of the cost of attaining them.[35]

It is noteworthy that the public library opened in Oldham in tandem with an industrial exhibition promoting the quality of British engineering and design. Moreover, sections of the museum (which was in the same building as the library) were to be given over to a permanent display of industrial wares.

In 1907, in Manchester, local businessmen and industrialists, organized by the Chamber of Commerce, formed a deputation to interview the Free Libraries Committee in an 'endeavour to establish a complete expert branch of the free libraries replete with up-to-date information on the position of all the industrial arts dependent upon scientific knowledge'.[36] Members of the deputation were drawn from the chemical and engineering sections of Manchester Chamber of Commerce, as well as the Society of Chemical Industry, the Manchester Gas Engineers Association and the Manchester Chemical Club; generally it was said to command the support of 'many bodies interested in science, chemistry, geology, electrical and general engineering, and other industries'.[37] The effort was mounted against a backdrop of anxiety over German competition, coverage of which permeated the pages of the Manchester Chamber of Commerce's *Monthly Record*. The previous year (1906) was described in one issue as the moment when the German trade challenge had reached its zenith: 'the high-water mark in the economic development of the German nation'.[38] Among other materials the deputation called for an increase in the number of technical journals (and their location in a separate department) taken by Manchester's central library. Comparison was made with such provision in the United States. It was reported by the Chamber of Commerce that the New York Public Library took 6,000 periodicals (many technical) per annum, compared with Manchester's 370.[39] Technical data, it was said, were essential in order to meet the German challenge. However, even the spectre of German European economic hegemony, as raised by Manchester's commercial and industrial community in 1907, was not enough to force the establishment of a separate technical library, the library committee arguing that technical literature in existing reference services was sufficient.[40] Manchester's business community had to wait until the First World War for an expanded technical collection housed in its own accommodation.

Technical education

Technical education was a prime concern of the pre-1914 public library. Its role in this respect had legislative backing.[41] The Public Libraries Act (1855) allowed for the provision of science and art classes subsidized by the Department of Science and Art, established in 1853 (the Select Committee on Public Libraries, it should be recalled, dealt extensively with the importance of library lectures). This power was reiterated in the Public Libraries Act (1884). The Technical Instruction Act (1889), allowing local authorities to raise a one penny in the pound rate for technical education provision, was adopted by many library authorities; in areas where library committees were already providing technical education classes the relief on the library rate was considerable. In a large number of cases – around a hundred by 1901 – technical schools and public libraries shared the same premises.[42] However, the 1902 Education Act placed responsibility for all technical education in the hands of education committees. The public library thus lost a role which it had been permitted to perform for half a century. Kelly has argued that this resulted in a loss of status.[43]

Nevertheless, the public library's image continued to benefit from the increasing emphasis on raising educational standards as a means of economic regeneration: the institution persisted in being an important source of literature and data relevant to economic activity.

Any explanation of Britain's post-1870 economic problems should be multicausal, incorporating not simply economic phenomena but an analysis of political and social institutions.[44] The social institution of education has thus provided one point of departure for economic historians. Specifically, technical education has been given a label of failure similar to that posted on the post-1870 economy.[45] Historians who have spoken in terms of general economic failure have referred in a derogatory fashion to the 'regulatory' nature of the British state, as compared to the concept of the 'development' state most closely associated with Germany. In other words, Britain did not achieve the level of state control conducive to economic stability.[46] Education – especially technical and scientific – is seen as one of the victims of disadvantageous regulatory control, one result of which was the failure to invest in innovative, high-yield, science-based industries such as electrical engineering, chemicals, dyestuffs, pharmaceuticals, glass optics and scientific instruments.

A mature industrial economy, it is argued, cannot function efficiently without adequate educational and research provision. It is claimed that human capital formation, defined as 'investment by individuals in their own education and training, and by states, firms and other institutions in the provision of education and training facilities', is as important as gross domestic fixed capital formation (for example, buildings and machinery) in determining economic growth.[47] A low level of research and development is offered as an important factor for understanding poor British export and productivity performance in the past.[48] Yet a correlation between education and research on the one hand and economic performance on the other is uncertain.[49] In modern times, for example, a relatively strong research and development input has in some instances failed to guarantee satisfactory economic growth.[50] Historically, technical innovation could have been derived primarily from increased demand rather than educational advance.[51] The nature of demand is also a factor. In 1868 Jacob Behrens (a spokesman for the Associated Chambers of Commerce) informed a committee on scientific instruction:

> It is perfectly true that in some, even in most, instances the superiority of foreign produce may consist merely in a more careful attention to what we are here too much in the habit of considering small matters. Sometimes it is in the finish, or a closer study of each country's peculiar taste or special requirements.[52]

Finally, it is possible that industrial progress has depended as much on low wage costs and periods of peaceful industrial relations as on scientific advance: the report of the Select Committee on Scientific Instruction (1868) argued that these were the major reasons why European rivals were progressing so quickly.[53]

Notwithstanding the lack of evidence linking educational advance with economic growth, technical education came to be seen by many in the late nineteenth century as important to economic regeneration. 'What England seems to need most,' observed a writer on industry in 1904, 'is a quickened activity and a higher technical skill.'[54] In an Oldham library lecture of 1892 it was argued that technical education was a suitable replacement for the perceived decline in apprenticeship (in reality apprenticeship proved durable).[55] The Industrial Revolution, it was said, had poisoned the close relationship between master and apprentice. Following the introduction of mechanized production, explained the lecturer:

> Master and man in most trades belonged to quite a different rank, the master often being a wealthy man, and never entering his workshop. The apprentices or learners had to learn in the workshop, not from the master but from the workman alongside of them. The workman had no interest whatsoever in teaching the apprentice, and he was jealous of him as a competitor in the market in a few years ... Thus it followed that the old system of apprenticeship had been killed in great part by wholesale manufacture. Therefore, as the wholesale system had ruined apprenticeships, they must enrich and make effective apprenticeships by giving education wholesale instead of retail.[56]

Such arguments in favour of technical education, as a means of replacing the declining traditional means of training, were no doubt compelling.

But there was also considerable opposition to technical education. In industry it was widely viewed as expensive, a viewpoint possibly derived from the atomistic nature of British industry, characterized as it was by small enterprises operating in a highly competitive environment with constant pressure on profit margins.[57] Some employers believed that technical education encouraged those engaged in it to share with others the technical secrets of their own enterprise.[58] Workers of independent character, it was said, rejected its supposed association with charity.[59] Many trade unions objected to technical education because it was seen as mostly beneficial to employers; only craft unions welcomed it as a means of replacing lost skills.[60]

The extent of opposition to technical education is a possible reason why historians have perceived it as having failed. Because it has been considered to be a key factor in economic performance it is easy to see how the notion of deficiency in technical education was applied to explanations of economic decline. This is not surprising given that some contemporaries not only objected to technical education *per se,* but took the view that current provision was inadequate: it was based on deficient elementary education; evening classes meant irregular attendance by weary workers; and teaching was poor.[61] But failure can only be established in relation to some conception of what constitutes success. The benchmark against which British technical education was measured was the German system. The librarian Stanley Jast declared in 1903 that the British only 'play' at technical education.[62] The place given to science in German education was widely admired. With regard to higher scientific research this admiration was perhaps valid.[63] However, in respect of non-university science and technical education there is little evidence to suppose that the German model was the one which Britain should have emulated. Misplaced admiration of the entire German technical-scientific establishment was perhaps the product of xenophobic fears of increasing German power (and the accompanying Anglo-German antagonism) in military matters and in international politics.[64]

The type of technical education (as opposed to higher scientific research and learning) provided in Germany was of a 'general' nature. Floud has distinguished between 'general' and 'specific' approaches to technical training.[65] The former is defined as the assimilation of skills which are transportable: a worker's knowledge is not confined to the operating processes of one firm. 'Specific' training, on the other hand, describes the assimilation of skills applicable to a specific job and firm. 'Specific' training was a characteristic of the United States, where apprenticeship (which was not narrow, but bestowed a wide range of skills) was weak and the 'American system' of specialized machinery widespread. 'General' training was a characteristic of Germany, where technical education was compulsory, and, where assimilated, taught skills could be practised in any firm – though there was specialization in terms of the categorization of institutions by trade. Britain, Floud argues, fell somewhere between these two extremes. Contrary to widely held belief, apprenticeship persisted, thereby giving workers a wide range of skills and flexibility. To this manual proficiency was added part-time education in *theory*. Such education was attractive in that it entailed no formal qualifications. These were in any case unnecessary as there were no formal barriers to vertical mobility, 'time-serving' being an important factor in promotion. Yet 'specific' skills were not neglected, and continued to be taught in the workshop.

This 'middle way' was conducive to producing highly motivated, promotion-seeking, intelligent yet practical workers: it was these who, very often, formed the supervisory grades and, being endowed with both 'general' and 'specific' skills, were of substantial benefit to the industries in which they worked. Whereas Britain might have been less successful than Germany in higher scientific fields, at lower levels (particularly the intermediate) late Victorian and Edwardian technical education cannot be classed as a failure. As More has written, 'contrary to what is sometimes said or implied by historians, Britain provided more technical education for more workers than most countries did'.[66] The result of the British system was a steady supply of proficient foreman, overseers and lesser managers. The need for these was noted at the time:

the great aim of a system of Technical Education whatever system be adopted, must be to pick out the best men, and so train them that they be fitted for responsible positions, foremen, overmen, and the like. It is a universal cry, both from masters and men, that there is a want of good foremen. The employer suffers from scamped work and wasted material, while the men feel they are put under control of one who is selected because he is a good 'slave driver', as they say, not because he is the most competent man to plot out the work, and to supervise its execution.[67]

Employers acknowledged the efficacy of good supervision and so keenly sought workers with such skills.[68] But theoretical technical education did not just produce intelligent industrial supervisors. Many workers in industries such as gas and electricity needed to know the theoretical basis of currents and pressure, even if they did not achieve substantial promotion.[69] Further, theoretical technical education served the rapidly growing white-collar occupations (clerks as a percentage of the occupied population increased from 2.9 per cent to 4.6 per cent between 1881 and 1911).[70] The clerks who flocked to enrol in evening classes assimilated theoretical knowledge which was eminently practical in developing the mental faculties appropriate to their work – though commercial subjects like shorthand and bookkeeping, it should be added, had little theoretical content.[71]

In the light of these arguments the theoretical content of British technical education is not a cause for regret. Those who framed the Technical Instruction Act (1889) knew exactly what they were aiming at, and its value. Before 1900 the term 'technical instruction' meant the teaching of principles. 'Technical education', on the other hand, implied the transmission of practical skills specific to a particular job; that is to say, purely vocational learning. In the twentieth century the meanings have been transposed.[72] Late-nineteenth-century public opinion was confused over the matter. If a definition of technical education was requested from the average citizen, proposed the *English Mechanic* in 1887:

> The answer which will be given with some hesitation will probably have some not very distinct reference to instruction in the use of tools ... or will, perhaps, be some mention of chemistry, or other branch of science, or, as a final resort, 'something to meet the German competition'.[73]

Such confusion did not characterize technical education legislators in 1889: 'instruction' stood for theory, and the latter, when applied to the production process, for value. As early as 1868, evidence had been given to the Select Committee on Scientific Instruction on the value of principles in learning:

> I should be the last to say that philosophy without practice, was the needful thing, but neither is practice without principles; indeed I believe that the need now felt is for instruction in the 'principles' of science. Practice is learnt empirically, but the principles, the laws of nature and their relations to each other, are not taught in the workshop or laboratory, and are not understood. The need is disguised when people talk of 'technical education'; it is not education in 'technicalities' which is wanted, this is learnt during apprenticeship, but education in the principles which are practically applied, but not understood, and, therefore, not made the most of.[74]

This advice was adopted in the 1889 Act which allowed rates to be spent on: 'instruction in the principles of science and art applicable to industries'.[75]

The theoretical nature of technical education as defined by legislators and as taught in practice meant that it was to a significant extent a form of secondary education. As much as for their intrinsic value science subjects were promoted as 'the best discipline in observation and collection of facts, in combination of inductive with deductive reasoning, and in the accuracy of both thought and language'.[76] Technical education also helped to foster reading skills irrespective of content. As the librarian W. E. A. Axon wrote:

> The object of reading is not simply to get information, to stuff your mind with crude facts; it is to train your mental faculties so as to have them always obedient to the word of order, and ready at any time to perform any duty you may impose upon them. This can only be done by mental discipline, whether by the study of classic literature, or of English literature, or of history, or of ethics, or of political economy, or of natural science or of mathematics.[77]

By building on elementary education skills, therefore, technical education enlarged the constituency of intelligent workers: 'an intelligent artisan is always preferable to an ignorant one', a textile manufacturer informed the Technical Instruction Committee in 1884.[78] In 1901 Quentin Hogg (founder of the polytechnic movement) urged workers to put intelligence as well as power into their work: 'There was a time when the workman were called *hands* but the time was coming when they would be called *heads*.'[79] Further, intelligence can produce adaptability and receptiveness to new ideas. Theoretical technical education made for flexibility in a workforce subjected to recurring division of labour; Adam Smith's *Wealth of Nations* (1776), it should be recalled, had advocated education as an antidote to the narrow-mindedness of manufacturing employment.[80] Hence, at the Manchester Technical Schools annual prize-giving in 1890, Sir Philip Magnus urged that:

> the artisan student must look to technical education to correct the personally injurious effects of the increasing development of division of labour in every trade ... Emerson has well said that by division of labour 'the art is improved, the individual is deteriorated. The incessant repetition of the same handiwork dwarfs the man, robs him of his strength, wit and versatility. Efforts should be made to develop individualism'. It is in the technical school that individualism is encouraged as a set-off to the socialism of the factory. In the technical school, the intelligence is cultivated as supplementary to the mechanical training of the workshop.[81]

The development of the public library before 1914, in terms of its economic role, is made more understandable by the preceding discussion on technical education. Public libraries, like technical education, were seen as receiving inadequate attention from the state in the fight for economic survival. An article in *Greater Britain* in 1891 called for state aid for public libraries, and noted:

> The English, we must admit, are a commercial nation, and England's position as a nation is due to her trade. Now we are being outrun by other nations, and if England is to hold her place among the leading powers of the world, she must

adapt a complete system of education of which public libraries are the 'sheet anchor'.[82]

Education was at the time considered essential for economic regeneration. A pro-public library circular in Lewisham in 1896 announced:

> In our ceaseless competition with foreign nations it is our duty, if we do not wish to fall behind in the race, to provide the very best opportunities for people of all classes in the matter of self-education, and for the acquisition of useful information.[83]

Scientific and technical education was especially attractive in this regard. In opening the Eastbourne Public Library and Technical Institute in 1904 the Duke of Devonshire asserted that 'it is through the study of science that we alone can hope to maintain our national progress and prosperity'.[84] A Bermondsey worker in 1900 went as far as to produce a 'beautiful and perfectly finished model of Bermondsey public library'; it was explained that England was behind Germany in technical education, but such latent talent as the worker's modelling displayed could be developed by the greater opportunities which the public library offered.[85]

The public library provided the materials which complemented the theoretical nature of technical education (though some materials, notably for art and design, had practical uses).[86] True, a municipal library could sometimes be a dumping ground for literature not required elsewhere:[87] the librarian F. T. Barrett called for 'the most liberal and comprehensive admission and preservation of the waifs and strays, the flotsam and jetsam of literature'.[88] None the less, there is considerable evidence to support the argument that the public library was a crucial compendium of technical education provision. Beyond the fact that some public libraries provided their own theoretical class instruction,[89] one of their major roles was to supply the books and periodicals that technical education students required.

In 1904 the Library Association sent out a questionnaire to public libraries asking, among other things, how they encouraged serious reading.[90] Answers to this question highlighted the close relationship between public libraries and technical education institutions. Chelsea replied that 'we are the library for the South West London Polytechnic Institute ... its teachers and its students are given special facilities.' Camberwell related: 'we assist students at our school of arts and crafts in every way. Technical and art works of a special character are provided, and full lists exhibited in the classrooms.' Wimbledon answered: 'There is close connection between the Technical Institute and the Library.' It was said that the 'junction of the library with the Technical School is ... a most fortunate arrangement: it strengthens both institutions.'[91] The latter arrangement was very necessary: few technical education institutions could afford their own libraries,[92] unlike in Germany where libraries were attached to the majority of institutions which delivered technical education.[93]

Technical literature in public libraries was not just for the enrolled student. Workers not taking courses were invited to use the library to keep abreast of developments in their trades.[94] In 1904 Bingley's librarian reported that books dealing with the town's trades were occasionally exhibited, and when this happened 'typewritten invitations were posted in all the workshops asking those interested to come and examine their trade books'. It was said that 'The manner in which these are appreciated has far more than exceeded our highest anticipations, especially for apprentices.'[95] Propaganda supporting the campaign for a public library in York in 1881 promised that 'Artisans in every trade will enjoy the opportunity of reading the best books, and seeing the best papers bearing upon their particular handicrafts.'[96] Thomas Greenwood believed that apprentices, in particular, benefited from public libraries: 'The arts and mysteries of manufacture are no longer taught by word of mouth alone ... the master workmen of the nineteenth century speak through books to all.'[97]

Public library technical literature was also at the disposal of the professional. In his seminal paper on technical libraries, given to the 1903 Library Association Conference, Stanley Jast defined the technical library's constituency as large, ranging as it did from unskilled to professional workers: 'the fully-fledged architect, or engineer, or anything else, must keep himself abreast of the literature of his profession or trade – the technical library will provide him with the means of doing so'.[98] Aside from the professional societies it was believed that the public library was the best means of securing contact with recent literature on any trade.[99]

Technical literature was expensive. Proceeds from the public library rate allowed for only moderate expenditure in this direction. Between 1890 and 1902 some libraries received funds for the purchases of technical literature from the revenue (known as 'whisky-money') raised by the Local Taxation Act (1890), which placed a duty on spirits. Liverpool's first grant of 'whisky-money' was £1,500. Such sums were welcomed, but only 26 libraries, it should be noted, benefited from 'whisky-money' in the 12 years it was available.[100] Yet the supply of technical literature in public libraries should not be underestimated. A report prepared for the London County Council's Technical Education Board in 1896 revealed a widespread demand for technical materials (in London's public libraries at any rate) and, to an extent, this demand was met. The librarian J. D. Stewart stated in 1910:

> Modern works on technical subjects of all sorts are receiving ever-increasing attention from the public libraries – in short, it is becoming recognised that there is a practical as well as a dilettante side to literature.[101]

He went on to list many libraries with a specialist technical collection. Some of the public libraries he noted are recorded here, along with their specialism: Bermondsey, Spa Road (architecture), Poplar (engineering and shipbuilding), Finsbury (metalwork and watchmaking), Wigan (mining), Bradford, Nottingham, Rochdale and Stalybridge (textile manufacturing).[102]

Even if public libraries did not specialize in a technical area they often produced separate catalogues of the technical works they possessed.[103]

Given that the supply of technical literature in public libraries was not insignificant, what effect did this theoretical learning have beyond direct application to a trade? First, technical literature was an encouragement to reading. This was particularly true of the lighter, popular technical and scientific journals. Sturges has argued that the public library's role in improving literacy was its major achievement: reading *per se*, whether technical literature or fiction, contributed to economic development even in such small matters as filling in forms or reading notices and advertisements.[104] Second, more intelligent and adaptable workers were produced. In opening the Eastbourne Public Library and Technical Institute, Sir Gilbert Parker MP explained that information and knowledge were not an end in themselves, 'they were only the materials for reason to work with'.[105] Similarly, the librarian and technical educationist J. J. Ogle believed that the engineering classes and the literature his library supplied in Bootle did not so much help to teach workers a specific trade as imbue broader skills like 'care, accuracy, thought, possibly invention'.[106] Third, to quote Ogle again, the teaching of broad principles which constituted technical education counteracted 'the cramping effect on a workman's intelligence of the present day minute sub-division of labour'.[107] Technical literature would help to negate the monotony and narrow vision which slavery to a particular process brought with it. In this respect, the architect M. B. Adams – who knew well from his own professional experience the damage to creativity which division of labour wrought – was correct in identifying the public library's aim:

> to emancipate our workers from the growing tendency encouraged by divided labour, which reduces them to the level of unthinking machines. We must teach the artisan to think for himself by showing him how to develop his mind.[108]

Fourth, the very intelligence, flexibility and receptiveness to ideas, mentioned above, were characteristics of the supervisory grades who attended public libraries in not insignificant numbers. In 1881 a promoter of the public library's technical instruction role stated:

> Managers and foremen, and leading men engaged in structural work, are constantly reading up in order to be proficient at the particular and various work committed to their charge.[109]

Fifth, white-collar occupations, most noticeably clerks and teachers, used the public library in large numbers as a method of obtaining a 'rounded' education.

Thus, the fact that technical education, as stated above, was at times barely distinguishable from secondary education had implications for the public library, which, after all, consistently promoted itself as a post-elementary 'continuation' school. Technical education via the public library was essentially secondary education. This was recognized by employers, some of whom were public library benefactors. Employers generally saw little direct relevance to their industrial concerns of stocks of technical literature.[110] The provision of employees' libraries in firms has a long history.[111] But these were stocked with a high proportion of fiction.[112] The primary aim was not to further directly a worker's technical skills (unlike in Germany where works libraries had a high non-fiction content[113]); workers in any case mostly read for amusement.[114] Employers saw reading *per se* as profitable – in the broad sense of producing better workers. This was the idea behind the provision of a library for East London Post Office employees (the East London Postal and Telegraphic Employees Town and Suburban Circulating Library and Literary Institute, which was situated at the district office in the Commercial Road and which circulated books to branch offices). Its aim was 'to promote mental, moral, and social improvement among the different classes, especially the junior, by good literature'.[115] It is likely that when employers supported the idea of a local public library – as was the case in towns as far apart as Northwich and Reading[116] – they did so for exactly the same reason. If public libraries stocked technical literature, all the better; its value was not in its content, however, but in its improving effect. The fact that public library technical literature counted for little in terms of 'specific' technical training should not detract from any economic role which the public library set itself.

Commercial information and political economy

If it is accepted that a 'secret of business is to know something that nobody else knows',[117] then it is surprising that so little interest was taken by British employers before 1914 in the collation of commercial information for research purposes. In modern times speedy, accurate and appropriate information has been considered an important ingredient of business success: 'A central source of reliable co-ordinated information makes economic sense for commercial and industrial organizations.'[118] This was not apparent to the vast majority of enterprises operating in Britain before the First World War – a war which was to change radically attitudes towards research. In the United States the importance of business libraries and information bureaux, both private and public, was widely recognized: research collections were assembled by some of the largest business houses, including General Electric, Price Waterhouse and the American Telegraph and Telephone Company. A library was recognized as a business asset which 'rightly administered can serve men who are doing things as well as those who are thinking things'.[119] From the 1890s business in the United States was also served by public provision of commercial information.[120] By 1916 the American public commercial library was recognized as a 'common feature of industrial life'.[121] The public library as a whole in the United States was clearly seen as an institution evincing an economic role, able to deliver 'visible, tangible, material results'.[122]

The reason why British businesses eschewed commercial information is not clear. Lamb has suggested that international economic hegemony meant that there was no real incentive to organize research in either commercial methods or industrial processes; after all, the Industrial Revolution had occurred largely without the aid of sustematically organized information and its stuctured dissemination.[123] It would be wrong, however, to assume that there was no provision of information for commercial purposes before 1914.

The public library from its inception (as noted in Chapter 5) incorporated a commercial information role, if not always in reality then as a broad objective of the movement. The Guildhall Library, when it was rebuilt in 1873, included 'a collection of books, directories, codes, manuals and trade papers useful to those wanting business information'.[124] In the planning of this collection it had been advocated that in any public library a 'room be used as a Library of Reference, free to all respectable persons desirous of making temporary use of dictionaries, maps, plans, works upon commerce, banking, etc.' Such a room, it was noted, 'exists in most large towns, and is much frequented by merchants, traders and others'.[125] Dependent upon the definition of 'large town', this was possibly an exaggeration. But large public libraries did stock commercial literature. One of the reasons for establishing a public library in Liverpool was said to be that 'there is not a place [in the town] where even a Gore's dictionary, or tide-table, or an almanac can be consulted as a matter of right by anyone desirous of doing so'. Adding to this statement, the leader of the campaign for a free library in Liverpool, J. A. Picton, asserted: 'Viewing the need for a public library from an economic standpoint, the benefit of an institution to those engaged in commercial and industrial pursuits would be manifest.'[126]

Even the public libraries of small towns provided some basic reference works useful to commerce; something as ephemeral as a railway timetable can be deemed to have had a commercial worth. By the early twentieth century a small public library like Croydon could possess a substantial commercial collection. In 1910 the Croydon Chamber of Commerce met at the public reference library to be informed of the materials available. Information could be found, it was said, on commercial geography, trade routes, the products and exports of various countries and the present commercial position of the country. There were maps, directories, railway rates, data on the manufacture of specific goods, news clippings on trade questions and books. The library boasted that it could answer almost any commercial question: 'Not long back they were asked as to the duty rates payable on certain articles in Belgium.'[127] The aim was to set up a commercial information desk in the library, similar to arrangements made in American libraries.[128]

Commercial knowledge was also available in a physical form in the numerous museums attached to free libraries. There were a number of motives behind museum provision. William Ewart had seen them as a means of technical (design) education, as did Thomas Greenwood later.[129] Moralizers saw them as useful instruments of counter-attraction. Religious propagandists supported them as places where 'the works of the Creator [were] shown forth in the preserved monuments of his bounty, wisdom and skill'.[130] They were also a source of commercial education: visible evidence of foreign tastes and products was supplied. As Greenwood explained:

> Manufactured goods which suit for South America do not suit for Australia, and there has for some time been too much of the happy-go-lucky about the style and shape of certain goods for some foreign markets, the prevailing idea being that what is suitable for one market will be suitable for all. A greater mistake could not possibly be made, and in order that employers and employees may themselves see the patterns required in other markets, no place presents so suitable and convenient a depositary as the museum of a Free Library. The town which takes up this subject vigorously will be the town which against all comers will hold its own ground. Manchester should have its museum of cotton goods, Leeds and Bradford their museums of woollen, Sheffield of tools and cutlery, Nottingham of laces and muslins, Bristol of boots and shoes and other goods, and Liverpool and Glasgow of almost every commodity in which for foreign markets the patterns differ.[131]

Finally, there were extensive patent collections held by public libraries.[132] Ostensibly, these were classified as technical information. However, they also had a commercial value (the boundary between definitions of technical and commercial materials has never been precise) in revealing the commercial intentions of competitors. The importance of housing patents in public libraries was explained by J. S. Rowntree in campaigning for a public library in York in 1881:

> An interesting feature in the histories of the libraries at Leeds and at Bradford is the large amount of attention which the 'specifications of patents' receive. These specifications are presented by the Government to the various towns and cities. The City of York duly receives them ... but having no proper place in which these specifications can be kept and made easily accessible, it is sometimes found more easy ... to go over to Leeds and search for them there, than it is to refer to those which are kept in the office of our City Surveyor ... the number of persons who referred to the specifications in the City of York last year may have been 25, while in Leeds it was said to have been 2684 and Bradford 1500.[133]

The type of reader who used patents, or other forms of commercial data for that matter, is unclear. It is likely, however, that the constituency which consulted commercial data (as opposed to literature on commercial subjects like bookkeeping) was not as wide as that which sought technical information. A leading annual commercial directory announced in 1890 that 'public libraries have special attractions to commercial men'.[134] Commercial knowledge was considered to be of importance primarily to those in control of production. The journal *Commercial Education* stated in 1912:

> But that our knowledge of the causes which induce a boom in trade will ever be so complete as to permit us always to enjoy unexampled prosperity is not to be expected. Everything is subject to flux, and the utmost that can be hoped for, is that fuller knowledge will enable us so to regulate production as to avoid the slump that has invariably followed a period of trade activity ... The great danger

that the manufacturers of the world have now to guard against is the danger of over-production.[135]

Guarding against over-production was, arguably, a coded message for 'necessary' unemployment (which could always be explained by too high wages). The need to convey such a message to groups which did not to any great extent use commercial information was a leading theme in the work of a Board of Trade committee appointed in 1898 to investigate the dissemination of commercial information.[136] Central government had long recognized the importance of commercial data to its operations. A commercial department within the Board of Trade emerged in the second quarter of the nineteenth century. A statistics department of the Board began operations in 1828, had a library by 1834 and librarian by 1843; in 1872 it merged with the Board's commercial department. Its major tasks were to record changes in foreign and colonial tariffs and collect trade statistics.[137] Some of this information was published, much of it in the *Board of Trade Journal*. Commercial departments were also set up by the Foreign and Colonial Offices. Reports on trade matters from foreign consuls were edited and published by the Foreign Office and distributed to Chambers of Commerce (Consular Reports). The Colonial Office published official reports from the colonies (Colonial Reports). The process by which commercial data were collected and disseminated was thus complicated and confusing: there was little coordination between the three commercial departments except for the information and news of commercial treaties and agreements which the Foreign Office released for publication in the *Board of Trade Journal*.[138] The aim of the Committee on the Dissemination of Commercial Information (1898) was to find a means of greater cooperation between the commercial departments so as to obtain a wider distribution of data in the economy. The constituency it identified went beyond the business community to include the working classes. But the new coordinating body which the report recommended – a Commercial Intelligence Department under the control of the Board of Trade, with a room in Whitehall open for enquiries[139] – was not relevant to ordinary people. The public library was seen as a more accessible conduit: some large public libraries already took a selection of government publications (including patents and, in some cases, Consular Reports).[140] Part of the committee's remit, therefore, was to see 'how far it was possible for assistance to be rendered by the authorities of public libraries in disseminating commercial information'.[141] A circular enquiring into the extent of demand and existing resources for commercial information was thus sent to 14 public libraries (nine in England). It was found that 'the authorities of such public libraries as we have addressed have generally displayed much interest in the question referred to us, and expressed a willingness to afford every distinction in their power'.[142]

However, a reading of the replies to the committee's circular (printed in Appendix No. 7 of the Report) reveals an exaggerated assessment of demand for commercial information. While, for example, Nottingham replied that there had been 'increased demand during recent months for information respecting trade with the Colonies', Bradford stated that there was 'not the demand for commercial information ... which might have been expected, having regard to its [Bradford's] position as a trading centre'.[143] It is therefore likely that government viewed commercial information as a means of propaganda: supply would induce a demand conductive to its objectives. The basic motive behind the proposed dissemination of commercial information to the working classes was that it would

> make them more fully acquainted with the conditions of foreign trade competition and cost of production. It is suggested that the general diffusion of such information might tend to prevent disputes and stoppages of work, which sometimes result in the diversion of industry to competing countries.[144]

The committee had heard from several witnesses how industrial conflict might be avoided if workers were better informed in commercial matters. A representative of the South Scotland Chamber of Commerce and member of his local public committee, T. Craig-Brown, explained that: 'Workmen aim exclusively at increase of wages or decrease of hours, without considering whether in the long run their action may not lead to diminution of employment.' As unions were now claiming a greater voice in management, he continued, 'it seems desirable that workmen seeking to exercise this new influence should be educated to do so wisely'.[145] T. R. Morgan, of the Cardiff Chamber of Commerce, spoke of the problems in the coal industry caused by lack of commercial knowledge:

> the workmen do not realise the amount of competition there is, and therefore they are led away with the idea that there is no coal to compete with South Wales coal ... and they become very much harder in their terms of fighting for wages.[146]

Similarly, J. S. Jeans of the British Iron Trade Association, referring to a current engineering dispute, explained that 'if the workmen had been well posted in the conditions of Continental and American competition this wretched engineering struggle would have never taken place'.[147] These exhortations to a fuller understanding of political economy reflected the economic pressures affecting society: workers, it was believed, required constant re-education in economic principles.[148]

There is no evidence that public libraries became fully fledged agencies of the Board of Trade's Commercial Intelligence Department,[149] though all free libraries were made aware of the department's existence shortly after its foundation in 1900, and no doubt referred to it from time to time.[150] The amount of commercial indoctrination for which the state had hoped was clearly not achieved through the public library. However, what the work of the Committee on the Dissemination of Commercial Information reveals is a belief in the potential of commercial knowledge to reduce industrial and social tensions. Workers needed to understand the dangers of pricing themselves out of a job; for if wage demands were not restrained, ran the argument, production costs would rise, foreign producers would benefit and unemployment would increase. High-brow commercial data might not have found their way into working-class reading, but more digestible materials, such as popular scientific periodicals and books on economics and geography, were read. It is plausible that local public library providers, many of them industrialists, recognized, as did the Committee on the Dissemination of Commercial Information, the value of commercial literature as a means of education in political economy. This was not a new aspect of public library provision. As outlined in Chapter 3, the institution's potential for fostering the powers of reason which would assist a fuller understanding of the workings of capitalism had been recognized from the outset. As William Brown had explained in opening in 1861 the Liverpool library buildings he had donated:

> Many of you recollect the ignorance and want of thought which prevailed among a large body of the working classes thirty or forty years ago. When they had any dispute with their master about wages, or anything else, they thought they were revenging themselves and punishing him by breaking and destroying his machinery, forgetting that his capital and his works were the instruments with which they had to earn bread for themselves and their families. Far different is their conduct now. Education has made such progress that they are much more intelligent. They see that such suicidal conduct would be as bad as the carpenter destroying the tools by which he lives. It is now pretty well understood that the more we improve our machinery, the more we increase our customers throughout the world, and the more hands are wanted to make articles to meet the demand.[151]

There was a close similarity, therefore, between the social motive behind commercial education and that behind the technical education which the public library also enthusiastically promoted. Technical education has been seen as productive of a 'spirit of reasonableness' and reduced radicalism;[152] commercial knowledge was also viewed as a force for social and industrial discipline.[153] Moreover, both were education *per se*, at once favourable to economic progress and the social stability associated with it. As a member of Oldham's public library committee stated in 1881, in urging the establishment of a free library against the backdrop of intensifying foreign competition, 'Our largest rate of all is our education rate. We never grumble at its amount, because it is in education that we find our national safety and progress.'[154]

Other economic benefits

Public library promoters were keen to publicize a range of economic benefits beyond the more directly advantageous dissemination of technical and commercial knowledge. Moreover, these tangible benefits were characterized by clear social stability imperatives, by virtue of their furtherance of values of enterprise and of a belief in the market.

A public library was a social institution which helped a locality retain its educated, experienced and skilled labour. In fighting for a public library in York, J. S. Rowntree stated that:

> A large Free Library is an element that distinctly enters into the calculations of persons in fixing their place of residence. I have heard superior artisans say that the libraries of Leeds, Bradford and Sheffield were attractions which they missed in York.[155]

This assertion can be supported by evidence from fiction. W. Riley's *Way of the Winepress* (1917) is set in the 1880s and tells the story of a young man, his mother and a young woman who, having fallen on hard times, are befriended by a well-to-do cotton manufacturer in the busy fictional town of Broadbeck. The manufacturer sends them to an isolated manufacturing village to learn the business of spinning, but being educated people they regret that they have lost the use of the Broadbeck free library 'with its store of hidden treasure, and ... the night-classes to which we had looked forward as a hopeful possibility'.

Similarly, just as a library could assist local employers to hold on to high-grade, mobile labour it could also attract respectable, wealthy residents and 'visitor' users who brought business to a town. This was especially true in respect of resort towns: it was said that the Leamington Spa Public Library had 'established itself as an important attraction from the visitor's point of view'.[156]

Public libraries were an early form of labour exchange. Fluidity in the labour market was encouraged by the use of the public library newsroom for seeking out vacancies:

> It is a well-known fact that thousands of men during the year find employment through reading the advertisements in the various places in the newsroom, and at nine o'clock in the morning to the minute, scores of men seeking work may be seen to go straight to the advertisement columns, leaving the news for a more favourable opportunity.[157]

Some libraries posted up newspapers on 'situations vacant' boards in entrance halls or outside the library. This was occasionally done before the library opened. An assistant at a free library in Marylebone (not a rate-aided institution) in the 1890s recalled:

> Arriving (theoretically) at 7.30 to cut the Situations Vacant ads from the Telegraph and the Chronicle, fasten them to the boards and fix them to the little windows on either side of the door. There was always a small crowd of 'out o'works' waiting.[158]

Public libraries also attempted to find employment for people in the colonies. The Leeds Public Library announced that:

> Intending emigrants to any part of the world, particularly to the English Colonies, find the public library of great use. Applications are frequently made to the Librarian, at the central Library, who can give most impartial information as to prospects, resources, climate, wages, etc., of each country.[159]

The librarian J. Potter Briscoe included in his list of basic requirements for any large public library an emigrants' information service.[160] Close links were developed with the government's Emigrants Information Office.[161] Emigration was not just of economic benefit to those seeking prosperity overseas; it was also proposed by the authorities as a method of relieving social pressures built up by the unemployment problem.[162] In *An Ideal Husband* (1895) Oscar Wilde's Lady Markby remarks: 'The fact is that Society is terribly over-populated. Really someone should arrange a proper scheme of assisted migration. It would do a great deal of good.' The public library assisted in the alleviation of such anxiety by providing information to would-be emigrants.

Finally, contiguous to its role as a moralizing agency the free library claimed to provide a means of reducing secondary poverty caused by unwise expenditure on unnecessary items. 'It is a well understood thing', wrote Greenwood, 'that in promoting the prosperity of material things, public libraries did more than anything else to advance the cause of temperance and thrift'.[163] Although the public library cost the ratepayer money, it was said that savings could be made from the reduced ignorance and idleness that it brought.[164] Janetta Manners advocated libraries in the belief that the abstinence from strong drink which they encouraged 'frequently doubles men's wages, for there are many who spend more than half they earn in liquor'.[165] Support for a public library in Camberwell came from one correspondent to a local newspaper who argued that, viewed as an economic question alone, it was costly to maintain a 'savage Horde among the civilised'.[166] At the opening of new buildings for Liverpool's library in 1861 the memory of George Stephenson was invoked to fortify the rhetoric of self-help as a remedy for poverty; to be successful in life, it was said, 'you must be temperate, you must be frugal, you must persevere', as the great engineer had.[167]

The public library's cultural (and moral) message was thus an intrinsically economic one too. As the political economist Samuel Fothergill stated:

> Intelligence, order and virtue contribute most powerfully to the increase and preservation of wealth, or to that physical and social well-being which affords the conditions of the highest culture. On the other hand, idleness, dissipation, vice, and crime, while they are fearfully destructive of existing wealth, are equally hostile to its production and accumulation.[168]

This moral-materialist argument was certainly highly appropriate to the ethos of the public library.

John Passmore Edwards

The way social (including moral) and economic concerns could intersect at the point of the public library is further illustrated in the life and work of John Passmore Edwards, who, around the turn of the century, donated numerous public libraries (as well as technical schools, medical institutions and settlement houses), mostly in London and in his native West Country.[169] Edwards is second only to Andrew Carnegie as Britain's most famous public library benefactor. He had accumulated his wealth in publishing, his primary motive being money: 'I determined to establish a periodical, thinking that thereby I should be able to build up a fortune, if not to win fame.'[170] (He had seen how his father had made his money through independent and hard enterprise – a carpenter by trade who diversified into brewing and market gardening[171]). During his time in publishing Edwards ran a large number of publications of great variety.[172]

He was throughout his life a free trader: his advocacy of Corn Law abolition had earned him the antipathy of the Mayor of Penzance, who at one stage threatened him with imprisonment.[173] He was also active in the peace movement: he had opposed the Crimean War and described the South African campaign in 1900 as 'criminal, cowardly and costly'.[174] His hatred of war was partly based on Christian principles.[175] But like others he also saw it as the antipathy of the international harmony which free mutual trade would ensure. Prosperity brought about by economic liberalism was thus at the core of his desire for better human cooperation; science and trade were the instruments of mutual coexistence.

Edwards was influenced by utilitarianism. Part of the reason for his benefaction, he once said, was 'to promote the greatest and most lasting good of the greatest number. In doing this I have selected institutions most likely in my judgement to minister to the physical well-being and the general advancement of the people'.[176] He was particularly interested in the contribution which science could make to progress, including the reduction of social exclusivity. This was manifest in his ownership (from 1869) of the journal the *English Mechanic*.[177] The journal's aim was to disseminate science and art instruction cheaply. The journal, in its own words, was taken by 'the skilled mechanic, the manufacturer, the amateur, the searcher after knowledge, and by men who have acquired knowledge'. Its readers were members of 'an industrial and intellectual guild', in effect 'the largest mutual aid society that ever existed'.[178] The journal would have been the ideal helpmate to young adults taking evening classes, combining as it did practical and theoretical knowledge.[179] Its commitment to science was unequivocal:

> Science is poking its nose into everything; it looks upon nothing as too sacred for investigation. Never mind how old a book is, or how long an institution or faith has existed in the world, never mind the number of millions who have believed in it or have been swayed by it, the scientific enquirer treats it as an everyday thing, analyses it, and if necessary turns it upside down or inside out. He tests its usefulness or its reality by the silent, but, in the long run, certain process of verification.[180]

Edwards saw science as the engine of progress. This belief became more important to him as anxieties loomed in the late nineteenth century over the nation's economic future. The public libraries he donated must be viewed in this context. At the opening of the Canning Town Public Library in 1893 he was reported to have urged the extension of technical education:

> for the sake of the community, for our industrial development, and for the sake of the Empire itself. He was anxious to some extent about the future commercial position and ascendency of this country. America was driving us hard in one direction, Germany in another, and Switzerland in another ... therefore it was essential that all the facilities possible should be placed within the reach of the working man and the artisan ... What would benefit the working man would benefit the community, and consequently the Empire.[181]

Edwards's outlook can thus be located firmly within the National Efficiency movement. The aim of his benefaction was:

> to build up the weak, and to afford ampler opportunities for the strong to do the best for themselves and the community ... this in my opinion must be done more energetically than hitherto, or England may be distanced in the supreme race to which nations will be summoned during the coming century.[182]

Yet Edwards combined these practical, utilitarian impulses with emotional, humanitarian concerns. His biographer wrote of Edwards's 'sympathy with the suffering portion of humanity'.[183] It was said that his aim was to 'serve his fellow man, raise the educational standards of the people, and lift the poor and helpless out of the mire of misery and moral degradation caused by ignorance'.[184] To this end he entered Parliament as a Gladstone supporter in 1880 (though he vacated his seat two years later having found political life not 'such a fruitful field of usefulness' as he had expected).[185] He made a greater social impact through his publishing and benefactions, which were sometimes combined. His ownership of the *Echo*, for example, sprang from philanthropic motives. He devoted the whole of its profits to benefaction, whether of drinking fountains, hospitals, convalescent homes or public libraries. He described the paper as 'devoted to the public good ... not for individual gain or sectional advantage, but for the benefit of the people'.[186]

One of Edwards's best known good works was the money he gave (£6,000) for the Whitechapel Public Library in London's East End – the library for which the idealist Samuel Barnett of Toynbee Hall had vigorously campaigned. At the opening ceremony in 1892 Edwards revealed the motives behind his benefaction:

> I do this not merely from a sense of duty, but because I think it is a distinguished privilege to assist in lightening or brightening the lives of our East End fellow citizens ... I have long felt that the East of London has stupendous uncancelled claims on the wealthy and well-to-do West End of London, and it affords me unalloyed gratification to wipe out a small portion of that indebtedness.[187]

These philanthropic sentiments[188] were no doubt inspired, as those of others were inspired, by a desire for greater social stability to calm the West End's fears of the East End.[189] As noted above, Edwards certainly possessed a desire for greater social harmony among people and peoples.

He despised competition that was destructive. In 1896, at the opening of the Nunhead Public Library, he was reported as saying:

> Man has been called a fighting animal; if so, there was no necessity for him to show his fighting qualities on destructive battlefields. There was no better form of rivalry than that between parishes in their endeavours to distance each other in works of public usefulness [such as public libraries].[190]

His philosophical motivation in this context was partly religious.[191] But his relationship with Samuel Barnett in providing a free library for White- chapel perhaps has implications beyond Barnett's committed Christianity: for Barnett was also an idealist thinker who put philosophical investigations into practice (see Chapter 7). Edwards's speech at the opening of the Whitechapel library, quoted above, couched as it was in the language of fellow citizenship and social obligation, bears a close resemblance to the themes which idealists were articulating at the time. Elsewhere, moreover, Edwards lectured enthusiastically about 'duty', which he distinguished from philanthropy. A 'philanthropic spirit is good', he wrote, but

> a dutiful spirit is better. Duty is a beneficent mistress. Her teachings and claims are prior to and mightier than the teachings and claims of philanthropy. Whilst a prevailing purpose of philanthropy is to mitigate human ills, a prevailing purpose of duty is to prevent them. There would be little necessity for the exercise of mercy or benevolence if right and justice ruled and regulated human affairs.[192]

The sense of duty to which Edwards subscribed was a central theme of idealism. If it is true that Edwards displayed an affinity with idealism then it is apparent that a concern for humanistic culture – about which idealists were obsessed, believing it to have metaphysical origins and to be the source of harmony and happiness – could exist, through the medium of the public library, alongside empirical utilitarian imperatives. Edwards appeared to accommodate both idealist and utilitarian sentiments. Public libraries were worthwhile, he believed, because

> they encourage seekers after technical knowledge, and promote industrial improvement ... [and] because they teach equality of citizenship and are essentially democratic in spirit and action.[193]

Further, in his autobiography, he finished by stating his own philosophy in words borrowed from great thinkers of the past. As befitted a man of science and utilitarianism he quoted John Stuart Mill and Herbert Spencer; but he also invoked the romanticism of Ruskin and Carlyle[194]. The question of Edwards's idealist leanings cannot be resolved here. However, there is enough of the spirit of idealism in his utterances and writings, and those of his contemporary public library promoters, to invite an analysis of idealism as a possible supplement to – though not a replacement for – the utilitarian momentum of early public library development.

CHAPTER 7

THE IDEALIST FLYWHEEL

The economic role which the public library evolved rendered the institution thoroughly 'useful' in the eyes of many who promoted it. As an instrument of materialism the public library corresponded to the utilitarian schema of stability based on a security of economic expectation. Utilitarianism offers a theory explaining much, though not all, of the early development of the public library. The momentum which utilitarianism provided meant that facets of the philosophy surfaced frequently in the public library debate (not only was there continuing stiff resistance to free libraries, but also vigorous discussion within the movement itself concerning objectives and methods) throughout the pre-1914 period. Such was the intensity of utilitarian forces helping to shape the early public library that, for instance, its legitimacy as an agency purveying so-called impracticable and merely recreational reading was seriously and persistently questioned.[1] For while it is true that utilitarians warmed to the idea of state-assisted rational recreation for diversion, they did so gradually, in stark contrast to those who recognized readily the social criticism of a brutalizing industrial world in need of soothing aesthetic culture.

Given that the embryonic public library movement was so strongly informed by what was at the time the most influential form of intellectual thinking – utilitarianism – it is important to the formulation of a theory of public library development that the philosophy which superseded utilitarianism be investigated too. That philosophy was 'objective' idealism, which, certainly by the last quarter of the nineteenth century, had become the most prominent philosophical school in British universities; its propagation was most intensely supervised by members of Oxford's Balliol College, and by Thomas Henry Green (see below) in particular.[2] (Consideration is not given here to 'subjective' or 'acosmic' idealism – closely related to phenomenalist thought – which states that reality is not independent of the mind, and that whatever exists is mental; material objects being merely ideas.)

An investigation of idealism is further warranted because many aspects of early public library development associated with utilitarianism not only continued to be visible after that philosophy's influence began to fade, but were amplified during the era that idealism came to dominate. Idealists and utilitarians alike pursued reasoned action, state intervention, political pluralism, equality of opportunity, the notion of citizenship, self-betterment, educational improvement and, above all, social stability within a fundamentally unchanged capitalist order. Each of these objectives was a major concern of the public library, which, having been born of utilitarian values, gradually developed an idealist vocabulary.

Epistemology and ethics

It is paradoxical that utilitarianism and idealism stood shoulder to shoulder in the fight for books on the rates, in that the two philosophies were, at a fundamental level, divergent. Utilitarians argued that reality and sense-experience determined ideas and character: knowledge developed *a posteriori*. They believed that individuals were like the atoms of Newtonian theory, each atom being exposed to exterior forces, thereby moulding humans into essentially asocial, isolated and mechanistic beings. Whereas utilitarians attempted to subordinate the mental to the physical, idealists taught the reverse of this relationship; prominence was given to ideas, to the ideal and to the inwardly creative human spirit.

The critical line of fracture between idealism and utilitarianism is epistemological. The spectrum of the source of substantive knowledge ranges from the Platonic view at one extreme to that of the early empiricists at the other. Plato argued that experience could not in itself yield knowledge, since the circumstances and objects which constituted experience are constantly changing. Rather, the source of true knowledge was the human spirit and its intellect, which drew its sustenance from the unchanging sphere of the 'forms' or 'universal truths'.[3] The nativism championed by Plato, and others since, thus proposes that the fount of knowledge is innate and that knowledge can exist *a priori*, having been arrived at by thought alone, regardless of sense-experience. Nativists point, for example, to the mental structures of mathematical reasoning and language acquisition as evidence of powerful, innate forces. While the image of an infant's mind crammed full of substantive knowledge is clearly unacceptable, the idea that the mental – like the physical – development of human beings is innately determined, or programmed, is a cogent argument. In this regard it is argued that even if an individual developed in isolation, without access to socializing education – the stereotype being the fictional Tarzan among his apes – he or she would at some predetermined stage come to *know* that 'two plus two equals four'.[4] Similarly, it has been argued, most notably by Noam Chomsky, that our knowledge of grammatical structure in our language faculty is innately formed and requires only some experience of a language's lexicon and context to trigger it into action. How else, the question is posed, can children learn so much linguistic complexity so quickly, with only a meagre exposure to language?[5]

Victorian and Edwardian idealists clung to the idea of nativism, particularly in terms of an unquestioning, 'given' faith in the metaphysical. They were confronted in their epistemology by an empirical tradition, encompassing utilitarianism, which was rooted in an enthusiasm for the power of environment and the malleability of human nature. Both John Locke's *Essay Concerning Human Understanding* (1689) and David Hume's *An Enquiry Concerning Human Understanding* (1748) spoke for much of the Enlightenment in its condemnation of Plato's autonomous rationalism, in its questioning of original sin and in its belief in the perfectibility of humankind. Empiricists have not, historically, rejected all forms of innateness.[6] For example, the principle of association among ideas, the ability to record experiences in memory (we do not learn how to learn from nothing) and Aristotle's proposal, made in his *Metaphysics*, that 'all men by nature desire to know'[7] have all been cited by empiricists as evidence of innate structures. However, this is not incompatible with the teaching that we cannot have *substantive* knowledge *a priori*. Empiricists countered the idealist belief that substantive ideas could be imprinted on reality. As such they denied the existence of as yet inexplicable forces which delivered moral goodness not through experience, but by means of residual qualities shared by each of us as members of a metaphysical whole.

To depict an epistemological scene of mutually exclusive, warring camps would be misleading. Chapter 3 described how John Mill's neo-utilitarianism evolved from a critical assessment of mechanistic learning; a realization that the senses, beyond being useful, could be enjoyed for their own sake. The culture of the aesthetic which Mill embraced echoed the teachings of the German metaphysicians and the English Romantics. As such, his philosophical reflection constituted a mellowing of utilitarianism's traditional hostility to doctrines which espoused the existence of 'native' human qualities. It has been suggested that the easing of empiricist attitudes to nativism continued after Mill's death; not so much owing to *his* legacy, as to that of Darwin. Early empiricists rejected nativism outright because to accept the innate existence of substantive knowledge was to endorse a non-scientific explanation (God), out of tune with the secular criticism which typified the Enlightenment. However, once Darwin had raised the possibility of a Godless universe, empiricists found they could endorse nativism with an easier conscience – in effect, with a scientific conscience susceptible to metaphysical perceptions shorn of divine implications.[8] This resulted in a freer run for nativist doctrines, including metaphysically based idealism.

The nativist-metaphysical basis of idealism dovetailed with its ethical stance. Idealists could not accept the utilitarian view that an action was morally correct only if, as a consequence of it, utility was increased. This *teleological* conception of moral action allowed human motivation to be cast in a calculating, mechanistic mould. Convinced of the ability of the individual to self-form elements of character, idealists thus spoke of moral action in a *deontological* sense. That is to say, individuals did not always act according to a consequentialist analysis. Rather, the human spirit was unpredictable. It could even inspire actions – such as sacrificing one's life for another or for a cause – which, while appearing morally correct, did not overtly enhance personal happiness. In rejecting crude consequentialism, idealists thus highlighted the capacity of the human mind to act under the influence of *absolute* motivations, like obligation, love and duty. Naturally, this deontological view of ethics invested considerable faith in the ability of humanity to exist in a truly *social*, harmonious way; it was a view which despised the social atomism and hedonism which raw utilitarians attached to human instinct.

Classical and Germanic roots: self-realization

Idealists and utilitarians were at odds with each other not just on philosophical matters of epistemology and ethics, but also on a range of practical issues, contention over which flowed inevitably from the divergence of the two schools' fundamental intellectual positions. The most worldly rift was between, on the one hand, the utilitarian objective of building a practical-minded, commercial, industrial nation, and, on the other, the idealist spiritual criticism and suspicion of a mechanized and progressive, yet alienating and brutalizing, society. Idealists rejuvenated the long-standing opposition to utilitarian materialism – an opposition which early thinkers like Coleridge had inspired. What partly accounts for the prominence of idealism approximately from the mid-1870s until the First World War was the rapid pace of industrial, urban and cultural change (despite the economic depression of 1873–96) which paralleled the philosophy's heyday. As work became more specialized, and society more complex and rushed, idealism duly appealed to the aesthetic, non-materialist side of the human spirit.

However, industrialization was not the creator of idealism: it had a much longer pedigree (much longer than that of utilitarianism). Its entrance on to the Victorian philosophical stage was far from being its debut appearance in a prominent intellectual role. British idealists drew their inspiration 'from common roots in Greek and German thought – above all in Plato, Aristotle, Kant and Hegel'.[9] From the intellectual tradition of Classical thought was borrowed the example of a civilized and harmonious existence in the Greek *polis*, where individuals acted morally as educated citizens of a sophisticated political society.[10] Plato's *Republic* was an abiding influence on idealism. His ideal society contained three classes of citizen: artisans and labourers to satisfy society's material needs; soldiers to defend the city-state; and rulers, or guardians, to organize social life. It was a society characterized by self-sacrifice and duty to others (although it should be stressed that Plato was no friend of pure democracy as a means of furthering social interdependence). This was manifest in the bravery of the citizen soldier, who asked no reward for his courage; and in the devotion to public service on the part of guardians who pursued an élitist intellectualism, not for the benefit of their own class's well-being, but for the dissemination of wisdom and knowledge to society as a whole.[11]

Whereas Plato's works were embraced by a wide spectrum of nineteenth-century intellectuals, Aristotle's appeal was narrower. In respect of idealism, however, Aristotle's influence was, perhaps, more crucial than Plato's. Aristotle's *Ethics* became the idealists' bible. It has been said that its practical content – the numerous references made to everyday life – made it an eminently readable text. It praised the collective social life of Greek civilization and emphasized the potential for social improvement without challenging fundamental, established social structures. Aristotle's *Ethics* became the key document for analysing the definition and worth of good citizenship in the late Victorian and Edwardian eras.[12]

In respect of idealism's metaphysical ingredient, however, it was Plato who provided the critical arguments. Plato's doctrine of the 'forms' or 'ideas' proposed the existence of changeless, eternal, non-material essences; there was an ultimate standard, for example, of beauty, of courage and of justice. The greatest of the 'forms' was the 'idea of goodness' – an innate desire to be virtuous.[13] Plato conceptualized an ultimate 'good' which dwelt beyond natural existence. Its nature could not be readily understood: it was like the sun, dazzling if gazed upon directly. Given the impossibility of self-inspection of the soul individuals could only come to know their own souls by looking at the souls of others, the brightest of which was that of God, who encapsulated the 'idea of goodness'.[14] Only an élite few, said Plato, could even begin to approach a comprehension of 'goodness'.[15]

'Good', in the Platonic sense, was described by Aristotle as intrinsic. Acts which were intrinsic could be undertaken for their own sake, as worthy ends in themselves. By contrast, Aristotle's favoured view of 'good' was extrinsic: an act was good if – as the utilitarians came to believe – it was a means to a good end; if, in other words, it was instrumental to the teleological growth towards perfection.[16] As Aristotle states in his *Ethics*: 'Every craft and every enquiry, and similarly every action and project seems to aim at some good; hence the Good has been well defined as that at which everything aims.'[17] Aristotle did not perceive an absolute 'good', as envisaged by Plato. Rather, he saw 'good' as belonging to human action and thought; actions could be good even in the absence of a timeless 'universal' of 'good', because the ultimate consequence of such actions was human perfection.

Victorian idealists drew heavily on Plato's metaphysics. However, they combined the Platonic idea that we were innately linked to a metaphysical entity with the Aristotelian notion of evolution towards a perfection *yet* to be achieved, by either humans or the superior being. Idealists' adoption of classical philosophy was bolstered by their exploration of German neo-hellenism. Under the influence of the Enlightenment, German philosophers had carried forward the metaphysical and ethical themes of Greek learning. Central to idealism were the teachings of Kant, especially his belief in the existence of original feelings beyond sense impression. The most important of these, Kant argued, was the sense of duty. His thinking in this respect was influenced as much by contemporary social change as the message of classical philosophy. The eighteenth century saw the breakdown of long-standing control mechanisms of custom, tradition and ritual: person as object. This constituted a liberation for the individual. However, greater freedom brought disintegrative tendencies in its wake. It became clear that there was a duty incumbent upon individuals to develop a self-activated moral consciousness: person as subject.[18] Kant stressed the value of moral autonomy in resolving the conflict between duty and inclination; thereby removing moral values from the body and locating them in the human spirit. He argued that moral action was dictated by reason from within, not by law or custom or public opinion from without.[19] Reason, he said, gave sense-experience its structure and coherence; it was our transcendent morality which enabled us to interpret and shape reality, rather than serve as its passive victim.

Kant differentiated between knowledge which was in itself eternal (*noumena*) and that which was derived from our sense impressions contained within space and time (*phenomena*). This proposition was supported by later German metaphysicians such as Fichte, who argued that knowledge did not come through natural experience but was part of a supernatural cosmic establishment outside space and time. Fichte taught that nature, including the human race, owed its being to an Absolute Ego whose motivation was that the underlying purpose of all things should be ethical. Consequently, Fichte stressed the importance of the cohesive, sharing nation state – a message of mutual assistance which struck a chord with the anti-Napoleonic national spirit of the Prussian people. The required spirit of national community could only be achieved, said Fichte, if education was made available to all citizens without distinction. Only then could full participation occur. Fichte's writing, not surprisingly, influenced the education reforms instigated in Prussia following its traumatic defeat by Napoleon in 1806.[20]

Hegel, too, believed in the state's duty to promote education, which was 'the art of making men ethical'.[21] His theory of knowledge combined the work of Kant and Fichte with Platonic-Aristotelian thinking. Like Aristotle he conceived of a teleological growth towards perfection; his dialectic of 'thesis' versus 'antithesis', producing 'synthesis', was conceived as a process approximating to the truth. Education was central to this process and, like Plato's guardians, he supported the idea of a class of élite teachers. These would be charged with the dissemination of knowledge. Hegel said that this duty had a cosmic significance. To assimilate knowledge was to 'realize' oneself: to become more conscious of one's existence. Moreover, individuals were merely part of a larger consciousness – referred to as Thought or Spirit or Absolute. Thus, individual self-realization contributed to the self-realization of the Absolute. Men and women were vehicles of the Absolute in its eternal quest for full consciousness; for, having begun as a featureless unity, it could only reproduce itself in the growing consciousness of humans. In short:

> Individual men [and women] find their own self-realization in their own thinking about themselves; and as they themselves are vehicles of Spirit, so Spirit too, realizes itself in their self-realization.[22]

This metaphysical conception of reality had implications for moral action. If all individuals were part of the struggle to realize an ideal essence, it followed that they were not wholly 'atomistic' but 'social'. Individuals were contributors to a common purpose which was intrinsically good, and in working for a common good an understanding of 'good' would be furthered. Hegel thus agreed with Kant that moral action could be dictated from within by reason. He added, however, that social forces also had a part to play because humans were pre-eminently outward looking. Of relevance here is Hegel's idea of civil society, which he defined as the intermediate phase between family and state. In civil society individuals, aided by law, were free to pursue their own self-interest, but within the restrictions of being interdependent with other individuals. Civil society possessed legal and economic institutions mutually beneficial to all. Hegel stressed a sense of community existing alongside concerns of self-interest. The fact that he looked to the ancient Greek *polis* as the model of civil life is no coincidence.

T. H. Green

German scholarship, especially that of the metaphysicians, found considerable favour in Britain. Coleridge, Carlyle and Thomas Arnold all promoted it. Matthew Arnold went to Prussia and observed German idealism in action in the state schools. As a consequence he came to regard

> the German concept of 'Culture' as the path to the successful operation of the inevitable democracy of the future, the corrective to the 'anarchy' which Englishmen were certain was the more descriptive synonym of 'democracy'.[23]

The belief that the state diffusion of culture to the masses could provide a 'unifying church' was shared by a great number of leading late-nineteenth-century academics. The chief Hegelian proponent of culture as a socially stabilizing agent was T. H. Green (Fellow of Balliol College, Oxford, between 1860 and 1878; after which time he served as Professor of Moral Philosophy until his premature death in 1882). Green discovered Hegelian philosophy as a Balliol student in the 1850s. (British idealists of this period were often known as the British Hegelians.[24]) His tutor, Benjamin Jowett (who also taught Matthew Arnold), had introduced it to Oxford after having visited Germany in the 1840s. It supplemented and invigorated the tradition of Greek learning at Oxford, and enriched the thinking of those who had already read German philosophy.[25] Balliol became the magnet for imported German ideas.

Green fused the Greek and German intellectual heritages.[26] The essence of his idealist philosophy was expressed in his *Prolegomena to Ethics* (1883) and *Lectures on the Principles of Political Obligation* (1895). Influenced by the Platonic-Hegelian tradition, Green believed that the physical world rested on metaphysical forces ruled by an eternal consciousness (in connection with this, his former religious beliefs will be discussed below). It was the human capacity for reason, he taught, which linked individuals to, and enriched, the eternal force. The divine purpose would be furthered by raising the consciousness – extending the self-realization – of individuals. Further, increasing the *number* of individuals whose consciousness was raised similarly advanced the self-realization of the eternal essence. Green defined 'real goodness' as 'a will to be good, which has no object but its own fulfilment'.[27]

For Green, the common cause of self-realization meant that individuals should be well disposed to one another. The idea of self-realization as the end of moral conduct has been seen as a synonym for self-interest. But Green emphasized that individuals could only realize themselves *in relation to others*: one first had to look inwards before one could look outwards.[28] Like the Greeks, and Hegel, he said that society was made up of free yet law-abiding persons, 'each his own master yet each his brother's keeper'.[29] He stressed the 'principle of human brotherhood' and is said to have coined the phrase 'political obligation'.[30] He employed a number of terms interchangeably – 'common interest', 'social good', 'public interest', 'common well-being' – to mean the importance of duty to others.[31] Green argued that spiritual natures, unlike material gain, could be enhanced by non-competition and cooperation.[32] He himself put theory into practice by engaging in the civic life of Oxford. He became a town councillor in 1876; his home was open to townsfolk of varied social backgrounds.[33] In his own life, therefore, Green attempted to fulfil the objectives of 'citizenship', a word central to his vocabulary.[34]

Green believed that citizenship was furthered by education. No worldly subject interested him more. He advocated basic schooling to combat crime, and to prevent social and political unrest. Education would remove class differences: by levelling up, not down. He wrote of 'unconscious social insolence' at the top of society and 'social jealousy' at its base; what was needed was 'a freemasonry of common education'. In order to diffuse culture and education teachers had to go 'to' their pupils, not vice versa. This *outreach* would accelerate the process of self-realization because educational advance – in terms of both standards and numbers affected – would teach citizens to be more aware of their own nature and their relation to others.[35]

Green's political philosophy existed as an extension of his ethics. Spiritual perfection he saw as no pipe-dream, but as realistically attainable. The state was to be the vehicle whereby individuals and the Absolute achieved self-realization. He viewed the state from the Greek perspective: it was a political community, not an overbearing machine. Far from being the enemy of liberty, the state, as 'servant', helped to lower obstacles to liberty by providing and maintaining the basic circumstances conducive to a fuller realization of human potentialities. He was not dogmatically opposed to state control, believing that each case for intervention had to be decided on its merits; after all, without protection from the state private property would find it difficult to thrive. In the footsteps of John Mill he explained that 'All that one can do to make another better is to remove obstacles and supply conditions favourable to the formation of good character.'[36] The state had a duty to remove, among other things, disease, the affliction of drink and the scourge of ignorance, each of these being an impediment to self-realization. His support for the state came more from its embodiment of 'community' than its potential for political equality, for he did not consider the right to vote as the guarantor of either a good society or the achievement of self-realization. He lamented, for example, Disraeli's victory in 1874, attributing it to the economic boom and materialistic tendencies of the early 1870s which had made the populace politically apathetic and, hence, less communal.[37]

The idealism which Green and others propagated, despite the often impenetrable style in which it was communicated,[38] was, like utilitarianism before it, no coffee-table philosophy. It produced – particularly via Balliol – a stream of educationalists, social workers, higher administrators and statesmen. It influenced political reality in the area of revisionist New Liberalism, which called for more social legislation; but it also complemented Gladstone's traditional liberal view of the societal role of the individual – that is to say, the individual with social duties aside from his or her concern for maximizing personal potential.[39] The citizenship which Green and his Balliol descendants taught became associated with a wide range of institutions, from Empire to school lunches, from democracy to national insurance.[40]

The commitment to social duty and the necessity of engaging in society were nowhere more clearly seen than in the late-nineteenth-century settlement house movement (the provision of cultural centres run by middle-class do-gooders for the benefit of the inner city's poor and demoralized), which received much of its nourishment from idealism.[41] Further, the intention to diffuse culture for the purpose of self-realization was encapsulated in the adult education movement, which idealism strengthened. The idea of university extension education was first suggested by an Oxford professor of philosophy, William Sewell, in *Suggestions for the Extension of the University* (1850).[42] Through the influence of idealism, Oxford University began extension lectures in 1878, Green being chairman of the organizing committee. (Extension lectures *per se* were inaugurated by Cambridge University in Nottingham in 1873.) An increased student participation was seen in the early twentieth century in the university tutorial class system and the Workers' Educational Association (WEA): these enshrined the idealist objective of teachers going 'to' the students.[43] The influence of idealism on adult education was carried through into the First World War. It is significant that responsibility during the war for the educational aspect of reconstruction was given to H. A. L. Fisher, upon whom Green had made a deep and abiding impact.[44] Furthermore, A. L. Smith (Master of Balliol 1916-24) became chairman of the Ministry of Reconstruction's Adult Education Committee. It was this committee which was given the responsibility of investigating the future of the public library; its recommendations being taken up by H. A. L. Fisher, Minister of Education, in the formulation of the Public Libraries Act of 1919, which abolished the rate-limit and extended library provision to the counties.

Moderation: religious influences

Though widely influential in terms of social reform, idealism did not seek radical social change. Idealism called for the refinement, not the overthrow, of capitalism. Its reinterpretation of liberalism in a corporatist direction in no sense challenged the almost universal acceptance of capitalism. Idealism advocated a better life for citizens without overturning the foundations of the established social and economic order. Green attributed poverty not to capitalism but to landlordism. He defended possessive individualism and private ownership of property on the grounds that they contributed to the common good by aiding individual development and self-determination. Green's friends mistakenly saw him as a socialist. This may have been because of his advocacy of increased state activity; yet Green saw the state as a means of ameliorating, not obliterating, capitalism. He urged social reform without socialism[45] and voluntaryism before state action. He laid stress on a moralized capitalism in which 'social' principles came to be accepted, in the sense of individuals evolving, in accordance with Darwinian theory, towards a realization that the higher pleasures of life were the most valuable.[46]

Idealists like Green criticized utilitarianism. They did so not because of a distaste for any utilitarian enthusiasm for unbridled free enterprise, but because of the utilitarian preoccupation with pleasure as the definition of 'good'. According to idealists, this narrow perception of 'good' meant that utilitarianism could not provide the degree of intellectual underpinning which a stable and secure society required. Idealists, on the other hand, said that they could and did provide the appropriate moral arguments. Idealism became a new justification for the market ethos.[47] Idealists saw disputes between capital and labour as unavoidable, but believed a stronger sense of citizenship and a greater readiness for self-sacrifice would be the arbiters of differences. They saw no role for sectional class militancy in producing change. (It is significant that during the First World War, when class politics reached an extremely high intensity, idealism appeared impotent and duly lost ground.[48]) The lack of radicalism in idealism was identified by some workers engaged in adult education who saw the idealist providers of WEA and university extension education as agents for indoctrinating capitalism.[49] An idealist such as the historian R. H. Tawney, who believed that capitalism endangered individual liberty and prevented self-realization, was very much the exception rather than the rule.[50]

To what, then, may we attribute idealism's popularity and political moderation? Idealism grew quickly because of the social soil in which it was rooted. The late nineteenth century saw a new awareness of social problems. Mid-nineteenth-century reformers and philanthropists were, arguably, more interested in the moral welfare than the material conditions of the poor: moral elevation was generally seen as more important than economic advance (though this was not ignored) in bringing about social cohesion and stability. But the economic gains and moral improvement experienced by some working-class groups in the mid-Victorian era highlighted the importance of economic factors in lessening social problems.[51] Thus, when social investigators began, from the 1880s, to publicize the exact extent of poverty[52] – Booth revealed that 30 per cent of London's population was living below the poverty line – the news pricked the conscience of respectable opinion. The 'rediscovery of poverty', and the associated fears of moral decline fanned by national economic performance, was not consistent with the material advance of the mid-Victorian period. As Samuel Smith MP wrote in 1885: 'the bulk of the nation has made wonderful progress both morally and materially in the last 40 years', yet 'there remains a large deposit of human misery in our midst, wholly untouched by the progress of the nation.'[53] The moral philosophy of idealism appeared to offer a solution to the social divisiveness afflicting the nation; it is no coincidence that its popularity soared at the very moment that moral regeneration once again became a burning issue.

Idealism's extensive influence is also explained by its religious dynamic. The message that idealism conveyed was not new: it had a Christian texture. Indeed, given the abstract and metaphysical nature of idealist writing (unlike the more worldly output of the utilitarians) it is, perhaps, doubtful if the philosophy could have become so influential if not for the familiarity of its underlying Christian themes.[54] Idealism can be best understood as a surrogate for the Christian faith. It appealed to a 'transitional' generation confronted by scientific and historical scholarship, most notably the secular theories of Darwin.[55]

For intellectuals like Green, idealism became a prop to a wavering faith. His Germanophilia was derived from his spiritual introspection: 'Green looked to German philosophy to reconstruct his beliefs.'[56] This is not to say that Green and his fellow idealists forgot their Christian roots. Christian values were retained, albeit in a modified form. Idealists echoed Christ's teaching relating to the 'brotherhood of man'. Green sought an altruistic society 'in which to every rational agent the well-being or perfection of every other agent shall be indulged in that perfection of himself for which he lives'.[57] To an extent, therefore, idealism echoed the Greek concern for a harmonious, interdependent citizenship. In fact, it can be argued that Christians were, in effect, the 'children' of the Greeks: they merely provided zeal in the pursuance of Greek virtues.[58] Green, and others, certainly combined Greek learning with Christian philosophy. Idealists took up the Evangelical belief in redemption. Evangelicals did not share the Puritan belief that poverty was essentially a product of sin. They argued, to the contrary, that citizens generally became poor as a result of external circumstances, not internal spiritual blemish. Hence, remedial action, to change circumstances, was appropriate to a reduction of poverty and an improvement of morals. Idealists were in this Evangelical tradition when they argued that state action, to deliver fertile environmental conditions, could be advantageous to moral and material welfare. The final link between idealism and religion was the adherence to metaphysical belief. Idealism duplicated metaphysical aspects of the Christian faith. Idealists employed religious language and analogies to emphasize the duties of citizenship in the context of an absolute essence existing beyond space and time.[59] Because they believed that individual lives could inform an eternal consciousness, idealists were able to speak of the immortality of individual souls[60] – the performance of duty would resonate down the ages.

Troubled in the age of Darwin by the question of the existence of heaven, idealists evolved a doctrine of the construction of heaven on earth.[61] It must be emphasized, however, that idealists like Green did not reject the notion of God entirely. They argued that humanity sensed, naturally and innately, the existence of a divine consciousness. Green himself assimilated Kant's belief that God – the 'Great Unknown' or 'Unconditioned' – was beyond human knowledge and understanding.[62] The idea of God being 'unknowable' certainly fitted with the proposition that God was infinite: it also placated internal anguish arising from the questioning of one's faith.

Henry Jones: a case study in duty

Clearly, idealism possessed a substantial religious ingredient. This becomes more evident if an examination is made of the philosophy of the Hegelian idealist Henry Jones. Beginning intellectual life as a Calvinistic Methodist preacher, Jones went on to study philosophy at Glasgow University, and to win a four-year scholarship in Germany; he eventually occupied the position of Professor of Moral Philosophy at Glasgow University.[63] Jones's contribution to idealism, in terms of originality, was slight. He has been described by one commentator as merely one of 'Green's parrots'.[64] For the purpose of this study, Jones's lack of originality is no disadvantage. On the contrary, his thinking might be taken as reflective of the broad sway of pre-First World War idealist thought.

Jones despised utilitarianism. He observed that the 'hedonism in morals, and the individualism in politics' which characterized utilitarianism had, by the early twentieth century, 'become utterly inadequate to our times'.[65] Jones refuted the epistemology of utilitarianism. He proclaimed the subordination of environment to consciousness:

Spirit is more and higher than any material or natural force ... the natural world is itself the symbol or phenomenal manifestation of Spirit.[66]

He believed it was

the presence of the ideal element in every act of man, his pursuits of purposes, mean or noble, which he has set before himself, that distinguishes him abruptly from the brute.[67]

Rather than undermining Jones's metaphysical beliefs, the new theory of evolution appeared to strengthen them. For Jones, Darwin had shown that the 'whole order of Nature is in movement', as was the 'whole scheme of Spirit'.[68] That movement was in a positive direction: social progress. The age was characterized by a new spirit of freedom. Consequently, he was able to boast that idealism 'lifts the lowly, it asserts the rights of the weak, and breaks the power of the strong'.[69] The 'levelling upwards' of humanity represented the 'victory of the living thing over its own limits'.[70]

Jones saw the exercise of duty as one of the main functions of the spirit and as the root of happiness.[71] He proclaimed the state to be the most effective vehicle for the discharging of one's duty to others. Within the context of the state, the relationships derived from duty helped to knit humanity together in a way which, far from being 'irksome', in fact acquired 'priceless worth'.[72] Jones was fluent in the language of citizenship and duty:

The citizen has but to stand in his station and perform its duties in order to fulfil the demands of citizenship. He is like an organ to the organism ... the state, on its part, if it is itself enlightened and worthy of such a citizen, will put forth all its force in case of need, in order to protect him and sustain him in his rights; for he is there on 'its' account.[73]

He conceived of freedom as 'life "within" the state' and the 'life "of" the state within its members'.[74] The state was a microcosm of the eternal consciousness: in the case of both the state and the Absolute, the development of the individual was crucial to the well-being of the 'whole'. Moreover, Jones argued that because duty was an 'absolute obligation' it must have been imposed by a universal and 'unerring authority'.[75]

The moral and metaphysical collectivism which Jones and other idealists proposed echoed the long tradition of Christian charity. It also struck a chord with socialistic prescriptions for earthly progress. Yet idealism was patently not socialism. Not only did its religious dimension ensure that it acquired a moderate and reformist nature; its anchorage in the mainstream values of nineteenth-century liberalism similarly rendered it progressive rather than revolutionary. Jones expressed well the social stability objective of idealism when he wrote:

A political society which cares only for some of its members, while the others are denied the rights and obligations of citizenship ... can command only a limited loyalty.[76]

The social stability implications of tearing down barriers to self-development were clearly understood by idealists – and certainly not in any socialistic way.

That idealism was close to the liberalism of John Mill in respect of collectivism for self-realization is clear. Yet it was not accusations of Leftist collectivism which came to undermine it. On the contrary, it was idealism's perceived attachment to the collectivism of the absolutist Right which weakened and eventually destroyed it as an effective intellectual and political force. Ironically, the German philosophy which made idealism such a dominant force served also to sully its name. The conflict with Germany, between 1914 and 1918, led many British intellectuals to reject their former adherence to German thought. The war shattered the idealist belief in the Hegelian view of the state. The Hegelian theory of the state was said to be at the bottom of German aggression. The state was relieved of its potential to empower (in the tradition of the Enlightenment) and given, instead, a potential to enslave.[77] Thus, although idealists like Jones could say that 'war has come upon us as a Duty',[78] his previous championing of German philosophy laid him open to frenzied attacks, such as that of J. A. Hobson (and others like Bertrand Russell who led the Cambridge assault on idealism)[79] in 1916, when he accused him of mouthing 'the pure milk of Prussianism'.[80]

Although it was idealism's attachment to the creed of the state which determined its downfall *after* 1918 (for its influence in the reconstruction strategy of the war and immediate post-war eras was noticeable) it should not be assumed that this attachment formed the core of idealist intellectual development *before* the Great War. The influence of German philosophy was crucial, yet it is best perceived as an ingredient which was thrown into an existing 'foundation' mixture of Greek and Christian thought. Idealism did not burst unheralded on to the political and philosophical scenes in the last quarter of the nineteenth century. The input of German thought, evolving from Kant through Fichte to Hegel, was part of its evolving heritage. But the lengthier aspect of its heritage was classical and religious in character. The influence of the ancient philosophers was seminal: Wordsworth pointed out that even if Plato's *Republic* was made widely available few would read it; 'and yet', he added, 'we have embodied it all'.[81] Such a process of embodiment was certainly applicable to idealism.

The broad church movement and Christian socialism

As argued above, idealism also embodied a strong religious dynamic, and in concluding this analysis of the philosophy it is appropriate to return to this key theme. Idealism evolved, in part, from the world of early Victorian religious theology. A generation before idealism's rise to popularity broad church reformers, in the tradition of Coleridge, had advocated a spiritual offensive by active, self-sacrificing citizens against the selfishness of commercial society. In the Evangelical tradition they questioned the utilitarian doctrine defining happiness as pleasure. Broad churchmen looked towards ecumenicalism in the hope that a universal Christian effort would precipitate the 'cooperative' society which Chartism had failed to deliver (a liberal Anglicanism embracing other forms of Protestantism was in itself cooperative). An attempt was made to shift religious belief away from a preoccupation with biblical truth and personal salvation towards a pragmatic interaction with society: especially the pursuance of religion for the social good and for corporate redemption. This was evident in the work of the Christian socialists who, perplexed at the defeat of Chartism, sought to relieve workers from exploitation by providing for their cultural uplift. The Working Men's College, established in 1854 by F. D. Maurice, Charles Kingsley and others, was an example of the kind of partnership between church and secular society at which Christian socialists aimed.[82] The Christian socialist ethos was almost identical to that of idealism. The idea of the settlement house, for example, came not from the latter, as is widely believed, but from the former. The Christian socialist D. J. Vaughan was both an uncle of Green and a formative influence. The languages of Christian socialism and idealism were remarkably similar. For example, Kingsley anticipated the notion of an eternal consciousness being strengthened by individual self-development in his perception of accumulated human wisdom as the guarantor of civilized behaviour:

> Every lesson which you learn in school, all knowledge which raises you above the savage or the profligate (who is but a savage dressed in civilized garments) has been made possible to you by them [the wise] ... Either the knowledge itself, or other knowledge which led to it, is an heirloom to you from men whose bodies are now mouldering in the dust but whose spirits live for ever before God, and whose works follow them, going on, generation after generation, upon the path which they had trod while they were upon earth, the path of usefulness, a light to the steps of youth and ignorance. They [the wise] are the salt of the earth, which keeps the world of man from decaying back into barbarism.[83]

Further, like idealism, Christian socialism's advocacy of cultural diffusion was reformist. F. D. Maurice explained:

> We believed and felt that unless the classes in this country which had any degree of knowledge more than their fellows were willing to share it with their fellows, to regard it as precious because it bound them to their fellows, England would fall first under an anarchy, and then under a despotism.[84]

It was this emphasis on culture as a social bond, for stabilizing a capitalist order fashioned in a gentler mode, which similarly helped underpin the early public library movement.

A recognition of the religious – especially broad church and Christian socialist – roots of idealism demonstrates that idealist thought had attained an influence in social and political affairs long before its sophisticated articulation by intellectual giants like Green. As such, it is simplistic to think that the informing of intellectual life, by utilitarianism and idealism, can be separated into two distinct periods. Utilitarianism and idealism overlapped in terms of periodization. They also overlapped in respect of their constituent facets: there was common ground to be found on a number of principles. This will become evident in assessing the coincidence of idealist values and the free library ideal. The free library was a baton which utilitarians had no trouble in handing on, in a staggered fashion, to idealist promoters similarly competing in the race to disseminate culture.

The intersection of idealist and public library philosophies

Idealist thought, including its religious dynamic, was clearly represented in the development of the public library movement before 1914. It is true that the contemporary literature of the public library provides little evidence that idealist philosophy was widely read by the institution's protagonists,[85] and even less evidence that the material which was read proved directly influential. However, it is significant that the utterances of public library protagonists bore a remarkable resemblance to the language of idealism and the pious vocabulary of its Evangelical origins. Certainly, the ethos of the early public library can be fitted neatly into the framework of idealist thought – the fit being tight enough, in fact, to allow serious consideration to be given to the theory that idealism provided the major intellectual momentum to pre-1914 public library expansion. Idealism acted as the flywheel for much cultural development, partly through the free provision of literature in a communal, civic setting. It is no coincidence, perhaps, that the heyday of idealism, between 1880 and 1920, was the very period when the public library experienced its most substantial expansion.

Declared motives of early public library promoters matched the purpose of Evangelical belief. An illuminating document in this regard is the record of the speech given by the Baptist minister, George Dawson, at the opening ceremony of the Birmingham Reference Library in 1866, in which he reiterated much of what he told the Select Committee on Public Libraries in 1849.[86]

Dawson described a library as 'one of the greatest causes, as it is one of the greatest results of man's civilization'. He did not discount its materialist, utilitarian role. In a library, he said:

> a man gets himself ready for his calling, arms himself for his profession, finds out the facts that are to determine his trade, prepares himself for his examination.

But he stressed more the library's cultural role as a vehicle for citizenship. It was a

> solemn chamber in which a man can take counsel with all that has been wise and great and good and glorious among the men that have gone before him, – (cheers).

This wisdom allowed the heat of discussions – ecclesiastical, political and social – to be dissipated: 'When a man has worked himself into this unwise heat a good place for him to go is a great library, and that will quiet him down admirably.' He related that in the name of conciliation he took pleasure in arranging in his own library the great literature of the past side by side, according to their divergences: he put radical beside Tory and 'they lie down together as the wolf and the lamb'. A library in Dawson's eyes was for 'all'. He praised the 'spirit of corporate ownership': it was 'a Holy Communion, a wise Socialism', because the institution was 'at the service of the whole people'. The library was 'all things for all men: the highest to kiss the lowest'. Enshrined in the library's civic character – much was made of the fact that Birmingham, unlike many other towns where philanthropy operated, provided its library solely from the rates – was the 'proclamation that a great community like this is not to be looked upon as a fortuitous concourse of human atoms, or as a miserable knot of vipers struggling in a pot [each] aiming to get his head above the other in the fierce struggle of competition.' Corporate management, he said, secured 'permanence of guardianship' for the library's contents. Moving on to a metaphysical plane he wished to make it understood that the library owed *its* existence to the existence of the town, and:

> that a town exists here by Grace of God, that a great town is a solemn organism through which should flow, and in which should be shaped, all the highest, loftiest and truest ends of man's intellectual and moral natures.

Elsewhere Dawson repeated his message of citizenship and duty. In a collection of sermons published in 1878 he remarked upon:

> a decay of public virtue in this land ... By public virtue ... I mean that public spirit which makes a man prefer, before his own prosperity and well-being that of the town or country to which he belongs.[87]

As an antidote to this decay he prescribed the self-sacrifice of 'doing good' which he defined not in:

> a mere ecclesiastical sense, – in the way of giving tracts, attending chapel services, and psalm-singing, – but doing good as in the sight of God whom we worship; doing good on the scale of God, that is, as far as the measure of our ability.[88]

From the viewpoint of authentic analysis there is perhaps a danger in reading idealism back into Dawson's comments. Moreover, it would be naive not to acknowledge other influences at play. In his Birmingham speech, for example, he stated the utilitarian 'multiplication of utility' argument in praising the shared ownership of cultural institutions: 'I may wish to study the skeleton of a whale, but my house is not large enough to hold one.' Yet, notwithstanding the pitfalls of retrospective analysis and the utilitarian influence on the municipal development of which he was a part, Dawson's outlook must surely be located in the idealist camp. In 1877, the year after Dawson's death, one tribute related that 'to the last the intuitional, rather than the scientific, method determined the substance of his thought'; in keeping with the idealist notion of a harmonious 'whole', Dawson described the public library as 'the largest and widest church ever established'.[89] His social philosophy was intertwined with that of Joseph Chamberlain, who, at the opening ceremony of Birmingham's new library in 1882, described the institution as 'a kind of Communism which the least revolutionary among us may be proud to advocate'.[90] In the 1880s, a statue of Dawson was erected (under a Gothic canopy, moreover, as befitted his romantic, idealist leanings) in Birmingham's city centre, alongside that of Chamberlain. This was surely symbolic of the common ground which existed between the two on the question of 'civic communism'. It also illustrates Dawson's faith in the city and its civic élites as the best provider of local services; as opposed to the model of self-governing, neighbourhood parliaments (along the lines of the anarchistic Anglo-Saxon 'folk-note') which operated in places like Sheffield during the Chartist era.[91] Central to the New Liberalism of the late nineteenth century was the stout defence of shared ownership of large-scale corporation facilities as a means of fostering individual and social progress. The idealist recommendation of pulling down barriers to self-realization was nowhere more evident than in the advocacy of free libraries by 'positive' liberals like Dawson.

The continuing idealistic and religious underpinning of the public library movement is illustrated in the work of Samuel Barnett, Vicar of St Jude's, Whitechapel, and first warden, from 1885, of the Toynbee Hall settlement house, both in East London. Barnett urged that we ask ourselves 'what we can do to increase the reverence which looks up to God for strength and the charity which is empty of self, what in a word we can do to induce a belief in the existence of good'.[92] His solution to this question was that people should show greater sensitivity to the plight of others, a sensitivity which he saw as, to a degree, forthcoming:

> One of the signs of the time is a new consciousness of other's needs ... The desire to serve is forcing men to new, and sometimes strange activities; it exists in all and waits for expression.[93]

He believed that 'good works' – carried out by all – would give society a greater cohesion. Barnett preached that the 'haves' must not despise the poor, and the 'have-nots' must not arouse hatred against the rich: 'Capital must become more right-hearted, and labour more right-headed.'[94] But he believed the onus was on the well-off to help solve problems of poverty and ignorance. This was not to be done by the distribution of 'doles', which were 'fatal to the independence of the people' and only perpetuated problems,[95] but by an invigoration of municipal life and institutions. It was within the power of civic authorities to enforce sanitary conditions, to make every house healthy and clean, and to provide common rooms which would serve as libraries.[96]

Barnett supported the campaign for a municipal library in Whitechapel. He led the effort to raise £5,000 for the project (to which was added a payment of £6,000 from Passmore Edwards) and to win the vote for adopting the Public Libraries Acts.[97] He looked upon free libraries as wholesome gifts: the best gifts were aimed at 'developing the high in the low, at bringing out the manlike qualities in those who live as animals'.[98] But improvement had to come 'by growth from within and not by accretions from without'.[99] A library was a basic requirement whereby citizens, if so disposed, assimilated culture and rejected sensual pleasures:

> The workman knows about livelihood; he might also know about life if the great avenues of art, literature and history, down which come the thought of ages were open to him. He might be happy in reading, in thinking, or in admiring, and not be driven to find happiness in the excitement of sport or drink.[100]

Like other idealists, he viewed the realm of citizenship as international and not confined to the family and civil society. At the stone-laying ceremony of the Whitechapel library he asked:

> How can we call upon voters to decide upon tariffs if they have no knowledge of the conditions of the races of the world? How can we ask Englishmen to govern India if they have no knowledge of the natives and their condition of life. There must be knowledge if the world is to go on in its career of progress. We hope that the books to be contained in this library will be the means of distributing knowledge.[101]

Finally, his conception of a library was based on its appeal as an intrinsically democratic, corporate institution: 'Books spoke alike to rich and poor.'[102] Moreover, a library was a meeting place for rich and poor, for the cultured and those seeking culture, for provider and recipient. All the best 'good works', Barnett said, were done 'with' not 'for' people: 'Doing which helps must be with the people, among friends; not for the people to strangers.'[103] Such a philosophy contradicted atomistic profit-seeking society. He was, not surprisingly, critical of machine production and its division of labour because it robbed workers of the joys of life.[104] He saw libraries as cultural antidotes to alienation. He praised the libraries of London's working men's clubs and was pleased to see that among the most patronized works were those of social critics such as Dickens, George Eliot and Charles Kingsley.[105] In his opinion, literature sparked imagination, thereby allowing people to escape their drab lives and thoughts of money.[106]

There is also evidence of idealism acting as an influence on library managers. The first chairman of the Woolwich Public Libraries Committee, C. H. Grinling, is a case in point. In 1906 Thomas Aldred wrote to his fellow librarian Walter Powell that:

> Grinling is a university man. Educated for the Church he at the last moment declined to take orders on objection to some doctrinal point, and so devoted his life to social work. He is a man of undoubted ability, but likely to end his days in a lunatic asylum. Over study or other causes, cause him at times to go 'queer' or half 'dotty' – to use a Lancashire term.[107]

Arguably, Aldred's assessment of Grinling confuses madness with idealist fervour. Having come down from Oxford in 1884 Grinling trained as a social worker under the Barnetts at Toynbee Hall. Aldred's description was also mistaken in that Grinling was ordained a Deacon in 1884, and was later to become curate of St James's, Nottingham. In 1890 he left Nottingham to become secretary of the Woolwich Charity Organization Society. When in 1900 Woolwich became a metropolitan borough

Grinling was elected to the council, where he 'set a swift pace in urging for better housing, wider education, health services, open spaces – indeed, all those amenities which made for a broader life for the people'.[108] He was given the Freedom of the borough in 1937 and remained in Woolwich until his death in 1947.

One of the amenities to which Grinling devoted his life was the public library. He viewed the public library in wholly idealistic terms:

> To the wise man his mind is a Kingdom ... The man is truly rich, whose mind, not whose house, is richly stored with precious things; and he only can attain to beneficent power over others who first learns to wisely rule himself. Harmony within oneself, harmony within nature, with the spirit of humanity, finally harmony with the Universal Mind are prizes we should seek ... valuing all material possessions, and books not least, for their serviceableness in this quest.[109]

He linked the metaphysical concept of the 'Universal Mind' with practical affairs by speaking of the public library's relevance to the notion of community:

> Libraries are workshops, and may become ten thousand times better workshops than they are to-day, when we recognise that work is the activity of body and mind and soul, which has as its conscious aim the development of the life of the individual as a member of the social whole.[110]

Grinling was committed to the civic ideal, which he believed Woolwich had 'held aloft'.[111] He came to express the hope that

> the democracy of the days to come is community, not majority, rule; that the round-table solution of all its [Woolwich's] problems is the ultimate basis of human advance.[112]

Further, his idealism was typically characterized by a social criticism of industrialism. He had a keen interest in natural history.[113] He hoped to restore a sense of kinship not just between the different races of mankind, but between mankind and the animal world: all living things were part of a 'natural whole'.[114] He aimed for:

> Freedom from all that is ugly and unnecessary in our lives. Acceptance of all that is strong and beautiful.[115]

His moral sense was tinged by an awareness of the 'natural' existing within the 'supernatural':

> It is freedom we seek and the fruits of freedom – great heartedness, mutual devotion, entry into the full inheritance of nature, man, and all that lies beyond.[116]

The revealed motives of Grinling, Barnett and Dawson do not by themselves constitute conclusive evidence that idealism infected public library philosophy. What is significant, however, is that many other public library promoters were saying similar things. The public library's association with citizenship – and with all that citizenship entailed in terms of political socialization, the civic ideal, the efficacy of state action and duty to others – provides evidence of idealist influences at work.[117] No word occurs more often in the public library debate around the turn of the century than that of 'citizenship'.[118] The Plumstead Public Library was said to teach the 'dignities and graces of citizenship'.[119] In 1908, the Mile End Public Library offered a lecture on 'good citizenship'.[120] The librarian W. B. Sayers described a 'successful juvenile book' for a public library as one designed 'to promote the higher life of the child and to direct him to good citizenship'.[121]

Citizenship, as far as idealists were concerned, extended beyond national frontiers. The librarian Stanley Jast once wrote that 'The school of intellectual internationalism is the reference library ... through it you contact the world.'[122] Generally, however, the word was applied to national and local institutions[123] – especially political and governing institutions. Citizenship required a measured approach to political debate. In 1886 a clergyman campaigning for a public library in Lambeth was reported to have told his audience:

> The safety of England lay in the way the voters were educated. Libraries would strike hard against demagogues, for men would be better able to think for themselves, and would not be left at the mercy of demagogues for their ideas.[124]

Similarly, the librarian J. J. Ogle wrote that 'ignorance is a danger to the community ... knowledge means death to iconoclastic agitators'.[125] Public libraries set out to provide balanced coverage of potentially controversial matters:

> The less we look at things in a party spirit the nearer we shall be to attaining perfection, whether in political, religious or social matters.[126]

The desire to avoid controversy persisted, and this often led to an apolitical approach. Public library lectures reflected this neutral stance. The season of lectures in a Stepney free library in 1900 was made up of uncontroversial themes such as 'Queen Victoria: her life and reign', 'The Tower of London', 'A journey to the North Pole' and 'Ants and their ways'.[127]

The public library encouraged political participation but deep within the boundaries of the existing political process. Such political participation was crucial to the success not only of national but also of local structures. The idealist Bernard Bosanquet wrote of libraries existing in a communal, parochial setting. He looked forward

> to a society organised in convenient districts, in which men and women pursuing their different callings will live together with care for one another, and with all the essentials, the same education, the same enjoyments, the same capacities. These men and women will work together in councils and on committees ... they will have pride in their schools and libraries, in their streets and their dwellings, in their workshops and their warehouses.[128]

The free library was often said to be the most popular civic institution. In 1904 a Northampton newspaper declared that the town

> prides itself, and not without reason, upon its equipment as a municipality. And

among the institutions comprised in that equipment there is none that appeals more strongly to the inhabitants of the town than the Free Library; none which is more closely appreciated or more fully taken advantage of.[129]

As expressed by idealists, citizenship in the context of the civic ideal encapsulated the notion of social obligation to fellow citizens. Yet the respect for social duty was not the preserve of idealists. Utilitarians had also spoken of dutiful citizenship. At the opening of Liverpool Public Library in 1860 Henry Brougham predicted:

> I have no manner of doubt that it [the public library] will tend to make the members of the different communions more religious, men more orderly and better subjects, and that the whole community will be improved in its duties towards man, and in its duties towards the government, and in its duties towards Heaven, by the improvement which it will derive from this institution.[130]

However, although overlapping occurred, idealist and utilitarian interpretations of dutiful citizenship were essentially divergent. Utilitarians approached citizenship from the standpoint of individualism. The protection of individual rights by law would ensure harmonious social interaction. The law would control and improve individual action. Conversely, idealists approached citizenship from the standpoint of humanity's intrinsically social nature. Men and women were socially dutiful because of an innate ethical sense. Utilitarians believed that institutions such as the public library would foster powers of reason – and it was reason which guaranteed social peace. Idealists hoped the public library would encourage existing and autonomous feelings of social awareness to flourish.

This divergence can be observed in attitudes to self-help and culture. The history of the public library movement is riddled with the rhetoric of self-help. 'Cholera could have travelled no faster',[131] wrote Asa Briggs of self-help: certainly, the public library acted as a channel down which the self-help message could flow rapidly. Utilitarians and idealists alike would have agreed on the egalitarian implications of self-help: that all individuals should be given the opportunity to progress in life. However, the public library movement's perception of self-help changed as utilitarianism waned and idealism found favour. Early utilitarian promoters spoke in terms of the social utility of self-help; individuals relying on their own efforts would stand a better chance of maximizing their own happiness, thereby making a greater contribution to the happiness of society. Self-help in this respect was closely associated with character-building and the Puritan work ethic: 'I believe all true and genuine culture', said William Priest at the opening of Liverpool Public Library, 'consists essentially in hard work.'[132] By the next generation, however, public library pleas for self-help were couched more in idealistic terms of realizing one's own potential. In 1911 a public library supporter in Dartford explained that: 'Every mind was made for growth, for knowledge, and its nature is sinned against when it is doomed to ignorance.'[133] By 1932 the librarian Stanley Jast was able to write of the public library's power to offer 'self-development in an atmosphere of freedom'.[134] Jast's analysis of the purpose of the public library drew on the pre-1914 idealist quest for a society permeated by culture. Culture at its most authentic was that which an individual *freely* developed for personal and communal enlightenment. As the Mayor of Darlington put it in 1885, in introducing the theme of self-culture to an assembly commemorating the opening of the town's public library, the new facility would increase 'the literary zeal of the inhabitants of Darlington' and 'promote an ardent desire for true culture which they all needed to have'.[135] The pursuit of culture in which idealists engaged had a spiritual basis – humanity was bound together by a metaphysical force hungry for cultural sustenance. The pursuit of human perfection was linked, according to this proposition, to a metaphysical perception of ultimate good. Utilitarians, on the other hand, tied as they were to the potential of social or environmental engineering, could not conceive of the power of the inward spirit. Their interpretation of self-realization, good citizenship and cultural improvement was essentially secular. In respect of these issues idealism thus represents a leavening of utilitarianism. Expressed motives of public library provision, such as those involving citizenship, self-help and the acquisition of culture, were modified. They became less earthly, scientific and utilitarian, and more metaphysical, romantic and spiritual in the meaning they conveyed to public library promoters and patrons.

Utilitarians had promoted, partly through the agency of the public library, a citizenship which emphasized individuality within social relations. Idealists, on the other hand, in supporting the communal nature of the public library, subordinated individual to social commitments. They preached the sanctity of a common life. The pursuit of culture was a 'shared' concern. The public library epitomized this commitment to 'share'. Its support of the university extension movement – which encapsulated the notion of the permeation of culture – should be noted in this regard. So should the perceived voluntary basis of library provision. Speaking in 1928 at the fiftieth anniversary celebration of the opening of Wigan Public Library, Stanley Jast reminded his audience that the plentiful 'book harvest of the present' was essentially the result of past 'communal support', as well as 'communal sacrifice' and the readiness of individual citizens to 'rate oneself [to accept an extra financial burden through voting for higher local taxes] as a voluntary act of goodwill'. In the true spirit of cooperation it was said in 1869 of the new public library in Doncaster that it stood for the notion 'that no one in the social scale is or can be independent of one another; that all hang together'.[136]

What citizens got out of the public library, as opposed to what they had to put in, also encouraged a communal attitude. In this regard, T. H. Green's analysis of the influence of fiction, the staple diet of the free library reader, is worth surveying. Green's first impression of the modern novel was negative: 'Instead of idealising life ... it sentimentalises it. It does not subordinate incidents to ideas.'[137] However, despite his perception of the novel as an inferior work of art (partly because novels involved copying, and copying was not art),[138] he did assign it an important social purpose. He believed it could remove 'barriers of ignorance and antipathy'. He was thinking here largely of class misunderstanding. The novel, he said, 'brings man nearer his neighbour, and enables each class to see itself as others see it'. Citizens were thus released from the 'tyranny of sectarian custom' – something which made the modern novelist a great 'leveller'.[139] In pursuing the idea of the social ramifications of novel-reading, Green estimated that it did make a contribution to the pool of self-realized culture which humanity had a duty to increase. He accepted that, 'While the minds of the lower orders acquire from novel-reading a cultivation which they previously lacked, the higher seem proportionately to sink.'[140] But the fact that novels wrought a modicum of culture in the majority of people, and acted negatively on only a minority of citizens, meant that the balance sheet of culture, in respect of novel-reading, remained 'in the black'.[141] Moreover, the modicum of culture which 'the many' received was beneficial in terms of being 'preparatory to some higher development'.[142] For Green, therefore, the reading of fiction, whether it was encouraged by the public library or other means, was to be welcomed – because it contributed to a common life in terms of both the shared stock of culture and social cohesion.

Further, as 'light' reading came to be more accepted in the decades immediately preceding the First World War the utilitarian belief that all culture and education should have a practical outcome was gradually watered down. At the same time, the idealist belief in the intrinsic worth of aesthetic culture, as well as in its value as a counteractive force to the rush and monotony of industrial life and work, gained ground. Thus, in 1902 the *Church Family Newspaper* could be found advocating the reading of library books because they relieved pain and suffering of body and mind; served as 'a means of distraction from everyday life ... to beguile the tedium of hours of sickness and loneliness and sorrow'; and, at the end of a hard day, provided workers with something 'that will amuse and interest them, and soothe their tired brains'.[143] Again, in Doncaster in 1869 it was said that the library provided 'some rest from daily toil, some recreation from the constant strain from work, some relief from the monotony of labour, which ... is apt to become routine and mechanical'.[144] To a large extent, therefore, the public library and its books offered a respite from the hectic pace of an urban existence. As buildings, public libraries provided tangible, yet also spiritual, havens in a world of industrial frenzy and, to borrow William Ewart's phrase, 'social collision'.

The idea of the public library as a spiritual retreat was shared by the man who took over from Ewart as the movement's chief parliamentary advocate. Sir John Lubbock (later Lord Avebury), at an opening ceremony in 1891, told his audience that 'A library is a true fairyland, a very palace of delight, a haven of repose from the storms and troubles of the world.'[145] Lubbock was a strident and active supporter of public libraries.[146] In 1903 he celebrated, in a moralizing tone, the fact that there were now 'public houses' all over the country 'not for the sale of beer, but for the free use of books'.[147] His support was given in the true spirit of idealism; his personal philosophy encapsulated the idealist vision. It was said that he 'possessed a missionary zeal for the intellectual enlightenment and moral elevation of the public'.[148] Lubbock was adamant that education not be about the utilitarian assimilation of 'dry facts'.[149] Rather he stressed the aesthetic aspects of learning, not least as an antidote to the ravages of industrialism upon the individual spirit. Thus, he wrote that whereas the primitive savage and the agricultural labourer both had a varied existence,

> The man who works in a shop or a manufactory has a much more monotonous existence ... He is confined, perhaps, to one process, or even one part of a process, from year's end to year's end. He acquires, no doubt, a skill little short of miraculous, but on the other hand, very narrow. If he is not himself to become a mere animated machine, he must generally obtain, and in some cases he can only obtain, the necessary variety and interest from the use of books.[150]

Lubbock conceptualized the spread of learning in terms of an idealistic Commonwealth of culture. He viewed the literature of England not only as 'purer' and 'nobler' than any other, but also as the birthright and inheritance of every Englishman.[151] The great readers of the next generation would not be the doctors, lawyers, shopkeepers or manufacturers, but the labourers and the mechanics.[152] With this in mind he took it upon himself to produce a list of his one hundred best books, for the guidance of his mutually dependent and growing Commonwealth of culture.[153] By invoking, in one of his commentaries, the biblical 'tree of knowledge' Lubbock imbued his yearning for a community of culture with a metaphysical dimension, as befitted a pure idealist:

> We may make a library a true paradise on earth, a Garden of Eden without its one drawback; for all is open to us, including, and especially, the fruit of the Tree of Knowledge, for which we are told that our first mother sacrificed all the Pleasures of Paradise.[154]

For Lubbock the fruit of the 'tree of knowledge' constituted life's highest pleasure. He saw the process of acquiring knowledge as a 'privilege and a blessing';[155] and of all the privileges enjoyed by society, he stressed that 'there is none, perhaps, for which we ought to be more thankfull than for the easier access to books'.[156] Lubbock believed, above all, that the privilege of reading good books, as provided by public libraries, produced the highest pleasure possible: communal feeling. The purpose of learning, he said, was 'to root in us the feeling of unity with our fellow-creatures';[157] true happiness came from being dutiful to others. He thus declared that: 'To shut oneself up from mankind is in most cases, to lead a dull, as well as a selfish life. Our duty is to make our self useful.'[158] Linking oneself to others in the context of an idealistic 'whole' made the individual happy which, in turn, contributed to the general happiness.[159]

Idealist notions of a common life, as expressed through the philosophy of Lubbock and the public library movement he promoted, became more difficult to convey after the outbreak of war in 1914. With the war came the idea that the infiltration of German philosophy into British intellectual thought had proved pernicious.[160] The assertion that the state (its purpose enshrined in institutions like the public library) formed the 'supreme community', no longer rang true. To an extent, therefore, the reputation of the public library was perhaps weakened by having been positioned within the civic network. However, it is possible that it was also weakened by its intention of disseminating culture. Its emulation of the German commit- ment to culture is clear. In 1886, Lord Acton wrote that 'the familiar type of German scholar ... [was] the man who complained that the public library allowed him only thirteen hours a day to read'.[161] In the half century before the First World War the English public library thought it recognized a similar raging thirst for culture – in the realms, moreover, of 'sweetness and light', as opposed to a residual though not unimportant demand for non-spiritual, vocational training. After 1914, as a result of the sullied image of strategies designed to enlighten the masses with culture, the public library was never again able to recapture fully its role as primarily a dispenser of spiritual learning. However, the fact that, commencing in the First World War, and certainly in the context of the public library, utilitarian impulses mounted a counter-offensive against idealism should not discourage a detailed analysis of the aesthetic, spiritual concerns of the public library before 1914. Such concern ran deep; nowhere more so, paradoxically, than in the desire of a stereotypically non-spiritual, materialist-oriented middle class to evolve an authentic, robust and, above all, distinct cultural identity.

CHAPTER 8

CULTURAL CONCERNS: IN SEARCH OF AN ASSERTIVE MIDDLE CLASS

In the previous chapter it was argued that pre-1914 idealism remained firmly attached to the virtue of free enterprise. The alternative view, the replacement in the late nineteenth century of stereotypically atomistic utilitarianism by collectivist idealism as the major philosophical determinant of social policy, might be construed as a softening of middle-class commitment to market industrialism and aggressive individualism. This anti-enterprise hypothesis would certainly prove useful, tactically, to ideologues in our own time seeking a restructuring of the economy disadvantageous to the proponents of welfarism. Of the multifarious explanations of Britain's economic decline one of the most celebrated has been the surrender of enterprise. It is argued that in the twentieth century, most notably after 1945, enterprise was 'crowded out' by the enthusiasm of Keynesian economic managers and humanitarian idealists for directing scarce resources to an unproductive welfare state.[1] Others attribute the problem of enterprise to deeper historical roots located in the second half of the nineteenth century, thereby allowing the history of the romantic period of industrialization before 1850 to be mobilized in a justification of modern market economics.[2] It is argued that the response of entrepreneurs to international competition and to developing technology based on science was not sufficiently adventurous, in stark contrast to the thrusting qualities of business heroes of proto-industrialization.

The shortcomings of entrepreneurial leadership, as discussed in Chapter 6, have been clothed in an accusation of 'failure'. This accusation has followed hard on the heels of other negative assessments of the pre-1914 industrial middle class. First – a view that has the longest tradition – the culpability for the squalor which characterized industrial society has been directed towards excessive bourgeois greed and materialism (a view which, it is worth contemplating, stands in sharp relief to the economic failure thesis noted above). Second, this bourgeois avarice seriously damaged cultural standards in the arts and in traditional learning, to such an extent that the Arnoldian criticism of philistinism has stuck. Third, in the face of continuing aristocratic influence no pure, rigorous middle-class cultural identity was allowed to emerge: the values of traditional élites were emulated.

In total these denigrations represent a bleak picture of social evolution on the part of the substantial middle class. On the other hand, considerable space has been devoted by historians to the confident and aggressive way in which middle-class power-holders 'despatched' an emergent and potentially threatening working class. In particular, attention has focused – though some would say over-zealously – on the success of strategies of social control. It appears, therefore, that the social history research of recent years has wished to have it both ways: assessing the middle class as having failed, yet at the same time presenting it as having succeeded in constructing a strong class identity in relation to the lower orders, and thus to the industrial society as a whole.

This chapter mobilizes evidence from the history of the public library to defend the culture of the Victorian and Edwardian middle class. Two aspects of culture are at issue here. The first is the social control notion of 'culture as ideology', which incorporates the term 'mass culture' (including its inference of manipulation) constructed through communication medias like public libraries. The second is the 'whole way of life' interpretation of culture, which, as the most appropriate for the study of the public library, is best understood by adopting the Tylorian line of evolution from barbarism – a combination of scientific materialism and intellectual-aesthetic improvement leading to a civilized society (as discussed in Chapter 1). Middle-class support for public libraries, as argued in Chapter 6, displayed an aggressive pursuit of prosperity; to which was added not only a keen attachment to intellectual culture, as was demonstrated in Chapter 5, but also, paradoxically, a desire to reduce squalor in the tradition of the Romantics. In combination, these concerns helped to fashion a way of life – a culture – which was authentic and free from overbearing aristocratic influence. Indeed, in the context of the public library, considering the anti-privilege utilitarian foundations of the institution, it is difficult to accept any other interpretation of middle-class consciousness. Regarding the latter, a middle-class solidarity is clearly evident in the mechanisms, including public libraries, which various elements adopted for the control of those yet to be rescued from barbarism. In this sense 'culture as ideology' – in effect the ideological position of the middle class – shades into that aspect of culture which describes the entire personality of the social group. However, the example of the public library shows that while the notion of the transmission of culture is not invalid it does require careful treatment and refinement. The idea that the public library and other agencies held the working class in a cultural tutelage is simplistic. The institution was as much concerned with the creation of a liberated working-class culture. This purpose sat alongside the concern to create a genuine middle-class culture. Public libraries thus represented a story of cultural success, for both the middle and working classes.

Middle–class 'failure' versus 'success'

The idea of middle-class 'failure', in Britain and elsewhere in Europe, has been a point of recent heated debate for historians.[3] The debate on the shortcomings of the English middle class was invigorated in the mid-1960s by Anderson and Nairn.[4] Their aim was to explain the absence of revolutionary ambition among the working class by analysing the relationship between aristocracy and bourgeoisie in the period since the political upheavals of the seventeenth century. Although they acknowledged the importance of 'history from below', they claimed it was only relevant if accompanied by an analysis of 'history from above'.[5] England was perceived as having (in the seventeenth century) the least pure bourgeois revolution of any experienced by a major European country. It was an agrarian and not an urban élite which emerged triumphant from the Civil War and the Glorious Revolution, and which became, in the eighteenth century, a virile capitalist class through agrarian innovation. The industrial bourgeoisie which emerged during the Industrial Revolution was confronted by the simultaneous appearance of a threatening proletariat. To safeguard its future, the bourgeoisie gravitated towards the aristocracy, which had its own reasons for welcoming such an alliance. As Nairn explains:

> Afraid from the beginning of the power of the new labouring masses brought into being by and for the Industrial Revolution itself, intimidated by the spectacle of the French revolution and all it signified, the English middle class quickly arrived at a 'compromise' with the English ancien regime. Because of its basically capitalist structure (tenant-farming carried on by wage labour for profit) and its absence of legal definition as a privileged estate, the aristocracy was such that a 'compromise' of this sort was possible.[6]

The result of this amalgamation was a 'fusion' of cultures, but one in which that of the old order dominated. The middle class sought to ape aristocratic values, which enjoyed a renaissance under late-nineteenth-century imperialism; extending and strengthening the Empire placed a premium on the aristocratic trait of leadership, and supercharged the monarchy.

These cultural arguments have been adopted by some historians in attempting to explain a perceived malfunction in the British economy over the past hundred years. The dominance of traditional over utilitarian values produced a 'gentlemanly' capitalism which eclipsed manufacturing and extractive industries.[7] Enterprise was slanted in the direction of commercial and financial pursuits related to the international economy. The British educational system was 'geared not to the production of industrial managers or scientist, but to the socialization of gentlemen into the cultural symbols of an elite'.[8] The stigma attached to 'getting one's hands dirty' pushed some of the ablest into careers in the City (of London) – an enterprise complex which concerned itself less with industrial degeneration at home than with the movements of capital in world markets. Arguably, the dominant capitalist objective had, since the early nineteenth century, been to make Britain not the 'workshop of the world', but the 'Venice of the nineteenth century'.[9] Most of the largest fortunes of the nineteenth century were made in commercial ventures and financial services: there were few equivalents in Britain of the industrial robber barons in the United States. Hence, it is argued, industrial business cannot be seen to have evolved a fully independent culture or cohesive consciousness.[10] Rather, there was:

> a slavish imitation of the landed aristocracy and its mores in the countryside or the West End of London, and most certainly in the life-styles of their sons and grandsons.[11]

However, the cultural assumptions underpinning the case for entrepreneurial failure have been challenged.[12] The argument that the industrial middle class failed to develop a coherence commensurate with its economic power should not, perhaps, carry with it the inference that commercial capital, by contrast, achieved a high degree of homogeneity and agreement. As Daunton has pointed out, the City was itself divided on a number of fronts, not least that of protection.[13] Further, one of the implications of the argument that cultural fusion produced gentlemanly capitalism is that a residue was produced of inward-looking industrialists, uncultured and, typically, Northern and of a Nonconformist persuasion. The image was caricatured by Dickens in his *Hard Times* (1854), a powerful socio-economic criticism of the Victorian industrial world. The local schoolmaster, Mr Gradgrind, was made to epitomize all that was inhumane in Coketown. He wished to imbue his students with 'facts' so as to assist their material existence: Dickens tells us that he 'had a particular pride in the phrase eminently practical, which was considered to have a special application to him'. When Mrs Gradgrind discovered that her children had been doing something as 'fancy' and as useless as peeping at the local circus she told them to 'Go and be somethingological directly'.

For many reasons the stereotyped image of insensitive and uncultured élites in Northern industrial towns is misplaced. First, although Gradgrinds could be found in such towns, they surely also existed elsewhere: in debating the Public Libraries Bill in 1850, the protectionist Tory member for Lincoln, Colonel Charles Sibthrope, was reported to have said that 'he did not like reading at all, and he hated it when at Oxford'.[14] Second, early industrialists were as likely to be Tory and Anglican as, stereotypically, dull, utilitarian and dissenting.[15] Third, commerce (and agriculture) and industry were symbiotic, not insulated from each other.[16] Fourth, there has been an imprecise definition of the aristocratic values which industrialists supposedly fell short of or which they clumsily aped. Fifth, social critics like Dickens were publicists who had an interest in exaggerating fictional characters like Mr Gradgrind.[17] Sixth, the anti-business literature and sentiments, which critics like Weiner cite, have a strong pre-industrial heritage,[18] and are even evident during the heroic era of proto-industrialism. Finally, as W. D. Rubinstein's *Capitalism, Culture and Decline in Britain 1750–1990* (1993) argues, the entire case for the cultural failure of an ignorant, unsophisticated middle class, unable to adapt and innovate in an increasingly complex, competitive and technical climate, is based on the acceptance of manufacturing as the leading sector, historically, in Britain's industrial experience. Yet recent work (for example, P. J. Cain and A. G. Hopkins, *British Imperialism, Vol. 1: 1600–1914, Vol. 2: 1914–1990*) has pointed to the historic strength, and long-term domination indeed, of (mostly southern led) commerce and finance; manufacturing being a mere interlude in an otherwise non-industrial saga. In other words, if the story of industrial development is denied a label of success, it follows that middle-class entrepreneurial and associated cultural failure is similarly difficult to ascribe.

Further, it is not certain that the social critics whom purveyors of the 'gentlemanly' capitalism argument sometimes invoke were consistent in their denigration of middle-class businessmen. Matthew Arnold can, on the one hand, be found labelling the middle classes as Philistines. In his essay *Democracy* (1861) he wrote:

> They want [lack] culture and dignity; they want ideas. Aristocracy has culture and dignity; democracy has readiness for new ideas, and ardour for what ideas it possesses. Of these, the middle class has the last only: ardour for the ideas it already possesses. It believes ardently in liberty [for example, religious toleration], it believes ardently in industry; and by its zealous belief in these two ideas it has accomplished great things ... Now, all the liberty and industry in the world will not ensure these two things; a high reason and a fine culture.[19]

On the other hand, in his essay *Equality* (1878), Arnold perceives a cultural refinement among the middle class: 'Serious knowledge, high accomplishment and refined taste' were to be found in a large class of gentlemen in the professions, the services, literature and politics, and to these 'a good contingent is now added from business also'.[20]

Arnold does not distinguish here between business which was commercial and that which was industrial. However, even the latter – so often scorned as the haven of anti-aesthetic greed – displayed a high degree of cultural achievement. Art was bought, and often commissioned, by entrepreneurs. A significant amount of the work of the Pre-Raphaelites, for example, originated with a thematic request from a wealthy, 'new money' patron. Bell argues: 'From the very first these painters [the Pre-Raphaelites] found their market among those whom contemporaries would have considered an ignorant and philistine clientele, the "self-made" men and manufacturers of the North.'[21] Making money and engaging in cultural pursuits were clearly not incompatible. As Seed writes of Manchester's wealthy unitarians, they showed that it was possible 'to be an ardent disciple of political economy and of Wordsworth's poetry, to ruminate in a Byronic melancholy on the ruins of Greece while one's capital accrued surplus back in Lancashire'.[22] Moreover, cultural identity could be preserved even if exposed to traditional ways of life. Gunn writes:

What needs to be emphasised in analysis of the nineteenth-century bourgeoisie is the importance of not assuming a simple correlation between social behaviour, ideology and economic practice. It was perfectly plausible for a Victorian industrialist to ride with the local hunt, build himself a castle in the country, and adopt a 'neo-feudal' pose of paternalistic employer, without consciously compromising in any way the imperative of capitalist production or class commitment.[23]

A bulging bank balance derived from industrial enterprise by no means inferred cultural malnutrition. In fact, accumulated industrial capital was often put to good work in the name of culture. The philanthropic whims of business élites found culture to be a highly suitable receptacle in terms of its beneficial effects on the moral fabric of the populace, on the status of civic life and on the confidence of the middle class.[24] Moreover, cultural institutions like public libraries helped to knit together disparate sections of a town's middle class.[25] They were not simply sites of contact for manufacturing social cohesion between the respectable classes and the masses, but instruments of negotiation on questions of middle-class politics, religion and sources of income (distinction to be noted between industrial, financial and merchant capital).

That efforts were required to deliver middle-class cohesion is exemplified by the struggle over the domination of the Leeds Library in the first half of the nineteenth century.[26] The Leeds Library was founded in 1776. Membership was limited to 500 and was transferable. From the outset the membership and the committee were dominated by an Anglican élite, a state of affairs which continued into the nineteenth century by virtue of the transferability of shares. Even in the 1830s and 1840s, when radical dissenting politics began to make its mark, other cultural formations were consistently thwarted in their attempts to gain influence over library policy. For example, Anglican censorship was stiff: in 1844 Mill's *A System of Logic* (1843) was rejected on four occasions by the committee. The early history of the Leeds Library demonstrates a lack of cohesion in the ranks of the middle class. In this particular cultural institution rifts were not resolved. However, this was not the case in other sites of cultural endeavour, such as the public library, which was so often acclaimed as a melting pot of religious and political differences.

Concern for cultural improvement was something which straddled the middle class. This was the case not only in matters such as literary and art appreciation, which constitute the traditional, popular definition of 'culture'.[27] Science, too, was considered a cultural pursuit. T. H. Huxley argued that although there had been a tendency to idolize 'rule of thumb' as the source of prosperity, science made a contribution to culture in its powers of observation and criticism; skills which were, moreover, intrinsically 'human'. Science, he said, ennobled character and could be used to help analyse social action (culture in the anthropological sense).[28] Romantic idealists are usually seen as the arch-critics of scientific materialism, yet Arnold concurred with Huxley in seeing science as a road to culture. He had faith in its civilizing power because it was conducive to what he called human 'expansion' (the full and free development of individual existence): 'curiosity', he said, was in an intelligent being 'natural and laudable'.[29] He believed that all learning, even in the humanities, had a scientific basis, if it was 'systematically laid out and followed up to its original sources'.[30] Further, it has been argued that science stood for moral edification because of the values of improvement and utility associated with it. But it went further than polite knowledge; it expressed the values of technological progress, of intellectual enlightenment and of modernity. Science became an expression of the cultural values of the new manufacturing élite even if the latter related more to its symbolic value than to its practical applications.[31]

Victorian middle-class culture was 'authentic' in that it was able to fashion a separate identity for itself. Whereas Anderson and Nairn might have been correct in seeing utilitarianism as too narrow and culturally deficient to underpin effective hegemony, they overlooked the influence of political economy – the articulated ideological justification of science, machinery, progress and materialism.[32] The power of bourgeois ideas about economic life was pervasive, particularly in the absence of alternatives. Moreover, economic ideas were often sanctioned by ideas on moral conduct. This was especially true of religion: divinity and economics ran together.[33] In an early critique of the Anderson–Nairn thesis, E. P. Thompson disputed the idea that the aristocracy continued to be the political masters: the best-remembered politicians are Lloyd George, Peel, Disraeli, Gladstone and Bright, not Lords Derby, Palmerston or Salisbury.[34] Moreover, the political self-confidence and sovereignty of the bourgeoisie in its native urban setting was unquestionable. These factors point to a robust bourgeois culture with an authentic and distinct ideology. It was the middle classes, many believed, who provided the prosperity upon which social stability rested. As Arnold wrote:

> The great middle classes of this country are conscious of no weakness, no inferiority; they do not want anyone to provide anything for them. Such as they are that believe the freedom and prosperity of England are their work, and that the future belongs to them.[35]

The argument that the middle class was successful culturally (aesthetically cultured) and possessed an authentic, distinct cultural outlook (or identity) gains support from the evidence of public library history. Aspects of public library development strongly contradict the idea of middle-class failure; though not to the extent of suggesting that all middle-class groups, by any means, championed culture.[36]

Despite extensive working-class use, public libraries were essentially institutions of the middle classes: provided by them, run by them, and used by them in considerable numbers. It is a paradox of the middle-class failure argument that London – where businessmen were presumed to have assimilated culture – was so slow to develop its municipal libraries. In the

City, however, a library was established and made public. In 1869 it was urged that a new building for the Guildhall Library would 'respond to the cravings of every wise and thoughtful man that the Capital of this vast Empire may be the Capital of Intelligence'.[37] It was said that

> Among the bankers, merchants and tradesmen of our City there are men who have felt it an honour to enrol themselves in the ranks of literature, whose fame hereafter will depend more upon their contributions to literature and science than to anything they may have done in the accumulation of wealth; such men – honoured and respected in all circles, possessing the confidence and respect of their fellow-citizens – we call upon to be up and doing in this matter.[38]

This enthusiasm for culture among the wealthy middle class did not, according to one account, spread to some industrial areas. It was stated in a history of Sheffield libraries that such matters

> seemed to have no meaning to the men of most influence in Sheffield, whose standard of culture was low compared with other towns. They had no conception of the many-sided value of books, which had so little, in their view, to do with 'getting on'.[39]

Elsewhere, however, the substantial middle class supported public libraries. Wealthy and powerful groups in Bolton gave generously for the establishment of a town library in 1853.[40] Manchester's library was described in a letter to the mayor as an institution 'worthy of the wealth and power' of the city.[41] When a wealthy merchant, William Brown, donated new buildings in Liverpool in 1861 it was said that: 'Commerce is again lending her protectorate to literature and to art, as in the brief prime of Florence and of Genoa.'[42] It was argued that the benefaction belied the image of commercial men as 'hard fisted' and 'grasping', who made 'their desk their altar, and their money their God'. Rather, it showed that 'commerce does not confine its energies within its own and special range'.[43]

Commercial and industrial enterprise alike gave financial support to public libraries. By virtue of the large sums involved the main source of this support – though subscriptions for establishing libraries came from all classes – was the *haute* bourgeoisie. Those who ran libraries – committees and librarians – were largely from intermediate middle-class groups, generally less wealthy and influential. (Throughout much of the period the working classes were not represented on committees.[44]) Library committees saw, from time to time, political squabbles.[45] But it was not as intense a battleground for rival ideologies as housing and education.[46] Many library committees, unlike other committees, had a high proportion of non-sectarian co-opted members chosen for their standing as local moral leaders or as 'men of letters'.[47] Businessmen also found their way on to library committees. Councillor W. H. Reeves, Chairman of the Northampton committee and the person responsible for the new library building of 1910, was described as 'an energetic man of the best business type ... it is fair to say that he has enhanced that reputation, and also local opinion of his ability for public affairs, by the splendid way he has pioneered this scheme.'[48] Despite the reservations of Edward Edwards, who argued that men of education were little represented on councils and hence gave little support to library schemes, it was generally the case that those who ran libraries had a not insignificant respect for culture.[49] Public libraries were the shop windows in which was displayed the burghers' liking for culture. As the *Islington Gazette* stated in discussing the suburb's new library system:

> The prosperity, intelligence and virility of a municipality may be gauged by the number and nature of its institutions. Point to a borough's educational and philanthropic institutions and its other agencies for uplifting the people, and it will not be difficult to judge of the characters of the men to whom the administrative work of the district is instructed.[50]

The cultural purposes for which middle-class providers established and ran public libraries were shared by middle-class user groups. The extent of the latter should not be underestimated. The Norwich reference library was described shortly after its opening as 'for the learned, and interesting to the learned only'.[51] The 'Rochdale pioneers' objected to a public library for the town because they had already provided reading rooms for their own members and found little point in taxing themselves for an institution which they believed was for use by trading, shopkeeping, middle and upper classes.[52] Further, it should be stressed that middle-class interest in social reform (including library provision) was not solely based on control imperatives: the middle class might benefit directly from social policy. As John Bright stated, 'there was no greater folly than starting a coach by which the middle class will not travel'.[53]

But was middle-class use based on motives for establishing public libraries other than a pure desire for cultural affluence? It has been argued that the establishment of institutions such as public libraries was merely a defensive reaction to stinging accusations of philistinism – no more than a boastful exuberance, in keeping with Ruskin's observation that 'advancement in life' actually meant 'becoming conspicuous', not through 'the mere making of money, but the being known to have made it', in this respect via spending on culture.[54] In her study of leisure in late Victorian and Edwardian Bristol, Meller has written that the 'provision of cultural facilities devoted to the formal concept of Liberal Culture ... sometimes became the spearhead of an attempt to salvage the reputation of the city'.[55] The same motive has been attributed to early-nineteenth-century initiatives in 'mucky' Leeds.[56] Perkin has argued in connection with middle-class spending generally that it was socially emulative of aristocratic consumption patterns.[57] Some such spending on cultural artefacts and pursuits was possibly suspect on these grounds: an enthusiasm for books could have been a symbolic expression of social position rather than a product of intellectual interest, as was often the case in the classical era, where to possess a private library (each of Cicero's 18 villas had one) was a normal badge of luxury and achievement worn by the crude and newly rich.[58]

The argument that middle-class culture was mostly for 'show' is, however, questionable. For example, there is no financial evidence to support the idea that the wealthy bought art *only* as an investment[59] (articles could only 'impress', after all, if they commanded an appropriately high price). Though a certain amount of spending and enterprise in the cultural field (private and public) was no doubt symbolic, it should not eclipse a sincere motive of educational advance for the middle classes. 'What a sad want I am in of libraries, of books to gather facts from!' wrote Carlyle.[60] He and others were enthusiastic in establishing their own shared repositories of knowledge.[61] As late as 1887 a Sunday School promoter could state:

> I have not found the best libraries in the houses of my richest friends ... How many middle class houses one enters to find that the library is represented by a few volumes, chiefly presents or school prizes, in a little bookcase.[62]

Clearly, middle-class library supply did not meet middle-class literary demand. Hence, public libraries found both support and a user base among the middle classes. Backed by civic finances, extensive and useful collections could be formed, thereby offering a service which the fiction-orientated subscription libraries could not.

Notwithstanding the intense competition between municipalities to produce institutions symbolic of a town's supremacy in civic and commercial achievement, public libraries were genuine attempts to satisfy a yearning for cultural profit among middle-class providers, administrators and users. For some, materialism was a mere 'stepping stone to those intellectual endowments and higher characteristics which were the real guarantees of national progress'.[63] In suggesting a public library for Blackpool the borough's Treasurer argued that 'While looking after the rolling shilling they must not neglect the cultural and intellectual side of a progressive community.'[64] The public library was frequently presented as a medium for transmitting into the present the accumulated wisdom of the past: the 'work of perfection', as it were, could not proceed without reference to recorded cultural achievement. Carlyle wrote that

> Every one able to read a good book becomes a wiser man. He becomes a similar centre of light and order, and just insight into things around him. A collection of good books contain all the nobleness and wisdom of the world before us.[65]

Emphasizing the rich history of culture was the aim of the library's stock generally, and the local history library in particular. Local collections did not just add to a sense of civic unity, they also safeguarded the past cultural achievement of the locality. The custodial role of the public library was epitomized by its local history department, which stressed a respect for the endeavours of citizens' ancestors. Librarians at a Library Association summer school in 1897 were told:

> Nothing needed more enforcing at the present time than a sense of reverence for the past, and nothing was more likely to excite reverence than the sight of an

early printed book, and of the exquisite care with which the early printers did their work.[66]

Other aspects of service which evinced culture were music libraries, and the art galleries and museums run in conjunction with public libraries. Art galleries and museums deserve extensive separate consideration, which cannot be afforded here. But something can be said about music departments which, though not found in every medium or large library, certainly made an early appearance in some. The circulation of music by public libraries began in 1859, in Liverpool.[67] By 1913 Bournemouth had a music library of over 3000 volumes housed in a lavishly styled separate room in the new library recently opened.[68] In 1892 it was estimated that about thirty public libraries stocked sheet music and scores: these included Manchester, Birmingham, Leeds, Sheffield, Dulwich, Peckham, Reading and Norwich. It was reckoned that the 'middle classes are doubtless, on the whole, the most frequent borrowers, but in several towns the working class are also keenly appreciative of the advantages of the music department'.[69]

That science could aspire to cultural status was reflected in public library content and ethos. The benefactor of the Liverpool Public Library, William Brown, linked science – which, in its stock and in its museum, his new library promoted – with civilization:

> How immeasurably increased has been our intercourse amongst ourselves and with the world, by our intelligent engineers and our skilled workmen! All this is the work of enlightened pioneers – men of science. Without their aid mankind would be semi-barbarians.[70]

Further, as discussed above, Passmore Edwards's motives in supporting public libraries showed how the institution could accommodate science as both a practical and a cultural pursuit.

Culture disseminated through the public library was also espoused for its economic benefits (as Chapter 6 demonstrated). At the opening of the Loughborough free library in 1886 a local manufacturer was reported as having called for a 'higher mental culture' to fight German competition precisely because

> the people of Germany were so much higher cultivated. They were cultivated scientifically, artistically, literally, and generally, and if they wished to hold their own as the greatest producing nation of the world, they could only meet the competition of the Germans by raising themselves in every point at least to a level with, and he hoped to a higher level than, the Germans of the present time.[71]

Culture clearly had a 'value'. Those who have disputed the argument that the nineteenth-century middle class in some way 'failed' have themselves failed to spell this out. While they are correct in seeing that the middle class, in various degrees, succeeded as entrepreneurs, as aesthetes and as possessors of a separate cultural identity – and evidence from the public library supports this argument at every point – there is little recognition of the contemporary awareness that culture could generate material gain. In fact the middle-class respect for the culture of improvement coincided with money-making to produce a distinct cultural identity which was not compromised by the values of traditional élites. This was evident in the recognition that cultural institutions, like public libraries, could serve as aesthetic solvents for the squalor which the pursuit of prosperity had produced.

Culture as a solvent for squalor

The symbiotic relationship between humanistic culture and materialism was clearly visible in the public library movement's reaction to industrialism's squalor – defined here as a combination of environmental ugliness and the alienation (arising from narrow, monotonous work) which accompanied the division of labour. At face value this statement is a paradox: the public library's role as an agency for aesthetic enlightenment did not fit with either its dispensing of practical knowledge to fuel industrialism or its civic prominence in *industrial towns*. This apparent contradiction was captured in the way Dickens's Mr Gradgrind viewed his local Coketown library in *Hard Times*:

> There was a library in Coketown, to which general access was easy. Mr Gradgrind greatly tormented his mind about what the people read in this library ... It was a disheartening circumstance but a melancholy fact that even these readers persisted in wondering. [Wondering being the cultivation of the sentiments and affections, as opposed to mechanical, utilitarian learning.] They wondered about human nature, human passions, human hopes and fears, the struggles, triumphs and defeats, the cares and joys and sorrows, the lives and deaths of common men and women! They sometimes, after fifteen hours' work, sat down to read mere fables about men and women, more or less like themselves, and about children, more or less like their own. They took Defoe to their bosoms instead of Euclid, and seemed to be on the whole more comforted by Goldsmith than by Cocker. Mr Gradgrind was forever working, in print and out of print, at this eccentric sum, and he never could make out how it yielded this unaccountable product.

Perspective was given to the ugliness of industrialism in Thomas Carlyle's *Past and Present* (1843), which made a notable impact on Victorian culture, finding an audience (including Ruskin and Engels) particularly among those 'spiritually adrift and anti-materialistic'.[72] As a counterpoint to preoccupations with money and progress Carlyle drew a picture of an aesthetic, ordered, hierarchical life in a twelfth-century English abbey. It was a society governed by justice and an aristocracy of talent in contrast to the vulgar, democratic impulses which Carlyle thought were afflicting early Victorian society.[73] Carlyle's evocation was based on an idealized vision of the past and a dislike of profit-seeking, atomistic society; sentiments previously articulated by Carlyle. His aim was to draw attention to 'a superior heroic society that indicted the prosaic present'.[74] He had no apparent sympathy with the pursuit of material ends:

> We have profoundly forgotten everywhere that 'cash-payment' is not the sole relation of human beings; we think, nothing doubted, that it absolves and liquidates all engagements of man ... Verily, Mammon-worship is a melancholy creed.[75]

He yearned for a world rid of squalid mass manufacturing:

> How silent ... lie all Cotton-trades and such like; not a steeple chimney yet got on end from sea to sea! ... Side by side sleep the coal-strata and the iron-strata for so many ages; no Steam-Demon has yet risen smoking into being.[76]

Later social critics drew greater attention to the effect of machine production on human existence. J. A. Hobson, a critic of unfettered capitalism, wrote of the mind-numbing monotony which industrial employment brought with it: division of labour robbed workers of the power to think and reason. He explained that

> The defect of machinery, from the educative point of view, is its absolute conservatism. The law of machinery is a law of statical order, that everything conforms to a pattern, that present actions precisely resemble past and future actions. Now the law of human life is dynamic requiring order not as valuable in itself, but as the condition of progress. The law of human life is that no experience, no thought or feeling is an exact copy of any other. Therefore, if you confine a man to expending his energy in trying to conform exactly to the movements of a machine, you teach him to abrogate the very principle of life.[77]

The problem in the late nineteenth century was that machines were proliferating and getting quicker, even in old industries like cotton spinning. Yet, this acceleration was not matched by a commensurate increase in the workforce: that is to say, labour was being increasingly sweated.[78]

There is evidence that the late nineteenth century was marked by an intensification of labour in both old and new production methods. On more than one front workers found themselves under increasing pressure, affecting the basic quality of life.[79] William Morris neatly captured these trends when he described how machines had 'driven men into frantic haste and hurry' instead of relieving them of work burdens as the early political economists had predicted.[80]

But it was not just life at work which became increasingly sordid. Industrial development had also stained the environment: life was noisier and dirtier. The idealist Samuel Barnett in 1894 wrote:

> Cities increase and the country becomes more and more empty. Observers shake their heads as they walk through the long, dull streets, and breathe the close air, and see the pale faces of the people ... Their hearts sink at the thought of the future, and they find themselves saying that cities will crowd in a blacker, incessanter line, that the din will be more, the trade denser, and that they will never see an ennobling sight, or drink of the feeling of quiet again![81]

William Morris in his *News from Nowhere* (1890) commented:

> England was once a country of clearings among woods and wastes, with a few towns interspersed ... It then became a country of huge and foul workshops and fouler gambling dens.[82]

The suggested antidotes to squalor were manifold, and included recreation via the public library. By the late nineteenth century the idea had taken hold that recreation did not have to be purely rational.[83] This was in keeping with Dr Johnson's definition of 'diversion': 'something that unbends the mind by turning it off from care'.[84] As society became richer, it was said, the opportunity for recreation increased, not just in terms of higher mental culture,[85] but also in terms of reading for amusement (non-fiction as well as fiction). The public library complemented the increased demand for recreation in an industrial environment. Public library books on natural history, for example, were quite popular. This was not only the result of Darwin's influence but was connected with the long-standing belief that 'God made the countryside, man the towns'. Thus, unitarians were advised to make regular visits to the countryside or natural history museums to bring them nearer to God;[86] and a museum (in association with a library) was proposed for Exeter partly because 'natural science leads to religion, natural religion leads to revealed religion ... they thus form one golden chain leading us to God'.[87] But interest in natural history could also be autonomous and secular, as in the case of the early eighteenth-century handloom weaver William Heaton, who, along with fellow-workers, formed a library on insects, and collected various items of natural science interest.[88] Further, public library books on travel and geography – illustrating far-off lands untouched by machines – were also popular free library issues. In her advocacy of public libraries Janetta Manners related that 'Those who dwell in towns love to read of beautiful countries, and many look forward to the possibility of some day visiting fresh scenes.'[89]

But it was not simply by means of their contents that public libraries countered squalor. Although the librarian Zebedee Moon might have complained that his Leyton library was subjected to 'the fiendish yells and other ear splitting noises interjected by the human voice and mechanical instruments of torture',[90] public libraries generally provided, as argued in the previous chapter, havens from the hectic activities of life. As Stanley Jevons noted, 'To many a moneyless weary man the Free Library is a literary club; an unexceptional refuge from the strife and dangers of life.'[91] The public library's appeal to loafers says much, indeed, about the serene, unmolesting atmosphere therein.

The public library also combated 'the dullness of the daily life of the masses'.[92] It afforded the workman

> a relief form the dullness and monotony of his task ... By perusing the books in the library, the working man can obtain for nothing, a relief a thousand times preferable to that which he seeks at such a cost in other places. In establishing such an institution you open out to the working man an inexhaustible fountain of the most refined and most refining pleasure.[93]

It was suggested that library recreation might counter dehumanizing specialization:

> In our manufactures the division of labour was carried to a high pitch. This

added, no doubt, enormously to the rapidity of production and to the excellence of workmanship, but it also tended to cramp the mind. To counteract this books were more and more necessary.[94]

The public library's role as a solvent for squalor was seemingly contradictory. On the one hand the institution was a product of industrial society: it became a common feature of industrial towns and was frequently underwritten by industrial benefactors. On the other hand it was firmly rooted in the social criticism which accompanied industrialism. An answer to this contradiction would appear to coincide with one of the traditional reasons for providing the various amenities which improved the quality of urban living. 'Who can quarrel', wrote William Morris, 'with the attempts to relieve the squalor of civilised town life by the public acquirement of parks and other open spaces, planting trees, the establishment of free libraries, and the like.'[95] An unfettered pursuit of the 'cash nexus' was simply not possible. It was counter-productive in that it produced problems of control. Hence, an amelioration of conditions was important if capitalist production was to continue. In Northwich the public library was assisted by the manufacturer John Brunner in this same paternalistic spirit (he provided holiday pay, pensions, sickness benefit, continuing education and a working men's club); one that characterized the running of his concerns.[96] In such instances a public library was a point of intersection where scientific materialism and culture met. It is true that this has been seen as a point of collision. At the opening of a branch library in East London in 1931 the novelist H. M. Tomlinson, in a statement that contained no awareness of the compatibility of culture and materialism, said that public libraries

> were important in this age of machinery when standards of truth and beauty were in danger of going under a mass of tarmac and electric pylons, and individuality and personality were going under the same steam roller.[97]

Yet the pre-1914 public library represented a marriage, with inevitable moments of friction admittedly, between the two.

The public library's cultural concerns assisted capitalism. From the 1870s onwards references to the public library as a centre of 'sweetness and light' abound. Thomas Greenwood wrote in 1886: 'Centres of light are these libraries, if not sweetness, and the sweetness lies in the appreciative light in which they are held.'[98] Matthew Arnold, the author of 'sweetness and light', might have criticized industrialism, but his aim, and that of most other social critics of the age, was a spiritual reform of capitalism, not its extinction. The public library ideal occupied the same standpoint, straddling a line between mindless materialism and passionate radicalism.

The history of the public library raises questions about the assessment of the pre-1914 period as an era of great 'loss' brought about by the greed of uncultured Gradgrinds. A degree of 'loss' and a presence of Gradgrinds cannot be denied. Yet the picture is not simple but textured. Industrialism's major promoters were not stereotypes: a respect for culture can be identified, at any rate, in their encouragement of the public library. It was possible for a town to be both wealthy and intelligent, and led by 'industrialists in search of gentility'.[99] What needs to be emphasized is not the middle class's subordination to aristocratic values and its nervousness in the face of rising working-class power; but its strength, confidence and independence, and the implications which these had for social stability.

The middle-class pursuit of social stability was based, in part, on a desire to commune with nature. The latter was characterized by an inherent harmony and stability. By instilling society with the 'natural' it too could become stable, while at the same time retaining its hierarchy. The Ruskinian idea of providing beauty where once there was squalor was encapsulated in the public library ideal.

In 1890 William Booth (founder of the Salvation Army) published his *In Darkest England and the Way Out*. The title was indicative of the social criticism of industrialism and the commensurate desire to smooth its rough edges. One route out of the darkness was the public library, a civilizing agency which aimed to dissolve squalor and improve the quality of life. It is thus a paradox of the pre-1914 public library that it was so often promoted by 'money' which was destructive of the environment, yet can also lay claim to being one of the first tax-based 'green' institutions. In this respect it was illustrative of a middle-class culture which was not narrow and dull, but dynamic and textured.

Social control and hegemony

The argument that early public libraries were authentic and successful middle-class institutions begs the question of their status as instruments of social control; in that the working class, which formed the bulk of the readership, were exposed to the hegemonic ambitions of middle-class providers and their subaltern library managers. This is certainly the clichéd view of modern public librarianship, as often rumoured by librarians with little interest in library history. It is doubtful, however, if this cliché can withstand critical analysis. Before such an analysis can be made, however, a brief assessment of the social control thesis, without reference to the public library, is required.

Social control is a term diffuse in meaning. One historian has denigrated it as having claimed 'the title of top historical cliché of the 1970s', when historians first mobilized the notion seriously.[100] Historians have undoubtedly misused the term. It remains, none the less, a neat sociological description of the mechanism for the regulation of social behaviour; for whenever

> we use such terms as persuade, restrain, discipline, coerce, penalise, reward, direct, manage or regulate to describe aspects of the activities of individuals, groups, organisations or society, we are talking about the exercise of social control over peoples' bodies, minds and behaviour.[101]

In this respect control pervades our lives – employers control workers, librarians control readers and parents control children (or vice versa). For some theorists this pervasiveness hinders the formulation of theories explaining human behaviour. Thus, a narrower version of social control has also found favour. As Cohen argues, social control is

> the organised ways in which society responds to behaviour and people it regards as deviant, problematic, worrying, threatening, troublesome, or undesirable in some way or another.[102]

The keyword here is 'organised', indicating an adhesion to formal, pre-meditated methods. Clearly the concept of social control is contentious, with conceptualizations ranging from the exercise of dictatorial power to questions of power underpinning commonplace relationships and behaviour.

To elaborate, it is worthwhile turning to the thoughts of a modern sociologist. 'For society to survive', writes Popenoe,

> it must have ways to condition the actions of people to make them want to conform to social norms most of the time. This is accomplished with mechanism or processes of social control. There are two main types of social control process: internal and external. One consists of those internal processes that cause people to be self-motivated to act in a conforming manner. The other consists of external pressures on people to conform through the use of various formal and informal social sanctions.[103]

The internal social control highlighted by Popenoe occurs when people accept as part of their identity, and usually without reservation, the norms of a group or society as a whole. Informal controls are the result of how people perceive the potential for negative reaction from others: that is to say, self-regulation through the fear of peer response to disapproved, deviant action. Taken together, these internal and informal aspects produce the definition of social control in its classical and enduring sense, as formulated by the pioneer sociologists around 1900.[104] It was not until the 1930s, under the impact of the Great Depression and the rise of totalitarianism, that sociologists departed from these formulations of social control as they became fascinated and preoccupied with issues of power. It was then that social control was 'transformed into a pejorative term which came to mean conformity and social repression'.[105] It is in this sense that many historians have made use of the term. They are interested in the policing of people not by themselves but by others (which in a class society would logically mean the implementation of methods for exercising class control).

In recognition of the fact that techniques for the policing of others can be both punitive and oriented towards a 'softer' approach of indoctrination or persuasion, Barrington Moore has pointed out that

> To maintain and transmit a value system, human beings are punched, bullied, sent to jail, thrown into concentration camps, cajoled, bribed, made into heroes, encouraged to read newspapers, stood up against a wall and shot, and sometimes even taught sociology.[106]

'Main force' is naturally essential to the maintenance of social authority, but it is not effective as the only means of control. Even in the most abrasive of dictatorships punitive coercion needs to be complemented by the organization of consent via psychological means – if only to control the personnel of the coercive organs themselves.[107] Mostly, it is this 'softer' dimension which has intrigued historians and sparked an interest in social control as a theory explaining the historical development of subordinate groups.

The period which has attracted most analysis by theorists of social control coincides with the birth of the public library movement. This was the mid-Victorian era of unprecedented material progress and social peace – though agitation and protest were by no means absent[108] – which Briggs has referred to as 'a great plateau bounded on each side by deep ravines or dangerous precipices'.[109] Historians have pointed to the emergence during this period of an élite stratum within the ranks of the working class;[110] others, it must be said, have disputed the existence of a cohesive 'labour aristocracy'.[111] It is argued that structural shifts in the economy precipitated a new breed of worker skilled in the processes demanded by technical change.[112] Recognizing these changes, so the theory develops, bourgeois ideologues sought to incorporate the skilled élite of the 'engineer's economy' into their own value systems by stressing the efficacy of the free market, as well as virtues of self-help, independence, respectability and thrift. The means of transmission in fashioning the 'buttress' class was the establishment by the middle classes of institutions for the working class.[113] Such a strategy was crucial in view of the fact that historically – and certainly during the Chartist era – the artisan classes had displayed a tendency towards radicalism.[114] One historian has referred to the post-1850 'embourgeoisement' strategy as a process of 'liberalization': a replacement of radicalism by establishment, liberal political values.[115]

Other analysts have disputed the power and perception of middle-class activists in engineering radical changes in working-class culture.[116] Cultural control was undeniably attempted. Power is a fact in all societies. Social interaction, including the exercise of power, occurs through the exchange of messages which are 'formally coded, symbolic, or representational events of some shared significance in a culture produced for the purpose of evoking a significance'.[117] Those who control the communication of messages can become more powerful.[118] If power-holders open the sluice gates to the reservoir of their culture, so the argument continues, then they are attempting to irrigate and tame potentially threatening territory as yet untouched by the dominant ideology.[119] It does not necessarily follow, however, that irrigation is successful. In the nineteenth-century cultural control appeared to be, on occasions, highly effective, as Joyce has argued in respect of the Lancashire mill town.[120] However, all control strategies are open to detailed criticism.

The social control thesis, as applied to nineteenth-century class relationships, can be questioned on a number of counts. First, controllers were not a homogeneous group. Social control implies the existence of a single middle-class ideology. Yet, the middle class was a 'social composite embracing men and women of widely differing conditions and experience'.[121] It was divided into fractions of capital, and was itself subject to class division.[122] Middle-class *reformers* might have been more enthusiastic about such control efforts as social class mixing than members of their class generally; it is possible that the bulk of the middle class did not wish to recruit a distasteful working class into its ranks.[123] Controllers were not in any case conspiratorial. As F. M. L. Thompson has argued, employers managed workers, the police controlled crowds and ministers led their congregations; but they did not do these things with any significant degree of collusion.[124]

Second, values such as respectability, thrift, self-help and independence were not exclusively middle class. Each had a long tradition within working-class, especially artisan, culture. For example, private education run for and by the working classes was considerable; before the Education Act (1870) and ensuing compulsory attendance obliterated it.[125] Further, middle-class views of working-class respectability were mythical; respectability was not a constant, but could be worn or discarded as easily as a collar and tie.[126] This indicates a degree of autonomy inconsistent with notions of effective social control.

Third, attempted control sometimes resulted in problems which required further control efforts.[127] For example, the erection of Board Schools brought considerable protest. The deliberate driving of railways through troublesome working-class areas created enlarged problems of control arising from arbitrary demolition and eviction. It may well be, therefore, 'that what were intended as controlling agencies [and efforts] produced incidental effects which most people would regard as beneficial, while at the same time failing in their ostensible purpose'.[128] Social reform as a means of social control should be mentioned in this respect. Social reform has been interpreted as a medicine for an ailing social system. The beneficence of the state is presented to the working class, in piecemeal fashion, so as to siphon off discontent, and to protect fundamental social arrangements;[129] or, as Stansky has put it, 'The powers that be are rarely so rigid that they will snap rather than bend; they attempt to preserve the old by accepting the new on their own terms.'[130] But social reform *can* produce quite the opposite to the desired effect. This is most clearly the case with education reform, which can serve to liberate.[131] As Lenin wrote: 'Study is essential for intelligent, thoughtful and successful participation in the revolution.'[132]

Fourth, it is misleading to present the working class as helpless and naive victims of bourgeois-directed hegemony. While some influences might have been absorbed unwittingly, others might have been accepted deliberately because they suited the interests of the recipient.[133] There is evidence, for example, that organized labour was 'not a passive subject of elite manipulation, but tended to adopt a positive strategy of exploiting and optimizing the progressive potential of welfare measures', a chief attraction of which was their municipal basis and the anti-capitalist ethos this inspired.[134] A young boy might have joined the local church football team run by a moralizing cleric, not for religious but for sporting reasons.

Fifth, social control suggests the possibility of social equilibrium – that control efforts can restore a stable situation which has broken down. This does not fit with a Marxist analysis of ongoing social conflict. Arguably, institutions designed to spread middle-class values, far from being sources of stability and equilibrium, were in effect incitements to conflict with an emergent working-class consciousness. Institutions such as mechanics' institutes and working men's clubs did indeed become battlegrounds for power, as working-class users rejected aspects of middle-class patronage and management.[135]

Control attempts, generally, often had to be revised: controllers were not, after all, quarantined from those they were attempting to hegemonize. Control was negotiated.[136] Workers were not stuck in a subordinate mode, unable to resist bourgeois influence. Rather, the working class reproduced dominant values in a modified, negotiated form which took into account the needs of the working class. The reality of class hegemony in the nineteenth century was not its existence or absence, but its limited nature. Subversion was contained, but institutions protective of working-class culture were not eradicated.

This argument challenges the classical Marxist analysis, noted above, concerning the dissemination downwards of a dominant ideology from a reservoir of culture fashioned by powerholders. Marx argued that those who controlled the means of economic production also controlled all social relationships, including the means of intellectual production. Hence, the values of society's most powerful group – in the nineteenth century the bourgeoisie – permeated society. This is too simplistic a formulation. More persuasive is the notion of hegemony formulated in the inter-war period by the Italian communist Antonio Gramsci. The essence of Gramsci's hegemony theory is the idea of negotiation. As he explained:

> The fact of hegemony undoubtedly presupposes that the interests and tendencies of the groups over which hegemony is to be exercised are taken into account, that there is a certain ... compromise ... that is, the ruling group make sacrifices of an economic-corporate kind, but it is also indubitable that such sacrifices and such compromises cannot affect what is essential.[137]

In other words, faced with an oppositional culture, a ruling group can only maintain hegemony if it recognizes the interests and intentions of that culture and, moreover, enters into an accommodation with it. Moreover, in accommodating elements of the oppositional culture, the culture of the dominant group is by definition adjusted. However, the fact that only some elements of the oppositional culture are accommodated means that it too has had to compromise on values and intentions. Hence a negotiated position is reached. A process of social negotiation has taken place which, in Gramsci's terminology, represents a 'passive revolution'. Clearly, the idea of hegemony achieved through social negotiation smacks less of successful conspiratorial manipulation by dominant groups than of a shared cultural experience – a 'whole body of practices and expectations over the whole of living'[138] – manufactured, in part, by the cultural influences and interests of subordinate groups. The maintenance of cultural leadership through negotiation rather than obliteration has positive implications for social stability. Gramsci's scheme is an 'optimistic theory, implying a gradual historical alignment of bourgeois hegemony with working-class interests'.[139]

The pre-1919 public library fits well with Gramsci's interpretation of hegemony. Public libraries were vehicles of negotiation between middle-class efforts to influence popular culture, and working-class determination to resist such change. The public library mounted cultural control efforts; but, ultimately, these did not achieve the success anticipated, and were at times even counter-productive.

The evidence of attempted control is extensive.[140] Libraries were bestowed a potential for dissolving radicalism. It has been argued that they were initiated as 'an anodyne to the labouring masses' to prevent the rise of another radical movement like Chartism.[141] At the opening of the Manchester Public Library in 1851 the town's mayor argued that free literature was a reward for those members of the working class who had not supported the disturbances of the 1840s; the middle classes could not do too much for the 'well-disposed', he said.[142] The public library offered citizenship to those willing to eschew political extremism. Socialist literature was not welcome on the shelves. In 1889, the library committee at Portsmouth withdrew J. Traill Taylor's *The Veil Lifted* – an illustrated work describing the latest developments in spirit photography. The link in this context between spiritualism and radicalism should be noted. Spiritualism in the late nineteenth century was strongly plebian, anti-Christian and politically radical; it was a 'nursery culture' for socialism.[143]

Public libraries sought moral regeneration. It was hoped they would act as institutions of counter-attraction to rid society, among other things, of 'tipsy rowdies', to quote a supporter in Lambeth in 1874.[144] In 1893, in support of the continued Sunday opening of free libraries, it was argued that were it not for the availability of reading on this day current users

> would spend the afternoon or evening in perambulating lazily about the streets or in the parks, and as intellectual idleness is the father of follies, they would, as hundreds do at present, degenerate from lightness of behaviour into sinfulness.[145]

Restricting access to undesirable literature was another means of improving morals. Censorship of material on moral grounds was a feature of the public library from its inception.[146] 'What is indispensable', said the Portsmouth librarian in 1886, 'is that the pabulum provided should be morally wholesome.'[147] Librarians issued and exercised strict rules of conduct as if to emphasize moral responsibility. It has been argued that public libraries were institutions highly attractive to labour aristocrats seeking decorum, respectability and moral uplift.[148]

Public libraries were promoted as ideal places for social class mixing beneficial to the eradication of class conflict. Supporters of a library for Darlington reported that

> every man, and every woman, and every youth feels that the library belongs to him of her as much as to any one else; they go to it as a place in which they have a common share, and all classes meet and mingle on a level of common privilege: there is no gradation of first and second and third class ... Free libraries form, therefore, a standing protest against the system of caste, and supply some help towards bridging over the gulf between classes, which philanthropists so much deplore.[149]

The notion of the institution as a site for class reconciliation is one of the strongest themes which emerges from the evidence. The public library was intended as a 'conservative link ... between the manufacturer and the operative'.[150]

However, drawing on the weaknesses in the social control thesis outlined above, it is evident that middle-class control strategies did not necessarily hegemonize working-class users.

Evidence of working-class independence rather than subordination in public libraries can be drawn from fiction. The character of Myles, a young factory hand, in J. Fothergill's *Probation* (1879) is hardly an example of a socially controlled worker. Chapter 4 of the novel is set in the reading room of the Thanshope Free Library, where Myles is a frequent visitor to read such material as the *Westminster Review*, but also to admire a young woman who also often used the library. One evening in the library – when Myles was pleased to be reading an article which made 'a particularly hard hit at the governing classes' – the son of a local Tory manufacturer, Frederick Spenceley, strutted into the library and commenced making advances to the woman Myles had for so long admired. The woman was noticeably ruffled by these advances, but Spenceley persisted none the less. Myles intervened, telling Spenceley that he would fetch the librarian and tell him that Spenceley was not a member; for which a ten shilling fine was payable. 'Confounded radical place, this ... Not fit for gentlemen to live in', exclaimed Spenceley as he withdrew. In this instance it was not the worker who was downtrodden, but the 'would-be dandy in his gloved, perfumed, over-dressed vulgarity', thereby turning the tables on the social control thesis.

It is likely that workers used their local library for what they could get out of it: for example, as a means of self-education and liberation from the very forces, ironically, which had helped to provide the institution. The use of libraries for liberating purposes should not be underestimated. Autonomous working-class libraries had a long tradition. In Nottingham in the 1830s and 1840s, for example, a number of operatives' libraries had been formed, some in public houses: 'All these libraries appear to have been spontaneous working-class products; there is no sign of initiative by members of the upper and middle classes.'[151]

The establishment of libraries to quell disorder and reduce the incidence of bad conduct frequently backfired. In keeping with the theory that control leads to deviance, not deviance to control,[152] libraries often attracted individuals and groups intent upon causing trouble. At one extreme this deviant behaviour was violent, as in the case of the troublesome characters who kept busy the ex-policeman attendant at the Old Kent Road Public Library (c.1907-14).[153] Often located in rough neighbourhoods, libraries could be construed by the alienated as symbols of unwanted authority. Thus, in 1889, Southampton's librarian often had to be escorted home by a policeman to prevent him from being manhandled by local roughs.[154] On the other hand, the challenge to authority could merely be a matter of youngsters 'larking about'.[155] In the 1870s, at the Norwich Public Library, youths made constant attempts to embarrass the librarian by requesting Tom Paine's *Rights of Man*, which was reserved for adults only, the librarian having referred to it as a 'wicked book'.[156] In 1895 two youths, aged 18 and 19, were fined ten shillings each for disorderly conduct and swearing in a Leeds branch library.[157] In 1885 the services of a policeman were requisitioned to patrol the reading room of the Darlington Public Library, where the noise was at times what one 'might expect in a Corn Exchange, but not in a reading room'.[158] In 1871 the Exeter Library Committee was informed that

> much disturbance had been caused by the noisy and disorderly conduct of certain young men, and that several had been turned out by the officials from the Reading Room.[159]

These and other episodes of deviancy in the public library mark the institution out as a place where citizens, if they so wished, could express their resistance, both playful and violent, to the notion of citizenship as conceived by authority seeking to regulate their behaviour. This tended to negate the socializing role which the institution set itself. To an extent, the strategy of suppressing deviancy via formal cultural altruism was counterproductive.

None the less, to view the public library as a battlefield would be incorrect. It was more a theatre of cultural struggle characterized by a high degree of negotiation and compromise. This was evident in the long-running debate over the worthiness of fiction for inclusion in collections. Many public librarians – in Gramsci's terminology and in the context of this aspect of the discussion 'subaltern intellectual deputies' of the dominant class[160] – held élitist presumptions concerning the reading tastes of the working classes. The fear was that the mass consumption of literature, epitomized by the cheap romantic novel, would lower standards. This anxiety was expressed by Matthew Arnold when he wrote: 'All ages have had their inferior literature; but the great danger of our time is that this inferior literature tends more and more to get the upper place.'[161] A great deal of support for the public library was derived from the promise that the institution would help to cleanse society of its propensity to consume inferior literature. Such support would not have recognized present day models of service, which attach considerable importance to satisfying consumer demands. It has been argued that the general failing of nineteenth-century public librarians to monitor their market, in terms of the popularity of fiction, was owing to the slow pace of professional development; one aspect of professionalism being the assessment of user needs.[162]

The unwillingness of public librarians and their committees to assess user demand has been viewed as an exercise in control. However, as a manipulator of its audience in the field of literary taste the public library can hardly be seen to have been a *successful* agency of élite culture. This is not just because some librarians were no doubt sympathetic to the more popular forms of literature (the emergence of the cliché that to read *something*, even of poor quality, was better than to read *nothing*, should be noted here). It is more the case that the self-appointed protectors of higher literature were only partly successful in preserving the public library's élite cultural reputation. Not only fiction, but popular fiction too, was accommodated by the public library. A major reason for this was explained by *Library World* in 1904:

> The ratepayer pays for the library, and they will have the books that please them ... It is no use lining the shelves of a free library with the recondite works of scientists, educationalists and philosophers, or the classical treasures of the past, if people prefer the last brand-new flimsy tale that comes hot from the press.[163]

In the context of the fiction debate, especially in the quarter of a century before the First World War, the public library was made to take note of the consumer democracy dimension of the utilitarianism which had founded it. This did not result in the abandonment of any tendency the public library might have had towards paternalism or social engineering. Rather, it represented a negotiated settlement between the two alternatives of promoting the public library as either purely élitist or radically popular. What was obtained was a mixture – in varying proportions, in different places, at different times – of these extreme options. This was preferable in the eyes of high culture to rampant philistinism. It was similarly acceptable to popular culture, which, it must be emphasized, also engaged in a process of negotiation and compromise.

But to view the adjustments forced by the fiction issue as a surrender of the culture of improvement would be wholly wrong. The autonomous, voluntary consumption of serious literature for self-improvement was an abiding feature of Victorian and Edwardian working-class culture. When the Woolwich Trades Council and Royal Arsenal Cooperative Society jointly approached the Woolwich Local Board of Health in 1895 for help to establish a library they did so because they 'wanted a library to supply them with literature that would supplant 'penny dreadfuls'.[164] Serious reading, such as science, did not need to be pushed down readers' throats.

For example, John Urie, a Paisley handloom weaver and printer, recalls in his autobiography how in the 1820s he relished being taken by his father to lectures on science and engineering at the Encyclopedia Club.[165] The public library complemented the democracy of science. As the town clerk of Salford was reported as saying at the opening of the library and museum there in 1849, 'Science was universal and not exclusive ... it would therefore be a disgrace ... if there was anything like exclusiveness in any part of their scheme.'[166] By virtue of its universal appeal, science, as purveyed through the public library, could not conceivably be labelled social control – and much the same can be said of the pursuit of knowledge generally in libraries. Men of culture, said Matthew Arnold, were the 'true apostles of equality'.[167] Indeed, idealist exhortations concerning the diffusion of culture and the common good were aimed at all in society, not merely at disaffected, subordinate groups. After all, the greater the numbers pursuing culture, the nearer was brought the realization of the Absolute; thereby leading to the ultimate fulfilment of both the human spirit and its metaphysical creator.

In both its utilitarian and its idealist phases the broadly democratic, egalitarian ethos of the public library transcended blatant control imperatives. In respect of political knowledge, for example, the public library professed a neutral approach. This, naturally, did not apply to radical conceptions of politics as held by Chartist or, later, socialist antagonists. However, the vast majority of readers would have accepted, before entering the library and thus exposing themselves to establishment norms, that politics could only be realistically pursued within the narrow parameters of the existing limited liberal democracy.[168] Utilitarians and idealists invited all in society to share in the prevailing political citizenship, the public library being an important tool in this regard.

A major objective of the public library's middle-class providers was the stabilization of the social system. This was not to be achieved solely through the imposition of formal social controls upon a deviant, oppositional culture; for such controls were in practice less effective than the idealized expectations that preceded them. Also important was the vigorous middle-class quest for unity, confidence and cultural integrity; to be satisfied by the enlightenment, materialism, social cohesion and universality inherent in the public library. Although these aspects of the public library's ethos can be construed as cunningly disguised mechanisms for coercing sub-cultures – and may have fulfilled this role to a degree – they were more a reflection of a successful middle class pursuing cultural objectives, without an exaggerated reverence for other cultures, and convinced that its destiny and that of social stability coincided. Social stability achieved through a culture of improvement was a concept understood not just by the middle class, but by the working class too. The realization of this concept was clearly, for the public library, an ambitious social strategy. However, it was a strategy which many of the institution's librarians, contrary to the cloistered image bestowed upon them, were willing to follow.

CHAPTER 9

LIBRARIANS: THEIR SOCIAL ENGAGEMENT AND CONTROLLING DISCOURSE

The textured and complex nature of the motives behind early public library provision – as seen in its utilitarian and idealist underpinning, and in its apparently contradictory combination of social criticism and a material purpose – is not something which has been consistently recognized by either historians or public library theorists. The same might be said of the motivation of the institution's most visible promoters: its librarians. The male (mostly) and female librarians who, before 1914, worked at the coal-face of cultural dissemination have often been accorded a verdict of ineffectiveness. Throughout its history public librarianship has been berated, frequently from the inside, for not fulfilling a more 'educational', 'material', 'useful', 'relevant', 'communicative' role – the words in the literature might change, but the intention to convey a sense of redundancy does not. Contrary to this sentiment, it is argued in this chapter that stereotypical accusations of detachment should not be applied lightly to the profession of public librarianship in the pre-1914 era; though neither should an assertion of librarians' social engagement obscure an assessment of them as controlling experts in command of a discourse of profession-alism and power.

The scorning of librarians has a long tradition. As an undergraduate at Edinburgh University (1809–14) Thomas Carlyle dismissed as useless his 'gerund-grinding' professors and turned, instead, to self-directed reading in the search for his 'spiritual Delphi'. His tutors became the 'multifarious set of books' which he devoured in the university's library. In pursuing the path of self-education Carlyle received little help from the librarian. The library was chaotic: it had no catalogue. Moreover, the librarian was a clergyman who, said Carlyle, 'took the pay as a perquisite and did nothing'.[1] The tendency to denigrate the calling of librarianship has persisted. As one commentator has written:

> The term librarian still conjures up for many the totally inaccurate caricature of an elderly spinster, with glasses and hair in a bun, who spends all day either stamping dates in books or arranging books on shelves.[2]

While the self-image of librarianship has contained an element of 'people-directed' service, the public and media image has often been of 'cold introversion, pedantry and anti-life tendencies [that] are rampant.'[3] The specific area of public librarianship has not escaped criticism. For example, in 1942, Lionel McColvin's prescription for a reconstructed post-war service included the lament that 'reference [public] library work is the outstanding failure of British Librarianship'.[4] Such accusations of 'irrelevancy' have not faded. As late as 1987 the public library was said to be failing in its attempts to meet 'useful' information needs: lack of marketing techniques in the winning of business clients being offered as a prime example.[5] In the same year, a voice from the political right accused the public library of selling its readers short owing to its complacent and inward-looking nature.[6]

The danger to authentic historical analysis which the adoption of hindsight poses should be familiar enough to prevent modern media images of public librarianship being imposed on the profession's entire history. As far as the professionals of the pre-1914 era are concerned, it is misleading to assume the existence of an anti-social characteristic. Such an assumption perhaps derives from the need of early public librarians to popularize their service in a hostile environment. In order to retain a foothold in society's climb towards higher cultural achievement, public librarians could not afford to ridicule popularity. They thus opted, primarily, to satisfy a generalized readership – groups with the least generalized needs, the recognition of which by librarians would have been evidence of a more sophisticated professional approach, were marginal to the contemporary service model. The chief librarian at Harlesden articulated the tendency to 'generalize' and the lack of sophistication in 'needs analysis' when, in 1904, he explained that 'as public libraries must cater for all sections of readers the amount spent on one particular class of books [he was referring specifically to technical literature] must necessarily be limited'.[7] The failure of public librarians to segment their readership (though they did discriminate to a degree) should not, however, be taken as evidence of a desire to be distanced from society and its problems.

Status

In the absence of any great urgency to specialize, public librarianship in its early years struck a mostly literary pose. This was no doubt interpreted by some as confirmation of an in-built Arnoldian sense of detachment and condescension. The librarian Ernest Savage, in recalling his own pre-First World War career, wrote that 'Public librarians thought more of Shakespeare and musical-glass culture than of the crafts.'[8] The tendency of recent commentators to tarnish pre-1914 public librarians with the same brush, one of irrelevance and ineffectiveness, must not hide the fact that librarianship in general, including public librarianship, did incur some contemporary criticism. Librarians found the image of their being mere custodians of books a hard one to shake off.[9] The primacy of the 'custodial' role was firmly entrenched. In 1835, the librarian of the British Museum, Sir Henry Ellis, told the Select Committee investigating his institution that 'Librarians are living catalogues, and can usually be consulted to great advantage.'[10] Out of this 'gatekeeper' role, some accusations of stuffiness, exclusivity and reclusivity inevitably arose. To quote the colourful Savage again:

> The mid-Victorians, in their later days that my impatient youth knew, never dreamt of librarianship as it is, let alone as it will be. They hadn't the imagination. Their idea was books in a college, a club, a big country house; books kept apart for the wealthy ... books shut away in glossy cases more effectively than on chained open shelves. They took timid mousehole peeps at librarianship through the dust and the musty snuff from calf bindings.[11]

In a similar vein Melvil Dewey likened the English librarian to a 'superior servant ... appointed to look after the silver', keeping the books in immaculate condition, but discouraging rather than encouraging frequent disturbance of them.[12]

The image of the librarian as a custodian of high literature, exhibiting a passive, detached, fortress mentality, must have done something both to damage the corporate image of the public library and to determine the low status which the profession is seen to have endured throughout the period under consideration, if not beyond. Low status was reflected in poor remuneration, made even poorer in the light of the long hours which had to be worked, particularly in the early decades of the profession's existence. When Dartford Public Library advertised the vacant chief librarian's post in 1915, as many as 54 applications were received for the paltry £120 annual salary.[13] Clearly, a great many people believed that they could carry out what they considered to be the undemanding duties of a librarian, for which a commensurately low salary (relative to other professions) was paid. Despite the literary bent of the profession not all librarians could be regarded as quality bookmen (the word 'bookwoman' hardly applies as the profession was overwhelmingly male). In some instances librarians were no more than caretakers with little bibliographic knowledge. When the vacant librarian's post at Erith was advertised in 1905 the four applicants were a senior clerk, a sub-librarian, a library assistant and a school caretaker.[14] The duties of the librarian at Oldham's North Moor Branch involved looking after the building and grounds, while cleaning the premises was the responsibility of his wife.[15]

Although from the outset public librarians developed a sense of professional 'expertise', a process of professional 'training' barely existed; the idea prevailed that the best path to professional achievement was not one of theoretical education but the practical experience of 'learning by doing'.[16] Librarians did follow the example set by other professions in changing from apprenticeship to student-apprenticeship.[17] But generally this affected neither the profession's popularity nor its status. The Library Association held its first exams in 1885, for which only three candidates entered. In some following years there were no exam entrants at all. Although an improved and revised syllabus was introduced in 1904, along with Library Association correspondence courses, the numbers obtaining professional qualifications before the First World War remained extremely low. The study of librarianship, perhaps because of its highly practical content (in this respect it did not correspond to the traditional nature of technical education in Britain), was unattractive to potential librarians who could achieve their goal just as easily by time-serving. For employers too, professional qualifications commanded a low premium. As late as 1931 a survey of 177 public library authorities revealed that only 67 of these made promotion conditional on the possession of certificates obtained at library school or through the Library Association.[18]

Many of the first generation of public librarians had no prior experience of work requirements beyond their own use of libraries: silverplaters, booksellers and school teachers were all drafted into service.[19] Even in the 1880s, when second-generation librarians might have been expected to originate from within the service, appointments were being made from other professions, as at Northampton and Portsmouth where ex-army men were enrolled.[20] When H. E. Curran, deputy librarian at Liverpool Public Library, applied for the chief's post, he told Ernest Axon that he 'feared a rank outsider's appointment – journalist, barrister, university swell, or poor relation'.[21] An analysis of Munford's *Who Was Who in British Librarianship 1800–1985* (1987) shows that public librarians who did not enter the service straight from school did so from a wide variety of occupations. Prior occupations included teacher, chemist's apprentice, mill worker, watchmaker, watch engraver's apprentice, bookseller, bookseller's assistant, clerk, policeman, journalist, farmer, railway signalman, paperstainer, silverplater's apprentice, postman and photographer. Whether these librarians, or others, entered the profession as, variously, the 'refuse' of other callings, the 'failures' and 'refugees' of other occupations, is uncertain. Samuel Barnett wrote: 'The preachers whose words halt, the teachers who cannot keep order, but whose mission is to preach and teach, could find their vocation as librarians.'[22] If what Barnett postulated often occurred, then the 'fortress' mentality of public librarianship becomes more understandable, in that lack of confidence or thwarted ambition may have triggered 'defensive' attitudes.

Self-confidence is not seen as a quality which the profession displayed in abundance. The move towards professional training had been intended to boost the self-image and social standing of librarians, but was not a success. Whereas in the United States a full-time college of librarianship was founded as early as 1887 (by Melvil Dewey at Columbia), British librarians had to wait until 1919 for such an institution (founded at University College London). Yet the pool of practical experience from which librarians were expected to rise was not of the highest standard. Before the First World War it was the 'elementary schoolboy, and not always the brightest, [who] often became the library assistant, and from the material available librarians had to be made'.[23] Boy assistants were frequently castigated by the public for their poor service. A Darlington reader urged that 'the boy with the piping voice and shrewd face, who acts as assistant, be taught a little more civility than he seems to possess when ordinary folks go for books'.[24] When, in 1905, Islington became the first authority to employ *only* female assistants it did so partly because the 'experience in the big towns of the north was that boys were a failure'.[25] Arguably, the prevalence of 'closed access' libraries in the period under consideration did nothing to improve the skills of assistants. Hence, pay remained low, a state of affairs compounded by the statutory rate restriction, which gave little room for manoeuvre in the wages bill. Thus, an unfavourable two-way process evolved, in that low pay attracted a sub-standard workforce which, in turn, was unable to command any higher reward than its skill level dictated. Wages for assistants were indeed low: 5 shillings per week starting pay at Eastbourne (1896); and 25 shillings per week at Darlington for a junior assistant at the top of his grade, even after 11 years of service.[26]

The low standards and rewards, which operated at the base of what professional structure can be said to have existed, had a detrimental effect on the pay and conditions of professional librarians; this owing to the fact that most were expected to become professionals by rising through the poorly paid ranks. It was not only that years of enduring low pay taught librarians to expect little reward for their work (even someone at the top of the profession, like James Duff Brown, could command only £300 per annum in 1904).[27] As important was the fact that professional was separated from non-professional largely by mundane time-serving and not by a barrier of prestigious qualifications.

The status of library work was not enhanced, arguably, by the emergence of female staff. Whereas in the nineteenth century library work was virtually a male preserve (unlike in the United States), by the 1920s, largely because of the war, around 50 per cent of assistants were female.[28] Male librarians began employing women in preference, ostensibly, to inefficient boy assistants. The idea was common that women were suited to library work because of certain supposed innate qualities, such as domesticity, orderliness and a willingness to serve. One male Croydon reader, protesting at the poor work of boy assistants, called for the employment of women who would at least keep the shelves dust free![29] Women were also seen to 'surpass men in the moral virtue of patience', which naturally made them ideal material for library work.[30] James Duff Brown argued that he employed only female assistants, for efficiency. In reality, the prospect of cheap labour – 'Chinese labour', as one Islington councillor described the policy[31] – was an attractive one for a rate-capped service. Even when women got a chance at the top, cheap labour appeared to be a factor determining their success. Sidney Webb, a member of London University's Library Committee, which sought in 1904 a librarian for the institution, felt strongly that a woman be appointed because

> You will get a far better woman for £150 than a man. For this sum you could get a good, university educated, practically competent woman who would regard the job as a valuable prize and who would be more easily 'absorbed' or dispensed with in a year's time if need be. A man at that price would be either a callow youth who would leave us at the first chance; or a half-educated clerk; or a 'failure' without energy or grit.[32]

Women thus compounded the low status of library work not because of their effect on standards of service, which was positive, but because of the economic exploitation imposed on them by a male library establishment.

Confronted with the prospect of continuing low status, public librarians took steps to improve their position. By the early years of this century they were showing considerable interest in employment prospects, promotion and salaries; and corresponded with each other at length on these matters.[33] Poor remunerations and conditions must have been a constant spur to the professionalization process. But pay was not the only concern. Librarians sought to assert themselves in a wider social setting. Their immediate obstacle in this respect was the library committee. In the library's immediate hierarchical management structure their power and influence were limited, being generally subordinate to those of the committee. The latter, for example, often supervised the acquisition of reading material, as at Eastbourne in 1896 where a separate 'Book Selection Committee' was established.[34] The career of Edward Edwards at Manchester Free Library in the 1850s offers one of the best illustrations of friction between a librarian and his committee. Edwards's independence and disregard for supervision must have been sorely compromised by the grovelling apology he was forced to make to his committee for having fallen behind in his financial accounting of book purchases:

> It shall be my earnest dream not, under any circumstances, to allow my zeal to outstrip my discretion. I shall always feel that to secure the confidence and good opinion of this Committee is the best reward I can obtain for my utmost exertions in their service; and that by exercising a liberal forbearance in respect of any oversight which I so deeply regret, the Committee will have even a stronger claim than ever to an exact and unremitting performance of duty on my part.[35]

Thus, even in the case of Edwards, the co-pioneer of public libraries and the founder of professional public librarianship, the word librarian spelt 'servant' and not 'partner'.

The fact that a master–servant relationship characterized public library administration throughout the period in question must have proved doubly frustrating for librarians, since in the library setting itself their authority was unquestioned; notwithstanding occasional 'informal' inspections by committee members wearing their reader's hat. Faced with small staffs of inadequate ability and motivation, librarians were unable to delegate responsibility as they might have wished.[36] W. C. B. Sayers described the prevailing attitude as: 'I am Chief Librarian and all the suggestions needed I will make myself'[37] (though Sayers himself, it must be said, was one of the few who encouraged suggestions from his staff). Consequently, expertise was concentrated at the top of the staff hierarchy, mostly in librarians themselves, and this, librarians believed, committees failed to acknowledge.

Librarians also believed that their true worth went unrecognized in the communities they served. Criticism that the public library fulfilled merely a passive recreational role at the ratepayer's expense was repeated time and again during the period under consideration. Yet the notion of 'service' to the community has, historically, characterized professional practice, including that of librarianship. The formulation by professions of a differentiated body of knowledge has always had, to be sure, a monopolistic and therefore material value. In the nineteenth century, indeed, the professions contributed significantly to a belief in the efficacy of the 'market', giving the entrepreneurial ideal a non-industrial expression.[38] However, the ideology of service and reciprocal trust by the community did not recede in the face of strengthening competitive forces.[39] Even if professional groups saw themselves as élites aiming at class and economic improvement they were not, by virtue of their expertise, disengaged from society. Librarians corresponded to this assessment of the professional purpose. The formation of a professional body for librarians in 1877 (the Library Association) represented a commitment to social engagement. Pay and conditions were certainly part of its remit; in fact, many library committees prevented their librarians from attending the International Librarians Conference which gave rise to the Library Association, for fear of trade unionism.[40] But a key objective of the Association was also to raise standards of *service*.[41] Thus, when in 1892 the Association held its annual conference abroad for the first time (in Paris, 1892) it did so not merely for the purpose of prestige – though the venue no doubt held a certain attraction in this respect – but to study standards of service in French national and municipal libraries.[42]

The Library Association did not develop without its share of damaging internal strife.[43] Yet the activities of such a professional body were neither the only nor the most effective means of advancing professional status and standards of service. Far better results, some public librarians proposed, would be derived from making the library more educational, more materially useful, more 'economic' and business orientated. This, it was said, was the way to improve corporate respectability and raise the public library's social prestige. But to achieve these goals the public library would need to 'extend' itself – to a degree it had not done before – *into* society. It could no longer rely on the passive role it had mostly assigned itself since its inception. This is not to deny, as shall be argued below, that organizing and conserving materials, and making them available for use, did not constitute a form of service; it is rather that *reaching out* to society, to encourage the exploitation of what is conserved and organized, constituted a higher form of service. As T. H. Green argued, the ideal teacher must go to his or her pupils.

American influences

If public librarians were to escape taints of redundancy and superficiality there was little in the experience of the public library in this country upon which to construct a more outgoing, useful service. The concept of service was present, as seen in the desire to regenerate society's morals, but the practical mechanics of improving service were until the very end of the century largely unexplored. When the inspiration to improve service did arrive it came from abroad. From across the Atlantic, from the 1870s onwards, came a stream of fresh ideas on the techniques, and indeed objectives, of professional librarianship, into which public librarians were able to tap. The cross-fertilization of the British library profession from ideas generated by the profession in the United States is a recurrent theme in pre-1914 library literature.[44] Nowhere was the superiority of American public librarianship more emphatic than in the field of library-user interaction: 'Service was an idea that weighed heavily on the minds of American librarians.'[45] The public librarians among those active in the establishment of the American Library Association in 1876 – the so-called 'Men of 76' – did much to erode the image of the librarian as the mere custodian of literature. Contributions by Melvil Dewey and Samuel Green to the first volume of the *Library Journal*(1876–7) were typical of the service-orientated spirit of American librarianship, and testify to the relatively high regard in which the profession was found. Dewey had this to say about his profession:

> The time has at last come when a librarian may ... speak of his occupation as a profession ... The best librarians are no longer men of merely negative virtue. They are positive, aggressive characters, standing in the front rank of the educators of their communities, side by side with the preachers and the teachers.[46]

Dewey advised the public librarians to tailor their work to the 'wants of ... [their] special community'. Public librarianship was now a 'high calling', and so, said Dewey, he would not be astonished to find 'the ablest business talents engaged in the management of a public library'.[47] His insistence on business acumen in library administration complemented his desire to mechanize and standardize the library.[48]

Samuel Green, a vehement advocate of good relations between librarian and public, urged the librarian in 'popular' libraries to 'put himself out' in the cause of building a popular intercourse between staff and user. Enthusiasm, persistency in assistance, a courteous disposition and outward-looking techniques, all of which he had tried to instil into his own library's staff, had all come to be 'highly appreciated in the community'; not only in the realm of cultural elevation but also 'in regard to the scientific principles which underlie the processes of their daily occupations'. Green's reasoning was logical. Quite simply, the more assistance librarians were given, the more the idea of libraries would be supported. Service-minded librarians would earn respect for the library. For even though treating readers 'as equals' might leave them open to a 'neglect of deference', the librarian's 'superiority of culture' would always shine in the face of 'disrespect, impudence and conceit'.[49]

The service tradition in American public librarianship strengthened over time, coalescing with strands of the Progressive creed which taught that the intellectual-professional community was duty-bound to serve society and, in particular, those with least educational opportunity.[50] Also of importance was the burgeoning complexity of American industrial society. The decades on either side of 1900 saw rapid growth in the economy.[51] This was based on increased concentration, diversification, innovation and mechanization which, in combination, presented new problems of organization for management. Complex problems called for complex solutions. Thus, the management of external marketing and internal organization became more 'scientific'.[52] In keeping with the new scientific approach, the idea emerged that business decisions could no longer be based merely on 'the way the old man used to run the shop'. Personal experience no longer offered a safe basis for progress; and intensified competition demanded that executives be 'familiar with the best knowledge and thought of the day in order to keep up with the profession'. Hence, the turn of the century saw the beginning of a rapidly rising output of business literature, indicative of 'the tremendous demand that has recently sprung up for the wider and better knowledge of business that spells "efficiency"'. This demand came not just from management but also from workers keen to improve their skills and intelligence in a competitive world.[53]

American public libraries sought to meet the demand for economic and industrial information by establishing business libraries. An 'Industrial Library' was established in Providence in 1900, followed in the next few years by 'Useful Arts' departments at Cincinnati, Detroit and Cleveland.[54] It was in the context of these attempts to capitalize on the increased demand for business and trade literature that the service tradition of the American public library began to pay dividends. A close psychological link can be identified between, on the one hand, notions of library 'outreach' and, on the other, the complex needs of an optimistic business world and its aspiring groups and values. Successful outreach required efficiency; something which was highly compatible with the business ethic. In the late nineteenth century, American public librarianship began to take greater note of the world of business. It set out to offer an 'aggressive' service to complement 'hard-nosed' business needs; and there was a growing confidence that the public library could become as intrinsically 'useful' as business. In essence, increased and improved production in the wider world would teach librarians themselves to be more 'productive'. American librarians believed that this path could improve significantly their professional status: not only would the ablest business talents be attracted to librarianship, but the librarian would enjoy greater engagement and, hence, appreciation in society.

This analysis of the United States library scene has been important

because some British librarians were profoundly influenced by developments across the Atlantic. Public library service to business was just one of a
host of ideas which took root in England having first been tested in the
United States. The professional association and Dewey classification are
two further examples. Advances in American librarianship were reported
extensively in the British library press. This was the main channel for
informing librarians of new techniques and revised objectives (visits to the
United States were for the privileged few). However, the library press could
not by itself produce change; librarians would only react to wider social
change. In fact, contextual conditions similar to those which wrought
change in the United States also existed in Britain. First, in the late
nineteenth century, despite anxiety over economic performance, the pace
of business, work and life generally was quickening; science and innovation
were making a social impact. Second, librarians in this country also had a
'service' tradition upon which to build; they professed, after all, to be
involved in the business of diffusing education and culture, albeit in a
relatively passive way.

Materialism, science and service efficiency

Some public librarians sensed changes in the nation's economic life,
including the threat to national economic security, and began promoting
their institution's value in aiding 'useful' pursuits conducive to the advance
of materialism. In the late nineteenth century, public libraries began once
again to stress the importance of serious, 'productive' reading,[55] though not
necessarily at the expense of recreative reading, which was also strongly
supported by many. James Duff Brown testified in 1904 to

> the value of books in the practical affairs of life, and the adoption [by the public
> library] of a thorough method of bringing this recognition home to the general
> public by means of a propaganda suited to each district.[56]

He advocated, accordingly, that public libraries provide high-class scientific
and technical magazines as a means of attracting serious readers.[57]

A growing number of public librarians began to discuss the provision of
special services to business; their thoughts were not to be fully realized until
the First World War. As municipal employees, librarians could not wholly
engage with the entrepreneurial ideal, unlike professions with a direct
market relationship; but they could relate to it in a limited way by providing
industry and commerce with information and knowledge pertinent to their
competitive needs. Moreover, the fact that librarians had to 'sell' the idea of
'pertinent' knowledge to business (because the latter was not widely
convinced of its efficacy) was in its own way an entrepreneurial pursuit.[58]

Stanley Jast was one librarian who devoted a considerable period of his
career to the furtherance of services to business. In 1903 he read a paper
on technical libraries to the Library Association Annual Conference. This
'unusual and far-sighted' piece duly appeared as a publication in its own

right, as well as in the *Library Association Record*.[59] The following year he was able to view at first hand American public library services to business as the United Kingdom Library Association's official representative to the annual conference of the American Library Association. While in the United States he visited public libraries in New York, Brooklyn, Philadelphia, Pittsburgh, Cleveland, Buffalo, Albany, Boston, Newark and Providence.[60] This was a formative experience for Jast, who was later, as deputy (1915-20) and chief (1920-31) at Manchester, responsible for establishing high standard technical and commercial library services for the city.

Business provision was, for Jast, but one aspect of improving the 'service' ethic. He believed that in all its departments the public library should become more helpful and scientific in its methods of operating an 'open' policy. 'Openness' was, in the tradition of Edward Edwards, something which pro-business librarians like Jast both preached and practised. In a paper read to the 1898 Library Association Annual Conference, entitled *Some Hindrances to Progress in Public Library Work*, he staged a vehement assault on the 'officialism' of past provision. He denigrated the 'red-tapeism' of library provision, in which he included: grasping fines; complicated and intruding fines for reference book loans; the issue of borrowers' tickets being dependent on the signature of two ratepayers; and the borrowing of only one volume at a time, even if it was part of a multi-volumed work.[61] In his years as chief at Croydon (1898-1915) he attempted to combat these and other restrictive practices. His list of innovations is impressive. It included: a telephone link between central library and branches (1898); the issue of extra non-fiction ticket (1899); library talks (1899); open access in central reference (lending already open access) (1899); a library magazine – *The Reader's Index* – for the public (1899); a technical book exhibition (1901); photographs for loan (1903); a special exhaustive index of authors, themes and titles to current year's periodicals; classified reading lists on various topics; a subject catalogue; and an information service via a 'quick enquiry' card index.[62] Jast did not have the resources to develop fully an information service to business. Croydon was at the turn of the century a thriving small-scale industrial and commercial centre with a population of 12,000, largely self-supporting and separate from London except for its commuter population.[63] This made it ripe for the establishment of a technical and commercial library service. Though Jast was not able to instigate such a service, his library magazine, *The Reader's Index*, did contain numerous local trade advertisements, thereby forging at least one useful link with business.

If the Croydon public library could not serve business to the full it could become more 'open' by interacting more effectively with the public. Jast instilled into his staff the need to be more assertive and helpful, especially in the area of reference work. The assistant was placed 'among the readers ... to help students in any way he can'.[64] Staff were taught to be more sensitive to the public's needs:

> The reference library assistant is brought in close touch with people of different temperaments. Some are shy and awkward, others dogmatic and demanding, and others easily served. In each case he is compelled to use different methods of obtaining an idea of the reader's wants; and must always use tact. Particularly is this the case with the shy reader, who is often afraid to ask help and wanders among the books without being able to find what he is seeking.[65]

Jast believed that one way to help all readers was by means of the application of science to the problems of knowledge dissemination. Dewey Decimal Classification had made a big impact on his library thinking.[66] He was an enthusiastic propagandist for the 'scientific' classified catalogue, a tool which challenged the supremacy of the dictionary catalogue. Sound classification, he believed, was the key to a fuller exploitation of the liberating open access revolution; and he believed he was engaged in a momentous struggle, declaring that

> when the history of the library movement is written the facts that will stand out are the battle of the dictionary versus classified catalogue; the application of exact classification to shelf arrangement; and the battle for open access.[67]

One local newspaper described Jast's championing of such innovations as 'more important than the invention of the aeroplane'! Moreover, it was surprising, said the paper, that these innovations came 'not from the office, or the shop, or the factory, but from the learned, and, as some thought, dreamy atmosphere of the library'.[68] Jast believed science could help him and others improve standards of service. The librarian J. Y. W. MacAlister once said that the 'good librarian ... must be guide, philosopher and friend to all his readers'.[69] Particular stress was laid by MacAlister, Jast and others on the 'guiding' remit of librarians: to help others gain knowledge a sound, scientific organization of the library, incorporating high cataloguing and classification standards, was essential.[70]

In other areas where customer relations were obviously important the notion of 'service' was also changing – though not to the extent, it must be added, seen in public libraries. By the early twentieth century the department stores of Britain's large cities had made notable improvements in services offered to shoppers. In 1880 David Lewis' opened a Manchester outlet (following the opening of shops in Liverpool in 1856 and in Birmingham in 1885). The new store sought to attract working-class as well as middle-class customers. Consequently it adopted a policy of encouraging customers to come into the store and browse without the imposition of any obvious pressure to buy. It was a strategy which other stores emulated. Furthermore, before the First World War, many stores installed accommodating facilities such as lifts, escalators, rest-rooms and restaurants.[71] In 1909 the American Gordon Selfridge opened his Oxford Street store. This he tried to make an informal, 'family' establishment with the inclusion of roof garden, bargain basement, ice-cream soda fountains for children, large and brightly lit shop windows, perfumery counters placed just inside the main entrance to seduce passers-by with enticing scents and adverts, promoting shopping as a leisure pursuit, which read: 'Spend the Day at Selfridges.'[72] But not until after the Second World War did retailing adopt what the public library had begun fifty years earlier: self-service, or open access in library terminology.[73]

Public librarians rightly saw themselves as pioneers in customer service. To be so they had to become scientists too. By the twentieth century librarianship had taken on a more technical appearance. In 1909 the Library Association declared: 'Librarianship has a technical side for which special training is necessary, and without this training no one is qualified to take up the position.'[74] This was a far cry from the early days of the Association, when it was ruled by 'gentlemen's gentlemen'.[75] By the turn of the century it was the municipal librarians who dominated: they were in the forefront of library innovation. Public librarians made contributions in advance of those running academic libraries: 'Any stuffy duffer who seemed no good for anything else on earth', said Savage, 'was jobbed into a learned library.'[76] It should be acknowledged, however, that some non-public librarians did make significant contributions, most notably in the field of bibliography. For example, E. W. B. Nicholson, essentially an academic librarian who helped to found the Library Association, was no die-hard when it came to supporting Sunday opening and open access.[77]

None the less, it was public librarians like Ernest Savage who were pioneering the new 'scientific' approach (it is no coincidence that he was trained by Jast at Croydon). In a *Library World* article in 1909, dealing with the representation of science in municipal libraries, Savage applauded the idea of extensive science collections. Science – in which he included literature which aided 'the side of our work which helps people earn a living' – was more important than reading for pleasure, which was of 'little permanent good'. He wished to promote literature of 'practical' value:

> Although it is pleasant for us to provide solace for a tired working man, and to provide a companion for the villa lady who can only afford a maid, yet my crass utilitarianism forces me to believe that it is better for our libraries to be educational institutions than philanthropic circulating libraries. I plead for less clap-trap and more science ... I want to see the public library recognised as an institution with a definite educational value, a definite business value; and less as part of the modern scheme of beer and skittles.[78]

The problem for public libraries, he continued, was that science was a sprawling area of human knowledge – a problem which was compounded by its relatively short shelf-life and the expensive nature of scientific publications. For local public libraries, with slim resources, a wide coverage of the literature was not possible. Hence, groups had to be *targeted*. The extent and nature of demand had to be assessed, and provision made accordingly. This process was particularly relevant to the needs of 'serious' reader groups such as technical school students. The process, in other words, was a 'scientific' assessment of need, aimed at furthering the consumption of 'useful' literature. In advocating both 'serious' literature and a 'scientific' process, Savage said he had laid himself open to being labelled nothing more than a 'crass and ignoble utilitarian'. He admitted only to being the last word of this description. And such was indeed the case. To promote serious science literature was utilitarian; and to devise scientifically how 'useful' literature would reach those who needed it was to enhance such a reputation.[79]

Further, as Jast had argued, the scientific instrument of classification could help to open up the library's treasures to readers. But classification was also useful to librarians seeking to improve their prestige; it became the symbol of the new drive towards enhanced professional status. In the 'closed' library, it has been argued, the catalogue was the main key to the stock. The public was thus given the chance to appreciate, in consulting the catalogue, the skilled and lengthy labour of the librarian who had produced it and who, many must have presumed, knew something of the content of the books listed. With the gradual emergence of the open access library, the catalogue (though this did not of course disappear) became less important in that readers were allowed to browse. However, this did not diminish public appreciation of the librarian, because a new method of 'revealing' the library – a scientific one – had emerged to supplement or replace the catalogue, and duly impress the public. Classification became the basis of the new link between librarian and reader because it attempted (reality has, of course, never matched theory) to arrange items on the shelves as readers would expect to see them.[80]

Public librarians were assisted in their migration towards science by the latter's rejuvenation in the nation's intellectual life. The intellectual community in the Victorian age – though the word 'intellectual' did not exist in the way we know it today until the late nineteenth century – consisted of 'men of science', 'scholars' and 'men of letters' (labels which reflect a contemporary and sexist perspective). During the Victorian age 'men of science' by and large took a back seat in intellectual activity. Literature, not science, was the hallmark of the intellectual élite. By the early twentieth century, however, science had staged a recovery, leading scientists having attained a higher social profile, and international reputations even. Despite the fact that economic, social and political élites remained bound to attitudes discouraging science, there was no denying the advances it had made in terms of knowledge, professional status, relevance to ordinary life and the confronting of things established – the way Darwinism confronted theology, for instance. But the effect of scientific discovery went much deeper. Science possessed, by the late nineteenth century, a 'silent and permeative genius' which deeply affected the nature of other disciplines, and helped to convert many other fields of intellectual activity into professional disciplines, including, to a degree, librarianship.[81]

Furthermore, science itself underwent a division of labour in the nineteenth century. The 'natural philosophy' and 'natural history' of the eighteenth century were transformed into physics and chemistry, biology and geology, each with its own distinct boundaries, techniques of investigation and specialized practitioners.[82] There was a proliferation of new sciences and sub-sciences. Two examples of emergent highly specialized disciplines were seismology (the study of earthquakes), named in 1858, and embryology (the study of rudimentary life forms), named the following year.[83] Moreover, the acquisition of a special name for a science usually indicated that it had achieved a distinct professional importance.[84] Thus, the evolution of the terms 'library economy' and 'library science' did not just indicate where librarians thought part of their future intellectual standing should rest, but revealed considerable status aspirations too.

Yet being 'at one' with science was no guarantee of improved professional prestige. It should be recalled that after about 1880 engineers fell from being the heroes of the industrial age to a position of diminished self-confidence; this was especially true of the 'electricals'. This had little to do with the qualities of engineers themselves, but with the economic climate in which they operated; their associated industries had begun to falter under mounting foreign competition and the engineering profession's reputation suffered accordingly.[85]

By contrast, the sphere in which librarians operated – broadly speaking, education – was, from the late nineteenth century onwards, one of expansion and optimism. Improved educational provision was required for advances in economic efficiency, as well as for a regeneration of society's culture and morals in response to the 'rediscovery of poverty' in the 1880s and the 'national efficiency' drive of the Edwardian period. In fact, it is necessary to stress – as the remainder of this chapter seeks to do – that public librarians did not, around the turn of the century, metamorphose into fully fledged, disinterested scientists, jettisoning their traditional role as moral agents of society. True, in order to enhance professional status some librarians sought to define themselves in close relation to the new scientific industrialism. But this was not something which detracted from a desire, or an ability, to disseminate culture – for the culture of improvement had come to include science alongside traditional learning. If anything, science had helped to strengthen this traditional role: it had shown that librarians were not obscurantists but could engage in inquiry and reform. This lesson could now be carried into the broader educational field, into 'liberal' adult education and the education of children. The notion of 'service', which science had helped advance, could now be further invigorated by an idealist commitment to widening the appreciation of culture.

The diffusion of culture and the service ideal

Throughout history librarians have been seen as embodiments of culture. The great library at Alexandria had, along with the city's museum, formed a literary research institution where the librarian was considered to be 'the most important personage of the intellectual entourage'.[86] The first librarians at Alexandria were true scholar-poets, not mere custodians of literature.[87] This intellectual image continued into modern times and was humorously described by Sayers in 1912:

unkempt, shabby, pre-occupied and absent-minded, climbing up ladders in a dim-lit dwelling-place of books, taking from the shelves volumes on which reposes the dust of generations, sitting upon the rungs of the ladder to read them, and ejaculating at intervals his invariable 'Prodigious' at the revelations of those worm-eaten folios – this is the cloistered, other worldly librarian of the imagination; a recluse, a scholar, and impractical, harmless and passive human automaton.[88]

Many Victorian and Edwardian librarians, including the municipal variety, were accomplished scholars and 'literateurs'. When Fulham's librarian, F. T. Barrett, died in 1905 he left a private library of three hundred volumes.[89] When the country's first school for librarians opened in 1919, eighty-nine of the ninety-nine students who enrolled chose 'Literary History and Book Selection', making it the most popular of the optional subjects on offer.[90]

This scholarly dimension did not mean that librarians had no conception of public service. Public librarians can be considered as part of the intellectual community which came under the heading of 'men of letters'; alongside poets, novelists, journalists, biographers, historians, social critics, philosophers and political economists. The one factor common to these groups was that each commanded some kind of 'market relationship' with the general reading public.[91] Public librarians did so in that they attempted, or so they often said, to meet readers' needs, though without the incentive of profit. As such they were interactive with society. They were not, however, servile to the public. It was part of the purpose of many of the professions to raise the moral tone of society.[92] This was certainly the case with librarians who, in part, perceived themselves as guides to a higher form of social life.

Librarianship was seen by some as akin to the 'gentlemanly' callings of medicine, the law and the church. Allegorically, librarians were sometimes allotted the pastoral-clerical role of shepherds of a flock.[93] As late as 1932 Stanley Jast was reminding librarians of Andrew Carnegie's words at the 1907 Library Association Conference, when the benefactor told his audience: 'Consecrate yourself to your profession for it is noble.' This was a sentiment and an assessment of a calling with which Jast fully concurred: 'To the priest the spiritual, to the doctor the physical, and to the librarian the intellectual ministry of man. It is a splendid part for us to play.'[94] The role of attentive public servant had been described by Thomas Carlyle in 1840:

> My notion of the librarian's function does not imply that he shall be king over us; nay that he shall ever quit the address and manner of a 'servant' to a Library; but he will be as a 'wise' servant, watchful, diligent, discerning what is what, incessantly endeavouring, rough-hewing all things for us, and, under the guise of a wise servant, 'ruling' actually while he serves. Like a Nobleman's Steward: that is in some sort the definition of him.[95]

The service in which Carlyle's 'stewards' worked was that of culture, their duty being to extend and enlarge it by diffusing literary knowledge. As the librarian of Edinburgh University wrote in 1923 after 46 years of library work:

Librarians are men who are not in the forefront in public. But they are certainly the stimulus to the soil of literature, and the dispensers of literary knowledge. Without them ignorance would bring forth a scentless flower instead of a garden of perfume. Librarians put the necessary tools into the hands of clergymen, statesmen and workers of all ranks. And their worth is not recognised as it should be.[96]

However, to be true servants of culture and, at the same time, improve their public reputation librarians needed not just to dispense but also encourage reading. Public librarians interviewed by local newspapers, and writing in their annual reports, constantly impressed upon the public the value of quality literature. Yet it was recognized that the process of making 'quality' readers was necessarily piecemeal, commencing, for the majority, at a rudimentary level. As Winchester's librarian explained in 1886:

> The great thing is to induce the people to read; and though it is perfectly true that the tastes of the majority may not coincide with our own, it is far preferable that they should read anything rather than they should read nothing.[97]

To coax readers – to maintain the library's popularity indeed – librarians were forced to make concessions to mass literary consumption. This seriously undermines any view of librarians as successful social controllers.

Interest had to be generated even in the lightest reading material, provided it was of an acceptable moral content. Sayers, in 1912, explained that librarians had a 'mission not only to provide reading but also to create readers'. They had to transform themselves 'from a passive into an active force in the community'.[98] Similarly, in 1909 the Library Association advised that, in every municipality, public library committee's principal efforts

> should be directed towards inculcating and stimulating the habit of reading both for recreation and mental improvement. The mere acquisition of books and their display in a public building will not of itself be sufficient to this effect.[99]

From the late nineteenth century, the idea that librarians required a higher profile was gaining popularity. Thomas Aldred, Southwark's librarian, explained in 1904 how he 'encouraged' reading: 'By the very best method, viz., personal recommendations to borrowers; and not shutting myself in an office working out details of utopian schemes.'[100] It appeared that librarians were, increasingly, leaving their offices to guide readers to their choices. Of the librarian at Portsmouth in 1886 it was said that 'the recommendations of a judicious adviser such as Mr Jewers [the librarian] are of great value'. Moreover, this allowed the librarian to take greater care of the readers' moral well-being; for although the ultimate choice was said to be 'affected by personal preferences', what was 'indispensable' was that 'the pabulum provided should be morally wholesome'.[101] Librarians believed that a substantial part of their clientele, made none the wiser by the catalogue, were baffled by the extent of choice, even in an open access setting.[102] In such cases, it was said, 'a well informed and affable librarian may be of the greatest service'.[103]

Presented here is the image of an 'engaging' librarian, actively aiding the reader in choosing worthwhile and morally sound literature. Librarians might not have taken on a 'confessor' role, as was sometimes the case in terms of the relationship between the shop assistant and the higher class customer.[104] But they did begin to pay closer attention to their clienteles in the hope of boosting reading and conveying culture. As noted above, science was an aid in this respect; so were practical schemes of open access, library talks, lectures, reading circles and exhibitions.

Supporters of open access pointed to its long tradition. Medieval libraries, though books were chained, were 'open' in the sense that staff were not required to fetch books. By modern times, in collegiate, proprietary, subscription and commercial libraries, the open library was almost universal. Many public library reference departments also had small sections of stock on open shelves (beginning at Cambridge, 1870).[105] But general lending services remained closed. However, in 1894, at Clerkenwell Public Library, James Duff Brown introduced open access to lending services. This was a revolutionary idea, enthusiastically supported by some: 'Mr Brown is become a Mahomet, and dingy Clerkenwell Library a sort of a librarian's Mecca, whence he spreads literally the true faith.'[106] Brown had first suggested open access in 1891, and was confirmed in its efficacy as an aid to education after his visit to the United States two years later.[107]

The main motivation behind the open access drive was the desire to spread culture by making the public library more educational. It was argued that allowing readers to browse would encourage them to read serious literature.[108] The indicator system, it was said, 'disgusted and disheartened many readers and would-be private students as open access could never do'. As a schoolboy and butcher's boy before the First World War, Albert Williams has described how using the closed access public library in Bolton was a complicated and crude business.[109] Readers warmly welcomed open access in the minority of places that it appeared before 1914.[110] Librarians hoped that this would not only encourage reading *per se*, but also develop a taste for 'useful' literature. Open access was thus promoted as an effort 'to get in touch with the educational work of the nation'.[111] It was viewed as an active educational force, one which enhanced the reputation of the library as the 'People's University'.[112] Moreover, to render the library more educational, free access not just to books, but to better books, was essential. As the librarian John Ballinger claimed:

> if our modern selection of books are to be of any actual educational help, they must contain choice and beautiful books, samples of fine painting, high class illustrations, and beautiful bindings, in order to present a more worthy standard of craftsmanship for teaching people improved ideas and workmanlike methods.[113]

To exploit good selection fully required improved *supervision*, which, it must be stressed, had two definitions. In 1907 the architect A. L.

Champneys made the following comments on library supervision:

> There is, it may be thought, something rather aggressive in the term and its
> acceptance, and it is a pity that there is no more agreeable word. Though
> supervision is undoubtedly a safeguard against malefactors and, as such, a
> benefit to the majority, the true spirit of it should be rather one of helpfulness,
> and the staff should be considered allies to the readers and not spies.[114]

Herein lies the twin definition of supervision in respect of library work. On
the one hand it has been considered a function of library management: an
attempt to enhance the smooth running of the library by maximizing public
accessibility. This would be achieved by concentrating staff in accessible
positions. Readers would have ease of access to staff for answering
enquiries: 'short lines for every process are essential', wrote one American
librarian.[115] Moreover, the financial savings which would arise from this
would be in the interests of both library establishment and users, not least
in terms of the extra money which could be spent on 'good' books. On the
other hand, supervision has meant the overseeing of a potentially disruptive
public; in effect, an expression of a desire not to 'help' but to 'spy'.

The fact that librarians thought they needed to spy on readers reveals,
perhaps, a degree of distrust of the public. Fears of public malevolence
increased with the arrival of open access. Librarians now had to watch not
only for mutilation of materials, but for their theft and misplacement also.
Yet there is evidence to show that the amount of theft from open access
libraries was minimal. George Dawson had told the Select Committee on
Public Libraries in 1849 that loss of books from mechanics' institutes
libraries was negligible.[116] One of the earliest libraries to offer freer access
was Salford, where there was no need to register for a book when obtaining
it for reference purposes:

> The check on the readers is entirely of a moral kind – a person so disposed
> could, without much difficulty, carry off the volume he had been reading; but
> 'not one case of this kind has yet occurred', and the conduct of all the readers
> has been most orderly and becoming. The readers know and feel that they are
> trusted, and this naturally makes them anxious to show that the trust has been
> well reposed.[117]

In the first four years of open access at Clerkenwell's lending library only
twelve volumes costing £1.10s.0d were stolen.[118]

Nevertheless, throughout the pre-1914 period, open access remained a
vexed question. Opposition to it was partly financial, in both a corporate
and personal sense. For poorly funded library authorities, adapting
premises and classifying stock was expensive. A popular view was that
open access was the dream of lazy librarians whose workload would be cut
at the ratepayer's expense. Some leading opponents of the system had a
significant financial stake in retaining closed access libraries. Alfred
Cotgreave, West Ham's librarian, became particularly vocal in his
opposition: his patented indicator for closed access libraries was, after all,
one of the most popular devices of its kind in use.

These financial concerns bolstered that part of the opposition to open access which was based on a distrust of the public. This opposition was not insignificant. One librarian described the open access idea as a 'plea for anarchy'.[119] Even open access enthusiasts devised means of 'safeguarding' their new system; by placing counters and shelving in appropriate positions for overseeing the public, and by placing wicket gates at entrances and exits. Councils and parishes were not slow to prosecute thieves, while posters, liberally displayed in libraries, warned of the penalties of mutilation and theft. But this continuing 'fortress' mentality could not prevent the emergence of a willingness to assist and liberate use and users. There was a growing awareness of the importance of supervision in terms of its positive definition. Open access revealed a new trust in popular use. Moreover, enshrined in it was the concept of 'service'. In a free access setting readers would, to an extent, have to help themselves. But they would also have the assistance of staff now released from behind the impenetrable barrier of indicator and issue window: 'A large amount of aid given to readers must take the form of personal assistance', remarked Portsmouth's librarian.[120] It should be noted, however, that supporters of indicators believed that their system also rendered service to the public, providing as it did an instant answer to a book's availability.

Open access stood for an enhancement of service to all, not just a privileged few. Distrust of users had never been determined by social class: that is to say, middle-class librarians spying on working-class readers who, stereotypically, had a propensity for stealing and mutilating. Such depredations had not been the preserve of 'the much-reviled lower orders'.[121] Thus, at Leeds Public Library it was considered 'not by any means clear that the better educated classes are not responsible for the filthy remarks so often to be found on the margins of books';[122] the Select Committee in 1849 had been told of the likelihood of theft and the need of a 'literary police' at as reputable a library as that of the Royal Dublin Society.[123] Just as both malevolence and the need to oversee were classless, so also, said open access enthusiasts, should be the notion of service to well-affected, education-minded readers who came from all social groups.

The new impetus to render a widely embracing service manifested itself in a whole range of extension activities. 'Extra-library activity' had existed in one form or another – most notably classes and lectures – since the early days of the public library.[124] For librarians, extension work was none the less a minor concern relative to the 'backroom' techniques of librarianship. In the late nineteenth century, however, the idea of 'extension' beyond mere fixed-site book provision gained popularity. Short library talks to the public (especially children) on the mechanics of library use – describing rules, issue and classification systems, the catalogue and other matters – became very popular. The library lecture underwent a renaissance. At Mile End, in 1893, a series of six lectures organized by the public library attracted 27,000 people.[125]

Briscoe and Axon: out of the cloisters

A novel means of engaging with the public was the reading circle. One of the chief proponents of this form of extension activity was J. Potter Briscoe (Nottingham's librarian), who saw it as a corollary to the 'bustling age' in which he lived:

> The hurry-skurry of city, town and society life seemed to need literature of a light and a scrappy kind; something which would not require much, if any, mental effort. Novels have therefore teemed from the press in greater number than has ever been published before in the history of literature; and snippet weeklies have been issued by publishers under scores of titles, and in ton loads ... The average reader is omnivorous and needs direction if he is to derive the greatest possible advantage from his reading.[126]

To meet readers' needs for direction, Briscoe continued, 'much thought has been given by the cultured, and others lower in the intellectual scale, who desire to do good to their fellows in their day and generation'.[127] In practice this often meant cooperating with the National Home Reading Union (founded 1889) which provided a magazine, book lists and group leaders (often librarians) to encourage the association of those seeking to advance their reading.

Briscoe also believed in giving short lectures on books and writers to attract readers and stimulate good reading.[128] He further asserted the need to reach out to minority user groups. The lack of library books for the blind was decried.[129] He urged and pioneered increased library use by the young.[130] He praised the work done by public libraries as agencies of the government's Emigrants' Information Office: this involved giving sound advice to those, often of little means, seeking a fresh start in the colonies, as well as protecting them against fraud, exploitation and hardship.[131]

These stances demonstrate a significant social commitment which Briscoe also displayed outside the library field. In Nottingham he was active in the temperance movement, as well as other church, charitable and social institutions: 'He appears to have had a finger in every conceivable pie of the town and a great love for being a committee member of one organization or another.'[132] His engagement in society was clearly evident in his library philosophy. The public library, he believed, was a 'local well-spring of learning'.[133] By using public libraries, individuals would 'be enabled to progress in matters which affected their callings and positions in life, and thus make them worthy citizens, good workmen, and acceptable members of society'.[134] It was the public library's duty to serve all, irrespective of class distinction.[135] In promoting reading of high character, he asserted, the 'librarian of the twentieth century must not spare himself for the common good'.[136] His view of librarians was that 'As a body, and as individuals, we are not selfish. We have some of the missionary spirit in us.'[137] This missionary impulse fitted well with Briscoe's wish to extend the library *into* society (it is probably no coincidence that his son, who followed him into librarianship, became a leading advocate of library publicity).[138] In 1886,

Thomas Greenwood wrote that 'The student and the book-worm do not necessarily make the best librarian for a Free Library, often, in fact, the very opposite.'[139] Greenwood might have been correct in stating this as a general rule. To Briscoe, however, it did not apply; a 'bookman born', he was also anxious actively to serve his community in its literary and cultural needs.[140]

There is no evidence to suggest that Briscoe was overtly or consciously influenced by educational idealism, even though his personal social philosophy and professional practice bear a striking resemblance to it. However, in the case of the librarian W. E. A. Axon, a contemporary of Briscoe, the suggestion of a link is much stronger. Axon became chief at Manchester and an active member of the Manchester Literary Club. He would have been aware of the interest of his fellow club members in the German philosophy which informed idealism.[141] He was aware of its impact: 'We have witnessed the vigorous development of German literature, essentially informed in the spirit of the new age.'[142] Axon was a man of erudite culture and learning. He was a product of educational self-help. He wrote to Edward Edwards in 1867:

> What knowledge I possess has been almost wholly acquired by the use of our Free Library [Manchester], which placed within my reach those aids to study and research which but for these institutions would be quite inaccessible to poor students like myself.[143]

Axon believed that the library could enable others to elevate themselves similarly:

> He who goes into a large library has the opportunity of communing with the greatest minds that have existed. If he imbibes some of their spirit, he must inevitably be a better man and a better citizen. Literature will liberalize his mind, give him broader views of life, a wider charity, a greater earnestness, and a deeper faith.[144]

He encapsulated his belief in the efficacy of culture in quoting Shakespeare:

> Ignorance is the curse of God;
> Knowledge the wing whereby we fly to heaven.[145]

For Axon, the library was 'an instrument of culture, of research, of moralization';[146] it was a 'universal provider' not only of information but of 'ethical inspiration and enthusiasm'.[147]

He freely quoted and praised the social critics of the age. He concurred with Carlyle that the 'true university of these days is a collection of books', and with Arnold that culture was in essence 'a study of perfection'.[148] He studied and admired the works of Ruskin who, according to Axon, taught

> that Art should be true to Nature, and that Man should be true to God. When Art loses its faith in Nature, it ceases to possess utility. When Man ceases to work Righteousness, there follow disorders and social perils of every kind. Ruskin beholds in our modern society an aristocracy which has abdicated its

functions, a middle class largely given up to greed, a working class struggling in the dark, but dimly conscious of injustice. He sees the fair fields replaced by 'jerry-built' houses, the lechery, the drunkenness, the brutality that disgrace our towns, and degrade men and women below the level of the beasts, and put them on a par with the fiends of the pit ... He has taught us also that it is an ill return for God's gift of delight in beauty and order to leave our brethren festering in misery and despair.[149]

Axon praised the fortitude of the Platonist Thomas Taylor, who, as a 'pagan' philosopher, stood firm against the denunciations of a Christian society:

it must be acknowledged that a man who devotes himself to poverty and to study in an age and country famous for the pursuit of wealth; who has the courage to adopt and the sincerity to avow opinions that are contrary to every prejudice of the time; who runs the risk of persecution and imprisonment; a man who 'scorns delights and lives laborious days', is entitled to our admiration and respect.[150]

Axon thus perceived the pursuit of learning as a work of 'Righteousness' (to quote Ruskin above), a sentiment which Samuel Barnett later echoed.[151] A librarian, he believed, had a duty to his fellow citizens both to conserve and to diffuse literature. He was an advocate of library lectures 'on the best book in a particular class or on a particular subject'.[152] Regarding the collection and conservation of materials he was motivated by the vision of the sustained growth of culture: from such passive work 'future knowledge may be wrought'.[153] The provision of literature was a social activity; and, like Briscoe's, his impulse to engage in society in the literary field was matched by social service in other areas. His obituary noted that he was not just a bibliophile but 'a humanitarian in its most ample sense'.[154] As a member of numerous social organizations and public bodies, including the Salford School Board and Moss Side Urban District Council, he 'took an active part in promoting all movements which in his belief would tend to the material and social amelioration of the people, and was accordingly a life-long advocate of education, temperance, peace, and food reform'.[155] Another movement that attracted his attention was that of the appreciation of art. As a member of the committee which proposed the establishment of an art museum in Manchester (and as a member of the Manchester Literary Club, which was closely associated with the idea) Axon was adamant that 'art should again become a teacher, an agent in social reform and the elevation of the people'.[156] He also applied this idealist philosophy to public libraries.

Social criticism and idealist influences

The image of librarians like Briscoe and Axon as social 'interveners' contradicts the received notions of passivity and introspection which have characterized the profession. Evidence from contemporary fiction further denies these charges. Published in 1908, the novel *Miss Lucy: a Character*

Study, by C. Coleridge, contains an unusual description of an Edwardian public librarian. It is the story of a woman, Lucy, whose personality becomes overshadowed by her loss of class status following the death of her rich guardian (her parents died when she was young), who leaves her penniless. Out of necessity Lucy is forced to marry below her station. Later in life she is dismayed when her daughter becomes engaged to the town's librarian, Kendal Ashford. Even though his family lived in 'a fine villa in Acton', and was above a game-keeper's family, Lucy cared little for the relationship; she considered her prospective son-in-law to be 'like the cock that thought the sun got up to hear him crow'. She was unimpressed by the fact that he had passed the higher Cambridge examinations and was getting good marks for papers on Browning at university extension classes. But for Kendal Ashford, the librarian, exams were an 'excitement'. They had qualified him for each step in life, including his post at the library: 'I went on getting all the education I could, and have got some credentials – I am still working for more – I want a London degree. There are many secretaryships, and excellent librarianships to be got.' Ashford had chosen a life of study and self-education in preference to a lucrative career in his stepfather's sherry firm: 'I hated disseminating alcohol, and I'd lived on a crust a day to study.' But he also preferred librarianship to selling sherry because it was 'something to be able to pull one's fellow creatures up a bit, and you don't do that in the wine trade'. Ashford was not a conventional character. He questioned his fiancée's father's integrity, his authoritarianism indeed, in hunting poachers, whom Ashford described as 'poor starving fellows'. He apparently had little concern for class distinctions. He cared not that he was marrying below him: 'I don't intend any class prejudice to stand in the way. It's beyond all that.' In this regard he was an independent spirit: 'I'd emigrate, or break stones, or work in a factory to be my own master. The assumptions of class are intolerable', he told his prospective parents-in-law.

This fictional representation, together with the previously described motivations of men of culture like Briscoe and Axon, of technicians like Jast and Brown, and, even earlier, of a man of inquiry like Edward Edwards, show that the image of the cloistered, socially disinterested librarian is a cliché. Librarians, especially those in municipal posts, tended to be integrated with the social criticism which characterized the industrial age. Though they had faith in the 'age of progress', this was curbed to an extent by hesitancy over the social disruption and conflict which industrialism wrought. They thus looked to moralize and to unite industrial society. They saw their institutions as schools of ethics. But what was the origin of this perception? Certainly religious influences (which in the United States contributed much to the New England-derived, genteel, gentry professionalism of librarianship) require an investigation which cannot be afforded here.

As far as secular explanations are concerned, it has been noted in Chapter 7 that the popularity of idealism corresponded with the explosion

in public libraries from around 1880. There is an intriguing similarity
between the philosophy of leading public librarians and educational
idealism. Librarians often spoke of the ultimate 'common good' at which
their work was aimed. They stressed the equality of opportunity which
libraries provided and the role which libraries played as generators of
democratic ideals. They believed that education through the library taught
duty, good citizenship and social obligation. These virtues librarians
themselves sought to practise by reaching out to readers, identifying their
needs (within the confines of what was morally wholesome) and guiding the
way to cultural elevation. Samuel Barnett believed this to be the librarian's
true vocation; that is to say, to ascertain

> the reader's mental equipment without appearing curious or arousing vexation.
> A recognition that such work was part of a librarian's duty would ... attract to
> the profession men and women desirous of rendering public service, or inspired
> by philanthropic ambitions. How better could men serve their generation than
> by acting as guides to enquiring minds?[157]

Barnett urged that librarians 'be missionaries rather than collectors of
books and makers of catalogues'.[158]

Refining the conservative image

There is little evidence that public librarians were especially enthusiastic in
studying the literature of idealism. From the evidence that someone has read
certain books it cannot in any case be assumed that he or she was influenced
by them unless, as in the case of Axon, individuals went on to cite and praise
those writings. But just because librarians cannot be shown to have drawn
directly on idealistic thought, there is no reason to argue that they were not
part of the idealist thrust of social policy in the half-century preceding the
First World War. It is true that librarians did not completely 'immerse'
themselves, as pure idealism would have dictated, in the society which they
served – but the same might have been said of settlement house workers. On
the other hand, they did not appear as detached and coercive as the teaching
profession in their quest to moralize society. On balance, librarians can be
said to have adopted a liberal, progressive outlook which, in the early period,
was formed from utilitarian ideas about the evils of exclusivity and inequality
of opportunity, as championed by social critics like Edward Edwards. By the
end of the nineteenth century these broadly corresponded to the New
Liberalism – a positive liberalism which, in the tradition of John Mill and
T. H. Green, sought the fulfilment of each individual's potential through a
modicum of collectivism. Librarians were of a liberal persuasion, and
perhaps often (though more research is required in the area of political
allegiance) with a capital 'L'. As Thomas Aldred wrote to Walter Powell in
warning him not to seek a library position in London,

> Work in London is not near so pleasant as in provincial towns, especially in
> liberal boroughs. Administrations here (in London) take their duties very

seriously and liberals, in particular, worry officials. You are better off in Birmingham if you attach any value to peace of mind.[159]

Because the public library was ostensibly apolitical, librarians have similarly been labelled with a political and social quietism which was intrinsically conservative. However, the image of the conservative-minded librarian of the pre-1914 era requires refinement. The provision of separate women's rooms and tables is a case in point. On the one hand these facilities might be taken as demonstrating that librarians sympathized with traditionalist attitudes to women. On the other hand, they can be seen positively, as a privileged treatment for women who would otherwise not feel able to use the library.[160] In other words, they can be viewed in idealistic terms, as facilities which enhanced the possibility of women's self-realization.

Librarians were burdened by a conservative image, partly because their first duty was to conserve literature. To diffuse culture one must first be its custodian. For librarians to assert their public-spiritedness, or people-commitment, was problematic. Sayers once observed that

> while intellectually the librarian is one of the most cultured of municipal workers, because he does not produce tangible material returns, and because he is grossly underpaid, he is too often regarded as the social inferior of other municipal workers.[161]

Since the inception of their movement public librarians had preached some kind of 'productive' message. To employers they had pledged intelligent, purposeful workers; to the latter the library was presented as an enticing source of material gain. Late-nineteenth-century economic anxieties boosted interest in this aspect of library work; a momentum which was to undergo a sudden acceleration during the First World War, when an economic role became the focus of public library purpose. In combining education for humanistic and economic progress librarians thus straddled the line of tension between scientific industrialism and cultural elevation. They supported both, and did not view them as incompatible: culture, they said, had economic benefits. This symbiosis was reflected in the profession's move towards science, which visionaries like Brown and Jast spearheaded. Their scientific aspirations fitted with the drive for economic regeneration; but scientific aspirations were also a means of furthering the traditional function of disseminating culture, in that science (for example, systematic classification and the considered planning of buildings) made access to knowledge and education easier.

Public librarians were intellectually intrigued by the potential of the application of science in libraries. They sincerely believed they were making an important and innovative contribution to progress. But they also saw science as a means of improving status and corporate respectability. The St Helen's chief, Alfred Lancaster, argued in 1900 that owing to technical book provision 'public libraries have reached a much higher position and are justly recognised as educational institutions'.[162] In all its aspects public librarians came to see their institutions as thoroughly educational – essential elements, in other words, in the national system of education. Such a position could only improve professional status. In this respect, it is significant that when public librarians acted as secretaries to science and art classes run by public libraries, as occasionally they did, salaries could virtually double.[163]

By classes and other extension activities the 'needful public sentiment', as one librarian put it, would be created.[164] Public appreciation was important to the material and status aspirations of librarians. By appearing as agents of educational endeavour they would be exhibiting the gentlemanly virtues of gentility and learning. In this respect public librarians might be seen to have been indulging in the formation of a middle-class consciousness. On the other hand, it can be argued that they were too aware of society's need for both stability and fewer class divisions to be excessively anxious about the claims of their own social class. The motivation was, rather, to serve society as a whole and rescue it from the ravages of industrialism.

In the final analysis, therefore, public librarians were neither conservative nor revolutionary. They were moderate reformers who aimed to reduce the social disorder and class conflict which they found so distasteful. This was to be done by conveying culture – not just to the lower orders, but to all social groups. As emissaries of culture they were not antagonistic to science but saw it as an aid to society's elevation. Science was manifest in the classification of stock and the provision of scientific, technical and business literature. Just as science brought order to the library, so also could it be applied to industrial society in the hope of improving the economic foundation of stability. Public librarians did not question the fundamental economic morality of the age. As Jast wrote in describing the constituency of the public technical library:

> It includes all who are engaged in business or profession, in buying and selling, skilled and unskilled labour of every sort, the great army of workers who have made England the England she is, and upon whose well directed education depends the England that she will be.[165]

These are unequivocally the sentiments of someone in broad sympathy with the fundamental social arrangements of industrial capitalism. What librarians did question, however, was the way in which the system had developed, creating social injustice, greed, ignorance and cultural deficiency. For the system to function smoothly these unattractive by-products needed to be ameliorated. It is in this context that the social criticism and cultural concerns of public librarians should be seen. The rounded, humane education which librarians advocated was not the antithesis of the utilitarian faith in scientific materialism, but its helpmate. A liberal, cultured and idealistic perspective, it was hoped, would help to soften the harshness of material progress and the utilitarian thought with which it was associated; thereby preserving those aspects of the progressive industrial capitalist society which they deemed worthy.

Public librarianship as a controlling discourse

In this refining of the conservative image of librarians care should be taken not to expunge perceptions of professional detachment, control and power. While it is true that early public librarians were more 'social' than has previously been assumed, they were also an integral part of the rising nineteenth-century phenomenon of professionalization, and the regulatory functions it delivered. Like all professions, librarianship contained status aspirations which translated into a fabrication of both power and expert knowledge. Of relevance here are the ideas of the historian and social theorist Michel Foucault, in particular his notion of the power of discourse.

In everyday usage a 'discourse' is taken to mean a formal, and often lengthy, coherent, rational treatment of a subject in speech or writing, producing a detailed line of argument. This process is seen to contribute to the construction of fields or bodies of knowledge which are perceived as being scientifically and objectively correct, or 'truthful'; or at least leading to the eventual discovery of truth. In many of his works, but most notably *The Archaeology of Knowledge* (1972) and *Discipline and Punish* (1977), Foucault employed a definition of 'discourse' which is critical of this conventional view.[166] Foucault was primarily concerned with the evolution of thought in the sciences (especially the social sciences) and the development of what he called technologies of power and domination. He contended that scientific truths, so called, can only be understood in the context of the motives of the 'expert' networks that produce them. Foucault questioned the conventional view of discourse in that it bestows upon the world of rational knowledge an aura of neutrality. Objectivity, said Foucault, is not achievable because the formation of all knowledge, or what we accept as 'knowledge', is inseparable from the exercise of power. For Foucault, knowledge comes from power, and vice versa. Power imbues knowledge, and knowledge is shot through with power. He did not simply mean that, according to the old adage, 'knowledge is power'; rather that knowledge is generally constructed so that power is established over those who have been excluded from its construction. Foucault thus employed the term 'power-knowledge' to describe a single configuration of social ideas and practices: knowledge and power as two sides of the same 'process' coin. It is this single configuration that constitutes discourses, a key feature of these being their origin in social practices: the social rather than the scientific production of knowledge. In essence, those in command of a discourse have the power to make it true, and to underwrite its scientific validity; in which case, said Foucault, the discourse can be called a 'regime of truth'.

Discourses transmit and reinforce power. They are one of the key systems through which power flows. Discourses can be produced by different individuals in different institutional settings, and the same discourse can be adopted by groups with contradictory (for example, class) interests. The power which flows from discourses is multi-levelled and is not dependent on power derived from other means (for example, income or wealth). Discourses operate, like power, at all points in society and are prosecuted by all social groups, from parents to presidents. Concrete examples of discourse-derived power are all around us. However, the power dimension of a discourse reveals itself most vividly when history enables us to explode the mythical nature of past accepted knowledge as promulgated by dominant social groups expressing 'norms' of thought: for example, with regard to the nineteenth century, the idea that homosexuality is a disease; or the medico-psychiatric arguments of the eugenics movement that, genetically, women and blacks suffer arrested development, and that madness is invariably inherited. These ideas were clearly based on socio-political values. Time will no doubt reveal if current discourses like management theory or the information society concept are merely social constructs, 'regimes of truth' indeed, promoting, respectively, control aims wrapped in a cloak of scientific neutrality and a technology-driven justification for the entrenchment of a modified capitalism.

When we are assessing scientific arguments it is thus important to take into account their implications regarding the construction and exercise of power; this is in keeping with the proposition that science is true *because* it is powerful. Sites of power are numerous, but a key site – and a further concrete example of a discourse – is that of the professional-expert. Discourses become embedded when those who form them prohibit or exclude those who do not. In terms of the discourse of a profession, this is translated into a distancing between expert and client. One of the key characteristics of professional authority (others being the establishment of a code of ethics, a professional association, a service ethic and restricted entry) is that non-experts are unable to judge the value of work or advice given by 'distanced' specialists. This means that the 'unknowing' have to confer a degree of trust in the expert. Specialized knowledge thus constitutes a 'lack of visibility' on the part of the non-expert, thereby placing the expert in a position of control.[167] It is a feature of modernity that individuals have confident expectations of experts and their knowledge. We have come to trust experts (though commentators on postmodernity would say less so) because we lack information; and we regard expert knowledge as truthful.[168] Experts are thus in an immensely powerful position not simply because they command a body of knowledge but because, as Foucault argued, they often use their position of 'exclusive' power to fabricate knowledge; to institute 'regimes of truth' over the 'unknowing'.

While there has been a fashionable backlash against the historical research and anti-totalizing theories of Foucault (in its location outside the Marxist tradition his 'microphysics' of power has attracted enemies by challenging decades of faith in universal and structuralist explanations), his arguments about how expert knowledge and professional authority are constructed remain enticing. Such is certainly the case in respect of the public library profession in its infancy, if not now. (It is indeed strange that although Foucault was concerned with analysing the construction and, in the broad sense, the classification of knowledge he never turned his attention to libraries and librarianship.) Librarianship has always evinced a degree of distancing between expert and client; this arising from the technical processes which librarians institute and operate in an exclusive fashion, as opposed to the social function of libraries, which is often shared by librarian and user. Jesse Shera's 'technicians in their white aprons' is a description of a type of librarian distanced from his or her client; it is also a description which generations of users might find familiar.[169]

In keeping with the idea that discourses are formed by drawing on other discourses, that discourses are made up of several statements working together to construct a 'discursive formation', the development of professional librarianship should be viewed as an amalgam of various social beliefs, values and activities. The main anchorage of librarianship is the search for order in the sphere of documentation, involving a concern for the classication of knowledge, and the development of housekeeping or management procedures for the safe custody and retrieval of materials. As discussed earlier, librarians developed this concern, especially the emergence of systematic classification, as a science. James Duff Brown viewed the classification of knowledge as a practicality of life. There was a 'unanimity of feeling', he wrote, regarding 'the necessity for systematic classification of some kind in every department of human life and effort': he explained that classification occurs in nature and in the activities of the costermonger organizing his fruit.[170] Richard Garnett, Keeper of Books in the British Museum, took a loftier view: 'The classification of a great library is equivalent to the classification of human knowledge, and may, if men please, become the standard or the symbol of conflicting schools of thought.'[171] Believers in library science thus infused their subject with rigorous dynamism: classification was said to be of relevance to all levels of human thought and activity. Moreover, the perfect classification of knowledge was seen as achievable. Librarians professed that: 'Order is Heaven's first law.'[172] The complement to the evolution of classification theory in the quest for order was the development of housekeeping and managerial techniques. This role flowed directly from the library's custodial-repository function: librarians' power being drawn from their position as 'keepers of supply depots concerned with inventory and control'.[173] This bureaucratic function, alongside the science of classification, constituted the scientific principles which, as stated earlier, Samuel Green said underpinned the processes of librarians' daily occupations. It was these scientific principles, moreover, which assisted and invigorated the social purpose (the various other statements of the profession's 'discursive formation') of librarianship: namely, the promotion of self-help and of cultural enlightenment delivered by ostensibly humanitarian, disinterested and benevolent individuals.

A strong case can be made for classing these various statements, and thus the discourse of librarianship itself, as merely 'regimes of truth', rather than scientifically and objectively truthful. Each can be considered in turn. The self-help ethic which librarians preached was in reality elusive, certainly in the context of social mobility. Whereas in the nineteenth century there was some movement between artisan and lower middle-class groups (as one would expect with the increased opportunities offered by industrial life) there was virtually none between the very poor (the majority) and the artisan class. The message of emancipation which the self-help ethic contained was thus a myth, inflated by librarians' rhetoric on self-realization and increased opportunity. In the same way that the truth of the self-help discourse can be doubted, the reality of the democratic thrust of cultural enlightenment can also be questioned. The mission of librarians to disseminate culture can be awarded a liberal dimension. However, in addressing the definition of culture, the question must be asked: 'Whose culture?' The argument might be made that librarians purveyed the culture in which *they* were most interested. Further, this paternalistic view mirrors the discourse of the benevolent reformer and philanthropist as the main motivators of library progress. As Wellard wrote in assessing the public library's history in traditional style in 1940, 'It is typical that social reforms are first conceived and promoted by a small group of enlightened and liberal individuals that believe that the masses can and must be elevated.'[174] However, one of the main contentions of this study, notwithstanding the recognition given in Chapter 4 to the importance of the individual on the stage of history, is that the motives of promoters cannot be divorced from the wider intellectual, ideological and social environment acting upon them. Finally, what of the adoption of science? It is clear that expert systems of classification were part of an over-ambitious project aimed at condensing, organizing and providing access to the entire stock of human knowledge; the most radical proposal being the indexing of information *in* documents, not simply of information *about* documents (witness projects like the International Institute of Bibliography established in 1895 and utopian schemes like H. G. Wells's encyclopedic 'world brain').[175] Yet the 'depth' subject access proposed and to be engineered by ostensibly detached scientists was and is by definition a highly subjective task. Any text has a multiplicity of meanings, most of which are complex and hidden. Exhaustive indexing is based, to a large degree, on the cultural outlook of the indexer and on what society and its groups at any given time define as knowledge. Thus, insofar as librarians espoused the new scientific documentation movement of the late nineteenth century (and the accompanying need to manage libraries and their stocks more efficiently) as a credible project pursuing 'truthful' knowledge, they were engaging in what might be considered a 'false' discourse, made all the more suspect by the inclusion in it of bureaucratic regimes of library rules, regulations and procedures existing under the presumptuous heading of 'library science' or 'library economy'.

Other 'regimes of truth' are more obvious: for example, the notion broadcast by early male librarians in support of female staff that women were suited to library work because of their innate patience, and their propensity for caring and domesticity; usually meaning an inherent ability to dust books and shelves, and to be gentle with readers. A more modern obvious example would be the adoption by librarians of the term 'information manager', which can be construed as a status-driven departure or, as one commentator has put it, 'a life-raft to enable them [librarians] to reach, if not climb aboard, the large platform of the general information industries'.[176] The identification of these and other regimes of truth outlined above does not call into question the revision made here of the past image of the public librarian as cloistered, introspective and wholly self-interested. It merely supports the argument that modernity and its expert groups, librarians among them, are inevitably touched by the tentacles of utilitarian, bureaucratic control.[177] The technical profession of public librarianship has often been given a democratic, idealistic gloss, the public library being, most famously, the 'people's university'. A Foucauldian analysis, however, reveals considerable profession-driven, status-derived concerns. The discourse of librarianship in its formative period pursued a project of truth which, while claiming a liberal purpose, included a strong dynamic of social control, though not in terms of the clichéd, Marxist interpretation of the concept.

CHAPTER 10

ARCHITECTURE: THE SOCIAL CAUSES OF DESIGN

The previous chapter showed how the development of a profession intersected not just with motives of provision to its clientele, but with wider social issues too. It is not surprising that librarians displayed a social dimension, for they were a highly visible element in what was an intrinsically social institution. They could be divorced from the broader workings of society no more than their institution. The visibility of librarians and their assistants, however, was less than that of the institution's architecture, to which a social function can similarly be attached. In some respects, indeed, it appeared that buildings were more important than the books they contained. The Public Libraries Act (1850) had permitted councils to spend money (raised through loans or rates) on buildings, but not on books: in fact, the word 'book' occurs only once in the whole Act.[1] For the user too, it was often the building which mattered most. This was particularly true of the Carnegie libraries, as one reader, mimicking the benefactor's Scottish heritage, explained in 1905:

> D'ye know what a libry is? I suppose ye think it's a place where a man can go, haul down wan iv his fav'rite authors fr'm the shelf an' take a nap in it. That's not a Carnaygie libry. A Carnaygie libry is a large brick and white stone impenetrible buildin with th'name iv th' maker blown on th' dur.[2]

A new approach to architectural history

Despite the considerable presence of the public library sensed by contemporaries, relatively little research has been attempted in the area of the institution's architecture; the more uniform, and some might say uninteresting, buildings of the modern era have perhaps blunted the zeal for investigation. There have been entertaining and informative, yet brief, assessments, such as those by Keeling, Desmond and Ball.[3] More exhaustive research has been undertaken by Smith and Dewe, from the perspective of benefaction and library architect respectively.[4] These studies have naturally taken account of some social use. However, no extensive, systematic research has been conducted into the social causation (from the viewpoint of motives of provision) of the public library built form, as has been the case in respect of work by architectural historians on other building types.[5]

Not that architectural history has always admitted data from outside its immediate domain of art. A parallel can be observed in the shortcomings of research in architectural and library history. Just as library analysis has lacked a broader historical perspective, so too in architectural history the tendency has been to view built form without reference to the society which conceived it, notwithstanding the employment of the shallow device of 'social background'. However, as with library history there has emerged in architectural history in recent decades a fresh approach – one which integrates the study of the built environment with that of non-design inputs. Arising from the general thesis that built forms 'exist in a web of non-material culture, made up of ideas, values, norms, beliefs and other phenomena which do not have physical properties',[6] a number of new questions have been asked, principal among them: 'What can we understand about a society by examining its buildings and physical environment?'[7] The answer to this question is that in any society buildings absorb (through the processes of design and construction) and, subsequently, reflect (in their final form) social, economic, political, religious and cultural functions. In short, the bond between built form and social form is indissoluble.

Art and design historians have largely ignored other history. Equally, historians and sociologists have underplayed art and design; yet these are not separate or distinct from society but part of a single process.[8] Exponents of this concept are not new.[9] It is only recently, however, that a new breed of writers – Girouard being a leader in the field (though some would argue, in a superficial way) – has gained recognition.[10] New approaches adopted in architectural history can be exploited by library historians to help them crystallize, or indeed reject, motives of provision. In accounting for the built form of the pre-First World War public library, motives connected with civic power, the pursuit of culture, social cohesion, self-help, social control, national economic performance and technical education can all be placed on the design agenda: for both the design process and final architectural treatment can tell us much about support for the public library ideal, thereby confirming or adding to evidence gathered elsewhere.

Style, symbolism and 'show'

The architectural evidence is extensive and varied. Style was eclectic. Of the hundreds of libraries built before the First World War some resembled Greek or Roman temples, others Renaissance palaces, Tudor mansions, Gothic churches or Scottish baronial homes; historical references were plundered from all areas of design.[11] The preoccupation with style and excessive aesthetic treatment has since been derided. As early as 1935,

when a considerable amount of visual evidence still stood, the librarian
B. M. Headicar concluded that

> A casual survey of existing public library buildings in this country promptly leads
> to the conclusion that it would be not altogether a bad thing if many of them
> could be swallowed up in a single night and provide an opportunity to put in
> their places structures which would be suitable for their purpose.[12]

In 1942 Lionel McColvin reported that 'as a class libraries are the worst
set of buildings to be found in the country'.[13] Later, in a much cited piece,
the librarian R. C. G. Desmond exclaimed: 'It is impossible to be
enthusiastic about public library buildings in this country and difficult even
to be charitable. They stand as shabby symbols of monumental dignity.'[14]
Because they had been subjected to a diversity of styles, Desmond
continued, public libraries had been too easily mistaken for churches and
chapels, banks and board schools, prisons or public wash houses. Further,
they had been badly planned (not fit for their purpose) and 'can appeal
only to perverse admirers of the Betjemanesque'.[15]

Betjeman himself, of course, rejected the derogatory broadsides on
Victorian architecture (these reaching a height in the immediate post-1945
modernist explosion) and helped initiate a new appreciation of Victoriana.
'Some of our finest architecture', he argued, 'was built by the Victorians,
and we must rid ourselves of prejudices about date and style in order to sift
the good Victorian architecture from the bad.'[16] The architecture of the
pre-1914 public library should be seen in this light. True, application of
style was haphazard, and this perhaps undermined the corporate image of
the institution. Yet diversity was the single most dominant characteristic of
Victorian architecture.[17] It was not confined to public libraries. Moreover,
there was a practical reason for variety in that there existed for public
libraries no central body determining style and planning unlike, say, in
board schools or inter-war underground stations designed by London
Transport.

Contemporaries were aware that much was yet to be achieved in public
library design. From the 1890s onwards librarians and architects were
highly vocal on the subject.[18] 'Where lies the blame?', asked the American
Charles Soule in 1912, in criticizing the past record of public library design
both here and across the Atlantic.[19] Soule proposed that in any design
project the motto adopted should be 'Firmitas, Utilitas, Venustus': that is to
say, 'Stability, Usefulness, Loveliness'. It was his opinion, however, that in
the past too much 'Loveliness' had been administered at the expense of
'Usefulness', and that the solution to this imbalance was that 'the library
should incontestably be assigned to the utilitarian extreme'.[20] 'The end of
building is convenience', he wrote, whereas 'the end of architecture as an
art is beauty, grandeur, unity and power.'[21]

Both the distinction between utilitarian and aesthetic concern, and the
subordination of the former to the latter, as identified by Soule and others,
carried some validity. But to exaggerate either inattention to utility or its

incompatibility with beauty would be a concession to retrospective analysis. Any library design, Victorian and Edwardian included, inevitably becomes outdated; even many modern designs, despite the technology available, may enjoy only a short period of praise before criticism sets in.[22] Modern planners might think their designs are more functional than those of their predecessors but, in reality, utility is always to be measured against the objectives of a service and the nature of demands on it.

To this extent Victorian and Edwardian library planners did not wholly fail to address function. Towards the end of the nineteenth century a great deal was being said on the matter, much of it in the context of national economic performance. Planners were aware, as today, that function was crucial. Moreover, if the definition of function is broadened to include an accommodation of fundamental social purposes, such as the celebration of the civic ideal or the exaltation of culture then, surely, the aesthetic tendencies of public libraries can be said to have been functional.[23] In this context, observations of the kind made by one commentator concerning Carnegie building grants – 'dissipated in many instances in the erection of palatial buildings'[24] – divert us from the functional symbolism for which they were designed.

In 1943 a finalist of the Royal Institute of British Architects' professional exams chose to approach the problem of library architecture from a perspective of function, arguing, in deference to the 'user', that 'if we realise that in a library building there is only the very human relationship between the reader and his book, we shall remember that the library building is not really public or civic, but personal and intimate, and need not be overpowering in its dignity'.[25] Modern approaches such as this ignore the useful role that architecture can play in giving meaning to human existence through the transmission of social messages. Public libraries of the pre-First World War era were symbolic. This is not surprising since architecture is one of the symbol systems – alongside language, gesture, expressive behaviour and pictures – which constitute the common experience of culture.[26] Moreover, architecture is a highly articulate, advanced symbol system capable of communicating complex meaning. At its simplest a symbol is a phenomenon 'which has a meaning additional to that which is communicated by its superficial configuration or stimulus profile'.[27] 'The Lord Mayor's coach was not for the Lord Mayor's benefit', wrote William Paley, 'but for society's: to excite the ambition of the prentice boy.'[28] John Ruskin argued architecture to be the most political of all the arts in that it imposes upon all who care to gaze a vision which is the philosophical expression of another individual (or group), irrespective of that philosophical expression being shared by those who view it.[29] Or, as Scruton has pointed out,

> Architecture is public. It imposes itself whatever our self-image ... Every man, whatever his tastes and aptitudes, is forced to confront the buildings which surround him, and to absorb from them whatever they contain of political significance.[30]

Architecture has a potential to impress itself politically, ideologically and socially on the unsuspecting observer. Victorian and Edwardian public library providers realized this and, accordingly, built to impress. The desire to impress formed the basis of the symbolism contained in the elevations and interior decor which they selected. The symbolic essence of public libraries was not primarily located in the use of allegory. Narrative, to be sure, was employed. Of the Darlington public library it was reported: 'it may be fairly claimed for its accessories (if we may employ such a term to describe stained-glass allegories, beautiful mouldings, busts etc.) that they will have an educative influence upon its frequenters all the more powerful because of their silent impressiveness'.[31] In Oldham it was proposed that the library be decorated with medallions of twelve literary, artistic and scientific 'greats' – Dante, Chaucer, Milton, Shakespeare, Turner, Mozart, Handel, Rubens, Stephenson, Watt, Crompton, Michaelangelo – presumably offering an invitation to follow in their footsteps. In such cases (which were common) form preceded function in an attempt to explain, in easily comprehended, pictorial language, the purpose of the institution.

A similar simplicity was at times evident in the employment of certain styles. Classicism was evocative of learning and pretensions to scholarship – partly because of the idea that classical architecture required more skill and knowledge to produce – and was used by architects accordingly;[32] the numerous museums of antiquity which sprang up in the nineteenth century lent themselves well to the newly discovered details of Greek architecture.[33] Classicism was an enduring style for all building types, despite the rise of the Arts and Crafts Movement; and a great many public libraries were fashioned thus. Gothic – which in its influential period achieved a high fashion status – was closely linked to civic prestige. It also had connotations of religiously derived moral earnestness and piety, values appropriate to the age. Gothic was applied to libraries but, interestingly, to few of those donated by Carnegie.[34] Arts and Crafts designs, which, by expressing originality, aimed to attract the attention of the ordinary passer-by, were perhaps indicative of a desire for greater social cohesion as perceived by the style's 'socialistic' inventors; the 'democratic' essence of the public library would certainly have been a plausible reason for employing designs from such sources.

No doubt, some buildings were erected with an 'iconographic implication' in mind.[35] However, it is likely that most architects were unconscious of such implications in adopting historical styles.[36] The authorial intent of architects can often, if not mostly, be separated from the existence of a hidden design agenda. If architects are influenced by cultural forces, which they surely are, they may be unable to recognize the details of this process. Just because an architect opts for a particular style, this does not mean that he is consciously promoting the full range of cultural interpretations of it. In the nineteenth century, the classical style, for example, was considered to be as much a part of Britain's heritage, resulting from the Roman presence over four centuries, as was the Gothic.

To have chosen a classical design was not necessarily evocative of any complicated propaganda intention. There is nothing surprising about architects plundering their history for the style – classical, Gothic or otherwise – that pleased them. It is thus not inappropriate to argue that public library designs perhaps owed more to the extensive portfolio available to architects than to any 'associational' value in the designs chosen. On the other hand, architects must have known that in some circumstances design could be mobilized to convey a desired message: for aesthetes like Ruskin or Pugin the Gothic was as much a principle as a style; and the same might be said of Palmerston's pursuance of a classical design for the Foreign Office. Accordingly, public library designs must to an extent have included principle and propaganda.

Generally speaking, however, narrative, in terms of both allegory and style, was a relatively minor concern of architect, library committee and librarian. Far more important were lay notions of substance, solidity, taste, repose, worthiness, dignity, enduring impression, size, splendour, monumentality, prominence and simple beauty. It was these basic ingredients – the most frequently invoked in the description of public library buildings by committees, civic élites and local newspapers – which conveyed readily the institution's social purposes. (It should be stressed that in assessing the causes of public library architecture the lay notions of providers and managers are as important as, if not more so than, the more technical considerations of the architect.) The central issue was the projection through aesthetic appeal (of whatever style or allegorical embellishment at hand) of an image designed to make a secular impact on those either ignorant or in need of a reminder of the public libraries' origins and worth. As such, the doubts raised in 1839 by the Society for the Diffusion of Useful Knowledge as to the desirability of separate public library buildings – 'It is men, not a building,' it asserted, 'that constitute a society, and it is by lectures and books, and not a public room, that the purposes of their association are to be obtained'[37] – were not shared by later generations of civic leaders, and to a certain extent their librarian and architect appointees, who displayed considerable concern for aesthetic treatment.

The evidence of aestheticism – defined here as the perception, even if mistaken, of an object as artistically tasteful or pleasingly eye-catching or both – is voluminous. Local newspapers, public library annual reports, the library and architectural press and opening ceremony souvenirs are littered with examples of ostentation. Of the Birmingham Public Library it was said that, 'wherever we turn, we find in the wealth of carving and the flush of colour evidences of originality and individuality, which indicate at once inexhaustible fancy and endless labour'.[38] Occasionally an unflattering description is to be found. The library at Poplar, opened in 1894, was said to have been 'entirely without pretension or ornamental features'.[39] The new Renaissance style library at Northampton (1910) was said to be 'without elaboration, and with an artistic restraint for over-ornament'.[40] Naturally, the rate limit enforced restrictions. Excessiveness was also curbed by strictures attached to Carnegie grants (though this was more a feature of later benefaction). The initial plans for the library in Luton, for example, were rejected by Carnegie's staff for not getting 'the most accommodation which can be had for the money consistent with good taste'.[41] Not all library committees were flamboyant in their building plans. Fulham's committee recorded that: 'It was their wish that a great deal of money should not be spent on adornment and embellishment.'[42]

However, these examples appear to be the exception rather than the rule. Within the financial means available library authorities generally aimed to make an aesthetic impact, even if sometimes the outlay affected literary provision. Thus, a journalist at the opening of Hammersmith Central Library wrote that his task was one of reporting 'miserable hypocrisy: for the average borough councillor loveth bricks and mortar pregnant with rich possibilities, to the complete exclusion of the classics'.[43] James Duff Brown attacked committees for harbouring

> such extraordinary ideas as to the purchasing power of the ratepayers' money or to the dollars so lavishly bestowed by Mr Carnegie ... for an inclusive sum of £5000 they imagine they are going to obtain a building as roomy as the Agricultural Hall or as ornamental and dignified as the British Museum.[44]

A great many libraries were made palatial. The new central library at Portsmouth (1908) was described as a 'palatial building ... certainly in extent and beauty the library can compare favourably with any in the Kingdom'. One person described it as 'fit for a King', adding that 'one cannot but be struck by the sumptuousness of the building'.[45]

Public libraries did not alone fall foul of aesthetic excess. In 1896 the Arts and Crafts propagandist Walter Crane denounced public buildings generally as 'inorganic', where 'decoration is considered merely as so much super-added or surface ornament, and often not so much to emphasise as to conceal structure, or to finish or to mark it'.[46] During the period in question 'official' architecture as a class was prone to elaboration and monumentality, the town hall offering the most obvious example.[47]

Furthermore, the library building type had historically been the subject of such treatment. The libraries of the ancient world were usually connected with colonnades, an intrinsically 'dignified construction' (though these also provided a functional reading environment in warm climates).[48] The sizeable ancient library at Alexandria was located in the city's monumental area contiguous to the Royal Palace. The library's ideological purpose was to glorify the culture and patriotic spirit of ancient Greece.[49] Yet most ancient and medieval libraries were situated in buildings used primarily for other functions.[50]

One of the earliest examples of external monumentality, produced in part by isolation, was the Radcliffe Camera (1749) in Oxford.[51] By the time public libraries came to be built, the idea of elaboration achieved through the external monumentality of a mono-purpose construction was well established. The same can be said of elaboration in the sense of making libraries monuments internally. An example of internal monumentality is the large 'hall' library, adorned with extensive wall shelving. This type of elaboration was first seen in the sixteenth century (the Escorial Library of the Palace Monastery of the Spanish Kings near Madrid being one of the earliest examples[52]), and became a familiar arrangement in nineteenth-century public libraries, especially their reference departments.

The erection of vast expanses of wall shelving in public libraries (especially Victorian), as at Birmingham in 1882, offers one of the best examples of superfluous ornament. This was historicism – the free use of a vocabulary of ornament drawn from the past – at its starkest. Since the inception of the 'hall' library concept in the sixteenth century, books had provided a ready means of ornamental display. From the Renaissance onwards books were placed on the shelves with their spine turned towards the spectator instead of being laid flat with their edges outwards. The rich decoration of the books, often enhanced by their arrangement in size and even colour, added to the decorative pretensions of the library.[53] In the phenomenon of the Baroque monastic library, for example, the design intention had been to create a fused unit, incorporating floors, ceilings, paintings, sculpture, furniture, fittings and, not least, the books which 'surpass their function and become the gilt tapestry that envelopes the total experience'.[54] In the new British Museum Reading Room (built in the 1850s) Panizzi eschewed statues and ornamental incrustations; the books were to be the ornamentation.[55]

A similar aesthetic experience was intended in many public libraries, whether conveyed through vast arrays of volumes or the supposed beauty of the shelving which supported them (though it should be remembered that good woods for shelving were often chosen for economy reasons in that they were durable).[56] Yet the sensible option, in terms of saving space, of keeping most of the books away from the reading room in separate stacks had been seriously advocated in the early nineteenth century.[57] (The first design for a library on such utilitarian lines was said to be that of Leopoldo della Santa, who in 1816 in Florence published a pamphlet entitled *Della Construzione e del Regolamento di una Pubblica Universale Biblioteca, con la Pianta Dimostrativa*. This included a plan, never carried into effect, advocating the use of separate book stores and reading room to save space.[58]) As the bookstocks of public libraries expanded so did the shelving needed to support them. Hence, galleries were added as a functional, though at the same time ornamental, device. As wall space became short, alcoves were introduced to provide more shelving. Yet public library readers themselves were not allowed to take books down from the shelves or, in some instances, use alcoves. The use of wall shelving, alcoves and galleries was therefore often highly ornamental, owing little to function.

This illogical, expensive and extravagant means of storage became self-evidently redundant once the issue had been raised in the early 1880s by William Archer, who as librarian at the National Library of Ireland in Dublin oversaw there the space-saving experiment of closed stocks and separate rooms, as opposed to the alternative of the vast hall housing decorative wall shelving.[59] Archer himself was probably influenced by the American librarian W. F. Poole.[60] The library press of the early 1880s conveyed a substantial debate on the 'wall shelving versus stack issue', highlighting the non-utilitarian nature of the former. From this time onwards, as Kelly has argued, there really was no excuse for designing in the traditional style.[61] But change was slow: library providers continued to find vast acres of wall shelving, served by galleries and supplemented by alcoves, as an aesthetically pleasing style.

This particular means of ornamentation is just one example of the considerable appeal made to the aesthetic faculty. Such an appeal was not new to library architecture. However, in the nineteenth century it became more widespread owing to the expansion of local government and the increased wealth of those who ran it. Hobsbawm has argued that the 'gigantic, awful and very expensive municipal buildings' of the second half of the nineteenth century were the result of both the vast surplus capital and savings accumulated in the first phase of industrialism, and the competition between municipalities for the best civic image.[62] This appears to be a plausible, fundamental explanation of the over-romanticizing and the propensity for 'show' in early public library design.

Civic society and its leaders

Civic pride and public library architecture went hand in hand. The librarian of the Royal Institute of British Architects wrote in 1939:

> If ever there was an architectural problem that should inherently be free from cliche, pompousness and all vile accoutrements of civic esteem it is the problem of designing a public library; and yet, if this is true, there is hardly a public library in England that can be produced to give whole-hearted support to the argument.[63]

It is a paradox of public library architecture that the successful business élites who populated many councils and library committees up and down the country, and who in making their money extolled the virtues of frugality and thrift, often opted for extravagance in library building. Many councils borrowed heavily to satisfy their desire for memorable edifices. The proportion of income devoted to the annual repayment of loans sometimes exceeded 35 per cent, thereby exerting pressure on salaries and book funds.[64] Monumentality and elaboration resulted, in part, from the fact that civic leaders wished buildings to be representative of their hierarchical position in the community.

The use of architecture by civic leaders to celebrate the towns which they dominated was seen in relation to other building types. Town halls (in which public libraries were sometimes situated), most notably after the Municipal Corporations Act of 1835, displayed in their architecture a commitment to town life and its improvement. For example, Manchester's classical town hall of 1825, built by the old Tory oligarchy at a cost of £40,000, was later eclipsed in terms of size and splendour by a fashionable new Gothic building of 1877, erected by Manchester's buoyant bourgeoisie at a cost of £1 million. This new town hall reflected, it has been argued, the confidence, power, wealth and deeply felt political sovereignty of the city's bourgeoisie.[65]

A similar representation of the 'substantial' middle class can be seen in the history of the public library in Birmingham. The city's first public library was built in the 1860s under the aegis of the 'economists' who dominated the council from the mid-1850s to the early 1870s. The mayoralty of Joseph Chamberlain, between 1873 and 1876, radically altered attitudes to local government spending.[66] One result of this was the striking monumentality of the new library built in 1882 – one of the best examples we have of public library size and splendour – in marked contrast to the frugality of its predecessor.

On account of their official standing, public libraries were subjected to a ubiquitous use of heraldry, and in their overall treatment were 'usually thought worthy of a certain dignity and substantiality'.[67] The use of architectural flamboyance to engage in civic rivalry has been noted above.[68] 'Show' was a means of competing against rival municipalities. Library committees commonly visited other towns to view their libraries when considering their own architectural plans.[69] 'Show' was also in keeping with ideas, drawn from the middle-class experience, on 'what a library should be'. Progressively in the nineteenth century, the libraries of large houses became general living rooms where books were displayed rather than used: the library became a mere drawing room lined with bookcases, and 'anyone wanting to study would have had to retire elsewhere'.[70]

The notion of libraries as things of display and ostentation was not therefore alien to the urban élites who provided public libraries. Moreover, the form which display took – that is to say, an often 'heavy' approach to internal decoration seen typically in showpiece reference departments – perhaps reflected the male domination of the architectural production and selection processes. Historically, the domestic library had been an essentially male room, often situated next door to other male rooms like those for billiards and smoking. Further, a masculine touch also characterized the dining room, which sometimes doubled as a library. It is possible, therefore, that male architects and committee members drew on their own and others' domestic situations in producing the rather formal interiors often evident in municipal libraries.

Public library designs endorsed rather than flattered middle-class self-confidence. They were not insincere monuments to the power of urban élites, but genuine barometers of their confident self-image. Accordingly, style should not be seen as an important issue. The choice of Gothic for the Bradford Wool Exchange of the 1860s has been viewed by one writer as backward looking and, by virtue of its medieval origins, illustrative of a middle-class sympathy with the traditions of landed society.[71] There is no evidence that when towns chose Gothic for their public libraries, or indeed classical styles which also had aristocratic overtones, they were expressing a social emulation of aristocratic values. It was not style – which in any case changed rapidly and was often chosen for its fashion value – but *substantiality* which mattered. When Betjeman wrote that the St Pancras Hotel reminded him of 'a pompous alderman with an enormous watch-chain, flaring tie and pearl tie-pin masking a bosom in which beats a worthy heart', he was thinking not so much of its Gothic treatment as its imposing image. There is no reason to suppose that civic leaders thought any differently about the pre-1914 public library.[72]

Library designs were essentially the work of civic leaders, not their appointed architects or their librarians. The latter had little influence with their committees. When Fulham was planning its new central library in the 1890s the building sub-committee (of eight) excluded the librarian.[73] Architects did not conform to the image of unfettered artists. Rather, they were 'tradesmen' architects.[74] Generally, they produced what committees wanted, or what they thought committees wanted. Designers proceeded on the basis of what had gone before and the instructions given to them by the committees, who, as noted above, travelled much to view and note existing buildings. In the Edwardian period such pictorial reference works as A. Cotgreave's *Views and Memoranda of Public Libraries* (1901) and J. J. Macdonald's *Passmore Edwards Institutions* (1900) must have had some influence on the recycling of established notions of how a public library should look. Architectural competition reinforced the control of commit-tees. Independent assessors were often appointed (more so later in the period) but their decisions were not necessarily accepted by committees, who might opt instead for a tame architect, perhaps a local man.[75] Competitions provided a wide choice for committees but encouraged a tendency to conform, whereas patronage arguably allowed for greater artistic freedom. As librarians noted: 'Competitive plans are usually insisted on; by such means the committee gains a variety of ideas and gets what it wants.'[76] Committees seldom looked for radical innovation in architecture. This resulted in friction between committees on the one hand, and librarians and architects on the other.[77]

Good or bad, in terms of aesthetic and functional quality, municipal libraries were none the less evidence of political sovereignty and local patriotism, the latter term being much used in the public library debate.[78] They reflected – despite the tendency to copy designs – the confidence and security of civic leaders and the urban middle class, who revelled in the prestigious appearance of the public library built form.

Benefactors

Few public libraries owed their origin or maintenance to civic society alone. Benefaction was widespread. Public library architecture made statements about the relationship between giver and recipient. Buildings reflected the social status of benefactors and demonstrated to townspeople the apparently selfless munificence of the gift. In York in 1881 J. S. Rowntree encouraged benefaction from any wealthy manufacturer or merchant so disposed, not just because a gift of a public library building would be an 'incalculable boon' for the city, but also because it 'might confer honour for themselves'.[79] In Darlington, where the Quaker Edward Pease bequeathed money for a public library, the entrance hall was decorated with a white marble bust of the late donor on a black marble pedestal.[80] Of the building as a whole it was said that: 'as it was erected as a memorial, no expense was spared by the donors to make it in every way worthy of the memory of its founder'.[81] Some benefactors took great interest in the progress of the buildings for which they had pledged money. For example, William Gilstrap, benefactor of the public library in Newark, sought the advice of J. Potter Briscoe in matters of detail, spent much time riding around the town searching for a suitable site and personally supervised the architectural drawings.[82]

Some idea of the public acclaim which the benefaction of a public library could generate can be gathered from A. Kenealy's *The Things We Have Prayed For* (1915). Passages from the novel describe the public library in fictional Croxford, donated some years earlier by a local businessman, Cooling Senior. The library was said to be 'a handsome and substantial building'.

> Cooling Senior had built and presented it to the town ... A man of large ideas, the gift was a considerable and costly one. He had spared no expense in construction or equipment. There were excellent reference and reading rooms; reading and writing rooms; class-rooms; a good if small museum; a picture gallery and a lecture hall. What it had cost him by the time all was completed nobody knew; though many speculated. It pleased his fellow townsmen to put the sum in large, round, ever-increasing figures. All were justly proud of it. No other town of its size had a Library to compare it with, in point of architecture or equipment.

When one evening the library played venue to the annual *conversazione* many speakers praised the institution and its benefaction: 'for the hundredth time' Senior Cooling was spoken of as 'the benefactor of the town in his munificent gift of our magnificent Library'. Clearly, magnificent buildings highlighted munificence.

Self-help

Benefactors consistently espoused the notion of the public library as an educator in self-help. Buildings were a celebration of this social philosophy, which proclaimed the moral supremacy and material efficacy of the free market. They bore physical testimony to the ability, supposedly inherent in all, to rise above one's station and achieve a measure of moral and material improvement beyond that bestowed at birth. References to past achievers, in keeping with the 'great man' approach to history, were freely deployed.

Allegorical sculptures of the 'greats' stressed the importance of culture, but also reminded onlookers that anyone could rise to cultural heights. It was related that at Fulham's Westfield Library

> Fancy scrolls along the walls are enriched with the names of all sorts and conditions of men, who, in various ages, have advanced civilization in all its branches.[83]

Whether or not such allegory made an impact is unknown. Obviously, providers saw it as worthwhile. Although not as important, perhaps, as monumentality and style, allegory could come into its own in certain circumstances – for example, in making the best use of a narrow street where a building's overall presentation mattered less. The allegory of achievement was also used internally. At Lincoln Public Library (1914) the aim was to make the marbled palatial entrance hall 'a pantheon of Lincolnshire worthies'.[84] However, allegory was arguably less decipherable than carved inscriptions. Often adorning doorways, these were clarion calls to self-motivation. Erith Public Library (1906) carried over its entrance the motto: 'Labour overcomes all things.'[85]

Nowhere was the symbolism of success and self-help more evident than in the built form of the Carnegie Library. Busts, paintings, ornamental carvings and the inscribed name of the benefactor were a constant reminder of the social morality which guided his life and with which he was synonymous. Tenets such as 'Work is no punishment, it is a blessing' or 'No young man ever lived who has not had his chance' would have been familiar to many Carnegie library users, perhaps endeavouring to emulate through educational improvement the benefactor's 'rags to riches' tale.[86] Yet irrespective of the books, the sheer physical presence of the building as a Carnegie benefaction was enhanced by the fact that he never gave money for books or subsequent maintenance: these were the responsibility of local citizens who, in true self-help fashion, would be taxing themselves to ensure the upkeep of an unexpected boon. A Carnegie building thus echoed the Christian message of exploiting a gift to its full potential, stating that even a few talents could be transformed into unthinkable success. As a London County Councillor was reported to have stated in praising the new Carnegie library at Mile End, opened in 1906,

> Mr Carnegie was one who knew his fellow men and tried to do what he could for them. The life story of that gentleman might well serve as a life lesson to all of them. From very humble surroundings, Mr. Carnegie had achieved wealth and amassed riches beyond the dreams of avarice.[87]

Such lessons were embodied in the bricks and mortar of Carnegie institutions. The name Carnegie was inseparable from both his moral message and the buildings designed to deliver it. In keeping with the need to attract would-be self-improvers, Carnegie libraries were treated with aesthetically pleasing, historical styles. They conformed to no specific architectural model, though free Renaissance and Edwardian Baroque were noticeably popular.[88] Rather, their similarity was in their substantiality and prominence, which often contradicted function. They stood as the epitome of ideal over practicality. A degree of function, social in form, none the less operated: the social message they conveyed was the ethos of the Carnegie philosophy stated in bricks and mortar.

Citizenship

Buildings which furthered the rhetoric of individualism sought, para-doxically, to foster social cohesion via a collectivist message. The concepts of the public library as a fountain of citizenship and a vehicle for social cohesion found expression in its architecture. The Arts and Crafts advocate Walter Crane asserted in 1896 that modern decoration of public buildings could be enhanced by 'the new development of municipal life and spirit in our towns', which fostered 'a sense of citizenship and local pride'. The public building, correctly decorated, 'would bestow a centralising and organic life and purpose to the vast jungles of bricks we call cities'. Once the organization of ordinary needs and utilities had been secured, said Crane, the 'collective' citizen 'should seek some higher and more comprehensive means for the expression of the aims and ideals of the community which should satisfy its needs, while stimulating the imagination and uniting the sentiments'.[89]

As a 'quasi-socialist' designer, Crane's faith in the ability of a well-designed public library to unite 'sentiments' and furnish a 'centralizing life' is not surprising. Yet such optimism was broadly felt. A prime concern for most library authorities was to site the library centrally so as to emphasize the availability of the institution to 'all' citizens. Librarians believed buildings should be 'near to the heart of the town's affairs, not poked away in some remote position serviceable only to the immediate residents'.[90] Even non-librarians believed that 'libraries should occupy prominent positions so as to attract people to them, not to be shut up in the background of some old building, or in a small street'.[91] Prominence would attract the 'goodwill' of the public, as Savage was later to advocate.[92] The requirement of central siting needed, of course, to be balanced against the desire for quiet surroundings conducive to rational recreation. The fact that planners often urged a quiet site was a reaction against the noise of many nineteenth-century urban environments. The yearning for quiet was one reason why reading rooms were often situated at the back of buildings, and why Sunday opening was suggested.[93] The noise issue was important, but was generally attributed less of a priority in the planning process than centrality. Peripheral siting contradicted the fundamental democratic, social and universal objectives of the public library. When Manchester Public Library moved to new premises in Kings Street in 1877 it did so because 'the Free Libraries are intended for all classes of the community ... and as the Reference Library is used largely by literary and scientific men and students, as well as by working men it appears indispensable that such Reference Library be in a central position'.[94] The frequent use of the word 'central' to describe a town's main library emphasized the importance attached to centrality. Naturally, not all libraries could be centrally sited. Tight budgets meant that central sites sometimes had to be passed over in favour of less well situated, but cheaper, adapted premises. In the early years, a high proportion of libraries were not purpose-built. Between 1850 and 1870, 17 out of 55 buildings used as public libraries were adapted premises.[95] Towns also established branches outside urban centres. By 1914, 533 library authorities in the UK were providing 345 branches.[96] However, the overriding public library phenomenon, in terms of both physical and symbolic presence, was the main town library. This was usually the flagship of a town's library network and was given, accordingly, considerable architectural treatment; though many branches, to be sure, also displayed elaboration and monumentality.

Flagship libraries needed to be not just centrally located and imposing in character, but preferably built in isolation.[97] An isolated building was more striking. For this reason some providers argued that the library should not share a building which also housed other institutions. When, early in the twentieth century, Northampton was considering a position for its Carnegie library a local newspaper objected to the library's planned inclusion in a multi-purpose building, proclaiming 'how much more complimentary to Carnegie to have a separate site'.[98] But many libraries did share buildings with other civic institutions and offices, or were adjacent to them. When this occurred the library's civic nature was underlined.

But libraries did not have to be contiguous to other official premises to evoke a civic message. The library belonged to civic society and all its social groups; it was a classless institution. As such, the idea was less to make the building appear civic (though this was not unimportant) than to make it as widely attractive as possible. A. L. Champneys argued that if the message can be conveyed that the building is 'for the public' then 'the success of the institution is more than half-assured'.[99] Because it was a communal utility it needed to be aesthetically attractive to all. Size and splendour were the lowest common denominators in this respect: public libraries needed to be 'landmarks' if they were to help encourage citizenship. As the library architect H. T. Hare argued,

> Every building should be a worthy landmark to the district where it is built, and should impress itself on the passer-by as a dignified expression of the public spirit which has promoted its erection.[100]

It was hoped that a public library which impressed, and hence attracted wide social use, would bridge the gulf between classes. Monumentality and artistry were seen as lasting investments in civic responsibility, the dividend to be paid in the currency of social stability.

In terms of internal design, the quest for citizenship manifested itself most obviously in newsroom design. Finances permitting, these were made spacious, not just because of their popularity, but also because of the practice of allotting each newspaper or periodical its own stand, reading slope or table space. This generous layout reflected the newsroom's niche in the politics of a 'liberal' pluralistic society. The 'liberal' notion of politics was similar to that of political economy in that it was believed that a point of equilibrium was arrived at by giving free reign to all the forces acting on the production and distribution of a particular commodity or service, or, in the case of social and political affairs, a particular issue. Via the 'furnace of debate', newsrooms would help to establish the 'truth'. In design terms this role was manifest in the vast array of fittings, each with its own journal, each offering ideas for the consideration of 'reasoning' users. Later, as the press became more concentrated, designers turned away from sprawling lay-outs and became more interested, most notably during the First World War, in utilitarian means of storing journals ready for speedy retrieval. There was, however, no overnight conversion to utilitarian methods (in fact, as late as 1988 Darlington Public Library was maintaining in its newsroom the multiplicity of reading slopes from the last century).

Culture

Public library landmarks were invitations to engage in civic life and to espouse citizenship through educational endeavour. Education, including the reading of 'good' fiction, was the means to culture, a liking for which was captured in the institution's architecture. Since antiquity library architecture has evoked an enthusiasm for culture. Libraries in the ancient world often resembled temples (or were given prominent places within them) because their contents – laws, rituals, songs, prayers, creation stories, biographies of the Gods – were treasured or sacred texts.[101] The 'temple' mentality of preserving such indispensable materials, which formed the basis of a culture, is identifiable in Victorian and Edwardian public library architecture. Public libraries, especially the largest, were said to be repositories of humanity's accumulated knowledge. Their architectural treatment often stressed the antiquity and tradition of learning. Thus, classical designs were not unpopular. These had never been absent from the British design tradition, but enjoyed unprecedented popularity after the results of detailed research into ancient Greek architecture had been brought to Britain in the 1750s. The architectural work of James Stuart and Nicholas Revett (the first volume of the Antiquities of Athens was published in 1762) was a 'landmark in the history of taste'. It generated a mania for Greek design.[102] 'We are all Greeks now', said Shelley.[103] The news of excavations at Pompeii (1863) stimulated a similar enthusiasm for the Classical era. Victorians looked to the cultural achievements of the ancients, and proceeded to congratulate their own social progress by copying classical architecture.

The public library built (in conjunction with a museum) in Preston in the 1880s was a prime example of the desire to ape Greek cultural performance. In choosing the Ionic style the architect was reported to have said that as the Hellenic race reached the highest standard in the plastic arts, literature and geometrical science, the suitableness of the style for the purpose of a building which is to be a repository of knowledge, of examples of the arts, and the specimens illustrative of the sciences, will be admired by all.[104]

It was not only Greek culture which was celebrated; Renaissance culture was also invoked. In his *Ideal City* (1894) Canon Barnett anticipated that in the perfect urban environment

> Halls, galleries, libraries, baths, hospitals, colleges, asylums, prisons (many of them brilliant with mosaic) will catch and raise the thoughts of men, as in the old days the thoughts of their citizens were caught by the public buildings of Florence and Venice.[105]

Memorial architecture of this kind signified a devotion to culture in an age when reference to the past and to non-utilitarian pursuits provided a respite from the onward rush of industrialism. Public libraries, like temples and impressive buildings of bygone ages, were in many respects set apart from the real world. As places for the reflective perusal of cultural achievement they were havens set aside from the hurry of daily life. This role was reflected in designs evocative of the intellectual excellence of past successful civilizations.

Yet as argued above, allegory should not be exaggerated. For lay providers and users, the concern for culture was conveyed more by grandeur and beauty than by style. Of the educational complex of buildings (which included a public library) proposed for Nottingham in 1876 it was said:

> If this be but the dawn of high popular culture, if the science of the present day, mighty as it is, be yet an undeveloped human power, and if the arts of eighteen hundred years ago are yet to hold their true refining influence, and shed a brighter lustre on futurity, then it is essential our Training Institutions should be designed on principles wide and unparsimonious, should have unstinted facilities for growth and permeation, and be endowed with generosity and freedom.[106]

The emphasis on size, however, did not eclipse appeals to the aesthetic faculty. In discussing the planning of small libraries, the *Building News* argued that 'The mental impressions made on the reader by the stones may be more elevating than that he receives from his reading.'[107] This echoed Ruskin's belief in the educative power of architecture, which, if artistically produced, contributed to 'mental health, power and pleasure'.[108] Pleasing architecture was a ready means of diffusing culture and improving taste.[109] It was hoped that beautiful buildings would encourage beauty in spirit and character too. Municipal patrons commissioned what they hoped would be works of art, as educational in their design as in their content.[110] As such, criticism of town élites deemed to have practised architectural barbarism is unfounded.[111] The middle class did not 'fail' culturally in the field of art. Despite the 'Gradgrind' image there is evidence (as offered in Chapters 5 and 8) to suppose that the middle class genuinely espoused art and architecture. The work of the architectural historian Mark Girouard is of relevance here, in that he accounts for young upper middle-class attachment to the fashionable Queen Anne style of the 1870s in their feeling of being more socially secure than their parents, who had been confronted with intense social unrest, most notably Chartist agitation. In the socially relaxed climate of the 1870s they were able to evolve a sympathy for 'sweetness and light'.[112] This Arnoldian interpretation can also be applied to public library architecture (of whatever style) which, plainly, displayed a confident enthusiasm for culture among middle-class providers. Buildings were frequently praised as 'tasteful' and 'dignified'. The East Ham Public Library carried above its portico the motif: 'Let there be light.'[113] The public library promoter Thomas Greenwood once urged: 'Let your Free Library be a public building doing credit to the intelligence of your town.'[114] The architect M. B. Adams recommended that public libraries be 'fitting caskets for enshrining jewels of knowledge'.[115] Public library architecture was pre-eminently a method of transmitting culture. This was the case in the anthropological sense of reproducing a society's culture; but more so in the aesthetic sense of diffusing culture to a brutalized populace.[116] 'To build ugly buildings', asserted the *Woolwich Pioneer* in commenting on a new library for the town, 'is a practice equivalent to building insanitary ones. The latter injure the body ... the former injure the mind in subtle and unnoticeable ways.'[117] The aim was to enrich the mind with the intellectual achievements of the past, as the librarian of Edinburgh University described his town's public library:

> As you enter the lofty hall with its myriad of pillars, see the busts representing in marble the lineaments of the intellectually great whose thoughts uttered by the voice, or given forth in the printed page gave vitality to the young life; look on shelves closely packed with books which carry the mind back to the most beautiful dawn that mortals could behold – the dawn of a printed literature, and we are lifted out of our ordinary thoughts. There is something impressive, 'reverential' in the building itself, as if it were filled with the spirits of the mighty dead who have made us heirs of the spiritual life of past ages.[118]

It is no coincidence, indeed, that many internal public library designs were based on academic models: libraries in Shoreditch (Haggerston) (1897) and Eltham (1906) were said to incorporate features of the Old Ashmolean in Oxford.[119] The public library was, after all, popularly presented as the 'poor man's university'. In this context design possibly enhanced cultural osmosis.

Social control

The fact that designs mirrored the quest for culture might easily be construed as an attempt to transmit middle-class values to a resistant working class. Built forms maintain social forms.[120] Buildings can indoctrinate and hence help to maintain power; ideals can be 'constructed'. Winston Churchill once said that 'the sociologist wants to know how men shape buildings and buildings shape men'.[121] For social control theorists, the operative word here would be 'shape': it encapsulates the idea that buildings do not simply incorporate society's ideas and beliefs but can be used by dominant social groups to maintain their position. This theory has commonly been voiced with regard to the public library. The social composition of committees, in respect of both elected and co-opted members, was radically different from that of the bulk of readers. It was committees which controlled the capital to construct buildings and which chose designs. Hence, it might be argued, architecture embodied the value systems of middle-class library governors. Social control was thus exercised, even if not explicitly stated. Working-class readers were consequently intimidated and alienated.

This is a crude analysis. True, library design can be used as 'a vehicle for social engineering aspirations', and as a means of maintaining power.[122] But with regard to the pre-1914 public library built form, control aspirations should not be mistaken for successful middle-class social control. Even if impressive architecture did humble some working-class readers – and there is not a shred of evidence to suggest that they were not immediately 'at one' with elaborate and monumental surroundings – its intention was to inspire.

Some providers believed that grandeur would drive away lower-class users. When Nottingham was considering a new building in 1867 one councillor warned: 'If they erected a fine, grand building ... the working classes would be kept away. They would never attend in their working clothes ... but would prefer a plain, substantial building erected without pretence.'[123] Similar sentiments were voiced concerning technical education institutions: 'It is thought by some persons that good rooms and pleasant looking institutions are apt to drive away the regular mechanic; and possibly, if they are made too luxurious, this may be the case.'[124] The idea, therefore, was to strike a balance between sparse utility and over-elaboration. In 1892 Bristol's librarian urged that a new library be 'one fit for a prince and not too good for a workingman'.[125]

The minimum condition was that a free library should 'attract'. Champneys believed that an attractive exterior and an agreeable interior were great inducements to the use of the library.[126] The architecture of Norwood Public Library was said to be 'distinctly inviting'.[127] An attempt was made to emulate the public house's potential for attracting a clientele: 'if gin palaces and the like are brilliant and handsome', said Birmingham's librarian J. D. Mullins, 'why should the opposition be enamoured of the dingy and the mean'.[128] Consequently, money permitting, few public libraries were designed like workhouses. This is not surprising. As institutions designed to attract, libraries were diametrically opposed to the deterrent principle of the workhouse 'Bastilles', even though both institutions aimed at a rationalization of labour under capitalism, and operated according to rigid regimes of regulation.

Attractive, comfortable surroundings were also seen as a means of rewarding library use. At the stone-laying ceremony for Leamington Spa's new Edwardian library the mayor explained that readers who, through the library, had improved themselves educationally and materially deserved a 'palatial' setting.[129] Moreover, it was believed that those interested in the 'aesthetic' would expect an artistic environment. The library promoter Janetta Manners wrote that 'judging from the delight working people take in illustrated papers, I believe they would enjoy their reading and recreation rooms all the more if it were found possible to beautify the walls'.[130] This was done in Hammersmith reference library, where books were kept in stockrooms to leave the walls free for hanging pictures: 'to leave it free for pictures', commented the *Builder*, 'would add much comfort to the quiet and comfort of the room'.[131] In this instance, the closed access system, a deterrent to some, was turned to good use as a means of attracting readers.

Architecture to impress was not a classical social control mechanism, though it was an attempt to influence society. But what of the considerable supervision built into public library architecture? Was this not an indication that working-class readers could not be trusted and needed to be educated into 'correct' methods of library use? A. L. Champneys believed that deference was paid to the 'shrine of supervision'.[132] Certainly, a great many changes were made to facilitate supervision. Glass screens were used to divide departments. Alcoves, the haunt of the malefactor, gradually became unpopular and were eschewed. To deliver a broad observational sweep, news-stands were swept away from the centre of rooms and replaced by wall-mounted reading slopes. Further, the supervisory potential of the library counter was exploited. The library counter is not just a physical, but also a psychological barrier.[133] It symbolizes the power of a library's staff over the user; and it can be positioned in such ways as to enhance, through supervision, that very power. The perfect model of supervisory power in this respect was provided by the circular Reading Room of the British Museum. Its staffed inner circle was just sufficiently raised to give a clear view of readers' desks radiating out from the centre. In the centre, commented one early description, 'is the 'quarter deck' of the Chief Superintendent, whose position commands a general view of all the tables and their occupants'.[134] The circular reading room was proposed as an 'ideal type' in Greenwood's widely read *Public Libraries* (1891).[135]

For those seeking to improve supervision there was no better model from which to draw inspiration than Bentham's panopticon. The design of the panopticon prison was determined by Bentham's belief in the efficacy of social engineering; in particular, the idea that an individual's character could be improved by external 'checks and spurs'. As he explained, 'Morals reformed – health preserved – industry invigorated – instruction diffused ... all by a simple idea in architecture', which he described as a 'new mode of obtaining power over mind, in a quantity hitherto without example'.[136] Bentham believed that prison should not merely protect society from the criminal, or merely dispense retribution, but also morally regenerate the offender in order to heighten his or her utility; he argued that prison education should aim to promote industry and responsibility, thereby facilitating a return to citizenship once a sentence had been served. One of the roles of the panopticon would be a cross between a technical education institute and a labour exchange, to which employers would come to choose recently trained workers.

The most striking feature of the panopticon was its design. The building was to be circular, with the governor and his staff at the centre of the complex, and the prisoners' cells at the circumference, all cells subject to constant observation. The essence of the scheme, however, was that observation was to be a one-way process. Superintendents could see prisoners, but prisoners could not see superintendents. It has been proposed that the panopticon plan displayed omniscience, omnipresence and omnipotence.[137] It was omniscientific in that character was to be changed empirically through functional architecture; omnipresent in that at no time could inmates determine that they were being unobserved; and omnipotent in that superintendents had absolute power over the incarcerated.

Parallels can be drawn between the 'moral architecture'[138] of the panopticon and aspects of public library design. The latter, like the former, often aimed to improve character and manufacture better citizens. A news-stand designed by the architect J. M. Brydon for reading rooms, for example, sought to 'ensure that people stand upright to read the paper and not lounge over it'.[139] Supervision was precisely calculated to prevent malefaction. Readers did not know when they were likely to be observed. It was not the library staff's job to observe continually; they had other duties to attend to. Readers would be aware, however, that at any time a librarian's gaze could fall on them. This was especially true in the case of elongated counters in open access libraries where stacks were arranged at right angles to the service point: as the architect M. B. Adams explained, the public 'never knew exactly who was looking at them or when they were being supervised'.[140] Arrangements for supervision thus increased the power of library staffs. Of the new library in Poplar it was said that, as a result of the counter's location, staff would be able to

> overlook and control the whole of the public portions of the building. The number of assistants will thus be of the fewest possible. With a different arrangement it would have been necessary to employ others for watching the evilly-disposed persons who, when unobserved, mutilate books and newspapers, and annoy others.[141]

There is no evidence that library planners studied the panopticon plan, but Bentham believed that his plan could be applied to other building types such as factories, hospitals, workhouses and schools (his Chrestomathic school of 1816 was also designed 'in the round' to give central surveillance); and it is certainly true that many libraries (public and otherwise) were given a circular design. What can be said is that the design principles of the panopticon fitted the requirements of other building types, public libraries included, in the field of social policy. However, library supervision should not be exaggerated. In practice, the public largely supervised themselves.[142] This echoed William Ewart's belief that the public use of a library, as opposed to exclusive admittance, created 'a kind of public police by their presence, which affords a kind of safeguard for the collection'.[143] In other words, authentic, 'informal' social control would operate, and for the most part surely did.

Further, just as the panopticon was designed to oversee all prisoners, so with public library supervision no distinction was made between readers, certainly not on grounds of class. There is no evidence that working-class readers were more intimidated than higher-class readers by supervision or, indeed, the library's general ambience. There is little evidence that any class of reader experienced intimidation; though this does not necessarily mean that none occurred. There might have been a general dislike of closed access, but that was not tantamount to coercion. It is true that early-twentieth-century library promoters looked back to a previous era characterized by a 'please do not touch' spirit. But this was, arguably, a retrospective and, hence, exaggerated analysis coloured by closed access and the modern commitment to make public libraries 'homes of the liberal studies and centres for the development of the true humanities of life'.[144] Recalling his early career, Sayers explained that producing an informal atmosphere by providing paintings, busts and ferns, in what was essentially a formal setting, created a reverence for books. In terms of the need to promote an educational image, this was a sensible ploy. It did not mean that in earlier years there was less reverence for books and more malefaction, for which greater control was required. Moreover, regarding the era as a whole, it is difficult to accept the picture of conflict between library establishment and user as painted by some, including Altick, who has written:

> in many places, the brusqueness of the assistants, the stern maintenance of discipline and decorum, and the inadequate and uncomfortable accommodations actually drove readers away.[145]

Such statements are highly contentious.

On the other hand, attention should not be diverted from the controlling aspect of the professional-expert discourse of librarianship discussed in the previous chapter; and the way, moreover, in which this discourse was reflected in the design and ambiance of public libraries. While it is important not to overplay the scolding image of library staff, the evidence that they drew status from fabricating an appropriate ambiance and from the implementation of efficient, supervisory and 'officious' designs is strong. Just as in the modern prison, as Foucault explains in *Discipline and Punish* (1977), detailed regulations, drills, timetables and the classification of inmates and their work tasks together orchestrated a 'dressage of the body',[146] so too in the library setting a reader was often faced by an array of operational procedures and rules, many of which found visual representation in the liberal deployment of prohibitive or explanatory signs and posters.

Of importance here is Foucault's theory of 'bio-power': the exercising of power via the (often subtle) domination of the body. Emerging in the late eighteenth century, the scientific disciplining of the body had by the middle of the nineteenth century, said Foucault, invaded a wide range of institutions beyond the prison. These included the asylum, the hospital, the school, the factory and the military. Although Foucault did not mention libraries his concepts of 'bio-power' and 'projects of docility' (the mechanisms by which the body is made subordinate to the objectives of those in positions of power) might easily be applied to them. It is possible to identify a strict coding of activities in early public libraries, especially after the open access revolution of the 1890s. These included the physical effects of the rising discourse of library science, such as the browsing of a now highly segmented and classified stock and catalogue; and the rituals of issuing and borrowing once selection had been made, and of returning items once read. Moreover, these activities were individualizing in nature, the aim being to dismember and calm the 'threatening', swarming crowd. 'Safeguarding' wicket gates in open access libraries imposed individual passage into the library. There was also the overbearing (though self-policed as well) regulation of silence; yet in an open access environment which unavoidably produced mingling of individuals in close proximity to one another, and which thus invited inter-reader communication. The imposition of regimes of silence highlighted the power of library staff by individualizing behaviour in a communal setting.

Evidence of controlling ambiance and design undermines the image of the early public library as a liberal institution. The most conclusive evidence in this regard comes from the panopticism of many open access lay-outs. Radial stacks, by facilitating the prospect (as far as the reader was concerned) of continual observation, defined the discourse of supervision not as one of assistance, as library science would have it, but as one of spying. The same control mechanism, as noted earlier, operated in rooms where stacks were positioned in traditional parallel formation at 90 degrees to long counters, thereby allowing staff a clear view of any aisle at any given moment; something which naturally kept the would-be malefactor guessing, and hence anxious to keep his or her body docile (physical docility mirroring, interestingly, the proclaimed ideological neutrality, or docility, of the public library). It is clear, therefore, that although the open access revolution and the designs which it inaugurated were wrapped in a discourse of liberation (self-service to aid self-help) and science (expert classification systems to facilitate browsing and cultural enlightenment), its real status might be described as a 'regime of truth' delivering docility and normalization via a disciplinary gaze and a propensity for intrusive, bureaucratic control. In this respect early public librarians might be described, to borrow Foucault's terms, as 'technicians of behaviour', 'engineers of conduct' or 'professionals of discipline'.

Function

Inattention to function in design has been one of the strongest criticisms laid at the door of public library provision before 1914. Writing in 1942 Savage stated that 'the worst period of library architecture was between 1895 and 1914. In later years building has been ... better adapted to its purpose'.[147] The move towards function has generally been located in the inter-war years. Ellsworth has argued that, just as there occurred

> a shift in interest from the purely bibliophilic aspects of librarianship to the use and users of libraries, so the new spirit in library architecture shifted from a purely aesthetic approach to a planning one based primarily on the use and users of buildings.[148]

But the idea that the First World War divided eras of non-function and function is too rigid an assessment. First, the post-1918 era has witnessed an enduring enthusiasm for an affected aesthetic. Classical designs, for example, were chosen for central libraries in Manchester, Marylebone and Kensington, as late as 1934, 1940 and 1960 respectively. Function has clearly not always been a priority. Second, there is extensive evidence of a concern for function long before 1914. Function in library architecture is not a modern phenomenon. For example, the practice of chaining books (which generally lasted up to the end of the seventeenth century) was, in an age of virtually irreplaceable manuscript and printed materials, highly functional; as were the bookcases, seats and desks to which the volumes were attached, and the location of these adjacent to windows offering natural light. In practice, therefore, in determining design, the notion of 'showing' a 'noble reading-room' was subordinate to the utilitarian need of effectively storing the books.[149] Further, some of the fittings of medieval monastic libraries, such as book-wheels and rotating desks affording selection from a stationary position, were patently functional.[150]

In the case of nineteenth-century public libraries the ingredient of function, including the discussion of it, was also visible. To make their libraries more user-friendly early-twentieth-century librarians were expected to study the requirements of architectural internal planning for their professional exams.[151] Committees also displayed an interest in design utility. In 1908 the Manchester committee sent a deputation comprising its chairman, deputy chairman and chief librarian to study libraries in the United States and Canada. After a six-week stay a report was prepared in which considerable attention was paid to advances in library architecture in the United States.[152] The report advised that 'Architectural effect be subordinate to utility and convenience.'[153]

However, utility could be included alongside architectural effect. At Darlington it was reported that the architect had produced 'a building not only highly artistic, but most admirably adapted for its purposes in every particular'.[154] Many aesthetically agreeable, historically styled buildings would have contained modern appliances to facilitate library work, as supplied by prolific inventors like Cotgreave. Moreover, aestheticism and function were not incompatible: domes erected over libraries might at first glance be interpreted as ornamental affectations, but were in reality often important sources of light. Domes fulfilled the double purpose of function and 'landmark' art (which in its way was functional in attracting readers).

The awareness of functional needs and the determination to do something about them were enshrined in the Carnegie Corporation's *Notes on the Erection of Library Buildings* (1911). This was a leaflet written by Carnegie's secretary James Bertram, published not for sale but for distribution to authorities using Carnegie money for construction. Its message was essentially a rebuke to the aesthetic tendencies seen to have characterized the Carnegie era. It urged a cut-back in the use of expensive ornament, such as in the use of columns, portals, stairways and domes. Further, in an age of expansion, development and specialization – for example, growing book stocks, open access, larger catalogues, services to children, and the appearance of departments for local history, music and technical literature – the Carnegie *Notes* thought it sensible to sweep away the idea of immovable internal barriers.[155] There is disagreement over the influence of the Carnegie *Notes*. Kelly has argued that the document subsequently benefited small library design.[156] One commentator has regarded its contribution to efficient design as negligible.[157] However, its degree of influence is not the issue here. More important is the fact that the document encapsulated a dissatisfaction with past design and reflected the existence of a vibrant debate on function. Function was very much *on* the pre-1914 public library design agenda.

Not that functionalists made deep inroads into the superiority of aesthetic concern. The pre-1914 era was one of categorization and clutter in library architecture. The Victorian obsession with categorization was reflected in the proliferation of library departments. J. Potter Briscoe stated in 1898 that any large public library required eight separate rooms: adult lending, children's lending, magazine room, patents library, reference library, news room, emigrants' information office and ladies room (though he personally opposed this).[158]

The architect A. L. Champneys said that as a general rule there should be 'a division of space into departments according to the various purposes for which the building is to be used'.[159] The result was generally one of 'clutter', often made worse by the awkwardness of siting libraries in town centres.[160] This was not out of keeping with traditions of design in other building types, including domestic buildings. Compartmentalization and confusion in internal planning were very much English characteristics in that, historically, the pursuit of privacy was more intense than elsewhere, certainly in comparison to the United States and France.[161] Late Victorian internal decoration was characterized by 'clutter'. The end of the nineteenth century, however, brought a 'great clean up'.[162] The general 'lightening of the load' in decoration was also visible in the internal planning of some public libraries. Thus, although planning in relation to function was not a priority of pre-1914 library designers, by the 1900s a growing awareness of it can be identified. First, the teachings of the progenitors of modernism placed greater emphasis than before on functional requirements. Second, concern over national economic efficiency was reflected in a desire to maximize efficiency in education administration through good design.

Proto-modernism

The roots of the modern movement are to be found in the Gothic Revival of the mid-nineteenth century. Pugin's *Contrasts* (1836) and *True Principles of Pointed Christian Architecture* (1841) advocated a return to medieval styles, not just because they were seen to be suited to industrial architecture, by virtue of their inherent flexibility, but also because of a yearning to restore pre-industrial religious zeal and social structure.[163] The Gothic Revival was born of capitalism's first great crisis. Medieval architecture, it was believed, could help to restore the stability which the fourteenth century was mythically perceived to have enjoyed. The momentum of the Gothic was carried forward into the mid-Victorian period by Ruskin, whose chapter 'On the nature of Gothic' in *The Stones of Venice* (1851–3) became one of the most influential pieces of architectural writing in the nineteenth century. Ruskin's departure point was not religion but a belief in the human integrity of medieval buildings produced by honest, skilled and 'interested' hand labour: that is to say, 'joyful architecture' in which artisans retained a profound knowledge of the art content of their work.

These architectural ideas developed alongside the social criticism outlined previously. The squalor of industrialism, and the class conflict it produced, led some social commentators, including designers, to seek inspiration in a pre-industrial golden age. William Morris embodied the double identity of social and design critic. He castigated machine production and its division of labour (though machines did have a place in his view of society as doing work that was revolting or destructive of self-respect), which robbed workers of pleasure in work and the people of a love of art: society's stability was thus endangered. Morris advocated the study of the art of the past ages to rid modern society of its divisions and sordid nature. He saw education as a great ally: it could not only illuminate bygone art and culture, but also make people realize the lack of dignity in their lives:

> Everyone who is pushing forward education helps us; for education ... when it reaches those who have grievances which they ought not to bear spreads deep discontent among them, and teaches them what to do to make their discontent fruitful. Everyone who tries to keep alive traditions of art by gathering together relics of the art of bygone times, still more if he is so lucky as to be able to lead people by his own works to look through Manchester smoke and squalor to fair scenes of unspoiled nature or deeds of past history, is helping us. Everyone who tries to bridge the gap between the classes, by helping the opening of museums

and galleries and gardens and other pleasures which can be shared by all is helping us.[164]

If questioned, Morris would no doubt also have approved of public libraries. He proclaimed that the architectural treatment of civic institutions was in itself an important educator:

> I want all the works of man's hand to be beautiful, rising in fair and honourable gradation from the simplest household goods to the stately public buildings, adorned with the handiwork of the greatest masters of expression.[165]

The Arts and Crafts school in which Morris participated taught a wide range of design criteria inherited from the Gothic. These included an honest selection of materials, choosing a style to fit purpose and location, promoting the integrity of creative labour, simplicity, practicality, function and the need to draw inspiration from the world of nature. Such objectives went beyond a narrow Arts and Crafts fraternity to influence architecture generally. The architect Richard Norman Shaw, for example, although he grew disillusioned with the Gothic, none the less championed vernacular design. The Queen Anne style, for which he is best known, corresponded to Puginian and Ruskinian criteria in that it was capable of construction by craftsmen with indigenous skills.[166] Moreover, Shaw developed Queen Anne into an essentially picturesque style which, in terms of internal planning, stressed the flexibility of room arrangement in contrast to, say, classical architecture, which allocated rooms geometrically according to a building's elevation. Picturesque internal planning was conceived, like nature, organically; as in the natural world, where forms grew and changed, buildings could be extended and adapted to fit their purpose.

It is no coincidence that M. B. Adams, the second most prolific public library architect of the pre-1914 age, was a student of Shaw. Adams believed that much contemporary design was pretentious:

> Most of the common architecture of our cities is simply ... both vulgar and expensive, seeking to impress by vainglorious noise, heralding its costliness from groundline to ridge as if obtrusive opulence might be accounted a virtue.[167]

Such 'monied imbecility' was to the detriment of function. He stressed that 'no building could be a success which was not well planned'.[168] 'The aim and object of an architect', he wrote, 'is to build beautifully – this is, of course, including convenience – for a building that is beautiful but inconvenient and unsuited for its purpose can be of no permanent interest or value'.[169]

Adams was not the only late Victorian or Edwardian public library architect to be interested in function. H. T. Hare, the most prolific designer of pre-1914 public libraries, showed 'unremitting inventiveness and functional planning' in his designs.[170] Both Adams and Hare were ahead of their profession in developing practical architecture.[171] Adams's lineage can be traced back, via Shaw, to the Gothic Revival. H. T. Hare's background was the Beaux Arts school, noted for its monumental, eclectic and historical architecture. This is not to say, however, that Hare or his contemporary public library designers were not influenced by the same ideas on function which informed and characterized the genesis of modernism, and which grew out of notable romanticizing of the medieval epoch.

Economic decline

The social instability to which architectural modernism was in part a response contained an economic dimension. If functional design was to help to stabilize social relations it had to address the problem of national economic malfunction. Functional design and economic efficiency are, after all, inseparable. Much of the landscape of the Industrial Revolution – mills, docks, viaducts, warehouses – was subject to a functional design imperative.[172] Moreover, it can be argued that much utilitarian, industrial architecture possessed an aesthetic quality, even though the world of traditional architecture tended to view the construction of rail sheds and factories – the Crystal Palace even – as engineering, rather than as artistic design.

It should be recalled that public libraries were first proposed in the 1830s and 1840s partly as a means of furthering design education among workers shorn of artistic skills by mechanization and division of labour. Ironically, the public library itself fell victim to sub-standard design; though, as previously explained, this should not be exaggerated. In the late nineteenth century voices were raised in support of a more efficient, functional architectural treatment. The fact that this period witnessed a strengthening in the recognition of the public library as a force for economic good was no coincidence. Anxiety over the economy's performance resulted in a call for increased efficiency in a whole range of economic inputs, labour and education included. Improvements in the organization of education would produce improved workers. But for education to improve, educational institutions needed to be designed more effectively. As far as the public library was concerned one designer, at least, became aware of the connection between economic performance and more efficient architecture.

M. B. Adams's modernist pedigree coalesced with his desire to produce public library buildings conducive to economic regeneration. In 1905 he stated the necessity of having good libraries to secure efficiency in what he termed educational administration:

> Personally I have no desire to assume the pose of a preacher; but I do wish to assert in the plainest possible language the practical necessity of ensuring to the public library its proper place in the solution of education administration.[173]

Efficiency in education was essential, Adams continued, because of increasing anxiety over Britain's position in the world economy:

> The need is obviously urgent, and the necessity is undoubtedly ripe, for the

simple and good reason that it is impossible to disguise the inevitable ...
Foreign competition, written large, leaves us no choice ... it can surely enough
only be recognised that circumstances beyond our control have settled for us,
once and for ever, the unrelenting demand for individual equipment and
educational efficiency if we are to hold our own in the cosmopolitan possibilities
of the immediate future.[174]

However, he questioned whether most public libraries were 'exactly
equal to the demands which are already asserting themselves in regard to
the ever-extending enterprise of education which in the near future is
calculated to assume still larger proportions'.[175] Adams believed that it was
crucial to pay special attention to the physical planning of public libraries in
order to secure the educational provision commensurate with being able to
compete in a dynamic world economy. Thus, because he disapproved of
'snippity news sheets' and praised the 'technical weeklies' and 'trade
journals', he accordingly advocated that more space be set aside in designs
for the reference department at the expense of the news/reading room.[176]

Adams made a strong case for the relevance of architecture to national
and even imperial prestige:

The architect's chief endeavour, notwithstanding the surmounting weight of our
commercialism, should be devoted to the production of thoughtful and artistic
buildings worthy of our national greatness and activity which distinguish the
political, ecclesiastical, and philanthropic enterprise of the Empire.[177]

He believed that to ensure national and imperial greatness there should be
a greater reliance on self-help. This philosophy could be shared by all. He
thus applauded

technical education projects intended for the bettering and amelioration of the
professional and working classes. It is impossible for any class to remain
indifferent in this matter, and no-one who has to earn his own living, to put it on
the bed-rock of existence, can afford to be left behind.[178]

In this context Adams's link with the benefactor John Passmore Edwards
should be noted. Edwards was committed to improving technical
education. One aspect of this was his ownership of the technical journal
Building News, on which Adams began serving in the early 1870s. This was
an immediate reason why Adams was chosen to design five Passmore
Edwards libraries.[179]

Another reason, a more significant one, was the belief he shared with
Adams in the efficacy of education to offset foreign competition:

He feared there were other nations who valued education more than ...
England and he would rather see a competition between nations in mind than in
trade.[180]

Just as Adams and Edwards shared an awareness of poor educational
provision, it is likely they also concurred on the importance of efficient
architecture in educational institutions.

The views of Adams and Edwards reflected the growing educational and
economic role of the public library. This was most clearly illustrated in the

growing number of public libraries sharing premises with technical schools, following the Technical Instruction Act of 1889. The linking of libraries to other educational facilities was not new. When in 1875 an educational complex was being planned in Nottingham it was urged that the library, museum, science school and university extension premises be housed under one roof because 'much greater efficiency and economy would be promoted by the association of these institutions in one building than by their being separately located'.[181] But the premium on such arrangements was increased by the economic anxieties of the late Victorian period. The architectural amalgamation of agencies became highly logical. A single edifice was advocated in 1902 for Leamington Spa's library, art school and technical institute because students 'could without leaving the building refer to books, prints, and art subjects which would be of immense value to them'.[182] The public library had always evinced some kind of economic role which was, in turn, reflected in the institution's design. The allegorical ornamentation – figures, statues, medallions, panels – which had decorated public libraries had frequently included references to science and industry alongside art and literature. In the late nineteenth century, however, 'architecture for economic growth', some believed, needed to go beyond mere allegory to a studied production of efficient buildings which would manufacture efficient workers.

Functional aestheticism

This architectural assessment has lent weight to the idea of the public library as an agency encouraging social stability. Aesthetic, 'landmark' designs reflected the strength, local sovereignty and cultural confidence of civic society's middle-class leaders and wealthy benefactors. They also served to diffuse a belief in citizenship, culture and self-help; the premium on designs for these purposes being increased as social tensions strengthened from the 1880s onwards. Anxieties over economic decline which accompanied social tension determined that functional design should supplement aesthetically derived social cohesion and tranquillity.

The intention was to deliver social stability via cultural and utilitarian design considerations. These were separate concepts and sometimes caused friction in determining design: the idea became popular that aesthetic treatment detracted from function. Yet design for culture and utility were not always incompatible. This was most clearly the case with children's library designs. Separate children's libraries and departments emerged from the 1880s. These often received more aesthetic attention than any other departments. When Sayers established a children's department at Wallasey immediately prior to 1914, he created 'a homely room, with a large bay window giving on to the lawn, around the interior of which I ran a continuous window seat'.[183] The aim here, and elsewhere, was to create a homely ambience. The children's library was to be a 'shelter' or 'half-way house': in short, 'a home away from home'. The intention was to attract children into the library by creating pleasant surroundings. This strategy had a cultural dimension in that children would be taken off the streets, which were said to corrupt them morally. Street life was also a factor in physical deterioration, which, in turn, affected economic efficiency: to rescue children from the street would be an investment in human capital. Further, it is possible that the separate provision of entrances and tables for girls and boys emphasized these cultural and economic motives by reinforcing established attitudes to the roles of the sexes. To be precise, there would be a strengthening in the perception of the distinctive roles of women: first as the moral guardians of the family, and second as homemakers for the requirements of male industrial and imperial armies.[184] Children's libraries, and their designs, thus aimed at a social stabilization to be delivered by mutually beneficial cultural and utilitarian concerns. It was a design imperative which reflected the symbiotic relationship between the pursuit of culture and that of utility: a relationship, indeed, which characterized pre-1914 public library objectives *per se*, not simply those in the field of architecture.

CHAPTER 11

CONCLUSION

The first serious proposals for municipal libraries in Britain coincided with the first major crisis of industrial capitalism, and the social tensions which accompanied that crisis in the 1820s, 1830s and 1840s. Utilitarianism – especially the brand which evolved under the direction of John Mill – provided a philosophical, yet also practical, response to emergent class conflict, social squalor, spontaneous working-class literacy and association, and anxieties over national economic performance. Utilitarians were highly active in the long campaign for free libraries which preceded legislation on the issue in 1850. The foremost protagonists of the public library ideal, William Ewart and Edward Edwards, displayed a range of utilitarian traits in their social philosophy. However, their interests, as well the interests of the Select Committee on Public Libraries (1849) which they dominated, were characterized not solely by stereotypical utilitarian concerns for hedonism, social atomism, improved social utility, material results and teleological reckoning, but also by an idealistic, deontological enthusiasm for spiritual refreshment and recreation, and for the diffusion of socially conducive humanistic and aesthetic learning. For example, in the assessment by Ewart, Edwards and the Select Committee of the public library's potential for art education, spiritual and material impulses coalesced: art was believed to offer an aesthetic elevation for the alienated, dehumanized spirit, while at the same time injecting a qualitative design dynamic into a worryingly inconsistent, and thereby socially divisive, manufacturing performance. Further, the very early public library move-ment embodied the hedonistic individualism of raw utilitarianism, yet shaped it – in accordance with the thinking of John Mill – into an altruistic incumbency placed on individuals to realize their potential in those higher pleasures, like education, which would benefit the social 'whole'.

From the outset, public library promoters were convinced that in addition to teaching aesthetic, humane knowledge their institution should fulfil a practical, economic role. The free provision of literature addressed material concerns, most obviously in terms of it serving as an investment in human capital formation to offset perceived economic malfunctions, especially after about 1870. The public library aimed to provide technical education for ongoing economic renewal. Moreover, the technical education it offered, whether for the trades or for clerks, was often of the general-theoretical kind – a pedagogic position which served to enhance the public library's reputation as a place of learning, science and culture (more about this later). In keeping with its place on the urban, industrial landscape, the public library was also promoted as an outlet for dispensing education in political economy. As a provider of information to business and to the trades, and despite its strong tradition of social criticism of industrialism, its aim went beyond a mere concern for prosperity to focus on the correctness of the market society. Advocates of free enterprise, many of them active benefactors, found the public library to be a worthwhile ally not only in the struggle to produce (some might say dragoon) a more effective workforce, versed in the laws of supply and demand, but also in the scheme to create an ordered approach to industrial relations.

Control was certainly a facet of the early public library's history. However, the notion of the public library as nothing more than an agency of dominant ideology has been rejected in this study. Control (power indeed) is a feature of any social circumstance, from the family to the operations of multinational capital. It was also integral to the ethos of the early public library; but it does not follow that social control engineered through the mechanism of the municipal library was conspiratorial or, more pertinently, successful. It is not feasible to apply to the early public library, in any wholesale fashion, theories of bourgeois-directed, conspiratorial domination. Hegemony was to a degree attempted, but was generally unsuccessful. For example, working-class readers made autonomous use of public libraries for economic gain and liberation; while strategies of control might be seen to have in themselves generated further problems of control, such as 'larking about', vagrancy and the nourishment of oppositional cultures. This is not to say that librarians should escape entirely from accusations of control. First, the fact that by 1914 many librarians had welcomed popular fiction into their institutions, thereby fully acknowledging a leisure role for the public library,[1] might be construed as a 'bread and circuses' type of control, diverting workers from the social tensions of the day. Second, the eagerness, especially after the open access revolution, to endow librarianship with a scientific-expert dimension, and with an associated, strengthened, 'self-help' purpose, was essentially a controlling 'regime of truth', in the Foucauldian sense. The emergence of library science was in keeping with the prevailing modernist, Enlightenment view that the establishment of 'truth' (discovered through reason) for humanity's emancipation was achievable. However, this liberal assessment is called into question by the obvious (from our historical vantage point) emptiness of the discourse of library science; in terms of the technical dream of perfect classification of, and access to, knowledge, or of the social utopia of individuals obtaining self-realization through culture not conflict. Once stripped of its emancipatory clothes (though in reality of course it never went naked in this respect) embryonic public librarianship as an expert system of knowledge is revealed, as much as any other profession, as in part a status-driven animal seeking what interests it rather than what is of concern to others. This was certainly the case with regard to the public library's regulatory and stereotypically authoritarian bureaucratic activities, in which librarians revelled and which were reflected in the (at times) formal ambiance and panoptic design of library buildings.

But the fact that public librarians extracted considerable power from the knowledge they commanded (their power, in turn, fabricating a new body of knowledge) does not mean that they – those who wished, at any rate – were able to hegemonize their largely working-class readership. On the contrary, they were forced to negotiate on a whole range of issues, the question of mass borrowing of fiction being a prime example. The institutionalization of fiction in public libraries was made possible partly by the acknowledgement given by some librarians of the potential of imaginative literature to elevate. This populist attitude (derived from the consumerist, hedonistic facet of utilitarianism) was reflected in the desire of many librarians to reform society by engaging in it, thereby confounding our received image of the librarian as a cloistered, detached professional. Far from acting as irrelevant bibliophiles, many public librarians took very seriously the social need to diffuse culture actively: for the teacher to go to the pupil, as T. H. Green advised. In attempting to fulfil this social purpose librarians sought to become more science-orientated, technological innovation in information storage and retrieval carrying with it the bonus of improved status. This symbiosis of science and aesthetic learning (the librarian being its quintessential purveyor) in the professional field was, interestingly, reproduced in the architecture of the public library. As befitted the civic context and the yearning for culture, providers sought to make buildings aesthetically pleasing; but they also paid close attention to function, especially after increased international competition demanded that education institutions be designed more efficiently, in the name of education-based economic regeneration.

Social engineering of this kind was rooted in the utilitarian doctrine. The latter did not, however, provide the major impetus to the public library's evolution during its period of rapid expansion in the half century before the First World War. This expansion was derived from a propagation of idealism, which succeeded utilitarianism as the flywheel of public library (and social policy) development, from about 1880. The rise of idealism coincided with the strengthening, in the late nineteenth century, of the 'idea' of society. Evolutionary (essentially Darwinist), socialist (partly Marxist, but mostly cooperative), corporatist (both local government and free enterprise) and historicist (essentially romantic medievalist) modes of thought coalesced to emphasize the status of society as an organism rather than as an aggregate: first and foremost, individuals were constituent parts of a social 'whole'. The growing awareness of the social context of life, or the 'group mind', was not just a feature of intellectual thought, for in the practicalities of life the organic model of social existence was present: in the emergence of mass circulation newspapers, mass entertainment, mass politics and mass culture, like books and libraries. In a way which helps to guard against the simplistic compartmentalization of group or individual philosophies, this 'social' ethic infected idealist (for example, social reformist) and utilitarian (for example, Darwinian environmentalist) thought alike. Just as apparently conflicting facets of utilitarianism and idealism could be found in the same individual, so seemingly disparate intellectual groups found common ground in the pursuance of a public spirit.[2]

One such piece of common ground was the shared civic and communal experience of the public library. Idealist thought had helped to foster the early public library ideal. But idealism's initial influence was overshadowed by utilitarian impulses. However, by the last quarter of the nineteenth century the tenets of idealism had become prominent in the debate on public libraries, as in other social fields. In a fashion which echoed the mature utilitarianism of John Mill, idealists decried self-interest as the basis of moral action, and championed instead agencies like the public library as instruments – in the vernacular of T. H. Green and others – of social fellowship. Idealists presented the public library as a method of cultural diffusion, the effect of which might engender a heightened awareness of the importance of duty. The promotion of social obligations, said idealists, would ensure that a capitalist society could continue to function – albeit in a modified, gentler and ameliorated form. Further, the 'hurried' society of the late nineteenth century spawned a ready acceptance of public library use for spiritual escape and renewal. This fitted well with idealist teachings on the pre-eminence of inner forces. The public library benefited from this philosophical perspective. In its early years it had been nourished by the utilitarian belief in the power of environment: hence its popularity among reformers as a means of social engineering. As a consequence of the increasing influence of idealism in the late nineteenth century, however, the public library's empiricist path was supplemented (not dislodged, it should be emphasized) by the idea that the assimilation of knowledge and ideas, through either serious or imaginative literature, was beneficial to the spirit.

The increasing interest in the existence of innate human qualities, as previously articulated by the English romantics and by the mature John Mill, coalesced with the advocacy and practical necessity of greater intervention by the state. Idealists pointed to the latent talents residing in each individual, and in doing so wondered at the limitless potential for self-realization – a vision which, for some idealists, included a metaphysical dimension expressive of humanity's intrinsically communal nature. However, for individuals to realize themselves, and thereby contribute to the evolution of the spiritual 'whole', they ideally needed an empirical helping hand. Limited state action was suggested as a means of lowering the barriers to self-realization; people could help themselves only if their environment was conducive to the process of inner-actualization. In this respect, the power of the state was viewed in a positive light. This outlook contrasts sharply with current dominant, negative attitudes, which admit neither the enabling potential of state influence nor the argument that state assistance need not be paternalistically directed and corrosive of independence. It parallels, however, the rejuvenation in the 1990s of the moderate British Left by the ethical vision of individual betterment and participatory citizenship based on a responsive collectivism.

The professional and the substantial industrial middle class which supported public libraries before the First World War had few inhibitions about the principle of the state as an 'enabler' and a facilitator of self-help. Providers did not apply this principle solely to the 'great unwashed'. The middle classes too were deemed to qualify for state assistance, for the purpose of their own self-realization. Contrary to widely held historical perceptions,[3] the public library was as much a middle-class as a working-class institution. The education and rationalism which the public library dispensed contributed to a flowering middle-class consciousness, not least in the way that the issue of good moral conduct contributed to the construction of a middle-class identity which contrasted markedly with the seemingly loose moral values of aristocratic society. Further, the public library's concern for the dissemination of culture demonstrated that the wealthy middle-class patrons who so frequently underwrote public library growth with their benefaction, propaganda and executive management of the institution do not conform to a stereotype 'Gradgrind', 'philistine' image. They were well aware of the 'improving' powers of culture in a society which had begun to worship progress and which, by definition therefore, required to have at its head a social class which was itself progressive and informed.

The middle classes who promoted public libraries saw themselves as envoys of civilization. Their cultural 'call to arms' was aimed at defeating the residual barbarism of pre-industrial society. The pre-First World War public library aimed to civilize industrial society by engaging in the mission to diffuse it with culture. The early municipal library was pre-eminently a cultural institution. Invoking the concept of culture in attempting to establish a theory explaining early public library development is neither vague nor intended as a poorly crafted catch-all assessment of purpose. Admittedly, culture is a word of multiple meaning. T. S. Eliot expressed the difficulty of capturing its elusive nature when he wrote that

> When the term 'culture' is applied to the manipulation of lower organisms – to the work of the bacteriologist or the agriculturist – the meaning is clear enough … When it is applied to the improvement of the human mind and spirit, we are less likely to agree as to what is culture.[4]

Notwithstanding the concept's complexity, however, it is not difficult, as commentators like Raymond Williams have shown, to separate out the identity of culture. The interpretation of culture employed in this study has revolved around the idea that culture entails the striving for improvement, in anticipation of the achievement of perfection, in all facets of *non-material* (whether political, aesthetic or spiritual) and *material* life.

In attempting to civilize industrial society – to render it, in effect, more cultured – public libraries hoped to assist in the stabilization of social relations. This was to be achieved in two ways. First, the provision of humane and idealistic learning which prepared individuals for the complexities of an urban-industrial existence reminded society of the values of tradition, dissolved feelings of alienation arising from industrial squalor and indirectly assisted material gain. Second, the encouragement of scientific and utilitarian learning, in addition to providing obvious direct and socially calming practical and material benefits, dovetailed with the 'liberal' education model in terms of intellectual principles of investigation, critical observation and reasoning.

The development of the English public library movement before the First World War coincided with an era of immense optimism, in stark contrast to the uncertainty of our (so-called) *postmodern* age. Notwithstanding both anxiety over foreign trade competition and the persistent social criticism of industrialism, Victorian and Edwardian England exhibited a profound faith in the possibilities of progress; a faith which remained largely intact until the cataclysm of the First World War created the first real doubts.[5] The public library was one of many social institutions nourished by the prospect of limitless improvement. It stood for individual and social development in the realms of both scientific and aesthetic learning. Its culture was the culture of perfection, in all aspects of human existence. Public libraries were part of an ambitious – even utopian – vision for the towns and cities of industrial society. They were conceived as significant ingredients in *modern* urban environments, which, ideally, were to be *planned*; taking their place alongside other instruments of a cohesive cultural existence, in a fashion not dissimilar to the mythical interpretation of life in the harmonious Greek *polis*.

That the public library has been more associated with the word police (of the moral kind) than the word *polis* (with its connotation of natural, non-imposed order) has served to bestow upon the institution a controlling and authoritarian image. As this study has argued, however, such an assessment requires careful reconsideration. It might none the less be possible to retrieve from the 'coercive agency' thesis something favourable to the public library's reputation: for the fact that the social control argument is applied in the first place indicates that whatever its failings the public library has never been a socially neutral institution. By definition, the social control thesis does not in itself entertain neutrality; and nor should we, in terms of the public library's past. In keeping with the idea of technological determinism (the notion that technology is a 'given', acting merely as a 'shaper' of social forces[6])there has been a tendency to allot a neutral role to the technology of collecting, organizing and disseminating free literature on the rates. In terms of historical analysis, the public library's image as an agency productive of social change (founded on the technology of library science) overshadows considerations of its existence being derived from the workings of a complex, 'ideologically active' society. The exception to this is the familiar and popular social control analysis. However, those who do not view the public library in a social control context perceive it as a 'commonplace' of urban life – of the political, social, economic and environmental arrangements we call modernism, roughly equated with the epoch of mature industrial society. Quite simply, the public library has never been something which, relatively speaking, has stirred the passions. As the librarian W. C. Berwick Sayers commented in 1938, 'even if the library penetrates into and permeates all modern life, it lacks that dramatic appeal possessed by things and events which live in the popular mind'.[7]

Yet the technology that is the public library, like the information technology of the modern age, has manifestly evolved from complex and intriguing social causes.[8] Public library development has been as much socially determined as it has itself determined social change. The most prominent aspect of this social determinism has been the public library's response to social instability. Far from acting as neutral social entities, public libraries have in the past functioned as correctives in eras of social crisis. Interest in the public library has noticeably quickened at crucial points in the evolution of industrial society. In the 1830s and 1840s, and again in the late nineteenth century, the stabilizing worth of the public library was broadcast in a particularly strong fashion. Subsequently, the pattern of the public library responding to deep-seated social and economic problems has persisted. This is evident in the part they played in the 'calming' reconstruction strategies and policies of the two World Wars;[9] in their serving as social facilities in the troublesome inter-war period;[10] in the social policy response to the economic shocks of the 1970s, out of which arose the advocacy of community librarianship;[11] or in the heritage and market reaction to the 'unemployed' 1980s and 1990s.

A key component in the social stability strategy of public libraries was the emphasis placed on technical education by promoters and librarians. The work of early public libraries was in line with the progressive contemporary interpretation of an education said to be 'technical'. The Royal Commission on Secondary Education (1895) was told by one of its witnesses that technical education was 'everything which prepares a man or woman for the walk of life which he or she intends to pursue'.[12] This would naturally include occupational preparation of a general kind: in other words, a general, rounded education. Further, in 1877, T. H. Huxley defined technical education as 'simply a good education, with more attention to physical science, to drawing, and to modern languages than is common, and there is nothing especially technical about it'.[13] The critical factor for Huxley was whether any technical education, so-called, exhibited a theoretical content; in which case it could be considered akin to liberal education. In particular, it might be considered part of that definition of culture, in the Tylorian tradition, which emphasizes the 'work of perfection', in all human affairs. Such a view of culture, with which – to reiterate the argument set out in Chapter 1 – the early public library coincided, was the antithesis of the orthodox utilitarian conception of education as the training of individuals to carry out particular tasks.[14] Raw utilitarianism taught that habit, learned through repetition, was more appropriate to the foundation of character and work efficiency than was theoretical thinking. The rationale of the public library was fundamentally opposed to this mechanistic perspective: for it aimed to produce wise citizens and 'educated' workers. In so far as it can be established, the public library was largely successful in its pursuit of this technical education (in the widest sense of the term) objective.

Generally speaking, the Victorian and Edwardian business community was not repelled by the public library's interpretation and dissemination of technical education – a marked contrast, indeed, to modern British employers' enthusiasm for the new vocationalism (training in narrow, directly marketable skills). Public libraries drew their business support from a wide variety of political and commercial backgrounds.[15] The evidence of this eclectic business input into public library provision suggests that, irrespective of commercial type, the education dispensed by the public library was deemed pertinent to production. The investment of the middle class in theoretical and general education agencies like the public library represents an episode of success in the history of middle-class culture. In terms of the wider definition of technical education, as in other respects, the notion of pre-First World War (especially northern industrial) middle-class 'failure' is mistaken: accusations of economic misjudgement and a philistine perspective do not stand up against the argument put forward in this study that a general education, as dispensed by the pre-1914 public library, is 'productive'; or the fact that agencies like the public library provided a wide access to learning and culture. While the industrial middle class saw the public library as an eminently practical institution, it also recognized its potential for dissolving the alienation and brutality which industrialism had created; though in the knowledge that culture possessed a material, tangible dimension. The public library thus occupied the paradoxical position of possessing an inheritance from the long-standing critique of industrialism – in the tradition of Coleridge, Arnold, Green and Tawney – while at the same time owing its existence to the culture of progress, whether scientific, industrial or humane.

Tracing the reasons for a perceived languid approach in the English industrial spirit back to the second half of the nineteenth century is not an exercise in which the history of the public library can offer much assistance. It is true that, stereotypically, the historical semiology of the public library is that of an institution emitting liberal studies-orientated 'sweetness and light'. W. C. Berwick Sayers once wrote that gratitude for the pioneering contribution of Edward Edwards had come from 'the unnumbered race of booklovers, readers and other seekers after the light'.[16] Arguably, however, other seekers after the 'light' – the 'light' itself indeed – encompassed both humane and scientific intellectual perspectives. Public libraries embraced the Victorian interest in science. Technical journals, trade books and special industrial collections were a feature of public library provision (public libraries, it should be remembered, were closely associated with the Technical Instruction Act (1889), which defined technical education not as manual instruction but as the teaching of general principles, which book and periodical learning naturally complemented). Despite the fact that public librarians were mostly arts-based, they did not march in unison behind any banner proclaiming that to be 'educated' was synonymous with being 'educated in the humanities'.[17] Librarians themselves, it should be recalled, invoked the power of science. In attempting to disseminate culture, to unite book and reader in the words of Ranganathan, they adopted a scientific classification of stock and an empirical approach for designing library buildings. Buildings themselves, indeed, could be found broadcasting the scientific message. One of the Latin mottoes carved on the front of Canterbury's public library (the Beaney Institute) read: 'Science is the image of truth.'

The promotion of science by the public library contributed to its credentials as a thoroughly progressive institution. Its status as a vehicle of progress and modernity was also furthered by its role as a radical 'satisfier' of rights. Against the backdrop of the enticing vista of the information society some librarians have come to speak enthusiastically of the right of access to information, both as a cure for information poverty and as a safeguard against the dangers of increasing concentration in information ownership. However, when speaking of rights in this context it is unlikely that most librarians recognise the dual meaning of the word. It is important to separate out the ideas of 'natural' and 'inductive' rights. Natural rights are absolute and non-negotiable, originating with the forces (the *natura*) which make humans what they are. The tradition of rights in this sense can be traced back to the Enlightenment, and was manifest in the proclamations accompanying the American and French Revolutions of the eighteenth century. To a large extent, the recent philosophy of the political Right in Britain has been influenced by a conception of natural rights, particularly in terms of a perceived innate desire of citizens to be as free as possible from the operation of the state, in accordance with the unbending laws of the free market. The political Left has also indulged in the language of natural rights: for example, radicals and idealists speak of the right to employment and to shelter.

The result of safeguarding natural rights (or moral rights, which Bentham called 'nonsense on stilts') may or may not be conducive to the common good, which is most certainly the criterion for supporting rights that are formed inductively. The theory of inductive rights would view the ownership of private property, say, as desirable because of its teleological effect on social utility, not because owning private property is of deontological value to the individual.[18] Both the utilitarian Mill and the idealist Green viewed the question of rights in this way. For example, each supported the right of citizens to enjoy limited state assistance as a springboard for self-realization. Had they not believed, pragmatically, that limited state action was for the common good, then they would not have promoted intervention as a right.[19] In other words, the decision to promote a basic right was derived from an inductive assessment of society – rights were to be induced by social circumstance and necessity. As such the right to a good library, supported by the state, could be conceived of in a positive way, as a means of educating citizens in how to be independent and how not to infringe the liberty of others; and not in a negative way, as an example of coercive, restricting state control.

Recent attacks on the public library (on the public sector generally, indeed) have, arguably, owed more to a negative than to a positive conception of liberalism and rights. This is a long way from the position adopted by pioneer promoters of the public library, manufacturers among them. Early public libraries were advocated in the great traditions of positive liberalism and urban culture.[20] Thus the Carnegie United Kingdom Trust reported in 1915 that

> The public library is a service essential to [the community's] well-being, and one which, like the question of public health and education, should be freely available to the whole community as part of its civic rights.[21]

Public library promoters supported the argument that individualism and individual rights could best be delivered by collectivism and the promotion of civic culture.

The utilitarian and idealist philosophies which underpinned the early public library movement were not exclusive monoliths. Nowhere was this more evident than in the concern to provide security (minimum standards of material and intellectual provision conducive to individual self-realization) and to protect rights. Over the issue of security, utilitarianism, contrary to its egoistic image, was as enthusiastic as idealism; the latter, perceived by some as socialistic, had at its base a commitment to individual empowerment and creativity. The issue of rights (and the security required to guarantee them) provide a clear example of how utilitarianism and idealism could overlap; of how their various components could coincide. However, as far as the satisfaction of rights via the early public library is concerned, it is the teleological perspective (most closely associated with utilitarianism) which took prominence. The public library, to be sure, incorporated, and still does, the deontological language of natural rights – witness its debt to romanticism, social criticism and aesthetic learning. But the institution's worth was conceived, for the most part, in a teleological fashion. Its greatest worth was seen to be the positive social utility it could generate, and the contribution it could make to social stability. While public library promoters might have viewed the right of the individual to self-fulfilment as 'natural', their overwhelming motivation was the belief that individualism in this regard was directed towards collective prosperity, and was recognized as such by individuals knowingly engaging in the civilizing process.

The triumph of teleology was also manifest in the unquestioning acceptance of the public library as a 'public good'. Utilitarians and idealists had a broad understanding of what constituted a public good. The social benefit of institutions like the public library could not be measured scientifically. However, a teleological reckoning in the form of discourse was possible, and was undertaken, most famously by the economist Stanley Jevons. As noted above, the utilitarian pioneers and business benefactors of public libraries were not narrow, calculating, Gradgrind stereotypes, but were teleologically convinced – even if they could not demonstrate it in accordance with felicific calculus – of the efficacy of culture to assist material progress. They recognized that the public library possessed a material, tangible dimension – not least in terms of the institution's ability to dissolve the spiritually and materially damaging alienation and brutality which industrialism had created. Similarly, idealist promoters acknowledged teleologically that a diffusion of culture through public libraries would reinforce capitalism – though in a modified form – by creating the harmony in social relations and the improved human existence from which prosperity would flow. Material advance was perceived as an externality of culture dispensed by the public library. Public libraries, naturally, provided commercial and technical information which was directly relevant to economic performance and individual prosperity. But they also facilitated material benefits indirectly. Public libraries attempted to fashion not simply more educated and, hence, productive workers, but also a more flexible workforce, schooled in theory as well as practice. As educators in citizenship, public libraries aimed to manufacture tamer, more reasonable and thus more profitable workers. Public libraries sought to diffuse an improved quality of life, serving as havens from the squalor and pace of industrialism, and offering a respite from the counter-productive monotony which the division of labour had wrought; yet, inevitably, releasing spiritually refreshed readers back into the fray of an acquisitive machine society.

In the final analysis, therefore, although criticized by the economizing, 'low tax' lobby of local politics, public libraries were widely viewed as beneficial 'public goods', by virtue of the material externalities of their dissemination of culture – this in addition to their value as agencies of a civilized way of life. Such indirect and 'cultural' means of securing prosperity might be considered apposite to today's complex, specialized and hurried society. It is by no means certain that the public library's *raison d'être* should be defined by any strong emphasis on economic benefits derived directly: for example, through the provision of services to business. As in the Victorian and Edwardian eras, economic benefits accrued indirectly might be considered as potentially more profitable than those accrued directly – and profitable not just in the material sense, but also in terms of the boost they give to humanistic culture as the basis of an improved, more just and more stable society. The problem is, of course, that in the utilitarian climate of the late twentieth century anything which cannot be measured is less likely to be described as worthy.

Today, advocates of commercialism and 'go-getting' tend to view humanistic culture and materialism as highly antagonistic facets of human existence. However, in the pre-1914 era, as this study has attempted to argue in relation to the public library, champions of progress and 'getting on' were prepared, unlike modern enterprise, to accept the pursuit of culture as highly complementary to their materialistic intentions. Consequently, attitudes to the provision of public services in the sphere of culture were generally positive, albeit within the context of a historic fear of centralization, state action and strong government. Nowadays, enterprise and economic liberalism express less zeal, relative to the general, high level of state intervention, for cultural public services. One possible reason for this is the context of national decline in which cultural (and other) public services operate. Whereas public libraries were once advocated as antidotes to the disquiet, disturbance and instability caused by progress, they are now advocated as agencies of stability against a backdrop of decline. This perhaps partly explains their continuing 'seedy', anachronistic and irrelevant image. The public library of the late twentieth century does not broadcast an over-arching, cohesive purpose. It does not, unlike its Victorian and Edwardian progenitor, possess a convincing sense of direction. Before the First World War, the public library movement announced a wholesale commitment to the battle to civilize society. The institution's promoters were unapologetic in their desire to imbue the populace with 'good taste'. This objective was neither narrowly patronizing nor entirely controlling. Rather, the 'taste' of which reformers spoke was essentially the quality of reason required for the making of those choices of action which delivered life's higher, purer pleasures – the most important of which were the innate quests for dutiful, non-atomistic self-realization and for social harmony achieved through altruistic improvement, though within the existing fundamental social relations of industrial capitalism. Early public libraries were ethical institutions. Their promoters were moral philosophers: they identified what was socially 'good', and endeavoured to act accordingly. Knowledge and learning were attributed a socially stabilizing, progressive purpose. In an era dominated by narrow vocationalism, specialization, materialism and the market, the past purpose of the public library needs to be recognized, both inside and outside the library world. In our uncertain, drifting postmodern age it is even more crucial than it would have been to make firmly worded statements on the ethics of public library provision, if not the crucial issue of access to information generally.

One such ethical statement might be that it is surely preferable that in the future public information services, including public libraries, be organized on a more flexible basis; one which locks into both general-conventional and marginal-alternative needs, and which challenges the rigid provision of the centralized, statist approach of the past, though without promoting the free market option wholesale. In this respect, that tradition of the public library defined by the state regulation of 'dangerous', alternative cultures will be weakened. On the other hand, the public library's other major tradition, that of redistributing opportunity, if not wealth, will be strengthened. In particular, such a radical reconceptualization of purpose will retrieve from the public library's past the modernist notion that the ultimate ends of knowledge are primarily social, altruistic and aesthetic; not individualistic, acquisitive and material.

APPENDICES

Appendix 1: Occupations of new borrowers at the Portsmouth Public Library 1887–1888

Accountants, clerks, etc.	93	Journalists	18
Apprentices	84	Labourers	45
Architects and draughtsmen	12	Lawyers and solicitors	19
Auctioneers and agents	17	Ladies	22
Bakers and grocers	28	Machinists	3
Basketmakers	3	Mariners and seamen	75
Booksellers and stationers	10	Merchants	5
Boot and shoe makers	15	Masons and plasterers	16
Brassfounders	7	Milliners and dressmakers	54
Brushmakers	12	Musicians	5
Builders and contractors	24	Nurses	3
Butchers	11	Officers: army and navy	45
Cabinetmakers, upholsterers		Oilmen	17
and polishers	9	Pastry cooks	6
Cabmen	3	Pawnbrokers	13
Carpenters and joiners	33	Pensioners: army and navy	65
Chaplains and ministers	8	Photographers	20
Chemists and druggists	12	Physicians, surgeons and	
Coalporters	2	doctors	11
Commercial travellers	7	Postmen	12
Coopers	2	Publicans	3
Carriers	4	Reporters	9
Customs and revenue officers	16	Riggers	15
Dairymen	7	Secretaries	12
Decorators, painters and glaziers	30	Scholars and students	124
Domestic servants	36	Schoolmasters and mistresses	87
Drapers, etc.	45	Shipwrights	116
Engineers	18	Smiths	25
Errand boys	13	Stokers	38
Factory hands	85	Tailors	16
Fitters	37	Tradesmen	11
Fruiterers, gardeners, etc.	17	Waiters	5
Gentlemen	9	Warehousemen	7
House and shopkeepers	74	Occupation not stated	952
Inspectors	22		
Jewellers	7	Total	2686

Source: Portsmouth Free Public Library, Report (1887-8).

Appendix 2: Occupations of new borrowers at the Leyton Public Library 1902–3

Accountants	10	Laundry employees	2
Agents and collectors	27	Library assistant	1
Apprentices and assistants	60	Machinists	17
Architects and surveyors	6	Married women	192
Artists and designers	6	Merchants and manufacturers	23
Bakers and confectioners	5	Milkman	1
Baths superintendent	1	Millwright	1
Bookbinders	2	Ministers	2
Boot and shoe makers	8	Musical instrument maker	6
Builders	4	Musicians	4
Bullet maker	1	Needlewomen	5
Butchers	2	Nurses	6
Cabinet makers, carpenters and		Oilman	1
joiners	12	Photographers	2
Caretakers and porters	4	Physicians and surgeons	4
Chemists	5	Plumbers, painters and	
Civil servants	8	decorators	15
Clerks, cashiers, etc.	342	Police constables	4
Coachmakers	3	Post Office officials	12
Cooper	1	Printers, compositors, etc.	28
Corn dealer	1	Railway employees	17
Customs and revenue officers	4	Saddle and harness makers	3
Cycle makers	2	Scholars and students	720
Distiller	1	Schoolmasters, mistresses and	
Domestic servants	18	teachers	183
Drapers and milliners	19	Shipwright	1
Draughtsmen	6	Soldier	1
Dressmakers	24	Stationers	4
Electricians	5	Tailors	7
Engineers, fitters, etc.	40	Tea dealers	2
Errand boys, etc.	25	Telegraphists	5
Fishmonger	1	Telephone attendants	2
Florist	1	Tobacconist	1
Furniture dealer	1	Travellers	34
Furriers	2	Upholsterers	2
Greengrocer	1	Waiters	2
Hairdressers	2	Warehousemen and salesmen	29
Hatters and hosiers	3	Watchmakers and jewellers	4
Ironmonger	1	Wood engraver	1
Ivory workers	2	Occupation not stated	589
Journalists	9		
Labourers	8	Total	2616

Source: Leyton Public Library, Report (1902–3).

Appendix 3: Occupations of female readers at the South Shields Public Library's lending and reference departments 1876

Lending

Actresses	2
Domestic servants	31
Dressmakers	48
Governesses and schoolmistresses	39
Housekeepers	8
Milliners	70
Pupil teachers	51
Saleswomen	38
Scholars	119
Scripture reader	1
Shopkeepers	8
Teachers of music	4
Widows	113
Occupation not stated	401
Total	953

Reference

Actresses	74
Dressmakers	42
Milliners	30
Pupil teachers	78
Servants	11
Students and scholars	76
Occupation not stated	109
Total	420

Source: Statistical Parliamentary Return by South Shields (1876).

Appendix 4: Volumes issued in the various subject classes in the lending and reference departments of the Leicester Central Public Library 1889–1890

Subjects	Lending	Reference
Theology, philosophy	909	1,969
History, biography	4,567	3,487
Voyages, travel	2,637	1,056
Science, art	4,756	8,296
Law, politics, commerce	250	325
Poetry, drama	915	1,442
Fiction	88,210	523
Miscellaneous literature	4,921	9,232
Juvenile literature	38,236	
Patents		2,743
Total	134,401	29,073

Source: Leicester Public Library, Report (1889-90).

Appendix 5: Illustrations of the various occupations of persons reading the same book at the Portsmouth Public Library 1887–1888

Ganot's Physics, issued 23 times

Artist	1
Cashier	1
Clerk	1
Drapers	2
Engineer	1
Fitter's apprentice	1
Dressmaker	1
Scholar	1
Shipwrights	2
Shipwrights' apprentices	8
Stationers	2
Stonemason	1
Occupation not stated	1

Major	1
Milliner	1
Optician	1
Plumber	1
Scholars	4
Shipwrights	2
Shopboys	2
Superintendent insurance company	1
Tailor	1
Teacher	1
Telegraph messenger	1
Writer, RN	1
Occupation not stated	11

England under Gladstone, issued 18 times

Clerk	1
Compositor	1
Dealer	1
Draper	1
Grocer	1
Housekeeper	1
Pensioners	4
Postman	1
Schoolmaster	1
Shipwright	1
Station master	1
Teacher	1
Outfitter	1
Occupation not stated	2

Smiles's Scotch Naturalists, issued 24 times

Carpenter	1
Carpenters' apprentices	2
Clerk	1
Grocer	2
Housekeeper	1
Nurse	1
Pensioners	2
Sailor	1
Scholars	2
Schoolmaster	1
Shipwright's apprentice	1
Teacher	1
Writers	2
Occupation not stated	6

Vambrey's Life and Travels, issued 42 times

Assistants	3
Brushmaker	1
Carpenter	1
Carver	1
Clerks	3
Coachman	1
Colonel	1
Dealer	1
Grocer	1
Housekeeper	1

Besant's All Sorts and Conditions of Men, issued 42 times

Clerks	2
Collector	1
Engineer, RN	1
Grocer	1
Gunner, RN	1
Housekeepers	3
Jeweller	1
Joiners' apprentice	1
Pastrycook	1
Pensioner	1

Salesman	1	Cashier	1
Schoolmistresses	2	Chemist	1
Shipwright	1	Clerks	12
Stationers	2	Clerk in Holy Orders	1
Teachers	3	Coal merchant	1
Writers	2	Commander, RN	1
Occupation not stated	18	Compositor	1
		Constructor	1
Grant's Aristotle, issued 29 times		Draper	1
		Dressmakers	2
Bootmaker	1	Electrical fitter	1
Captain, medical staff	1	Engineers	3
Carpenter	1	Fishmonger	1
Clerks	2	Fitter	1
Compositor	1	Furniture dealer	1
Domestic	1	Gunner, RN	1
Drapers	2	Hairdresser	1
Fitter	1	Housekeepers	5
Fitters' apprentice	1	Jeweller	1
Gold beater	1	Journalist	1
Grocer	1	Lieutenant-Colonel	1
HM Customs	1	Matron	1
Housekeeper	1	Newsagents	2
Painter	1	Portmanteau maker	1
Pastrycook	1	Postman	1
Shipwright	1	Scholars	6
Shipwright's apprentice	1	Schoolmasters	2
Shop boy	1	Schoolmistresses	2
Smith	1	Shipwrights	4
Tailor	1	Soda water maker	1
Traveller	1	Stationmaster	1
Warehouseman	1	Stationer	1
Occupation not stated	5	Steward, RN	1
		Surgeons	2
Haggard's King Solomon's Mines,		Surveyor	1
issued 111 times		Tailor	1
		Teachers	5
Bookseller	1	Telegraphist	1
Brushmaker	1	Upholsterer	1
Carver	1	Occupation not stated	34

Source: Portsmouth Free Library, Report (1887-8).

Appendix 6: Books selected at the Portsmouth Public Library by borrowers engaged in various occupations 1887–1888

A clerk

Stanley's History of the Jewish Church, 3 volumes
Fortunes Made in Business, 2 volumes
Fenn on the Funds
Money and the Mechanism of Exchange
Norman Conquest, 5 volumes
History of Belfast
India and its Native Princes
Tale of Two Cities

A civil engineer

Fortunes Made in Business, 2 volumes
Draper's Intellectual Development of Europe, 2 volumes
Ganot's Physics
Life of Henry Fawcett
Spiritual Wives, by Dixon
Wonders in Living Nature
United, a novel, by Sinnett
A Look Round Literature
Army Society, by Winter
Rider Haggard's Complete Works
Animal Anecdotes, by Page

A journalist

Light of Asia, by Arnold
Oliver Ellis, by Grant
The Devil's Advocate, by Greg, 2 volumes
Free Lance Tiltings in Many Lists
Russia Under the Czar, by Stepniate, 2 volumes
Serjeant Ballantine's Experiences
Curiosities of Law and Lawyers
Liberal Movement in English Literature
King Solomon's Mines
Suicide, its Philosophy, Cause and Prevention
Barnaby Rouge
Memoirs of a Physician, by Dumas

A labourer

Green's Short History of the English People

Greenwood's Little Ragamuffins
Graphic and Illustrated London News
Dombey and Son
Old Curiosity Shop
Tale of Two Cities
All Sorts and Conditions of Men
By Celia's Arbour
Ireland, Its Scenery, Character, etc., 3 volumes
Tales from Blackwood
Reminiscences of Abraham Lincoln
Harry Richmond by Meredith

A domestic servant

East Lynne, by Wood
The History and Life of Bishop Hannington
Lady Audley's Secret
Look Before You Leap, by Alexander
Canadian Pictures, by Marquis of Lorne
Girl of the Period, by Linton
She, by Rider Haggard
Dishes and Drinks, or Philosophy in the Kitchen
Life of Harriet Martineau
Mill on the Floss
Her World Against a Lie, by Marryatt

A schoolmistress

Adam Bede
Hostages to Fortune
Lost for Love
Motley's Rise of the Dutch Republic
Seaforth, by Montgomery
Oceana, by Froude
United, a novel, by Sinnett
Clouds in the East, by Baker
Health and Education, by Kingsley
Old Mortality, by Scott
Weaver Stephen, Odds and Evens in English Religion, by Parker
Royal Favor, by Wallis
Aurora Leigh, by Browning
We Two, by Lyall

A schoolmaster

Sweet Sleep and How to Promote It
A Diary of Two Parliaments, by Lucy
History of Crime in England, 2
    volumes
Biographical Essays
Wonderful Characters
Froude, Short Studies on Great
    Subjects, 3 volumes
By Celia's Arbour
Golden Butterfly
Ready Money Mortiboy
She, and Dawn, by Haggard
Society in London
Essays from the Spectator
For Cash Only
Mirk Abbey
History of English Literature, by Taine,
    4 volumes

A dressmaker

Cherry Ripe, by Mathers
Her World Against a Lie
Too Good for Him
Young Lady Treasure Books

Kidnapped, by Stephenson
Lady Audley's Secret
Oceana, by Froude
Lives of Robert and Mary Moffatt
Bootle's Baby, by Winter
Life of General Gordon
A Lady's Life in the Rocky Mountains
Middle March

A student

History of a Crime, by Hugo
Life of Frank Buckland
Unorthodox London
The Transvaal War
Burma, Past and Present
Three Years of Arctic Service, by
    Greely
Head Hunters of Borneo
The Congo, by Stanley
Autocrat of the Breakfast Table
King Solomon's Mines
Green's History of the English People,
    4 volumes
The Conquest of England, by Green
Burnaby's Ride to Khiva
He Would be a Soldier, by Jephson

Source: Portsmouth Free Public Library, Report (1887–8).

SOURCES

Archive sources

Bradford City Archives:

- Opening of the Bradford Commercial Library (1 May 1918). Manuscript list of invitations prepared by Bradford Public Libraries.

British Library Information Science Service:

- Collection of letters to the librarian Walter Powell (c. 1900), uncatalogued.
- Library Association questionnaire to public libraries (1904), uncatalogued.
- Letters to William Munford on the subject of public library benefaction (1950), uncatalogued.
- Newcuttings and scrapbooks, including press cuttings libraries (1897-1898), compiled by B. Matthews; and West Ham Public Library cuttings (1890-1933).
- Photographs and ephemera arranged by library authority, uncatalogued.

British Library Manuscripts Division:

- Letters from William Ewart.

British Library Reference Division:

- Manuscript diaries of Edward Edwards.

Crewe Public Library:

- Minutes of the Crewe Mechanics' Institute.

Ewart Family Records:

- Diaries and notebooks of William Ewart.

Greater London Records Office:

- London County Council, Technical Education Board, Minutes of the Science, Art and Technology Sub-Committee (29 April 1896).

Manchester Public Library Archives:

- Letters to Edward Edwards.
- Personal scrapbooks of Edward Edwards.
- Sir John Potter, autograph letters.

Nottingham Record Office:

- Report on the proposed educational buildings by the borough engineer [M. O. Tarbotton](March 1876).

Public Records Office:

- Records of the Board of Trade, Commercial Department (1901–17).

School of Librarianship, Wales:

- Plans and ephemera relating to public library architecture.

Scottish Records Office:

- Records of the Carnegie United Kingdom Trust relating to pre-1914 Carnegie benefactions.

Tower Hamlets Public Libraries:

- Correspondence of J. Passmore Edwards with the Limehouse Public Library Commissioners.

William's (Dr) Library:

- Free Christian Union Papers, including a letter from J. Passmore Edwards to Edward Enfield.

Public library records

Records held by the reference or local studies departments of the following libraries (or library authorities) include such material as scrapbooks, news cuttings, committee minutes, annual reports, library magazines, ephemera and photographs:

Bath, Birmingham, Bournemouth, Bradford, Bristol, Bromley, Crewe, Croydon, Darlington, Doncaster, Dumfries, Eastbourne, Hammersmith and Fulham, Islington, Lambeth, Leamington Spa, Leeds, Lewisham, Manchester, Nantwich, Northampton, Norwich, Nottingham, Oldham, Oxford, Portsmouth, Southwark, Swindon, Tower Hamlets, Westminster, Wigan, Winchester, York.

Parliamentary papers

Board of Trade, Advisory Committee on Commercial Intelligence, *Report*, Cmd 2044 (1904).

Board of Trade, Departmental Committee on the Dissemination of Commercial Information and the Collection and Exhibition of Patents and Samples, *Report*, Cmd 8962 (1898).

Chambers of Commerce, *Copies of answers to queries of the Vice-President of the Council [on Education] as to technical education* (Parliamentary papers 1867–8).

Committee of the Council of the British Association for the Advancement of Science, *Report on the best means for promoting scientific education in schools* (1867).

Hansard, *Parliamentary Debates.*

Parliamentary returns for public libraries (1876 and 1877).

Select Committee on Arts and Manufactures, *Report* (1836).

Select Committee on the Condition, Management and Affairs of the British Museum, *Report* (1836).

Select Committee on Inquiry into Drunkenness, *Report* (1834).

Select Committee on Public Libraries, *Report* (1849, 1850, 1851 and 1852).

Select Committee on Public Walks, *Report* (1833).

Select Committee on Scientific Instruction, *Report* (1868).

Stanley, Lord, *Circular [on technical and primary education] to Her Majesty's representatives abroad together with replies* (Parliamentary papers 1867–8).

A note on secondary sources

The discursive nature of this study, arising as it does out of its methodological imperative that library history should be placed in the context of both critical social theory and broader historical development, would produce an over-long and diffuse list of secondary texts. Priority in terms of space is therefore given to supporting notes which, by way of reflecting the social anchorage of the public library, are extensive. However, those interested in secondary sources on the history of the public library specifically can refer to Thomas Kelly's *History of public libraries in Great Britain 1845–1975* (1977), and for more recent sources to Denis F. Keeling's *British library history: bibliography* (1972 and subsequent issues).

NOTES

Unless otherwise stated all books are published in the British Isles.

1 In search of an analytical model

1. *Samuel Johnson's Dictionary of the English Language* (1827 edn) defined civility as 'freedom from barbarity ... Politeness ... elegance of behaviour ... Rule of decency'.
2. M. Demarest, Arnold and Tylor: the codification and appropriation of culture, *in* P. Scott and P. Fletcher (eds), *Culture and education in Victorian England* (1990), p. 41 (note 3).
3. *Samuel Johnson's Dictionary*, op. cit. For a recent, succinct debate on the definition of culture see C. Jenks, *Culture* (1993).
4. As explained by G. Turner, *British cultural studies: an introduction* (1990), pp. 42–3.
5. Chapter 1.
6. B. Willey, *Nineteenth century studies: Coleridge to Matthew Arnold* (1964), p. 265.
7. F. R. Leavis and D. Thompson, *Culture and environment: the training of critical awareness* (1933), pp. 1–3.
8. R. Williams, *The long revolution* (1965), p. 366.
9. R. Hoggart, *The uses of literacy* (1958), pp. 263, 274.
10. R. Hoggart, The abuses of literacy, *Guardian* (27 June 1991). Hoggart's position is applauded by P. Coleman, Much more than books, *in* M. Ashcroft and A. Wilson (eds), *Public library policy and strategic planning* (1990). R. Samuel, In defence of potboilers, *The Times* (7 March 1992) takes the opposite view to Hoggart's 'heritage' position, arguing that public libraries must be forward-looking and responsive to popular demand.
11. The 'chameleon-like' description of the nature of culture is taken from M. Tinko, Thomas Carlyle and Victorian culture, *in* Scott and Fletcher, op. cit., p. 19.
12. This is also the definition of culture pursued in the *International encyclopedia of the social sciences* (1968).
13. T. S. Eliot, *Notes towards a definition of culture* (New York, 1948), p. 30.
14. George Eliot can also be mentioned in this regard. See S. Graver, *George Eliot and community: a study in social theory and fictional form* (Berkeley, 1984).
15. P. W. Buck, *How conservatives think* (1975), p. 27.

16. The German perception of culture is explained by R. Williams, *Keywords* (1976). R. C. Benge, *Libraries and cultural change* (1986), pp. 11–13 also highlights Tylor. J. C. Powys, *The meaning of culture* (1930) defined a cultured individual as one who engaged in critical thinking, questioned dogmatic authorities and developed an original philosophy of life.

17. E. B. Tylor, *Primitive culture: researches into the development of mythology, philosophy, religion, language, art and custom* (1891), p. 1.

18. Ibid., p. 6.

19. Ibid., pp. 26–7.

20. Ibid., p. 27.

21. Ibid., p. 27. The tendency to grade culture and civilization is also apparent in the work of another early anthropologist, J. G. Frazer. See in particular his *Golden bough: a study in magic and art* (1890). H. Kuklick, *The savage within: the social history of British anthropology, 1885–1945* (1992) argues that early evolutionists and anthropologists regarded the peak of reason to be exemplified by Victorian culture, the rest of humanity being graded below it.

22. Demarest, op. cit., p. 36.

23. In his *Anthropology: an introduction to the study of man and civilization* (1881), pp. 23–4, Tylor wrote that 'Human life may be roughly classed into three great stages, Savage, Barbaric, Civilized'.

24. Arnold is often seen as the high priest of élite culture. It is interesting to note, however, that in *Culture and anarchy* he writes of culture as 'a general perfection, developing all parts of our society', as noted by Demarest, op. cit., p. 29.

25. T. C. Smout (ed.), *The search for wealth and stability: essays in economic and social history presented to M. W. Flinn* (1979), p. xvi.

26. C. Babbage, *On the economy of machinery and manufactures* (1835), p. 169.

27. J. P. Dunbabin, *Rural discontent in nineteenth century Britain* (1974), p. 18.

28. T. S. Ashton, *An economic history of England: the eighteenth century* (1955), p. 227, notes 15 different occasions in the eighteenth century when popular disturbance and poor harvests coincided.

29. See the introduction by T. Gourvish and A. O'Day to their *Later Victorian Britain 1867–1900* (1988), p. 2.

30. S. Fothergill, *The principles of political economy as applied to the wages question* (1872), pp. 4–5.

31. R. Quinault and J. Stevenson, *Popular protest and public order: six studies in British history 1790–1920* (1974), p. 24.

32. P. Laslett, *The world we have lost* (1971), p. 4.

33. E. J. Hobsbawm's discussion of economic fluctuations and social movements in his *Labouring men* (1964) argues that economic downswings provided inflammable material which was ignited in ensuing upswings. See also the conclusion to J. Stevenson, *Popular disturbances in England 1700–1870* (1979).

34. Fothergill, op. cit., p. 5.

35. *Stratford Express* (1 November 1890).

36. M. H. Harris, *History of libraries in the western world* (1984), p. 4.

37. *Stratford Express* (1 November 1890).

38. See R. Williams, *The country and the city* (1973) with regard to this last area of tension.

39. 1 October 1853.

40. R. S. Woodhouse, *The empiricists* (1988), p. 2. F. Copplestone, *A history of philosophy*, Vol. 8 (1966), pp. 301-2.

41. I. Britain, *Fabianism and culture: a study of British socialism and the arts c.1884–1918* (1984) argues that the view of the arid, uncultured, utilitarian Fabian is a stereotype.

42. The importance of models is discussed by R. C. Floud and D. N. McCloskey (eds) in the introduction to their *Economic history of Britain since 1700*, Vol. 2 (1981).

43. From 1964 a paper on library history was included in the Library Association syllabus for professional training.

44. P. Hoare, Library history, *in* D. W. Bromley and A. M. Allott (eds), *British librarianship and information work 1981–1985*, Vol. 1 (1988), p. 289, points to the existence of greater vibrancy elsewhere. T. Kelly, Thoughts on the writing of library history, *Library History*, 3:5 (Spring 1975), p. 168, regrets the insulated approach to much research. Witness, also, the broad approach evident in P. F. McNally, *Readings in Canadian library history* (Ottawa, 1986), and in the American library history periodical *Libraries and Culture*. R. Snape, *Public libraries, leisure and the provision of fiction 1840–1945: case studies of public libraries and library committees in Darwen, Blackburn and Wigan*, unpublished PhD, CNAA (Institute of Advanced Studies, Manchester Polytechnic, 1992) makes good use of wider history and theory.

45. See W. A. Munford, *William Ewart M.P. 1789–1869: portrait of a radical (1960)* and *Edward Edwards 1812–1886: portrait of a librarian* (1963).

46. M. I. Lattimore, *The history of libraries in Plymouth to 1914: a study of the library developments in the three towns of Plymouth, Devonport and Stonehouse which amalgamated into Plymouth in 1914*, unpublished PhD, University of London (1982). This has only one chapter on public library provision but its history is enhanced by a detailed introduction on the historical development of the area. Contextual occupational and educational data are particularly useful.

47. T. Dunne, *Bolton public libraries 1853–1978* (1978), p. 18.

48. Page v. The idea that libraries are 'created by society' is one of the seventeen principles of librarianship given by J. Thompson, *A history of the principles of librarianship* (1977), p. 204.

49. The following have lamented the absence of theory in library history: J. H. Shera, On the value of library history, *Library Quarterly*, 22 (1952). R. V. Williams, The public library as the dependent variable: historically orientated theories and hypotheses of public library development, *Journal of Library History*, 16:2 (1981). P. Sturges, Library history in Britain: progress and prospects, *in* D. G. Davis Jr, *Libraries and culture: proceedings of the (USA) Library History* Seminar VI, 1980 (Austin, Texas, 1981), p. 371 writes of the past, mistaken, subordination of social context to narrative.

50. W. A. Wiegand, The literature of American library history, *Journal of Library History*, 17:3 (Summer 1982), p. 319.

51. J. H. Shera, *Foundations of the public library: the origins of the public library in New England* (Chicago, 1949), p. 248.

52. R. D. Altick, *The English common reader: a social history of the mass reading public 1800–1900* (Chicago, 1957), p. 225.

53. Sturges, op. cit., p. 368.

54. K. A. Manley (with D. Keeling), Sunshine in the gloom: the study of British library history, *Libraries and Culture*, 25:1 (Winter 1990), p. 80. P. Sykes,

The public library in perspective: an examination of its origins and modern role (1979), p. 67, agrees that most social historians have been silent on the subject of libraries.

55. D. G. Davis Jr, Book reviewing in library history, *Journal of Library History,* 12:2 (Spring 1977), editorial comment.

56. A good example is D. Fraser, *Urban politics in Victorian England* (1976). This otherwise comprehensive study looks at the structure of politics in Victorian cities in respect of the provision of a wide range of services; though not public libraries which, while not political dynamite, surely evinced a political dynamic worthy of coverage.

57. W. C. B. Sayers, Public libraries and public education, *Westminster Gazette* (20 September 1907).

58. *Doncaster Gazette* (15 February 1924).

59. Sykes, op. cit., pp. 7–10.

60. W. E. Doubleday, *A primer for librarianship* (1931), pp. 113–14.

61. T. Kelly, *A history of public libraries in Great Britain 1845–1875* (1977), pp. 14–15. For a detailed analysis of the change from adoption by ratepayers' poll to adoption by council resolution see R. J. B. Morris, The adoption process for public libraries in the United Kingdom', *Local Government Review* (28 August 1976).

62. Quoted in St Martin-in-the-Fields Library Commissioners, *First report* (covering 1887–91).

63. See Brown's scheme for Islington's public library system, included in Islington Borough Council, *Minutes* (2 March 1906). Those who were not in a position to use libraries were said to include the incarcerated, the sick, the disabled, the very young and the very old. The *Croydon Guardian* (6 March 1915) reported the librarian Stanley Jast as saying that, discounting children under 10 years and persons over 70 years, 1 in 8 of the Croydon population used a lending library.

64. T. Kelly, Public libraries and public opinion, *Library Association Record,* 68 (1966). A great deal of apathy surrounded the public library question. A poll in Bournemouth in 1885 recorded a result of 749 in favour of adopting public library legislation, and 914 against – but 1665 did not vote; as related in C. Riddle, *The library movement in Bournemouth* (1913), p. 1.

65. A poster produced by the anti-library campaign in York in 1881 read: 'It is not right to ask a ratepayer for a pound, it is not right to ask him for a penny, and all talk to the contrary is moonshine'; York Public Library Scrapbook.

66. *Islington Daily Gazette* (27 July 1906).

67. G. Crossick, Urban society and the petty bourgeoisie in nineteenth century Britain, in D. Fraser and A. Sutcliffe, *The pursuit of urban history* (1983).

68. Handbill produced by the York Anti-Library Rate Committee; York Public Library Scrapbook.

69. Trades Union Congress, *Report* (1884), p. 46.

70. Letter from H. M. Robinson to A. Carnegie (21 November 1902), Scottish Record Office, records of the Carnegie United Kingdom Trust, GD281/3/205/L.

71. For an explanation of compounding see M. J. Daunton, *House and home in the Victorian city: working class housing 1850–1914* (1983), pp. 203–4.

72. H. Pelling, The working class and the welfare state, *in his Popular politics and society in late Victorian Britain* (1968).

73. P. Thane, The working class and state welfare in Britain 1880-1914, *Historical Journal*, 27 (1984) broadly agrees with Pelling's analysis (see previous note) but argues that each area of social reform should be assessed individually; some reforms were more popular than others. Further, although most would have preferred increased wages and regular work to social reform, the latter was occasionally welcomed as a decisive boost to living standards.

74. *Souvenir of the opening of the Alverstoke Free Public Library and Technical Institute* (1901), p. 11.

75. T. Greenwood, *Free public libraries* (1886), p. 140, argued that because ratepayer opposition was so vehement it was politic to proceed carefully: 'To make haste slowly', wrote Greenwood, 'should, therefore, be the motto of all friends of the movement'.

76. Figures from T. Kelly, *A history of public libraries*, op. cit., pp. 23, 112. The number of adoptions relative to the total number of local authorities was extremely small. In 1901, for example, there existed in England and Wales 67 county boroughs, 28 metropolitan boroughs, 1122 municipal councils and 14,900 civil parishes; Census of England and Wales, *Report* (1901), p. 14.

77. Daunton, op. cit., p. 202. Further, in the 1890s the rate of increase in rateable values began to slow.

78. See the table of adoptions in Kelly, *A history of public libraries*, op. cit., pp. 494-502.

79. *The Library*, 6 (1894), pp. 212-13.

80. Our great municipal libraries ... the Islington Public Libraries, *Sunday Strand* (May 1909), pp. 428-36. An analysis of London's public library history can be found in *Library Review*, 33 (1984).

81. Cited by E. Hobsbawm in his essay on the nineteenth-century labour market in his *Worlds of labour* (1984), pp. 147-8.

82. P. J. Waller, *Town, city and nation: England 1850–1914* (1983), p. 59.

83. One exception here is B. Wiltshire, *The public library in autobiography*, unpublished MPhil, CNAA (Polytechnic of North London, 1982), although the majority of works cited in this are of a middle-class origin.

84. The most extensive collections of Parliamentary Returns are those of 1876 and 1877. A comprehensive collection of annual reports can be found at the British Library Information Science Service. A detailed analysis of London's library users appeared in *London: a Journal of Civic and Social Progress* (26 April 1894).

85. E. A. Savage, *A librarian looks at readers: observation for book selection and personal service* (1950), p. 248.

86. The wording on a handbill, *Save the Christchurch Library*, advertising a meeting against the sale of that particular institution in 1919. Southwark Local Studies Library, PC 021 BCA.

87. An analysis of medium and large public libraries in the 1880s and 1890s has stated that the proportion of users was 63 per cent manual workers, 21 per cent professional and managerial positions and 16 per cent clerical and non-manual occupations; B. Lackham, *The Library and society* (1971), p. 5. (Luckham makes no mention, however, on how he arrived at these percentages). D. Gerard, *Libraries in society: a reader* (1978), p. 83, analyses these proportions and thus makes the point about over-representation.

88. Greenwood, op. cit. (1886 edn), p. 139.

89. R. J. B. Morris, *Parliament and the public libraries* (1977), p. 12.

90. The *Croydon Advertiser* (29 March 1890), in discussing a library for the town, argued that many treated the public library as a charitable institution: 'we have known ladies and gentlemen either from misconception or downright snobbishness, actually decline to avail themselves of the benefits of their library, simply because it was called the "free" library'. C. Kernahan, *The reading girl* (1925), p. 15, relates that she had been told by a middle-class woman that in using a public library she would feel 'very much as if I was making use of a soup kitchen - as if I were meanly availing myself of something intended for quite another class'. The Department of Education and Science, *The libraries' choice* (1978), p. 5, argues that the public library had a working-class image until the First World War, but that this image began to wane in the recession of the 1930s as the middle classes gave up their subscription libraries and flocked to the public library to economize.

91. J. Allred, The purpose of the public library: the historical view, *Library History*, 2:5 (Spring 1972), pp. 192-3.

92. J. S. Rowntree, *Free public libraries: an address delivered in the Festival Concert Room, York . . .* (1881), p. 9.

93. Calculated from South Shields' Parliamentary Return of 1876.

94. J. D. Brown, *Manual of library economy* (1907 edn), p. 406.

95. A. Robson, The intellectual background of the public library movement in Britain, *Journal of Library History*, 11:3 (July 1976).

96. A. Blakemore, *Rolling through the years*, p. 98, typescript, Shrewsbury Local History Library.

97. Free public libraries, *Westminster Review*, 42 (1872), p. 334.

98. R. Trainor, Urban elites in Victorian Britain, *Urban History Yearbook* (1985) argues that although there occurred a slight democratization of urban leadership before 1914 - in local government, for example - radical change did not come about until after 1918. Before the First World War élites remained well connected to the upper ranks of the middle class. However, their persisting social substance should not cloak their diversity.

99. T. Kelly, A history of public libraries, op. cit., p. v.

2   Foundations of the public library ideal

1. For example, the Library Association, *A century of public library service* (1950), p. 2, states that 'it is reasonable to say that on 14 August 1850, was *started* [emphasis added] a great social institution which has increasingly, throughout the century, been of incalculable benefit'.

2. R. J. B. Morris, *Parliament and the public libraries* (1977), p. 1.

3. T. Kelly, *Public libraries in Great Britain before 1850* (1966) notes a prolific independent provision.

4. A. R. Thompson, The use of libraries by the working class in Scotland in the early nineteenth century, *Scottish Historical Review*, 42 (1963). Also Chapter 8 of T. Kelly, *Early public libraries: a history of public libraries in Great Britain before 1850* (1966).

5. See the evidence of Sir Henry Ellis, Select Committee on the Condition, Management and Affairs of the British Museum, *Report* (1836).

6. This was a core message conveyed in the Select Committee on Public

Libraries, *Report* (1849), including the evidence of Edward Edwards (Q. 131), who blamed the lack of public libraries in Britain relative to other countries on the effects of the Reformation, the latter having destroyed, he argued, the monastic library which in other countries had been appropriated for fairly wide public use.

7.   R. Altick, *The English common reader: a social history of the mass reading public 1800–1900* (Chicago, 1957), p. 223.

8.   Between 1832 and 1839 the Religious Tract Society distributed through England and Wales over 4000 collections of a religious and moralizing nature.

9.   Libraries in Bermondsey prior to rate-supported libraries, Anon. (no date), Southwark Local Studies Library, PC 021 BER states that the John Street Wesleyan Sunday School in Bermondsey, South London, established in 1843, had 700 volumes in its library divided into a section for scholars and another for senior scholars and teachers.

10.   See the evidence of George Dawson (Q. 1216, 1329), Select Committee on Public Libraries, op. cit. William Lovett told the same committee (Q. 2771, 2773) that a quarter of the 200 coffee houses in London possessed libraries, and that one in Long Acre had over 2000 volumes.

11.   Select Committee on Public Libraries, op. cit. The evidence of Samuel Smiles (Q. 1993, 1994) and George Dawson (Q. 1366) testifies to this. F. M. L. Thompson, *The rise of respectable society: a social history of Victorian Britain 1830–1900* (1988), p. 213 states that this practice became increasingly common after 1850.

12.   T. Kelly, Early public libraries, op. cit., p. 241.

13.   T. Kelly, *A history of public libraries in Great Britain 1845–1975* (1977), pp. 3–4, 455–7.

14.   Select Committee on Inquiry into Drunkenness, *Report* (1834), p. iv.

15.   Ibid., p. vi.

16.   Ibid., p. vii.

17.   Ibid., p. ix.

18.   Ibid., p. x.

19.   Ibid., p. ix.

20.   Ibid., p. viii.

21.   Ibid., Q. 2017.

22.   Ibid., Q. 2028.

23.   Ibid., Q. 2017.

24.   Nineteenth-century beer consumption was at a peak in 1802–3. One of the driest years of the century was 1817. Thereafter, an upward trend lasted until 1835, at which point consumption was 25 per cent less than in 1802. This was followed by a fall from 1835 to 1855. F. M. L. Thompson, op. cit., pp. 312–13.

25.   Select Committee on Inquiry into Drunkenness, op. cit., Q. 2079, 2032.

26.   Morris, op. cit., p. 206.

27.   Hansard, *Parliamentary Debates* 29 (1835), col. 568.

28.   Ibid., col. 567.

29.   For the texts of these bills see *Parliamentary Papers: Public Bills,* Vol. 4 (1835), p. 49; Vol. 4 (1836), p. 713; Vol. 4 (1837), p. 61.

30.   Hansard, *Parliamentary Debates* 30 (1835), col. 652.

31.   Ibid., cols. 650–1.

32. Ibid., col. 649.
33. *House of Commons Journal* 90 (1835), pp. 561-2.
34. Hansard, *Parliamentary Debates* 29 (1835), col. 576.
35. Select Committee on Public Walks, *Report* (1833), Q. 861.
36. J. Manners, *Some of the advantages of recreation rooms, reading rooms and public libraries* (1885), p. 71.
37. M. Girouard, *The English town* (1990), p. 272. It is worth emphasizing that improved health through games and sports was not a concern of early reformers, and was not popularized until the rise of 'muscular Christianity' in the late nineteenth century.
38. Select Committee on Public Walks, op. cit., Q. 830-6.
39. Ibid., Q. 352.
40. The words which appeared on the final report in 1836 were 'Arts and their connection with manufactures'. However, the evidence was taken in two parts: first in 1835 on the subject of 'arts and manufactures', followed in 1836 by evidence on 'arts and the principles of design'.
41. Select Committee on Arts and Manufactures, *Report* (1836), p. iii.
42. Ibid., p. iii.
43. Ibid., p. v.
44. Ibid., p. iv.
45. Ibid., Q. 1353-4.
46. W. A. Munford, Pioneer ancestors, *Library Association Record*, 59 (1957). For a succinct description of the activities and aims of mechanics' institutes see S. Katoh, Mechanics' institutes in Great Britain to the 1850s, *Journal of Education, Administration and History*, 21:2 (July 1989).
47. M. Fogarty, An analysis of the reasons behind the decline and ultimate collapse of the Wolverhampton Athenaeum and Mechanics' Institute library 1847-1869, *West Midland Studies*, 12 (Winter 1979).
48. R. J. Morris, *Class, sect and party: the making of the British middle class. Leeds 1820–1850* (1990), p. 306.
49. Society for the Diffusion of Useful Knowledge, *Manual for mechanics' institutions* (1839), pp. 54-7 (written by B. F. Duppa).
50. *Museums Act* (1845), 8 and 9 Vict. c. 43.
51. Kelly, *A history of public libraries*, op. cit., pp. 10-11.
52. E.g. P. Sturges, Context for library history: libraries in eighteenth century Derby, *Library History*, 4:2 (1976) and The place of libraries in the English urban renaissance of the eighteenth century, *Libraries and Culture*, 24:1 (1989).
53. For example, Chapter 1 of W. A. Munford, *Penny rate: aspects of British public library history 1850–1950* (1951); and G. Jones, *Political and social factors in the advocacy of free libraries in the United Kingdom 1801–1922*, unpublished PhD, University of Strathclyde (1971).
54. There are two notable exceptions here: J. Noyce, *Libraries and the working classes in the nineteenth century* (1974); and P. Corrigan and V. Gillespie, *Class struggle, social literacy and idle time: the provision of public libraries in England as a case study in the organisation of leisure with direct educational results* (1978).
55. E. P. Thompson, *The making of the English working class* (1968), p. 781.
56. E. Hobsbawm, *Industry and empire* (1968), p. 74.
57. Ibid., p. 75.

58. Ibid., p. 58 points out that the price of 11 pounds of spun cotton fell by 62.5 per cent, 1812–1832.

59. A. Gamble, *Britain in decline: economic policy, political strategy and the British state* (1981), p. 8.

60. See E. Hobsbawm's introduction to F. Engels, *The condition of the working class in England* (1969), p. 14.

61. Ibid., p. 232, words of Engels.

62. Three succinct assessments are: R. J. Morris, *Class and class consciousness in the Industrial Revolution 1780–1850* (1979); D. G. Wright, *Popular radicalism: the working class experience 1780–1880* (1988); and R. Glen, *Urban workers in the early Industrial Revolution* (1984), particularly the introductory chapter. P. Joyce, *Visions of the people: industrial England and the question of class 1848–1914* (1991) diverges from traditional assessments by arguing that there has been a fixation with class and that it has been overplayed by historians.

63. E. P. Thompson, op. cit., pp. 9-10.

64. Ibid., p. 10.

65. Ibid., p. 12.

66. Ibid.

67. H. Perkin, *The origins of modern English society* (1969), p. 177.

68. For example, G. D. H. Cole and R. Postgate, *The common people 1746–1946* (1961).

69. J. Foster, *Class struggles and the Industrial Revolution* (1974). Perkin, op. cit.

70. E. J. Hobsbawm, The making of the working class, *in* his *Worlds of labour* (1984); and A. Briggs, The language of 'class' in early nineteenth century England, *in* A. Briggs and J. Saville (eds), *Essays in labour history* (1960).

71. G. Rude, *The crowd in history: a study of popular disturbances in France and England 1730–1848* (1964), p. 6.

72. Ibid., p. 6.

73. Ibid., p. 7.

74. E. P. Thompson, op. cit., p. 938.

75. C. Tilly, Britain creates the social movement, *in* J. E. Cronin and J. Schneer (eds), *Social conflict and the political order in modern Britain* (1982).

76. E. H. Hunt, *British labour history 1815–1914* (1981), p. 247.

77. Ibid., p. 219.

78. G. Pearson, *Hooligan: a history of respectable fears* (1983).

79. Hunt, op. cit., p. 237 writes: 'there is every indication that more determined attempts to challenge the government would have met equally determined resistance'.

80. M. Bentley, *Politics without democracy 1815–1914* (1984), p.127.

81. Wright, op. cit.

82. N. Kirk, *The growth of working class radicalism in middle Victorian England* (1985), Chapter 3.

83. M. I. Thomis and P. Holt, *Threats of revolution in Britain 1789–1848*, p. 128.

84. Bentley, op. cit., pp. 133-4.

85. Quoted in N. J. Frangopulo, *Rich inheritance: a guide to the history of Manchester* (1969), p. 50.

86. C. C. Armstrong, *Manchester as it was* (1875). Manuscript printed in the *Manchester Review*, 9 (Spring 1960).

87. P. Hepworth and M. Alexander, *Norwich public libraries* (1965), p. 10, points

out that this same flavour can be tasted in the foundation stone-laying ceremony for the public library in Norwich in 1852.

88. J. F. C. Harrison, *Robert Owen and the Owenites in Britain and America: the quest for the new moral world* (1969), pp. 136, 222.

89. Manchester Free Libraries, *The Builder* (23 March 1867).

90. Manchester Free Library, *Report of the proceedings at the public meeting held in the library* (1852), pp. 17, 19.

91. Ibid., p. 33.

92. Manchester Public Free Libraries, *Report of the proceedings of the public meeting on the occasion of the opening of the branch free library . . . of Chorlton and Ardwick* (1866), p. 7. Doncaster Borough Free Library and Newsroom, *Catalogue and inaugural ceremony* (1869), p. 18.

93. Pearson, op. cit., p. 164.

94. G. Himmelfarb, *The idea of poverty: England in the early industrial age* (1984), p. 385.

95. As explained by Pearson, op. cit., p. 159.

96. Himmelfarb, op. cit., p. 387.

97. C. Thomson, *The autobiography of an artisan* (1847), p. 170.

98. See introduction to V. Neuburg, *Literacy and society* (1971).

99. By 1871, however, the respective rates had increased to 80 per cent and 70 per cent. By 1891 rates stood at 94 per cent (men) and 90 per cent (women). By the turn of the century the sexes had achieved parity at 97 per cent. Rates derived from J. Walvin, *A child's world: a social history of English childhood* (1982), p.121; and A. Digby and P. Searby, *Children, school and society in nineteenth century England* (1981), pp. 3–5.

100. Digby and Searby, op. cit., pp. 3–5.

101. W. B. Stephens, *Education, literacy and society: the geography of diversity in provincial England* (1987).

102. V. Neuburg, *Popular education in eighteenth century England* (1971), p. 93. A nineteenth-century example of reading being more common than writing comes from the opening of the library at the Salford Museum in 1849. The idea that anyone obtaining a book should enter their name in the register was given up after a few days 'not only because it occupied so much time; but because many who came for books were unable to write, and some, rather than confess their inability, would go without the book they desired'. *Chambers Edinburgh Journal*, 15 (1851), p. 199.

103. See V. Neuburg, *Popular literature: a history and guide* (1977), and his Literature of the streets, *in* H. J. Dyos and M. Wolff (eds), *The Victorian city: images and reality*, Vol. 1 (1973); L. James, *Print and the people 1819–1851* (1978), and the first two chapters of his *Fiction for the working man 1830–1850* (1963); L. Shepard, *The broadside ballad: a study in origins and meaning* (1962).

104. *Seymour's humorous sketches* (1836), scene III.

105. G. E. Maxim, *Libraries and reading in the context of the economic political and social changes taking place in Manchester and the neighbouring mill towns 1750–1850*, unpublished MA, University of Sheffield, 1979.

106. J. Weiner, *William Lovett* (1989), especially Chapter 5; and B. Harrison, Kindness and reason: William Lovett and education, *in* G. Marsden (ed.), *Victorian values: personalities and perspectives in nineteenth century society* (1990).

107. W. Lovett and J. Collins, *Chartism: a new organization of the people* (1840); facsimile publication by the 'Victorian Library', with an introduction by A. Briggs (1969), p. 74.
108. This is a central theme of R. K. Webb, *The British working class reader 1790–1848: literacy and social tension* (1955). The working-class thirst for reading is similarly depicted by James, op. cit. and by Altick, op. cit.
109. J. Thompson, *A history of the principles of librarianship* (1977), p. 208.
110. Quoted in P. Cadogan, *Early radical Newcastle* (1975), p. 126.
111. W. Stafford, *Socialism, radicalism and nostalgia* (1987). Chapter 8 provides a discussion of Coleridge's *A lay sermon addressed to the higher and middle classes on the existing distress and discontents* (1817).
112. M. Kaly and G. Riddell, Turning back the clock, *History Today* (October 1988), p. 7.
113. Corrigan and Gillespie, op. cit.

3   The utilitarian flywheel

1. R. Johnson, Educating the educators: experts and the state 1833-1839, *in* A. P. Donajrodzki, *Social control in nineteenth century Britain* (1977), p. 83.
2. J. Plamenatz, *The English utilitarians* (Oxford, 1958), p. 1.
3. F. R. Leavis's introduction to J. S. Mill, *Mill on Bentham and Coleridge* (1950), p. 35. This being an abridgement of articles from the *Westminster Review* of 1838 and 1840.
4. E. Halevy, *The growth of philosophic radicalism* (1928), p. 6.
5. G. H. Bantock, *The minds of the masses 1760–1980* (Studies in the history of education theory, Vol. 2) (1984), p. 22.
6. E. Royle, *Victorian infidels: the origins of the British secularist movement 1791–1866* (1974), p. 128.
7. Ibid., p. 126.
8. Ibid., p. 133.
9. However, Bentham believed philanthropy was derived not from conscience or duty but from enlightened self-interest; this according to Mill, *Mill on Bentham*, op. cit., pp. 66, 70.
10. R. Pearson and G. Williams, *Political thought and public policy in the nineteenth century: an introduction* (1984), p. 19.
11. R. J. Halliday, *John Stuart Mill* (New York, 1976), p. 46.
12. Ibid., p. 22.
13. M. Sanderson, *Education, economic change and society in England 1780–1870* (1983), p. 49.
14. Halliday, op. cit., p. 22.
15. Mill, *Mill on Bentham*, op. cit., p. 109.
16. B. Simon, *Two nations and the educational structure 1780–1870* (1983), p. 49.
17. As argued by Mill, Mill on Bentham, op. cit., p. 710.
18. S. Hollander, *The economics of John Stuart Mill* (1985), p. 603 (note 3).
19. Mill, Mill on Bentham, op. cit., p. 109.
20. Ibid., p. 91. That Bentham did not start from scratch is an important point to stress. David Hume had used the term 'utility' frequently. However, he wrote of traits of character which were agreeable or useful; he did not speak of utility in terms of what actions individuals might best take. Previously, Francis Hutcheson defined virtue as that which gives pleasure, which was but a short

way from the Benthamite notion of equating utility with pleasure. *Encyclopedia of philosophy* (1967), Vol. 4, p. 100 and Vol. 8, p. 208.

21. Mill, quoted by F. R. Leavis in his introduction to Mill, *Mill on Bentham*, op. cit., p. 16.
22. Ibid., pp. 41–2.
23. Ibid., p. 61.
24. Ibid., p. 61. Johnson, op. cit., p. 83 argues that the Benthamites were detached in one important sense: they were essentially London-based, with little knowledge of industrial society outside the capital.
25. W. Thomas, *The philosophic radicals: nine studies in theory and practice 1817–1841* (1979), p. 1 explains that at a time of revolutionary threat in the early nineteenth century the utilitarians were viewed as potentially 'unsafe'.
26. F. Rosen, The origins of liberal utilitarianism: Jeremy Bentham and liberty, *in* R. Bellamy (ed.), *Victorian liberalism* (1990), p. 61.
27. Ibid. The theme of security forms the main theme of Rosen's discussion.
28. Hollander, op. cit., p. 649.
29. As argued, by S. Conway, Bentham and the nineteenth century revolution in government, *in* Bellamy, op. cit.
30. Thomas, op. cit., p. 3.
31. O. MacDonagh, *Early Victorian government 1830–70* (1977) discusses several favouring and resisting forces, beyond the Benthamite influence, leading to the legislative revolution of the time.
32. As argued by Thomas, op. cit., p. 6.
33. This is the essence of the argument offered by Conway, op. cit.
34. Thomas, op. cit., p. 4.
35. G. Wallas, *The life of Francis Place 1771–1854* (1898), pp. 85–6.
36. F. R. Leavis in his introduction to Mill, *Mill on Bentham*, op. cit., p. 29. For Mill's modification in respect of government intervention, see F. Copplestone, *A history of philosophy* (1966), pp. 36–44.
37. Halliday, op. cit., pp. 49–52.
38. Hollander, op. cit., pp. 618–38.
39. Mill, *Mill on Bentham*, op. cit., p. 93.
40. Quoted in G. L. Williams, *John Stuart Mill on politics and society* (1976), p. 40.
41. Mill, *Mill on Bentham*, op. cit., p. 90.
42. Ibid., p. 72.
43. Ibid., p. 71.
44. Ibid., pp. 73–4.
45. J. Gibbins, J. S. Mill, Liberalism and progress, *in* Bellamy, op. cit., p. 99.
46. Ibid. Gibbins offers a clear explanation of negative liberalism.
47. As explained by C. Wilmer, *Unto this last: and other writings of John Ruskin* (1985), p. 21.
48. S. E. Stumpf, *Elements of philosophy: an introduction* (1979), p. 70.
49. Ibid., p. 70.
50. F. Place, *Improvement of the working people* (1834), p. 9.
51. Sanderson, op. cit., p. 51. See also B. Harrison, Kindness and reason: William Lovett and education, *in* G. Marsden (ed.), *Victorian values: personalities and perspectives in nineteenth century society* (1957).
52. A key point made in W. H. Burston, Utilitarians and the monitorial system of education, *in Yearbook of Education* (1957), and in his *James Mill on philosophy and education* (1973).

53. Hollander, op. cit., p. 659.
54. Stumpf, op. cit., p. 69.
55. Gibbins, J. S. Mill, op. cit., p. 69.
56. Williams, op. cit., pp. 30-2.
57. Select Committee on Inquiry into Drunkenness, *Report* (1834), p. vi.
58. R. M. Young, Herbert Spencer and 'inevitable progress', *in* Marsden, op. cit.
59. Quoted in Mill, *Mill on Bentham*, op. cit., pp. 156-7.
60. Quoting from Mill's autobiography in F. R. Leavis's introduction to Mill, *Mill on Bentham*, op. cit.
61. See M. D. O'Brien's essay on free libraries (to be discussed here in Chapter 6) *in* T. Mackay, *A plea for liberty: an argument against socialism and socialistic legislation* (1892).
62. T. Mackay, *The dangers of democracy: studies in the economic questions of the day* (1913), p. 268.
63. Gibbins, J. S. Mill, op. cit., p. 101-2.
64. Ibid., p. 102.
65. Mill's realization that he had been too harsh on Bentham, and his consequential return to elements of Benthamite thought, is explored by Hollander, op. cit., pp. 605, 610-12, 638-60, who argues, for example, that Bentham did not speak of duty simply to one's own self, but also to others, in terms of avoiding actions which reduced happiness in others.
66. Wallas, op. cit., p. 41.
67. D. Fraser, *Power and authority in the Victorian city* (1979), pp. 3-4. Fraser does not see 1835 as a revolution, but it did allow for future widening of responsibilities in a municipal setting (p. 151).
68. Ibid., p. 19.
69. J. A. Roebuck, *A letter to the electors of Bath on the Municipal Corporations Reform Bill* (1835), p. 7.
70. Wallas, op. cit., p. 343.
71. G. Crossick, Urban society and the petty bourgeoisie in nineteenth century Britain, *in* D. Fraser and A. Sutcliffe, *The pursuit of urban history* (1983), p. 314.
72. Fraser, op. cit., p. 96.
73. N. McCord, Ratepayers and social policy, *in* P. Thane (ed.), *The origins of British social policy* (1978), p. 31.
74. A. Ryan, Utilitarianism and bureaucracy: the view of John Stuart Mill, *in* G. Sutherland (ed.), *Studies in the growth of nineteenth century government* (1972), pp. 40, 49.
75. J. Gibbins, Utilitarianism, conservatism and social policy, *in* L. Allison (ed.), *The utilitarian response* (1990).
76. J. A. Roebuck, *On the means of conveying education to the people* (1835), p. 7.
77. Brougham on the education of the people, *Blackwood's Magazine*, 17 (1825), p. 534.
78. J. Streintrager, *Bentham* (1977), p. 106.
79. J. Curran, The press as an agency of social control: an historical perspective, *in* G. Boyce, J. Curran and P. Wingate (eds), *Newspaper history: from the seventeenth century to the present day* (1978) argues that the respectable campaign against stamp duty was not motivated by libertarian impulses, but driven by the belief that a free press would work against radical disaffection and social instability.

80. Hansard, *Parliamentary Debates* 30 (1835), col. 654-5. Words of Mr Wakely.
81. H. Brougham, Practical observations upon the education of the people: addresses to the working classes and their employers, *Edinburgh Review*, 41 (1825), p. 509.
82. F. Place, *A letter to a minister of state respecting taxes upon knowledge*, pp. 3-4.
83. Ibid., p. 4.
84. Mill, *Mill on Bentham*, op. cit., pp. 41-2.
85. F. Rosen, *Jeremy Bentham and representative democracy: a study of the Constitutional Code* (1983), p. 7.
86. Quoted in Bantock, op. cit., p. 192.
87. C. W. Sutton, *Manchester Free Libraries: record of the Jubilee celebrations* (1903), pp. 23-4.
88. H. Silver, *English education and the radicals 1789–1850* (1975), p. 31; from James Mill's article on education, *in Encyclopedia Britannica (Supplement)* (1918).
89. Silver, op. cit., p. 29.
90. R. Altick, *The English common reader: a social history of the mass reading public 1800–1900* (1957), p. 131.
91. Sanderson, op. cit., p. 31.
92. See K. McGarry's comments on literacy in both his *Literacy, communication and libraries: a study guide* (1991) and *The changing context of information: an introductory analysis* (1993).
93. Quoted in J. Bentham, *The works of Jeremy Bentham*, Vol. 2, ed. by J. Bowring (1843), pp. 256-7; from Bentham's *Rationale of reward* (1825).
94. In 1845 the Manchester Mechanics' Institute ran lectures in the following areas: 'Introduction to political economy'; 'Production of wealth'; 'Distribution (rent, wages, profit)'; 'Interchange (value, currency, foreign commerce, restrictions)'; 'Consumption (individual, government)'. Manchester Mechanics Institute, *Outline of course of lectures on political economy*, Manchester Public Library Archives.
95. Silver, op. cit., p. 26.
96. A. Llewellyn, *Decade of reform: the 1830s* (1972), p. 9.
97. C. B. Macpherson, *The political theory of possessive individualism: Hobbs to Locke* (1964), p. 3.
98. Quoted in Bantock, op. cit., p. 173.
99. Simon, op. cit., p. 127.
100. Ibid., p. 132.
101. Ibid., p. 136.
102. Place, *A letter to a minister*, op. cit., p. 18.
103. S. Maccoby, *English radicalism 1832–1852* (1935), p. 272.
104. Hollander, op. cit., p. 722.
105. Simon, op. cit., p. 80.
106. Altick, op. cit., pp. 142-3.
107. Bentham, op. cit., p. 258, from his *Rationale of reward* (1825).
108. Burston, op. cit.
109. Quoted in F. A. Cavanagh, *James and John Stuart Mill on education* (1931), p. 127.
110. Ibid., p. 129.
111. Ibid., p. ix.

112. Ibid., p. xxvi.
113. Ibid., p. xxiv.
114. R. Porter and M. Teich, *Enlightenment in national context* (1981), p. 6.
115. Ibid., p. 14.
116. Ibid., p. 15.
117. Ibid., p. 15.
118. Fraser, op. cit., p. 161.
119. J. Harris, *Private lives, public spirit: a social history of Britain 1870–1914* (1993), p. 249.
120. *The autobiography of John Stuart Mill* (New York, 1924), p. 116.
121. Bentham, op. cit., p. 258, from his *Rationale of reward* (1825).
122. *Ceremonies connected with the opening of . . . a free public library and museum presented by William Brown to the town of Liverpool* (1861), p. 13.
123. *The Times* (26 January 1841).
124. Public libraries, *Westminster Review*, 8 (1827), p. 106.
125. Public libraries, *in* Society for the Diffusion of Useful Knowledge, *The companion to the British almanac; or yearbook of general information* (1850), pp. 54-5.
126. Manchester Free Public Library, *Report of the proceedings at the public meeting held in the library . . . to celebrate the opening of the free library* (1852), p. 31.
127. A. Brooks and B. Haworth, *Boomtown Manchester 1800–1850: the Portico connection* (1993), p. 29, identifies this as a prime aim of part of the collection in the private Portico Library in Manchester.
128. Benjamin Heywood was one such figure; ibid., p. 50. The term 'moral statistics' is appropriately employed by F. Driver, *The workhouse system 1834–1884* (1993), p. 10.
129. Hansard, *Parliamentary Debates* 30 (1835), col. 652.
130. Ibid., col. 654.
131. Select Committee on Public Libraries, *Report* (1849), pp. 251-2.
132. J. Hole, *'Light more light!' On the present state of education amongst the working classes of Leeds* (1969 facsimile reprint of 1860 edn), p. 124. See his numerous references to the importance of libraries in his *Essay on the history and management of literary, scientific and mechanics' institutions* (1970 facsimile reprint of 1853 edn).
133. The same point is made with regard to temperance objectives by B. Harrison, *Drink and the Victorians: the temperance question in England 1815–1872*, pp. 198-9.
134. E. Edwards, *Free town libraries* (1869), p. 22.
135. As argued by G. Jones, *Political and social factors in the advocacy of 'free' libraries in the UK 1801–1922*, unpublished PhD, University of Strathclyde (1971), p. 103.
136. G. Dawson, *Sermons on daily life and duty* (1878), p. 122.
137. T. Greenwood, *Public libraries* (1981, 4th edn), p. 64.
138. J. Gerrard, *Leadership and power in Victorian industrial towns 1830–1880* (1983), p. 52.
139. Quoted in J. Thompson, *A History of the principles of librarianship* (1977), p. 94.
140. *Free public library: to the owners and ratepayers of the city of York* (1881). A pro-adoption leaflet *in* York Public Library Scrapbooks.
141. Ibid.

142. E. H. Hunt, *British labour history 1815–1914* (1981), p. 232.
143. For example, see Select Committee on Public Libraries, op. cit., Q.1266, 1357.
144. Manchester Free Public Library, op. cit., p. 34.
145. Manchester Free Public Libraries, *Report of the proceedings . . . of the opening of the branch free library for . . . Chorlton and Ardwick* (1866), p. 18.
146. Ibid., pp. 20–1. Words of W. T. S. Daniel.
147. R. Slaney, *An essay on the employment of the poor* (1819), p. 12.
148. Ibid., p. 55.
149. R. Slaney, *The state of education of the poorer classes in large towns* (1971 facsimile reprint of 1837 edn), p. 23. This pamphlet was published in 1837 as a report of a speech on 30 November that year by Slaney in the House of Commons.
150. J. Allred, The purpose of the public library: the historical view, *Library History*, 2:5 (Spring 1972), p. 194.
151. Select Committee on Public Libraries, op. cit., Q. 1933-6.
152. Ibid., p. xi.
153. Greenwood, op. cit., pp. 59–60.
154. M. S. White, *Profit from information* (1981), p. 2.
155. Driver, op. cit., pp. 13–14.
156. G. Himmelfarb, Bentham's utopia, in her *Marriage and morals among the Victorians, and other essays* (1989).
157. Manchester Free Public Libraries, *Report of the . . . inauguration of the . . . Hulme Branch Library in Stretford Road* (1866), p. 9. Words of Rev. F. C. Woodhouse.
158. Pages 64–5.
159. William Ewart's notebook on imports and exports; item 57 of the Ewart Family Records.

4 The principal pioneers: Ewart and Edwards

1. S. E. Finer, The transmission of Benthamite ideas 1820-50, in G. Sutherland, *Studies in the growth of government* (1972). Finer labels the three stages: irradiation, suscitation, permeation.
2. R. Pearson and G. Williams, *Political thought and public policy in the nineteenth century: an introduction* (1984), p. 35.
3. W. Ewart, *Reform of the Reform Bill, and its anticipated results. A letter to a cabinet minister (1837)*, p. 29. University College, University of London, Manuscripts Department.
4. W. A. Munford, *William Ewart MP 1798–1869: portrait of a radical* (1960), p. xiii.
5. J. Hewitt, *To be sold by auction . . . two hacks* (January 1835).
6. Munford, William Ewart, op. cit., p. xiii.
7. Ibid. The only previous biography was a short sketch by G. W. Shirley, *William Ewart: a pioneer of public libraries* (1930).
8. E. Edwards, Libraries and the people, *British Quarterly Review*, 11 (1850), p. 80.
9. A perusal of his unpublished notebooks for 1853, 1856, 1863 and 1866 reveals a diversity of interests ranging from mortality in the Indian Army to the import and export trade with France, from banking to poor relief. Item 57 of the Ewart family records.

10. S. Ellis, *William Ewart's work for education*, MEd dissertation, Manchester University (September 1973). As far as can be ascertained the only available copy of this document is in the Ewart family records. The dissertation illustrates Ewart's educational reform interest regarding fine and applied arts; elementary, secondary and university education; repeal of taxes on knowledge; public exams; metric weights and measures; and public museums and libraries.

11. St Martin-in-the-Fields Public Library Commissioner's *First Report* (covering 1887-91).

12. Munford, *William Ewart*, op. cit., p. 179. The accusation of wavering was made in an election ballad of 1857 entitled *To the electors: wavering willie*, deposited with the Dumfries Public Library.

13. *Spectator* (9 December 1837). Referred to in J. Hamburger, *Intellectuals in politics: John Stuart Mill and the philosophic radicals* (1965), p. 176.

14. H. Martineau, *A history of England during the thirty years' peace*, Vol. 2, pp. 351-2, quoted in Munford, *William Ewart*, op. cit., p. 70.

15. Letter from William Ewart to Francis Place (26 June 1837). British Library Manuscripts Department, MS 37949f364, 1160 additional.

16. W. Thomas, *The philosophic radicals: nine studies in theory and practice 1817–1841* (1979), p. 2. Thomas (p. 300) places Ewart alongside the philosophic radicals Roebuck and Hume.

17. N. Abercrombie, S. Hill and B. S. Turner, *The dominant ideology thesis* (1984), p. 97.

18. Pearson and Williams, op. cit., p. 10.

19. Bentham himself led a closeted life, was never 'read by the multitude', and with 'many of the most natural and strongest feelings of human nature he had no sympathy'; J. S. Mill, *Mill on Bentham and Coleridge* (Introduction by F. R. Leavis) (1950), pp. 39, 61.

20. Pearson and Williams, op. cit., p. 10.

21. Thomas, op. cit. pp. 3, 10.

22. Shirley, op. cit., p. 3.

23. H. Silver, *English education and the radicals 1780–1850* (1975), pp. 28-9.

24. Thomas, op. cit., p. 12.

25. *Dumfries and Galloway Advertiser* (27 January 1869). An 1857 election ballad entitled *Address to the loyal and independent town of Dumfries*, deposited with the Dumfries Public Library, urged: 'If Just Reform, Free Trade, still take the van, Then art thou honor'd in thy chosen man ... Electors! don't forget the Hustings day - Three cheers for Ewart, Reform! then hip hurrah'.

26. J. Grant, *Random collections of the House of Commons from the year 1835 to the close of 1836: including personal sketches of the leading members of all parties by one of no party* (1836), pp. 278-9. Cited in Correspondence with William Munford, item 21 of Ewart family records.

27. Unpublished notebook on the import and export trade (covering 1828-33), item 56 of Ewart family records.

28. Munford, *William Ewart*, op. cit., pp. 181-3.

29. S. Maccoby, English radicalism 1832-52 (1935), p. 152.

30. J. Hamburger, The Whig conscience, *in* P. Marsh (ed.), *The conscience of the Victorian state* (1979), p. 26.

31. Pearson and Williams, op. cit., p. 17.

32. Hansard, *Parliamentary Debates* 57 (6 April 1841), col. 937.

33. Munford, *William Ewart*, op. cit., p. 115.
34. Shirley, op. cit., p. 5.
35. Article on William Ewart (by W. A. Munford), *Encyclopedia of library and information Science*, Vol. 8 (New York, 1972), pp. 260-1.
36. *Illustrated London News* (25 July 1848).
37. Hansard, *Parliamentary Debates* 48 (20 June 1839), col. 592.
38. Ibid., col. 589.
39. Hansard, *Parliamentary Debates* 14 (3 July 1832), col. 51.
40. Munford, William Ewart, op. cit., pp. 137-8.
41. Hansard, *Parliamentary Debates* 91 (20 April 1847), col. 1050.
42. Letter from Ewart to Edward Baines (10 September 1846), in the appendix to E. Baines, *Letters to the Rt Hon. Lord John Russell* (1846)
43. Ibid.
44. Letter from Ewart to Edward Baines (15 September 1846), in Baines, op. cit.
45. Hansard, *Parliamentary Debates* 50 (9 August 1839), col. 180.
46. Hansard, *Parliamentary Debates* 57 (6 April 1841), col. 942.
47. Hansard, *Parliamentary Debates* 11 (15 March 1832), col. 280.
48. Hansard, *Parliamentary Debates* 51 (28 January 1840), col. 732-3.
49. Hansard, *Parliamentary Debates* 57 (6 April 1841), col. 941.
50. F. Bedarida, *A social history of England 1851-1975* (1979), p. 75.
51. Letter from Ewart to Charlotte Rutson (9 April 1848), quoted in Munford, *William Ewart*, op. cit., pp. 174-5.
52. Hansard, *Parliamentary Debates* 50 (9 August 1839), col. 180.
53. Hansard, *Parliamentary Debates* 21 (7 March 1834), col. 1286.
54. Letter from Ewart to Charlotte Rutson (30 April 1848), quoted in Munford, *William Ewart*, op. cit., p. 175.
55. Ibid.
56. T. Greenwood, *Edward Edwards* (1902), p. 15.
57. Hansard, *Parliamentary Debates* 50 (9 August 1839), col. 180.
58. Ibid.
59. Ibid.
60. Ibid.
61. J. H. Wellard, *The public library comes of age* (1940), p. 101.
62. Hansard, *Parliamentary Debates* 10 (3 March 1832), col. 1148.
63. Ewart, op. cit., pp. 28-9.
64. Ibid., p. 21.
65. Ibid., p. 7.
66. Ibid., p. 32.
67. Ibid., p. 14.
68. Ibid., p. 30.
69. Ibid.
70. Ibid., p. 32.
71. Ibid., p. 14.
72. Ibid., p. 24.
73. Ibid., p. 22.
74. Letter from Ewart to Charlotte Rutson (May 1852), quoted in Munford, *William Ewart*, op. cit., p. 134.
75. Hansard, *Parliamentary Debates* 20 (27 March 1829), col. 1499.
76. Ibid.
77. Ewart, op. cit., p. 7.

78. W. A. Munford, *Penny rate: aspects of British public library history 1850–1950* (1951), p. 14.

79. P. N. Kaula, Centenary of William Ewart, *Herald of Library Science*, 9:3 (July 1970).

80. Munford, *William Ewart*, op. cit., p. 137.

81. Letter from Ewart to John Pink (1864), quoted in Munford, William Ewart, op. cit., p. 150.

82. Words of the librarian W. C. B. Sayers, *Library Association Record* 40 (1938), p. 352.

83. W. A. Munford, *Edward Edwards 1812–1886: portrait of a librarian* (1963), p. 7.

84. Richard Garnett quoted in L. S. Jast, *Inauguration of the Edward Edwards Monument at Niton, 7 February 1902* (1902), p. 3.

85. Greenwood, op. cit., p. 14.

86. Ibid., p. 69.

87. K. A. Manley, Edward Edwards: the first professional public librarian, *Library Association Record*, 88 (1986), p. 143.

88. Greenwood, op. cit., p. 7.

89. Ibid., p. 12.

90. Ibid.

91. E. Edwards, *The administrative economy of the fine arts* (1840), p. 325.

92. Munford, *Edward Edwards*, op. cit., p. 176.

93. Edwards's personal scrapbooks contain notes on a bewildering variety of subjects. Included are items on education, poetry, English language and literature, history of localities, history of European countries, history of ancient and modern libraries, foreign languages, and Napoleon. See Edwards's unpublished manuscript Scrapbook, Book 'E' on Libraries etc. (1860–76), Manchester Public Library Archives. The width of his intellectual interests is also shown in the contributions he made to the eighth edition of the Encyclopedia Britannica: these range from 'Newspapers' to the 'Post Office', and from 'Tea and the tea trade' to 'Woollen and worsted manufacturers'; Greenwood, op. cit., p. 149. W. A. Munford reminds us that his reading was remarkably varied, from Adam Smith to Mrs Gaskell; Edward Edwards in retrospect, *Library Review* (Summer 1963), p. 91.

94. K. A. Manley, Edward Edwards: a humble librarian at Oxford, *Library History*, 7:3 (1986), p. 74. Witness Edwards's two-volume *Life of Sir Walter Ralegh* (1868). He was truly a 'man of letters', as indicated by H. P. McCartney, Edward Edwards: man of letters, *Manchester Review* (Winter 1964–5).

95. E. Edwards, *Remarks on the minutes of evidence . . . on the British Museum* (1836). The investigation's full title was Select Committee on the Condition, Management and Affairs of the British Museum, which reported in 1836.

96. Munford, *Edward Edwards*, op. cit., p. 19. Edwards was unquestionably an economic liberal. In his youth he had been influenced by the democratic and economic ideas of the radical free trader William Fox. Sir John Potter (Manchester's mayor and first chairman of the town's public libraries committee) once referred to Edwards as 'a radical of the Cobden school'. Greenwood, op. cit., pp. 23, 114.

97. With the utilitarian Joseph Hume he was on terms of more than a passing acquaintanceship; Greenwood, op. cit., p. 13. He knew Ewart, certainly from

the late 1830s, when they both served on the governing committee of the Art Union of London.

98. E. Edwards, *Metropolitan university: remarks on the ministerial plan of a central university examining board* (1836), p. 9.
99. Ibid., p. 10.
100. Ibid., from A. Smith's *Wealth of nations*.
101. Ibid., p. 11.
102. Ibid., p. 15.
103. Edwards, Remarks ... British Museum, op. cit., (1839 edn), p. 9.
104. Ibid., p. 12.
105. Select Committee on the Condition, Management and Affairs of the British Museum, *Report*, Q. 1320-2, 1325.
106. Ibid., Q. 1313.
107. Ibid., Q. 4795.
108. E. Edwards, *A Letter to Sir Martin Shee on the reform of the Royal Academy* (1839), p. 12.
109. Ibid., p. 13.
110. Edwards, manuscript Scrapbook, op. cit., p. 189.
111. Jast, Inauguration, op. cit., p. 6.
112. L. S. Jast, *Libraries and living* (1932), p. 1.
113. Greenwood, op. cit., p. 127, quoting Edwards's *Memoirs of libraries* (1859). His social vision in the sphere of classification is commented on by Munford, Edward Edwards in retrospect, op. cit., p. 93.
114. Greenwood, op. cit., p. 44. Edwards told this to the Select Committee on the British Museum, op. cit.
115. Greenwood, op. cit., p. 86.
116. E. Edwards, *Free town libraries* (1869). Opposite p. 192 is a list of recent 'negligible' losses.
117. R. Altick, *The English common reader: a social history of the mass reading public 1800–1900* (Chicago, 1957), p. 223.
118. Further evidence of his utilitarianism is seen in his advocacy of central government grants and an inspectorate for public libraries; Greenwood, op. cit., p. 88.
119. Edwards, The administrative economy, op. cit., p. 271.
120. Ibid., p. 345.
121. Ibid., p. 272.
122. E. Edwards, *Remarks on the paucity of libraries freely open to the public ... in a letter to the Rt Hon. Earl of Ellesmere* (1849), pp. 34-5.
123. Edwards, Free town libraries, op. cit., p. 16.
124. E. Edwards, *A statistical view of the principal libraries in Europe and America* (1848), pp. iii–iv.
125. His diary for 1849 is filled with affectionate descriptions of his country walks with Ewart; Greenwood, op. cit., p. 69. He wrote, in 1867, a work entitled *Commons, parks and open spaces near London: their history and treatment considered in regard to Public health and recreation.*
126. Edwards, Remarks ... British Museum, op. cit., (1839 edn), p. 43.
127. Quoted in Greenwood, op. cit., p. 88.
128. Edwards, A statistical view, op. cit., p. iii.
129. Ibid., p. iv.
130. Edwards, Remarks ... British Museum, op. cit., (1839 edn). p. 44.

131. Edwards, The administrative economy, op. cit., p. 333.
132. E. Edwards, *A letter to the Rev. Thomas Binney on the present position of the education question* ... (1847), p. 25.
133. Greenwood, op. cit., p. 63, quoting from Edwards's Remarks on the paucity of libraries, op. cit. (1849).
134. Manchester Free Public Library, *Annual report* (1856), p. 9.
135. This principle is enshrined in the title of his Free town libraries, op. cit.
136. He told the Select Committee on Public Libraries (1849) that even great writers needed public libraries to further their intellectual pursuits. Highlighted by Greenwood, op. cit., p. 71.
137. Edwards's unpublished manuscript Diary (entry for 23 February 1848), British Library Reference Division.
138. Ibid. (entry for 25 February 1848).
139. One of his scrapbooks from later in his life contained two detailed newspaper articles on Disraeli: the first covering an attack of gout suffered by the Prime Minister; the second reporting on the unveiling of Lord Beaconsfield's (the name Disraeli took when elevated to the peerage) statue outside Parliament, on the second anniversary of his death in 1883. Edwards, manuscript Scrapbook, op. cit., pp. 25, 27.
140. Quoted in Munford, op. cit., p. 58, from *British Quarterly Review* 10 (1849).
141. Edwards' Diary, op. cit. (entry for 4 April 1848).
142. Ibid. (entry for 8 April 1848). Part of this entry read: 'On the way to the Museum, saw the disgraceful proclamation ... declaring the meeting ... illegal ... I resolved immediately wavering all minor disagreements to sign the petition for "The Chartists" '.
143. Ibid. (entry for 10 April 1848).
144. R. Cowtan, *Memoirs of the British Museum* (1872), p. 146.
145. Ibid., p. 147.
146. Ibid., p. 145.
147. Ibid., p. 157.
148. Select Committee on Public Libraries, *Report* (1849), Q. 3395.
149. Edwards, The administrative economy, op. cit., p. 312.
150. Edwards quoted by J. Thompson, *A history of the principles of librarianship* (1977), p. 77.
151. Ibid., p. 91, quoting from Edwards's Memoirs of libraries, op. cit.
152. That his respect for education was enduring is illustrated by the active support he gave, whilst librarian at Manchester Public Library, to the Public Schools Association, which helped pave the way for the Education Act (1870); ibid., p. 217.
153. T. Greenwood, Edward Edwards: some notes on his life and work, *Library Association Record*, 4 (1902), pp. 10, 24.
154. Quoted in J. L. Thornton, A mirror for librarians (1948). Taken from the preface to Edwards's Memoirs of libraries, op. cit. (2nd edn, 1901). Edwards had died before the second edition was published. However, Greenwood was able to rescue from Edwards's papers some sheets printed in 1885, a year before Edwards's death.
155. C. W. Sutton, Edward Edwards, *Library Association Record*, 14 (1912), p. 617.
156. See note 30. Also quoted in R. Garnett, To the memory of Edward Edwards, the pioneer of the public library movement, *Library Association Record*, 4 (1902), p. 1.

157. Munford, Edward Edwards in retrospect, op. cit., p. 91.
158. Quoted in Edwards's Manuscript scrapbook, op. cit. For a printed version of the section from the lecture *Of kings' treasuries*, beginning 'I say first we have despised literature', down to 'circulating libraries', see C. Wilmer (ed.), *Unto this last: and other writings by John Ruskin* (1985), pp. 274-5.

5 Culture, materialism and the 1849 Select Committee: the cultural materialism of art

1. Select Committee on Public Libraries, *Report* [including minutes and evidence] (1849), hereafter in the notes for this chapter referred to as 'Report'. The committee produced subsequent reports in 1850, 1851 and 1852. The reports of 1851 and 1852 were largely statistical in content, and are of little relevance here. The report of 1850 is noteworthy in that it contained further evidence from Edward Edwards, and from Antonio Panizzi (librarian of the British Museum) who had been enraged by Edward's criticism of the British Museum Reading Room expressed to the Select Committee in 1849.
2. T. Kelly, *A history of public libraries in Great Britain 1845–1975* (1977), p. 12 (note 3).
3. Free town libraries, *Westminster Review*, 42 (1872), p. 335.
4. The local tax charged in some areas, since 1845, for the provision of a museum had earned the derogatory title 'beetle rate'; evidence of George Dawson, *Report*, op. cit., Q. 1298. In debating the public library issue in the House of Commons in 1850 one Member 'supposed they would be thinking [next] of supplying the working classes with quoits, peg-tops, and foot-ball'; Kelly, op. cit., p. 14. *The Illustrated London News* (18 May 1850) stated in respect of free libraries: 'The education of the adult people by their own agency without the aid of government grants or the interference of officials and officious functionaries, is a result in the highest degree desirable, and will be one of the gratifying proofs of our advancing civilization.' Finally, it is important to note that the 1850 Act was a diluted version of the original, more interventionist Bill which had stipulated no minimum population level for a town seeking to establish a library, and which had made no arrangements for a ratepayers poll on the issue; R. J. B. Morris, *Parliament and the public libraries* (1977), pp. 23-4.
5. D. Fraser, *Power and authority in the Victorian city* (Oxford, 1979), p. 6.
6. Ibid., p. 6.
7. W. A. Munford, *William Ewart MP 1789–1869: portrait of a radical* (1960), pp. 184-5.
8. Ibid., p. 131.
9. Letter from Ewart to Edwards (26 March 1849), printed in J. J. Ogle, Edwards and Ewart and the Select Committee on Public Libraries of 1849, *Library Association Record*, 1 (1899).
10. Society for the Diffusion of Useful Knowledge, Public libraries, in the Society's *Companion to the British almanac; or, yearbook of general information* (1850), p. 53. In its review of the report of the Select Committee on Public Libraries, the *Athenaeum* (1 September 1849) was equally enthusiastic; the report was said to be 'one of the best blue-books connected with literature that Parliament has given to the public for a very long time'.

11. Society for the Diffusion of Useful Knowledge, op. cit., p. 53.

12. See, for example, T. Kelly, Public libraries and Public opinion, *Library Association Record* 68 (1966). Kelly argues that the main motives of 1849-50 were moral and educational, and in that order. By late century, the argument continues, the same motives behind provision are clearly identifiable, but education had by then taken preference.

13. J. H. Wellard, *Book selection* (1937), p. 9. In Wellard's opinion, appeasing the masses was one of three main motives to be identified in the Select Committee's deliberations. On the other two motives he concurred with Kelly's (see previous note) moral and educational assessment.

14. The central thrust of T. Greenwood, *Edward Edwards* (1902).

15. T. Kelly, *Early public libraries: a history of public libraries in Great Britain before 1850* (1966), p. 238. Similarly, W. J. Murison, *The public library: its origins, purpose and significance* (1971), p. 79 writes of the Act's partiality as a weak foundation of the British public library system. P. Sykes, *The public library in perspective: its origins and modern role* (1979), p. 33 has argued that the permissive nature of early legislation 'served to emphasise the aura of impoverishment which enveloped the library service in its formative decades'.

16. Report, op. cit., p. x..

17. Murison, op. cit., p. 50. Recently, P. King, *Privatisation and public libraries*, 1989, p. 26 has argued that past uncertainty over roles has accounted for current lack of purpose.

18. Report, op. cit., p. iii.

19. Ibid., p. iii.

20. Ibid., p. viii. It was anticipated (p. ix) that provincial free libraries would essentially be libraries of 'education', as opposed to national 'deposit' libraries of 'research'. However, the transfer of duplicates from 'deposit' to provincial libraries would bestow upon the recipients a partial 'research' status.

21. Ibid., p. xii.

22. Ibid., p. viii.

23. Ibid.

24. Ibid., p. iii.

25. Ibid., p. vii.

26. Ibid., pp. vii-viii.

27. In an article about the Marylebone Free Library (not municipal) *The Lady's Newspaper* (14 January 1854) stated: 'The advancement in the taste and knowledge of the working classes in this country is shown by the great improvement in the illustrations and matter of our cheap periodicals; and in the great demand for good and practical books, when the price comes at all within the means of the mass of English Mechanics.'

28. Report, op. cit., Q. 1276.

29. Ibid., p. viii.

30. In his essay *Civilization* John Mill warned that literature would become more ephemeral as the democratization of society proceeded, and as power drifted from individuals to the masses. To reverse the decadent trend affecting literature he appealed for 'national institutions and forms of policy calculated to invigorate individual character'. G. H. Bantock, *The minds of the masses 1760–1980* (Studies in the history of education theory, Vol. 2) (1984), p. 186.

31. Report, op. cit., Q. 2076.
32. Ibid., p. viii.
33. Ibid., Q. 2695-8. For a description of the social problems affecting early-nineteenth-century Spitalfields see P. McCann, Popular education, socialization and social control, *in* P. McCann, *Popular education and socialization in the nineteenth century* (1977), pp. 2-5. Spitalfields was characterized by economic distress, large numbers of weaving poor, a high and increasing density of population, a high incidence of juvenile delinquency, and a declining allegiance to the church. From the 1820s an 'islanded' bourgeoisie existed in perpetual fear of insurrection. William Lovett was asked if he knew of a liking for French novels among the working classes, and if he thought 'useful publications' would reduce the circulation of 'immoral and anti-social publications'; Report, op. cit., Q. 2814-18.
34. It was argued that public funding would not attract religious or political animosity because free libraries would not stock controversial material; Report, op. cit., p. x. The mechanics' institute manager John Langley reminded the committee that religion and politics were largely excluded from mechanics' institutes; Report, op. cit., Q. 2452.
35. Hansard, *Parliamentary Debates*, 109 (1850), col. 847.
36. Ibid., col. 846. In the same debate (col. 841) Brotherton said public libraries would 'provide the cheapest police that could be established'.
37. Report, op. cit., p. xiv. The Report (p. viii) also stated that: 'There can be no greater proof of the fitness of the people for these institutions than their own independent efforts to create them.' An increasing desire for self-education in many poorer areas was also noted; p. vii.
38. *The Times* (4 September 1852).
39. The former librarian of Yale related how in the USA book donations were commonplace; Report, op. cit., Q. 1662. The Report (p. x) stated that the public library was 'one of those cases in which a comparatively small aid may accomplish a large proportion of public good'. *The Times* (7 April 1854) referred to the 1850 Act as the 'point of the wedge' in terms of mounting library legislation. The *Athenaeum* (18 March 1854) stated that 'A Free Public Library in every large parish will soon be considered as much a necessity as the Baker's shop.'
40. See the evidence of E. R. P. Colles of the Royal Dublin Society; Report, op. cit., Q. 2844-8. The Report (p. iv) stressed the greater accessibility of libraries on the continent.
41. See especially the evidence of Samuel Smiles. Charles Dawson testified that the self-education which libraries gave was more valuable than taught education; Report, op. cit., Q. 1309. G. Jones, *Political and social factors in the advocacy of free libraries in the United Kingdom 1801–1922*, unpublished PhD, University of Strathclyde (1971), p. 134 has observed that the Select Committee was 'a body comprising industrialists, career politicians, litterateurs, an ex-officer, the son of a trader, and a child of the working class ... a significant proportion of the membership of the committee, either in their own persons, or in their family annals, exemplified the social mobility possible through study and application'.
42. The London missionary Charles Corkran spoke of the existence of cheap publications which touched upon the question of labour, and the relationship between master and men; Report, op. cit., Q. 2698. Charles Dawson

explained how free libraries could aid balanced political analysis and help reject demagogy; Report, op. cit., Q. 1266, 1318-20, 1323-7.

43. Report, op. cit., p. xi. For Meyer's full evidence concerning the Hamburg Commercial Library see Report, op. cit., Q. 2159-69 and 2208-12. Further information is given by C. W. Black, Commercial libraries, *International Library Review*, 5 (1973), p. 96. Hamburg's commercial library was established in 1735 - the earliest recorded institution of its kind - as a supplement to the town's main library. It became, and it is now, the library of the Hamburg Chamber of Commerce. Edward Edwards described it to the Select Committee as 'a model of what a library upon commerce ought to be'. A similar local chamber of commerce library was established in Bordeaux in 1845 and opened to the public in 1854.

44. Report, op. cit., p. xi.

45. Ewart's question to the Italian librarian W. Libri; Report, op. cit., Q. 1920.

46. Report, op. cit., p. xi.

47. Ibid.

48. Ibid.

49. Ibid., Q. 2503-4.

50. Munford, William Ewart, op. cit., p. 77. Greenwood, in his biography of Edwards, op. cit., p. 15, described Ewart's father as a 'well-to-do representative of the yeoman class'. Arguably, he was more than this. The son of a Scottish Presbyterian minister, he began as an apprentice to a firm of cotton manufacturers, but eventually built up one of the largest merchant enterprises in Liverpool.

51. S. Macdonald, *The history and philosophy of art education* (1970), p. 75.

52. *The Art Journal* 12 (1850), p. 248.

53. Q. Bell, *Schools of design* (1963), p. 46.

54. B. Denvir, *The early nineteenth century: art, design and society 1789–1852* (1984), p. 18.

55. Ibid., pp. 207-16.

56. See, for example, E. Edwards, *A letter to Sir Martin Archer Shee on the reform of the Royal Academy* (1839).

57. Art Union of London, *Annual Report* (1852), pp. 11-12.

58. Art Union of London, *Annual Report* (1846), p. 15.

59. *The Art Union Monthly Journal of the Arts* 10 (1848), p. 5.

60. National Association for the Protection of Industry and Capital throughout the British Empire, *Form of address [to the Queen] recommended by the National Association* (1850).

61. Quoted in D. K. Jones, *The making of the education system 1851–1881* (1977), p. 2.

62. *Art Union Monthly Journal of the Arts*, 10 (1848), p. 5. The Exhibition itself became a symbol of a new respect for order. The *Art Journal*, 3 (1851), p. 293 stated: 'I know no higher test of civilization than this: that a woman, neither of robust health nor intrepid spirit, could, without a moment's hesitation, go alone in the midst of 100,000 people of every class; certain of civility, order, decorum, and if it were needed, protection.'

63. *Report*, op. cit., p. xiv.

64. E. J. Hunter, *The role of the public library in the development of technical education in Great Britain and Ireland during the nineteenth century*, unpublished MA dissertation, University of Sheffield (1973).

65. *The Sunday question again: shall the free libraries and the art gallery be open on a Sunday?* (1871), p. 10. Librarians were to show persistent interest in the provision of materials for art education. One question in the Library Association's professional exams in 1909 asked entrants to: 'Describe the ways in which collections of pictures may be helpful to readers'; *Library Association Yearbook* (1909), p. 84. The *Library Association Record*, 19 (1917), p. 31 said pictures of authors and their haunts was a 'direct and simple method of developing literary skill'.
66. Report, op. cit., Q. 1754-5, 2425.
67. T. Kusamitsu, *British industrialization and design 1830–1851*, unpublished PhD, University of Sheffield (1982), argues that a deskilling of workers owing to the Industrial Revolution was a main reason for the growth of design education between 1830 and 1850: for example, in mechanics' institutes, schools of design and through industrial exhibitions.
68. Edwards sent copies of his book to a number of friends. One wrote back saying he was 'glad that the subject has met with so able and judicious an advocate. That the Book will do much good to the cause [of the arts] I cannot doubt and that the learning and research you have bestowed on it may be duly appreciated by the public.' Letter from Henry Hayward to Edwards (12 August 1840), Manchester Public Library Archives.
69. E. Edwards, *The administrative economy of the fine arts* (1840), p. 325.
70. Report, op. cit., Q. 3396.
71. Edwards, *The administrative economy*, op. cit., p. 36.
72. Edwards, Letter to ... Shee, op. cit., p. 13.
73. According to his great grandson, also named William Ewart, interviewed August 1988, the public library pioneer collected a sizeable library of books on art and architecture, a collection now dispersed. The unpublished Ewart family records (items 55 and 58) contain three small travel diaries (1821-2) and two large diaries (of Ewart's Grand Tour) which contain highly detailed descriptions of artefact and building design, and some sketches by Ewart of architecture and people.
74. *The public library movement in London ...* (1894), newspaper cutting, source unknown; Croydon Public Library Cuttings (1894-1900), p. 40.
75. Unpublished notebook on the import and export trade 1828-33, Ewart family records, item 56.
76. Macdonald, op. cit., p. 117, quoting Haydon. The nature versus mannerism controversy is explained in detail by Macdonald in his chapters on 'Academic principles' and 'Schools of design'.
77. Ibid., p. 121.
78. Ibid., p. 119.
79. As noted by J. Allred, The purpose of the public library: the historical view, *Library History*, 2:5 (Spring 1972), p. 289.
80. Macdonald, op. cit., p. 65.
81. Ibid., p. 70.
82. M. Harrison, T. C. Horsfall and the Manchester Art Museum, *in* A. J. Kidd and K. W. Roberts (eds), *City, class and culture: studies of social policy and cultural production in Victorian Manchester* (1985), p. 121, makes this point in respect of the middle-class art fraternity's attitude in general.
83. Macdonald op. cit., pp. 150-3.
84. Edwards's brother-in-law, Henry Hayward, was a prime mover of the union;

Greenwood, op. cit., p. 13. It is possible that Edwards was also a joint founder, along with the architect George Godwin; Ogle, op. cit., p. 623. Edwards's heavy involvement can be judged from his numerous Art Union correspondence included in *Letters to Edward Edwards*, Vol. 4 (1833-7) and Vol.5 (1838-9); Manchester Public Library Archives.

85. W. A. Munford, *Edward Edwards 1812–1886 : portrait of a librarian* (1963), p. 23.

86. The Art Union [of London], *Report on the meeting of 21 March 1837 to establish such a society* (1837), p. 2. The Union described itself as 'a society for the advancement of the fine arts'.

87. Ibid., p. 3.

88. Art Union of London, *Annual Report* (1846), pp. 13-14.

89. Art Union of London, *Annual Report* (1851), p. 10.

90. Ewart wrote in his notebook on the import and export trade (1828-1833) that: 'Commerce assists and profits by discoveries in Science'; Ewart family records, item 56.

91. *Report*, op. cit., p. vii.

92. *Report*, op. cit., Q. 1933-6; to the Italian librarian Libri. Ogle, op. cit., p. 623, has pointed out that the forerunner of the public Libraries Act, the legislation on free museums in 1845, had resulted from a meeting held in 1844 (which the library enthusiast Joseph Brotherton attended) to discuss means of improving popular taste.

93. Letter from Ewart to Sir John Potter (Mayor of Manchester) (15 August 1852). Sir John Potter, Autograph Letters Collection, Vol.1; Manchester Public Library Archives.

94. G. Tonelli, Taste in the history of aesthetics from the Renaissance to 1770, *in Dictionary of the history of ideas* (New York, 1973), p. 353.

95. The Third Earl of Shaftesbury writing in 1831, quoted in B. Denvir, *The eighteenth century: art, design and society 1689–1789* (1983), p. 63.

96. P. J. Anderson, Pictures for the people: Knight's 'Penny Magazine', an early venture into popular education, *Studies in Art Education*, 28:3 (Spring 1987). J. Seed, Commerce and the liberal arts: the political economy of art in Manchester 1773-1860, *in* J. Wolff and J. Seed (eds), *The culture of capital: art, power and the nineteenth century middle class* (1988), p. 63, argues: 'Art was everywhere in Manchester by the mid-nineteenth century', and points out that a particular working-class favourite was the 'penny portrait' or 'good likeness' (pp. 64-5). Janetta Manners, *Some of the advantages of easily accessible reading and recreation rooms and free libraries* (1885), p. 43, wrote that: 'The love of the poorer classes for pictures and illustrations is well known.'

97. E. Cooper, The people's art, *Art Libraries Journal*, 12:4 (1987) argues that notable art was produced at work, outside the daily routine; in leisure contexts; at home; for clothing; and by workers in contained communities like ships and prisons.

98. *Report on the opening of the Salford Museum and Library* (1849).

99. At the time technical education essentially meant design education.

100. T. Fawcett, Too much to look at, too much to read, *Art Libraries Journal*, 12:3 (1987), p. 8, explains that regarding art Ruskin viewed the reproduction, proliferation and mass production of images as inherently damaging to quality.

101. As concluded by Denvir, The early nineteenth century, op. cit.

6   Economic concerns: 'useful' knowledge and political economy

1.   W. E. Houghton, *The Victorian frame of mind 1830–1870* (1957), p. 183.
2.   Ibid., p. 190. Houghton's phrase.
3.   R. Duckett, Paradise lost? The retreat from reference, *Library Review*, 41:1 (1992), p. 10.
4.   The term 'useful' knowledge is used here in its materialistic sense. A nineteenth-century popular interpretation might also have included liberation from economic and political exploitation, as argued by R. Johnson, Really useful knowledge: radical education and working class culture 1790– 1848, *in* J. Clark, C. Critcher and R. Johnson (eds), *Working class culture: studies in history and theory* (1979).
5.   *Islington Gazette* (9 May 1887).
6.   M. D. O'Brien, Free libraries, *in* T. Mackay (ed.), *A plea for liberty: an argument against socialism and socialistic legislation* (1892). In an article entitled Reading and readers, *Sunday Magazine* (1893), p. 189, it was stated that O'Brien's essay had caused 'quite a stir', and had led people to ask 'if public libraries had been such an unmixed good as their promoters would have us believe'.
7.   H. Spencer, *Education: intellectual, moral and physical* (1861). O'Brien was part of the late Victorian Spencerian complex advocating rampant individualism and rejecting the collectivist direction of the politics of the time; as discussed by M. W. Taylor, *Men versus the state* (1992).
8.   See Chapter 1 of Spencer, op. cit.
9.   F. A. Cavenagh (ed.), *Herbert Spencer on education* (1932), p. xxi.
10.   C. T. Smout in the preface to the 1949 edn of Spencer's *Education*, op. cit.
11.   G. C. Peden, *British economic and social policy: Lloyd George to Margaret Thatcher* (1985), p. 3.
12.   Darwin's phrase from *On the origin of species*, cited by R. M. Young, Herbert Spencer and 'inevitable' progress, *in* G. Marsden (ed.), *Victorian values: personalities and perspectives in nineteenth century society* (1990), p. 155.
13.   Peden, op. cit., pp. 5–6. Also T. W. Hutchinson, *On revolutions and progress in economic knowledge* (1978), Chapters 3 and 4.
14.   S. Jevons, The rationale of free public libraries, *Contemporary Review*, 39 (1881), p. 385.
15.   The mistaken commentator is R. Altick, *The English common reader: a social history of the mass reading public* (Chicago, 1957), p. 146. The importance of information as a resource has nevertheless been challenged; see, in this context, J. Eaton, *Is information a resource?*, Department of Information Studies, University of Sheffield, Occasional Paper No. 4 (1987). Jevons's 'multiplication of utility' argument evinced a communal thrust. Yet the theory of marginal utility, which he conceptualized in the 1870s, was, if anything, atomistic; it was less to do with macro issues than micro inputs, as argued by J. Harris, *Private lives, public spirit: a social history of Britain 1870– 1914* (1993), p. 224.
16.   T. Greenwood, *Free public libraries* (1886), p. 111.
17.   *South London Press* (23 January 1892).
18.   Ibid., p. 163.
19.   Jevons, The rationale, op. cit., p. 388.

20. Poster advertising the lecture, Lambeth Public Library Cuttings, Box N/63/1/ 23(1).

21. *Croydon Guardian* (3 April 1915).

22. P. Gregg, *A social and economic history of Britain 1760–1972* (1973), p. 367. See also the index of gross domestic product given in Table 24 of C. H. Feinstein, *Statistical tables of national income, expenditure and output of the UK 1855–1965* (1972).

23. F. Crouzet, *The Victorian economy* (1982), p. 378.

24. The obsession with decline is shown in the titles of numerous recent books, for example: M. W. Kirby, *The decline of British economic power since 1870* (1981); J. Eatwell, *Whatever happened to Britain: the economics of decline* (1982); A. Gamble, *Britain in decline: economic policy, political strategy and the British state* (1981); M. J. Weiner, *English culture and the decline of the industrial spirit 1850–1980* (1981). D. N. McCloskey, Did Britain fail?, *Economic History Review*, 23 (1970), p. 446, wrote: 'Few beliefs are so well established in the credo of British economic history as the belief that the late Victorians failed.'

25. G. McCulloch, Science education and the historiography of national decline, *History of Education Society Bulletin*, 30 (Autumn 1982). R. C. Floud, Britain 1860-1914: a survey, *in* R. C. Floud and D. N. McCloskey (eds), *The economic history of Britain since 1700*, Vol. 2 (1981), p. 3.

26. K. Burgess, Did the late Victorian economy fail?, *in* T. Gourvish and A. O'Day, *Later Victorian Britain 1867–1900* (1988), p. 256.

27. S. B. Saul, Some thoughts ... on the performance of the late Victorian economy, in D. N. McCloskey, *Essays on a mature economy: Britain after 1840* (1971), p. 397.

28. Crouzet, op. cit., pp. 381-90.

29. J. Burnley, *The story of British trade and industry* (1904), p. 215.

30. P. Bagwell and G. Mingay, *Britain and America 1850–1939: a study of economic change* (1970), p. 8.

31. Burnley, op. cit., p. 214.

32. Crouzet, op. cit., p. 381.

33. See Chapter 8 of H. E. Musson, *The growth of British industry* (1978). Also, A. Reid, The division of labour and politics in Britain 1880-1920, *in* W. J. Mommsen and H. G. Husung, *The development of trade unionism in Great Britain and Germany 1880–1914* (1985), p. 153.

34. Greenwood, op. cit. (1887 edn), p. 36.

35. Oldham Free Library and Museum Committee, *Minutes* (27 July 1881).

36. *Manchester Chamber of Commerce Monthly Record*, 18 (1907), p. 288.

37. Ibid., pp. 288, 342.

38. Ibid., p. 138.

39. The Manchester Chamber of Commerce Report for 1907 was cited in the *Library Association Record*, 20 (1918), p. 107.

40. *Manchester Chamber of Commerce Monthly Record*, 18 (1907), p. 289.

41. P. Sturges, British legislation for public libraries and technical education 1850-1902, *in* P. Kaegbein and P. Vodosek (eds), *Staatliche Initiative und Bibliotheksentwicklung seit der Aufklärung* (Wiesbaden, Germany, 1985). T. Kelly, Public libraries in adult education, *Journal of Librarianship*, 2 (1970).

42. E. J. Hunter, *The role of the public library in the development of technical education in Great Britain and Ireland during the nineteenth century,*

unpublished MA dissertation, University of Sheffield (1973). Hunter gives an excellent detailed description of how public libraries were in effect the first technical education schools. He avoids, however, a theoretical discussion of the implications of this.

43. T. Kelly, Public libraries and public opinion, *Library Association Record*, 68 (1966), p. 249.

44. Both Kirby, op. cit., and Floud and McCloskey, op. cit., offer multicausal explanations.

45. See S. F. Cotgrove, *Technical education and social change* (1958).

46. B. Elbaum and W. Lazonick, An industrial perspective on British decline, *in* B. Elbaum and W. Lazonick (eds), *The decline of the British economy*. M. D. Stephens and G. W. Roderick (eds), *Scientific and technical education in early industrial Britain* (1981) explore in their conclusion the reluctance of central government in Britain, unlike in Germany and the USA, to intervene in education.

47. R. Floud, Technical education 1850-1914: speculations on human capital formation, *in* L. Jorberg and N. Rosenberg (eds), *Technical change, employment and investment* (Lund, Sweden, 1982), p. 82.

48. D. C. Mowery, Industrial research 1900-1950, in Elbaum and Lazonick, op. cit., p. 189.

49. Burgess, Did the late Victorian economy fail?, op. cit., p. 267. Also, it is argued that during early industrialization education was not just irrelevant to industrial change but itself suffered a decline in standards at the elementary level; D. K. Jones, *The making of the education system 1851–1881* (1977), p. 4.

50. For example, Britain in the 1950s spent more on 'R and D', as a proportion of national income, than any other country in Western Europe. In the same decade France and Germany were among the countries least committed to 'R and D'. Yet Britain's economic performance in the late 1950s and in the 1960s - when her 'R and D' of the 1950s would have been expected to start yielding dividends - was in stark contrast to that of France and Germany. D. S. Landes, *The unbound Prometheus: technical change and industrial development in western Europe from 1750 to the present* (1969), p. 521.

51. P. M. Heimann, The scientific revolutions, *in* P. Burke (ed.), *The new Cambridge modern history*, Vol. 13 (Companion Volume, 1979), p. 269.

52. Letter from Jacob Behrens to the Vice President of the Committee of Council on Education (24 January 1868), cited in *Copies of answers from chambers of commerce to queries of the Vice President of the Council [on Education] as to technical education*, Parliamentary Papers (1867-8).

53. Select Committee on Scientific Instruction, *Report* (1868), p. vii.

54. Burnley, op. cit., p. 215.

55. C. More, *Skill and the English working class 1870–1914* (1980), pp. 220-1.

56. *Lecture on technical schools* (1892), newspaper cutting, source unknown, Oldham Public Library Cuttings, Vol. 1 (1885-1903), pp. 28-9.

57. J. Wrigley, Technical education and industry in the nineteenth century, *in* Elbaum and Lazonick, op. cit., pp. 177-8.

58. More, op. cit., p. 218.

59. G. C. T. Bartley, Statistics and suggestions on the present condition of and the requirements for promoting technical education in England, *in* Liveries Company Committee, *Report on technical education* (1878), p. 72.

60. Cotgrove, op. cit., p. 23.

61. Bartley, Statistics and suggestions, op. cit., p. 23. However, More, op. cit., p. 212 argues that union attitudes were neutral.

62. L. S. Jast, Technical libraries, *Library World*, 3 (1900-1), p. 258.

63. See C. E. McLelland, *State, society and university in Germany 1700–1914 (1980)*, and R. Locke, *The end of the practical man: entrepreneurship and higher education in Germany, France and Great Britain 1880–1940* (1984). Also argued by More, op. cit., p. 198.

64. P. Alter, Science and the Anglo-German antagonism, *in* Gourvish and O'Day, op. cit.

65. Floud, Technical education 1850-1914, op. cit.

66. More, op. cit., p. 215.

67. H. T. Wood, Proposals for a system of technical education, *in* Liveries Company Committee, op. cit., p. 11.

68. Burgess, Did the late Victorian economy fail?, op. cit., p. 267; and Wrigley, Technical education and industry, op. cit., p. 169.

69. More, op. cit., p. 217.

70. Cotgrove, op. cit., p. 53.

71. Ibid., p. 55. The lower middle class was heavily engaged in adult education; G. Crossick, The emergence of the lower middle class in Britain: a discussion, *in* G. Crossick (ed.), *The lower middle class in Britain 1870–1914* (1977), p. 28.

72. P. W. Musgrave, The definition of technical education 1860-1910, *in* P. W. Musgrave (ed.), *Sociology, history and education: a reader* (1970). Musgrave argues that the term 'technology education', which has emerged this century, would be a better way of describing theoretical instruction. T. H. Huxley in his *Science, culture and other essays* (1881) defined technical education, in an essay on the subject, as 'the practicalities of workshop education'.

73. *The English Mechanic and World of Science* (14 October 1887).

74. Select Committee on Scientific Instruction, op. cit., Appendix 20. The centrality of principles is stressed by R. Barton, Scientific opposition to technical education in Stephens and Roderick, op. cit., p. 17.

75. The wording of the Act is given in Cotgrove, op. cit., p. 38.

76. Committee appointed by the Council of the British Association for the Advancement of Science to consider the best means for promoting scientific education in schools, *Report* (1867), p. 3.

77. W. E. A. Axon, Books and reading, *Library Chronicle*, 4 (1887), p. 45.

78. Quoted in Cosgrove, op. cit., p. 42.

79. Crewe Mechanics Institute: annual prizegiving distribution, newspaper cutting, source unknown (27 November 1901), Crewe Mechanics Institute Council, *Minutes* (21 October 1901), Crewe Public Library.

80. A. Smith, *Wealth of nations*, Vol. 2 (1910 edn), pp. 263-4, 269.

81. P. Magnus, The responsibilities of town councils with regard to education, *in* Manchester Technical School, *Introductory addresses on technical education teaching in its application to trades and industries* (1890).

82. Commerce and the compulsory provision of public libraries, *Greater Britain* (15 September 1891).

83. *Vote for free libraries* (1896). Circular, held by Lewisham Local Studies Library.

84. *Eastbourne Chronicle* (13 August 1904).

85. *Southwark Recorder and Newington Gazette* (12 May 1900).

86. Croydon Public Library provided a photographic collection covering manufacturing goods and processes. L. S. Jast, *Technical libraries* (1903), p. 5.

87. When Darlington Public Library opened in 1885 its stock was partly donated by the Society of Civil Engineers and the Society of Mechanical Engineers. *Newcastle Daily Chronicle* (23 October 1885).

88. F. T. Barrett, *On the selection of books for a reference library* (1896), p. 5.

89. A library was opened in Bootle in 1887. It immediately established theoretical science classes in botany, magnetism and electricity, physiology and geology. These classes encouraged the later establishment of a technical school. J. J. Ogle, *Educational work in Bootle 1884–1900* (1900).

90. *Library Association questionnaire to public libraries* (1904), British Library Information Science Service, uncatalogued.

91. Words of the Earl of Northbrook, *Souvenir of the opening of the Gosport and Averstoke Free Public Library and Technical Institute* (1901), p. 55.

92. Out of 550 technical education institutions in 1955 only 160 possessed a library. Technical college libraries: a symposium, *Library Review*, 15 (1955-6), p. 316.

93. *William Lowther's reply for Prussia to the Circular [on technical and primary education] of Lord Stanley to her Majesty's representatives abroad together with replies*, Parliamentary Papers (1867-8).

94. Workers using the Old Kent Road Public Library, donated by the gas manufacturer George Livesey, made good use of the books on the making of gas - books which the library stocked in large numbers. This was according to the former Camberwell Chief Librarian, W. J. Hahn, who in the *South London Press* (5 August 1955) recalled his early library career as a junior assistant.

95. Library Association questionnaire to public libraries, op. cit., return from Bingley. Fulham Public Library circulated lists of books to local workshops; Fulham Public Library Committee, *Minutes* (9 May 1910).

96. *Free public library: to the owners and ratepayers of the city of York* (1881), pro-adoption leaflet, York Public Library Scrapbook (1881).

97. Greenwood, op. cit. (1887 edn), p. 109.

98. Jast, Technical libraries, op. cit., pp. 2-3.

99. *Readers' index: the bi-monthly magazine of the Croydon Public Libraries* (1913), p. 86. In the same volume (p. 88) it was reported that the library authority had recently produced a special catalogue on the gas industry.

100. J. P. Lamb, *Commercial and technical libraries* (1955), p. 24.

101. J. D. Stewart, *How to use a library* (1910), p. 10.

102. Ibid., pp. 58-77.

103. For example, the Leicester Public Library, *Annual report* (1889-90) contained a two-page selection of technology books to be found in the central reference library.

104. P. Sturges, Public libraries and technical education: a re-evaluation, *Journal of Librarianship*, 18:3 (1986), pp. 189-90. Sturges argues that grand ideas about public libraries being multicultural and educational complexes have detracted from their fundamental objective of promoting the literacy essential to an industrial society.

105. *Eastbourne Chronicle* (13 August 1904).

106. Ogle, op. cit., p. 48.

107. Ibid., p. 48.

108. M. B. Adams, Public libraries, their buildings and equipment: a plea for state aid, *Royal Institute of British Architects Journal* (1905), p. 274.
109. W. H. Bailey, *On technical libraries: in relation to the more beneficial use of free libraries for trade purposes* (1881), p. 4. This was first read to the Manchester Association of Employers, Foremen and Draughtsmen.
110. M. R. Marshall, *A history of industrial libraries in Britain to 1960*, unpublished Fellowship of the Library Association thesis (1968).
111. Ibid. Some examples are given by Marshall. J. Manners, *Some advantages of easily accessible reading and recreation rooms and free libraries* (1885), p. 2, notes that 'many great retail houses provide libraries for the people they employ'.
112. *York Cocoa Works Library Catalogue* (1890). The catalogue contains 26 pages of fiction and just 11 pages of non-fiction. Periodicals taken were of the highly popular variety: e.g. *Aunty Judy's Annual, Every Girl's Annual* and *Sunday at Home*.
113. T. Hitchler, Krupp free circulating library at Essen, Prussia, *Library Journal*, 27 (1902). This library, the forerunner of the German public library, contained a high percentage of scientific and technical books, presupposing the strong influence of technical training. It was said that 'many preferred no book at all to a work of fiction'.
114. S. Shipley, The libraries of the Alliance Cabinet Makers Association in 1879, *History Workshop* (Spring 1976). The Association was politically conscious, yet most works were fiction.
115. Manners, Some advantages, op. cit., p. 4.
116. The Reading-based firm of Huntley and Palmer gave £5000 in 1882 for the establishment of a public library, and the Palmer family donated books and money; Letter from Reading Public Library to William Munford (1950), deposited in British Library of Information Science Service, uncatalogued.
117. Words of Aristotle Onassis, quoted in Industrial Group of the Library Association, *Industrial and commercial libraries: an introductory guide* (1986), p. 1. At the stone-laying ceremony of the North Islington branch library Sir Albert Rollit MP said: 'Knowledge is the basis of all business ... education is the basis of our public libraries', *Islington Post* (3 November 1905).
118. Industrial Group of the Library Association, op. cit., p. 1.
119. *Special Libraries*, 3 (1912), p. 161.
120. P. K. Mutchler, *Public library cooperation with business and industry*, unpublished MA dissertation, University College, University of London (1969), p. 2.
121. *Yorkshire Observer* (3 November 1916).
122. F. Crunden, The public library as a factor in industrial progress, *The Library*, 7 (1906), p. 388.
123. Lamb, op. cit., p. 22.
124. Ibid., p. 21.
125. W. S. Saunders, *Guildhall library: its origin and progress* (1869), p. 49.
126. Evidence of a witness interviewed by a Liverpool Council committee investigating the establishment of a free library for the city. P. Cowell, *Liverpool public libraries: a history of fifty years* (1903), p. 15.
127. *Croydon Advertiser* (19 November 1910).
128. *Croydon Guardian* (19 November 1910).
129. Greenwood, op. cit. (1886 edn), p. 335.
130. *Ceremonies connected with the opening of the building for a free library and*

museum presented by William Brown to the town of Liverpool (1861), p. 21. Words of Lord (Henry) Brougham.

131. Greenwood, op. cit. (1886 edn), p. 335.
132. Patents were taken by public libraries from early in their history. Certainly by 1873 Nottingham Public Library had a collection of patents; Nottingham Free Public Libraries and Museums Committee, *Minutes* (4 March 1873).
133. J. S. Rowntree, *Free libraries: an address delivered in the Festival Concert Room, York* . . . (1881), p. 12.
134. *Commercial London: a manual of business information* (1890), p. 197.
135. *Commercial Education* (10 December 1912).
136. Departmental committee of the Board of Trade to inquire into and report upon the dissemination of commercial information and the collection and exhibition of patents and samples, *Report* (1898), Cmd 8962.
137. S. Foreman, *Shoes, ships and sealing wax: an illustrated history of the Board of Trade* (1986), pp. 8, 15.
138. Departmental committee of the Board of Trade, op. cit., p. iii.
139. Ibid., p. x.
140. Ibid., p. viii.
141. Ibid., p. iii.
142. Ibid., p. 111.
143. Ibid., p. 154–5.
144. Ibid., p. viii.
145. Ibid., Q. 4.
146. Ibid., Q. 162.
147. Ibid., Q. 1395. C. Reed, *Why not? A plea for a free public library and museum in the City of London* (1875), p. 18 argued that a public library user 'examines into the real causes of those social changes by which his trade . . . is affected . . . He is not swept into the vortex of every sudden strike'.
148. M. Berg, *The machinery question and the making of political economy 1815– 1848* (1980).
149. Board of Trade Commercial Intelligence Department, *Minutes* (1901–17), Public Record Office BT11/3/C7065/09, make no mention of public libraries.
150. *Report to the Board of Trade by the Advisory Committee on Commercial Intelligence with reference to their proceedings* (1904), Cmd 2044.
151. Ceremonies . . . Liverpool, op. cit., p. 19. Such messages reiterated earlier calls to educate workers in political economy. At the opening of Manchester Public Library it was advised that workers should 'read and learn the laws which regulate capital and labour and no longer allow themselves to be the dupes of charlatans and deceivers'; Manchester Free Library, *Report of the . . . opening of the free library* (1852), p. 10.
152. P. W. Musgrave, Constant factors in the demand for technical education, *British Journal of Education Studies*, 14 (May 1966).
153. W. E. A. Axon, Bolton and its free library, *Papers of the Manchester Literary Club*, 5 (1879), p. 20, said that a knowledge of the cotton industry in which they worked would make operatives more efficient.
154. Oldham Free Library and Museum Committee, *Minutes* (27 July 1881).
155. Rowntree, Free libraries: an address, op. cit., p. 11. The mechanics' institute in Crewe (provided by the locomotive works) fulfilled a similar role. The railway employers in Swindon did not build workers' houses until it ran into

shortages of skilled labour; D. Drummond, *Crewe: the society and culture of a railway town 1842–1914*, unpublished PhD, University of London (1986).
156. Leamington Spa Public Library, *Annual report* (1916), p. 6.
157. E. R. N. Mathews, *Birmingham and Bristol: a few words about public libraries and museums* (1892), pp. 5–6.
158. Letter from Mrs. E. Cockburn Kyte to E. M. Exley (received 2 August 1956), Marylebone Local Studies Library. For a detailed discussion of late Victorian and Edwardian unemployment and government policies (including labour exchanges) devised to contain its social effects see J. Harris, *Unemployment and politics: a study in English social policy 1886–1914* (1972).
159. Historical summary [of Leeds Public Library] to September 1877, Sparke Collection [of extracts, documents etc. relating to the Leeds Public Library], Vol. 1 (1892–5), p. 1.
160. J. P. Briscoe, A well equipped library, *Library Assistant*, 1 (1898–9), p. 49.
161. The Leeds Public Library received applications from the Board of Trade's Emigrants' Union Office asking that literature on the subject be circulated to branch libraries in the area; *Leeds Mercury* (11 March 1898). The Emigrants' Union Office donated pamphlets to the Hammersmith Public Library; along with a special noticeboard for displaying information; Hammersmith Public Library Committee, *Minutes* (8 March 1898). Literature for emigrants has been seen as an early form of community information service; K. Whittaker, British public libraries and the emigrants' information service, *Library History*, 8:2 (1988).
162. For a discussion on emigration as a means of relieving casual employment and its social effects see G. S. Jones, *Outcast London: a study in the relationship between classes in Victorian society* (1971).
163. Greenwood, Free public libraries, op. cit., pp. 126–7.
164. Manners, Some advantages, op. cit., p. 13.
165. J. Manners, *Encouraging experiences of free libraries, reading and recreation rooms* (1886), p. 22.
166. *An appeal to the friends of knowledge*, newscutting, source unknown, Southwark Local Studies Library, PC 020 Cam.
167. Ceremonies ... Liverpool, op. cit., p. 14. Words of T. B. Horsfall.
168. S. Fothergill, *The principles of political economy as applied to the wages question* (1872), pp. 5–6.
169. J. P. Edwards, *Institutional buildings completed or commenced during the diamond jubilee of Queen Victoria* (1897). J. J. MacDonald, *Passmore Edwards institutions: founding and opening ceremonies* (1900).
170. Quoted in E. H. Burrage, *J. Passmore Edwards: philanthropist* (1902), pp. 26–7.
171. Ibid., p. 14.
172. These included: *Temperance Tract Journal, Public Good, Poetic Companion, Biographical Magazine, Peace Advocate, Building News, English Mechanic, Echo* (pioneer of the halfpenny daily for the working class); and he had part shares in *Hampshire Independent, Southern Echo, Salisbury Times*. List assembled from Burrage, op. cit., p. 29, and J. Camplin, *The rise of the plutocrats: wealth and power in Edwardian England* (1978), p. 81.
173. Burrage, op. cit., p. 14.
174. Letter from J. Passmore Edwards to the Limehouse Library Commissioners (3 February 1900), Tower Hamlets Local Studies Library.

175. Burrage, op. cit., p. 22.
176. Edwards, Institutional buildings, op. cit., p. 1.
177. In 1870 the name changed to the *English Mechanic and World of Science*, having absorbed three leading science journals. Its circulation, as explained in the issue of 23 September 1870, was thus said to be greater than all other science periodicals put together.
178. *English Mechanic* (27 September 1869).
179. The issue of 31 December 1869 contained items on: the production of prints, applied mechanics, steam engines and furnaces, gas manufacture, and divining rods. Letters took up a quarter of the issue. The theoretical side of the journal became more important as time passed. It became less concerned with lathes and more concerned with the principles of science.
180. *English Mechanic* (27 August 1869).
181. *East End News* (3 October 1893).
182. Edwards, Institutional buildings, op. cit., p. 2. He did not, however, advocate further Imperial expansion. He called for a consolidation of the Empire by improvements in national efficiency, 'to build up at home healthful, educated and prosperous citizens'; J. P. Edwards, *A few footprints* (1905), p. 51.
183. Burrage, op. cit., p. 7.
184. Ibid., p. 36.
185. Quoted in S. Koss, *The rise and fall of the political press in Britain*, Vol. 1 (1981), p. 189.
186. Ibid., p. 36.
187. Burrage, op. cit., p. 53. Also quoted as a private letter from Edwards to Canon Barnett in H. Barnett, *Canon Barnett: his life, work and friends*, Vol. 2 (1918), p. 5.
188. At the same ceremony Lord Roseberry said of Edwards that 'wherever he goes a suspicion of benevolence dogs his steps'. Quoted in Burrage, op. cit., p. 53.
189. Jones, Outcast London, op. cit., discusses the West End's fear of the East End.
190. Edwards, A few footprints, op. cit., p. 39.
191. Edwards subscribed to the Free Christian Union and offered his services beyond a mere cash donation. Letter from Edwards to Edward Enfield, Dr Williams' Library, Free Christian Union Papers, 24/133/78.
192. Edwards, A few footprints, op. cit., p. 39.
193. Ibid., p. 40.
194. Ibid., p. 48.

7   The idealist flywheel

1. R. Altick, *The English common reader: a social history of the mass reading public 1800–1900* (Chicago, 1957) argues that in the nineteenth century the public library could never quite shed its utilitarian heritage.
2. Other main figures included Edward Caird, F. H. Bradley and Bernard Bosanquet; P. P. Nicholson, *The political philosophy of the British idealists: selected studies* (1990), p. 1. The discussion of idealism in this chapter was formulated with reference to the following key texts: A. R. Cocoullos, *Thomas Hill Green: a philosopher of ethics* (New York, 1974); F. Copplestone, *A history of philosophy* (1966); P. Gordon and J. White, *Philosophers as*

educational reformers: the influence of idealism on British educational thought and practice (1979); A. Macintyre, *A short history of ethics* (1967); I. M. Greengarten, *Thomas Hill Green and the development of liberal democratic thought* (1981); M. Richter, *The politics of conscience: T. H. Green and his age* (1983).

3. P. Carruthers, *Human knowledge and human nature: a new introduction to an ancient debate* (1992), p. 2.
4. Ibid., p. 18. The distinction between the invention of numerals (numeric writing) and mathematical understanding should, of course, be emphasized.
5. Ibid., pp. 50-2 and 84-5.
6. Ibid., p. 9.
7. A. Stumpf, *Elements of philosophy: an introduction* (1979), p. 431.
8. This is the evidence of Carruthers, op. cit.
9. Nicholson, op. cit., p. 2.
10. See chapters on Plato and Aristotle in F. M. Turner, *The Greek heritage in Victorian Britain* (1981).
11. Macintyre, op. cit., pp. 36-9.
12. Turner, op. cit., pp. 323-6. A valuable commentary on the work is given by J. Barnes in his introduction to J. A. K. Thomson (translator), *The ethics of Aristotle: the Nichomachean ethics* (1976). Among the surviving works of Aristotle are two works on ethics: *Eudemian ethics* named after its editor Eudemus, and *Nichomachean ethics*, named after Aristotle's son Nichomachean. It is the *Nichomachean ethics* which concerns us here.
13. P. Huby, *Greek ethics* (1967), p. 28.
14. Ibid., p. 32.
15. Macintyre, op. cit., pp. 42-8.
16. Chapter 2 of Stumpf, op. cit.
17. Macintyre, op. cit., p. 57, quoting from Book 1:i of The ethics of Aristotle.
18. Gordon and White, op. cit., p. 16.
19. Ibid., p. 230.
20. Ibid., contains multiple references to Fichte.
21. Ibid., p. 51.
22. Ibid., p. 18.
23. M. Allot and R. Super (eds), *Matthew Arnold* (1986), p. xxii.
24. Nicholson, op. cit., p. 1.
25. Gordon and White, op. cit., p. 7.
26. Turner, op. cit., p. 359.
27. Ibid., p. 361.
28. Copplestone, op. cit., pp. 172-3 makes the point that, according to Green, true self-satisfaction was self-realization; not in the sense of seeking personal pleasure, but in searching for one's personal nature in terms of knowing oneself. Only in this way could others be understood. R. Sennett, *The fall of public man* (1977), has argued that to know oneself has now become an end in itself, instead of a means through which one knows the world, as Green urged. We are now absorbed with ourselves; the psyche has become privatized.
29. Turner, op. cit., p. 3.
30. Cacoullos, op. cit., p. 13.
31. Ibid., p. 112.
32. Nicholson, op. cit., p. 3.

33. Richter, op. cit., pp. 370-1.
34. Ibid., p. 344.
35. For an analysis of Green's philosophy of education see Gordon and White, op. cit., pp. 68-87.
36. From Green's *Prolegomena to ethics*, quoted in R. Bellamy, T. H. Green and the morality of Victorian liberalism, *in* R. Bellamy (ed.), *Victorian liberalism* (1990), p. 157.
37. Richter, op. cit., pp. 366-7.
38. Bellamy, op. cit., p. 133.
39. J. Vincent, *The formation of the British Liberal Party 1857–1868* (1972), pp. 246-7.
40. Turner, op. cit., p. 368.
41. S. D. Koven, *Culture and poverty: the London settlement house movement 1870–1914*, unpublished PhD, Harvard University (1987).
42. Gordon and White, op. cit., p. 101.
43. Ibid., pp. 91-111.
44. Ibid., pp. 156, 205.
45. Ibid., pp. 38-9.
46. Bellamy, T. H. Green and the morality, op. cit., p. 142. G. S. Jones, *Outcast London: a study of the relationship between classes in Victorian society* (1971), p. 7 discusses Green's evolutionist thinking.
47. The introduction to Greengarten, op. cit., gives an account of idealism's origins in capitalism.
48. Richter, op. cit., pp. 355 and 374-6.
49. B. Jennings, Revolting students: the Ruskin College dispute 1903-1909, *Studies in Adult Education*, 9:1 (April 1977).
50. See Tawney and social history, *in* J. Kenyon, *The History men: the historical profession in England since the Renaissance* (1983). Tawney was educated at Balliol, and later taught there. He joined the Fabians in 1905, the Independent Labour Party in 1909 and, following the establishment of a new constitution, the Labour Party in 1918. Tawney 'belongs with the non-Marxist ethical socialism of the Labour left', writes R. Terrill, *R. H. Tawney and his time: socialism as fellowship* (1974), p. 277.
51. G. Himmelfarb, *The idea of poverty* (1984), p. 528.
52. Jones, op. cit., pp. 290-6. Whereas in the 1870s discussion of the condition of London's poor was confined to specialist journals, in the 1880s the problem received a much wider press which warned of a social volcano threatening revolution.
53. S. Smith, The industrial training of destitute children *Contemporary Review*, 47 (January 1885), p. 107.
54. Richter, op. cit., p. 13. Gordon and White, op. cit., p. 222 argue that idealism's religious foundations are clearly evident, from the fact that idealism's decline coincided with the secularization of life after 1918.
55. Richter, op. cit., p. 19.
56. S. Wallace, *War and the image of Germany* (1988), p. 5.
57. Nicholson, op. cit., pp. 59-60.
58. Turner, op. cit., pp. 361-4.
59. Richter, op. cit., p. 345.
60. Gordon and White, op. cit., p. 222.
61. Bellamy, T. H. Green and the morality, op. cit., p. 133.

62. T. McPherson, *Philosophy and religious belief* (1974), p. 23.

63. Entry for Jones in *Dictionary of national biography*.

64. Nicholson, op. cit., p. 1.

65. H. Jones, *Idealism as a practical creed* (1909), p. 208.

66. Ibid., pp. 106–7.

67. Ibid., pp. 19–20.

68. Ibid., p. 23.

69. Ibid., p. 28.

70. Ibid., pp. 28–9.

71. Ibid., p. 117.

72. Ibid.

73. Ibid., pp. 123–4.

74. Ibid., p. 124.

75. Ibid., p. 125.

76. Ibid., p. 111–12.

77. Wallace, op. cit., p. 49.

78. Ibid., p. 44.

79. Ibid., p. 51.

80. M. Freeden, *Liberalism divided: a study in British political thought 1914–1939* (1986), p. 32.

81. Quoted in W. E. A. Axon, Thomas Taylor the Platonist, *The Library*, 2 (1890), p. 246.

82. See J. F. C. Harrison, *A history of the Working Men's College 1854–1954* (1954). J. Harris, *Private lives, public spirit: a social history of Britain 1870–1914* (1993), p. 224, comments on the shift of religion onto a more social stance.

83. C. Kingsley, *The temple of wisdom: a sermon preached to the boys of Wellington College* (1866), p. 9.

84. Maurice's address to the Salford Working Men's College, 1859, quoted in R. Williams, *Culture and society 1780–1950* (1957), p. 113. The 'socialism' in Christian Socialism should not be taken to infer extreme radicalism. 'Socialism' at the time often simply meant cooperation, and 'anti-socialism' meant competition; J. F. C. Harrison, op. cit., p. 8.

85. D. F. W. Hawes, *Reflections on some social, philosophical and educational influences on British library history 1880–1965*, unpublished MA dissertation, University College, University of London (1978).

86. Borough of Birmingham, *Opening of the free reference library . . . inaugural address by George Dawson* (1866).

87. G. Dawson, *Sermons on daily life and duty* (1878), p. 122.

88. Ibid., p. 25.

89. R. W. Dale, George Dawson: politician, lecturer, preacher, *Nineteenth Century* (August 1877), p. 52. M. Girouard, *The English town* (1990), p. 222.

90. T. Greenwood, *Free public libraries* (1886), p. 75.

91. Girouard, op. cit., describes Dawson's monument. D. Smith, *Conflict and compromise: class formation in English society 1830–1914* (1982), pp. 75–9, juxtaposes Dawson's civic gospel in Birmingham with traditions of anarchy and self-government in Sheffield. Dale, op. cit., p. 46 testifies to Dawson's sympathy with 'continental liberalism' in terms of its broader view of the functioning of government.

92. S. A. Barnett, *St. Jude's Whitechapel: seventeenth pastoral address and report of the parish work* (1890).

93. S. A. Barnett, *Sermon preached before the University of Oxford* (1884).
94. S. A. Barnett, St. Jude's Whitechapel, op. cit.
95. S. A. Barnett, Great cities and social reform, *Nineteenth Century*, 14 (July–December), p. 814.
96. Ibid., p. 814. He said it was 'as easy to build a library as an infirmary in every parish'; S. A. Barnett, Practicable socialism, *Nineteenth Century*, 13 (January–June 1883), p. 558.
97. H. Barnett, *Canon Barnett: his life, work and friends*, Vol. 2 (1918), pp. 4–5.
98. S. A. Barnett, Sermon, op. cit.
99. H. Barnett, op. cit., p. 11.
100. Ibid., p. 1.
101. Ibid., p. 5.
102. Ibid., p. 7.
103. S. A. Barnett, Sermon, op. cit.
104. Ibid.
105. S. A. Barnett's preface to T. S. Peppin, *Club-land of the toiler: exemplified by the workmen's club and institute union* (1895). Of 144 London clubs Peppin had knowledge of 109 possessing libraries (pp. 57–8).
106. H. Barnett, op. cit., p. 12.
107. Letter from Thomas Aldred to Walter Powell (26 February 1906), Collection of letters to the librarian Walter Powell, British Library Information Science Service, uncatalogued.
108. *The Times* (2 June 1947).
109. *Labour and public libraries*, newscutting, source unknown, Woolwich Public Library Cuttings, Vol. 1, p. 17.
110. C. H. Grinling, *Libraries as workshops* (1903). This was reprinted from the *Library Association Record*, 5 (1903).
111. C. H. Grinling's preface to *Twenty-five years of history of the Woolwich Labour Party 1903–1928* (1928).
112. Ibid.
113. Grinling edited, along with T. A. Ingram and B. C. Polkinghorne, *A survey and record of Woolwich and West Kent* (1909).
114. C. H. Grinling, *Fifty years of pioneer work in Woolwich* (1922), p. 25.
115. Ibid., p. 5.
116. Ibid., p. 32.
117. Only H. E. Meller, *Leisure and the changing city 1870–1914* (1976) has looked at the link between citizenship and the public library, but only briefly.
118. According to Richter, op. cit., p. 344 citizenship also occurs more than any other theme in the works of T. H. Green.
119. *Kentish Independent* (5 August 1904).
120. List of lectures given by Mile End Public Library in 1908. Tower Hamlets Local Studies Library.
121. W. C. B. Sayers, *The children's library* (1912), p. 1.
122. L. S. Jast, *Libraries and living* (1932), p. 57.
123. At a meeting of the West Ham (South) Radical Club it was said that public libraries would 'give men a firmer grasp of the duties of municipal and national life'. *Stratford Express* (29 October 1890).
124. Newscutting, source unknown, Lambeth Public Library Cuttings, Box iv/63/1/23(1). Words of Rev. C. E. Escreet.
125. J. J. Ogle, *The extension of the free libraries acts to small places* (1887), p. 3.

126. Reading and readers, *Sunday Magazine* (1893), p. 193.
127. St George-in-the-East Public Library, *First report* (covering 1895-1900).
128. From B. Bosanquet's *Essays and addresses* (1886), quoted in Gordon and White, op. cit., p. 119.
129. *Northampton Daily Chronicle* (1 October 1904).
130. P. Cowell, *Liverpool public libraries: a history of fifty years* (1903), p. 96.
131. A. Briggs, Samuel Smiles and the gospel of wealth, *in* his *Victorian people: a reassessment of persons and themes 1851–1867* (1965), p. 126.
132. *Ceremonies connected with the opening of the buildings for a free library and museum presented by William Brown to the town of Liverpool* (1861), p. 24.
133. *Public library for Dartford: personal expression of opinion*, newscutting, source unknown (8 September 1911), Dartford Public Library Cuttings (1900-59).
134. Jast, op. cit., p. 4.
135. *Public meeting in the Mechanics' Hall: the Bishop on self-culture*, newscutting, source unknown (1885), Darlington Public Library Newscuttings.
136. Jast, op. cit., p. 55. Doncaster Borough Free Library and Newsroom, *Catalogue and inaugural ceremony* (1869). Words of the Vicar of Doncaster.
137. T. H. Green, *An estimate of the value and influence of works of fiction in modern times* (1862), p. 23.
138. Ibid., p. 4.
139. Ibid., p. 30.
140. Ibid., p. 31.
141. Ibid.
142. Ibid., p. 32.
143. *Church Family Newspaper* (16 May 1902).
144. Doncaster Borough Free Library and Newsroom, op. cit., p. 7.
145. J. Lubbock, *Free libraries: a speech delivered at the opening of a free library at Rotherhithe* (1891), p. 8.
146. He was present at numerous adoption meetings and opening ceremonies; e.g. Metropolitan Borough of Woolwich, *Programme of proceedings at the opening ceremony of the public library in William St by . . . Lord Avebury* (1901).
147. B. Harrison, *Drink and the Victorians: the temperance question in England 1815–1872* (1971), p. 339.
148. *Dictionary of national biography*. At various times he was involved in the Working Men's College, the University Extension Movement and the London County Council.
149. J. Lubbock, *The pleasures of life*, Part 1 (1891), p. 192.
150. Lubbock, Free libraries, op. cit., p. 5.
151. Ibid., p. 8.
152. Lubbock, The pleasures, pt 1, op. cit., p. 72.
153. Ibid., pp. 89-93.
154. Ibid., p. 69.
155. Ibid., p. 181.
156. Ibid., p. 53.
157. Ibid., p. 182.
158. Ibid., p. 130.
159. Ibid., p. 2.
160. Freeden, op. cit., p. 31.
161. Wallace, op. cit., p. 7.

8   Cultural concerns: in search of an assertive middle class

1.   R. Bacon and W. Eltis, *Britain's economic problem: too few producers* (1976).
2.   M. Wiener, *English culture and the decline of the industrial spirit 1850–1980* (1981).
3.   The middle class is seen to have failed in Germany also. Unable to assert itself against the old order, it is argued, the way was left open for conservative forces to initiate two world wars, thereby supporting the cliche that 'that is the way the Germans are'. This line is exposed as simplistic by D. Blackbourne and G. Ely, *The peculiarities of German history: bourgeois society and politics in nineteenth century Germany* (1984).
4.   See essays by P. Anderson, Origins of the present crisis and T. Nairn, The British political elite, both in *New Left Review*, 23 (January–February 1964). Also see Chapter 1 of T. Nairn, *The break-up of Britain: crisis and neo-nationalism* (1977).
5.   P. Anderson, *Lineages of the absolute state* (1974), p. 11.
6.   Nairn, The British political elite, op. cit., p. 20.
7.   For an early exploration of this theme see D. C. Coleman, Gentlemen and players, *Economic History Review*, 26 (1973). Coleman argues that professionalism in business (i.e. modern professional management) has attained great influence in the twentieth century. Professionalism has incorporated the nineteenth-century dichotomy of 'educated amateur' and 'practical man'. In this marriage, however, the social values of the former have predominated. A less full, but earlier explanation of 'gentlemanly' capitalism was made by D. H. Aldcroft, The entrepreneur and the British economy 1870-1914, *Economic History Review*, 17 (1964-5), pp. 128-9 who wrote of the move from 'the furnace to the field' in explaining what he saw as the complacency which affected late Victorian and Edwardian entrepreneurs. The most enthusiastic support for this position has been M. J. Weiner, English culture, op. cit. Nairn, The break-up of Britain (1981 edn), op. cit., p. 23, extrapolates economic decline from his cultural analysis, blaming Britain's economic backwardness on 'Liberal, City Imperialism'. A succinct analysis is included in A. G. Hopkins, British Imperialism: a review and a revision, *Recent Findings in Economic and Social History*, 7 (Autumn 1988). Recent commentaries include M. J. Daunton, Gentlemanly capitalism and British industry 1820-1914, *Past and Present*, 122 (February 1989); D. Nicholls, Fractions of capital: the aristocracy, the City and industry in the development of modern British capitalism, *Social History*, 13:1 (January 1988); and H. C. Malchow, *Gentlemen capitalists: the social and political world of the Victorian businessman* (1991).
8.   J. Wrigley, Technical education and industry in the nineteenth century, *in* B. Elbaum and W. Lazonick, *The decline of the British economy* (1986), p. 162.
9.   K. Burgess, Did the late Victorian economy fail?, *in* T. Gourvish and A. O'Day (eds), *Later Victorian Britain 1867–1900* (1988), p. 262.
10.   Malchow, op. cit., p. 6.
11.   W. D. Rubinstein, *Men of property: the very wealthy in Britain since the Industrial Revolution* (1981), p. 248. True captains of industry existed only in towns like Oldham which were relatively insulated, and where members of the commercial classes were few – in such an environment manufacturing magnates enjoyed cultural superiority; W. D. Rubinstein, Wealth, elites and

the class structure of modern Britain, *Past and Present*, 76 (August 1977), p. 107.

12. A recent forceful rebuff is J. Wolff and J. Seed (eds), *The culture of capital: art, power and the nineteenth century middle class* (1988). The Anderson–Nairn thesis has been criticized for its generalizations. Even Anderson admitted that his essay was a 'crude and preliminary attempt to pose some of the development questions of British capitalism'; Anderson, Origins of the present crisis, op. cit., p. 39. What the thesis did, however, was to set in motion the debate on the nature and causes of Britain's perceived crisis: C. Leys, *Politics in Britain: an introduction* (1983), p. 13. E. P. Thompson, The peculiarities of the English, *Socialist Register* (1965), p. 312, wrote of the thesis: 'If it cannot be accepted as an historical statement, it is nevertheless an incitement to study and at an uncommon pitch of conceptual intensity'.

13. Daunton, Gentlemanly capitalism, op. cit., p. 156.

14. Hansard, *Parliamentary Debates* 109 (1850), col. 839.

15. Wolff and Seed, op. cit., pp. 5–6.

16. S. Gunn, The failure of the Victorian middle class, in Wolff and Seed, op. cit., pp. 23–4.

17. Dickens believed that important human values were not amenable to mathematical calculation. He sincerely questioned the influence of the statistician and the economist. He was not alone in expressing these objections. Realizing this, he dramatized objections to scientific materialism. He was a propagandist who was sensitive to the public's sense of right and wrong. He flattered the public's moral feelings by conveying, and enlarging, familiar topics into fiction. P. Collins, *Dickens and education* (1965), see conclusion in particular.

18. N. McKendrick, 'Gentlemen and Players' revisited: the gentlemanly ideal, the business ideal, and the professional ideal in English literary culture, *in* N. McKendrick and R. B. Outhwaite (eds), *Business life and public policy* (1986). McKendrick (p. 102) also supports the argument made in the previous footnote - that literature should not be taken at face value because of intervening factors such as the need for readership; as well as the fact that literary evidence can reflect social and political obsessions.

19. M. Arnold, *Democracy* (1861), *in* M. Allot and R. H. Super (eds), *Matthew Arnold* (1986), pp. 311–12.

20. M. Arnold, *Equality* (1878), *in* Allot and Super, op. cit., p. 437.

21. Q. Bell, The Pre-Raphaelites and their critics, in *Pre-Raphaelite Papers* (1984), p. 16, produced by the Tate Gallery. An example is James Eden, owner of a Bolton bleaching works who commissioned Millais's 'Autumn Leaves', as discussed by M. Warner, John Everett Millais' 'Autumn Leaves', *in* Bell, op. cit., p. 126. A similar argument is made by J. Wolff and C. Arscott, Cultivated capital: patronage and art in nineteenth century Manchester, *in* G. Marsden (ed.), *Victorian values: personalities and perspectives in nineteenth century society* (1990).

22. J. Seed, Unitarianism, political economy and the antinomies of liberal culture in Manchester 1830–1850, *Social History*, 7 (1982), p. 11. See also J. Harris and P. Thane, British and European bankers 1880–1914: an aristocratic bourgeoisie? , *in* P. Thane, G. Crossick and R. Floud (eds), *The power of the past: essays for Eric Hobsbawm* (1984).

23. Gunn, op. cit., p. 29.

24. M. E. Rose, Culture, philanthropy and the Manchester middle class, and M. Harrison, T. C. Horsfall and the Manchester Art Museum, both *in* Marsden, op. cit.

25. Wolff and Arscott, op. cit.

26. R. J. Morris, *Class, sect and party: the making of the British middle class* (1990), pp. 171, 284–5.

27. See J. Seed, Commerce and the liberal arts: the political economy of art in Manchester 1775–1860, and C. Arscott, Without distinction of party: the Polytechnic Exhibitions in Leeds 1839–1845, *in* Wolff and Seed, op. cit.

28. T. H. Huxley, Science and culture (1880) *in* his *Science and culture and other essays* (1881).

29. See Chapter 4 of F. G. Walcott, *The origins of 'Culture and anarchy'* (1970).

30. M. Arnold, *Literature and science* (1882), *in* Allot and Super, op. cit.

31. P. M. Heimann, The scientific revolutions, *in* P.Burke (ed.), *The new Cambridge modern history*, Vol. 13 (companion volume, 1980), p. 270.

32. K. Nield, A symptomatic dispute: notes on the relationship between Marxian theory and historical practice in Britain, *Social Research*, 47 (1980), p. 489.

33. R. Gray, Bourgeois hegemony in Victorian Britain, *in* J. Bloomfield (ed.), *Papers on class, hegemony and party* (1977), p. 78.

34. Thompson, The peculiarities of the English, op. cit.

35. Arnold, Democracy, op. cit., p. 311.

36. The library promoter George Dawson noted that the houses of 'the large part of the middle class' offered endless luxuries, but few books. Borough of Birmingham, *Opening of the free reference library . . . inaugural address by George Dawson* (1866).

37. W. S. Saunders, *Guildhall Library: its origin and progress* (1869), p. 56.

38. Ibid., p. 17.

39. Sheffield Libraries, Art Galleries and Museums Committee, *The city libraries of Sheffield 1856–1956* (1956), p. 22.

40. T. Dunne, *Bolton Public Libraries 1853–1978* (1978), p. 11.

41. Letter from T. N. Talfourd to Sir John Potter (18 May 1852), Sir John Potter Autograph Letters Collection, Vol. 2, Manchester Public Library Archives.

42. *Ceremonies connected with the opening of the buildings for a free library and museum presented by William Brown to the town of Liverpool* (1861), p. 64.

43. Ibid., p. 66.

44. The Chelsea Public Library Committee, *Minutes* (24 June, 22 July, 29 July, 26 August 1887) record that its meetings were held at 5 p.m., which would have excluded many working people from attending. The Fulham Public Library Committee, *Minutes* (1 August 1893) record a meeting held at 10 a.m.

45. T. Greenwood, *Public libraries* (1894), p. 352. E. Savage, *The librarian and his committee* (1942), p. 12.

46. W. E. Doubleday, *A primer for librarianship* (1931), pp.113–14. G. Lovell, Changes in the buildings in which we work, *in* Library Association, Home Counties Branch, *Looking both ways: the management of change* (1980), p. 25 argues that low political activity on library committees made politicians interfere in professional practice as a substitute for debating policy.

47. Library Association, *Establishment of public libraries* (1909), p. 7 advised that: 'Co-opted members should be selected for their local knowledge, their knowledge of books, and their interest in educational matters generally.' Of

Islington's nine council committees in 1907 only one, the library committee, had co-opted members; Islington Borough Council, *Minutes* (15 November 1907). In 1913 the Bournemouth Library Committee had six councillors and six co-opted members; C. Riddle, *The library movement in Bournemouth* (1913), p. 8. Note that the Public Libraries Act (1892) required that co-opted membership must be a feature of committees.

48. *Northampton Daily Chronicle* (9 June 1910).
49. E. Edwards, *Free town libraries* (1869), p. 22.
50. *Islington Gazette* (25 October 1907).
51. *Notes and Queries*, 92 (3 October 1857), p. 279.
52. J. Gerrard, *Leadership and power in Victorian industrial towns 1830–1880* (1983), p. 57.
53. K. Robbins, John Bright and the middle class in politics, in J. Gerrard et al. (eds), *The middle class in politics* (1978), p. 27.
54. C. Wilmer, (ed.), *'Unto this last' and other writings by John Ruskin* (1985), p. 256.
55. Meller, op. cit., p. 7.
56. R. J. Morris, Middle class culture 1700-1914, in D.Fraser (ed.), *A history of modern Leeds* (1980), pp. 200-1.
57. See Chapter 3 of H. Perkin, *The origins of modern English society 1780–1880* (1969) for a discussion on social emulative spending.
58. J. W. Thompson, *The medieval library* (1957), p. 5.
59. Rubinstein, Men of property, op. cit., p. 189 points out that the very wealthy had most of their money in stocks and bonds, or in cash in banks, or in loans to individuals and firms. Their chattels - houses, heirlooms, art treasures etc. - accounted for only about 3 per cent of total wealth.
60. Quoted in B. L. Dyer, *The public library systems of Great Britain, America and South Africa* (1903), p. 7.
61. The lack of libraries in London, and poor standards in the British Museum's library, encouraged him to commence the campaign for the London Library; F. Harrison (ed.), *Carlyle and the London Library* (London, 1906). In 1834 Manchester had at least 12 libraries; Manchester Public Library Archives, MS/f/310.6/M5/37. M. Guizot informed the Select Committee on Public Libraries (1849) that he was grateful for the existence of the London Library and other such institutions, as reported by E. Walford, *Old and new London* (1989, facsimile reprint), p. 189.
62. L. Watson, *What shall I read? Helps to the study of English literature* (1887), pp. 17-18, produced by the Sunday School Union.
63. P. Cowell, *Liverpool public libraries: a history of fifty years* (1903), p. 159.
64. J. Burkitt, *Blackpool libraries 1880–1980* (1980), p. 1.
65. Harrison, Carlyle and the London Library, op. cit., pp. 68-9.
66. *The training of librarians*, newscutting, source unknown, Press cuttings on libraries (1897-1948), compiled by B. Matthews, p. 13, British Library Information Science Service.
67. Cowell, op. cit., p. 52.
68. County Borough of Bournemouth, *Minutes* (12 May 1911). The Bournemouth Public Library *Annual Report* was included in these minutes.
69. *Magazine of Music* (March 1912).
70. Ceremonies ... William Brown to the town of Liverpool, op. cit., p. 31
71. T. Greenwood, *Free public libraries* (1886), p. 130.

72. F. Kaplan, *Thomas Carlyle: a biography* (1983), pp. 329, 339 and 439-43. The entry for Carlyle in the *Dictionary of national biography* says that this book made more of a stir than most of his writings.

73. G. B. Tennyson, *A Carlyle reader: selections from the writings of Thomas Carlyle* (1984), p. 407.

74. R. J. Smith, *The Gothic bequest: medieval institutions in British thought 1688–1863* (1987), p. 196.

75. T. Carlyle, *Past and present* (1843), p. 198.

76. Ibid., p. 88. On occasions, however, Carlyle displayed an ambivalent attitude to industrialism. For example, A. L. LeQuesne, *Carlyle* (1982), p. 53, cites him thus: 'Cotton-spinning has the clothing of the naked as its result . . . soot and despair are not the essence of it; they are divisible from it'.

77. J. A. Hobson, *The evaluation of modern capitalism: a study of machine production* (1906), p. 348.

78. Ibid., pp. 337-8.

79. See M. J. Daunton, *House and home in the Victorian city: working class housing 1850–1914* (1983), pp. 264-5 which argues that intensification of work led to increased domesticity. See also, E. J. Hobsbawm, Custom, wages and workload in nineteenth century industry, *in* his *Labouring men* (1964).

80. W. Morris, *Art socialism, in* his *Architecture, industry and wealth* (1902), p. 107.

81. S. A. Barnett, *The ideal city* (1894), p. 3.

82. Quoted in B. Trinder, *The making of the industrial landscape* (1982), p. 248.

83. Meller, op. cit., p. 5.

84. R. W. Malcomson, *Popular recreations in English society 1700–1850* (1973), p. 4.

85. This was noted by Greenwood, Free public libraries, op. cit., pp. 129-30.

86. G. Davison, The city as a natural system: theories of urban society in early nineteenth century Britain, *in* D. Fraser (ed.), *The pursuit of urban history* (1983), p. 353.

87. G. T. Donisthorpe, *An account of the origin and progress of the Devon and Exeter Memorial Museum* (1868), p. 10.

88. W. Heaton, 'The old soldier', 'The wandering lover' and other poems; together with a sketch of the author's life (1857), p. xix. His natural science hobby, he said (p. xviii), kept him from the public house.

89. J. Manners, *Some of the advantages of easily accessible reading and recreation rooms and free libraries* (1885), p. 35.

90. Z. Moon, *Evidence to Parliament in support of the Leyton Urban District Bill* (1904), Walthamstow Local Studies Library.

91. W. S. Jevons, The rationale of free public libraries, *Contemporary Review*, 39 (1881), p. 387.

92. *The free library movement* (1886), newscutting, source unknown, Lambeth Public Library Cuttings, Box iv/63/1/23(i).

93. Cowell, op. cit., p. 66.

94. *South London Press* (23 January 1892). Sir John Lubbock, Chairman of the LCC, speaking at the opening of Bermondsey Public Library.

95. Quoted in P. Sykes, *The public library in perspective: an examination of its origins and modern role* (1979), p. 33.

96. M. Eddison, *A little gem: Sir John Brunner and the Northwich Free Public Library* (1985).

97. *Sunday Observer* (8 March 1931) reporting on the opening of the branch library in Fairfoot Road, Bow, East London.

98. Greenwood, Free public libraries, op. cit., p. 123.

99. Arnold, Culture and Anarchy (1955 edn), p. 210.

100. R. J. Evans, *The forging of the modern state* (1983), p. 315.

101. A. Edwards, *Regulation and repression: the study of social control* (1988), p. 1.

102. S. Cohen, *Visions of social control: crime, punishment and classification* (1985), p. 1.

103. D. Popenoe, *Sociology* (1983), p. 239.

104. E. A. Ross, *Social control* (1901), examined the societies formed in the American West by the gold-rush. These societies incorporated persons from widely differing backgrounds, yet they became cohesive entities based on trust and fairness, without the controls of class direction and domination.

105. N. Janowitz, *Social control of the welfare state* (1977), p. 10.

106. B. Moore, *Social origins of dictatorship and democracy* (1969), p. 286.

107. R. Gray, Bourgeois hegemony in Victorian Britain, *in* J. Bloomfield (ed.), *Papers on class, hegemony and party* (1977), p. 84.

108. D. C. Richter, *Riotous Victorians* (1981), p. 163.

109. A. Briggs, *Victorian people* (1965), p. 9.

110. See E. J. Hobsbawm, The labour aristocracy in nineteenth century Britain, *in* his *Labouring men* (1964). For an authoritative discussion see R. Gray, *The aristocracy of labour in nineteenth century Britain* (1981), or for a succinct coverage R. J. Morris, The labour aristocracy in the history of British class, *Recent Findings of Research in Economic and Social History*, 7 (Autumn 1988).

111. Though the term was employed by contemporaries, a division between labour aristocrats and other workers is difficult to identify empirically; Gray, The aristocracy of labour, op. cit., pp. 9–12. D. G. Wright, *Popular radicalism: the working class experience 1780–1880* (1988) questions the existence of a labour aristocracy. However, one argument supporting the existence of an élite stratum is the widening of skilled–unskilled wage differentials between 1850 and 1873, and the low unemployment experienced by skilled compared to unskilled trades; K. Burgess, *The challenge of labour: shaping British society 1850–1930* (1980), p. 16.

112. See the examination of economic context in Chapter 1 of Burgess, op. cit.

113. See, for example, A. Chapman, *The People's Palace for East London: a study of Victorian philanthropy*, unpublished MPhil, University of Hull (1973).

114. 'Who says cobbler says radical', wrote E. J. Hobsbawm, *Primitive rebels* (1971), p. 109.

115. J. Foster, *Class struggles and the Industrial Revolution* (1974), describes how the 'revolutionary conscious' Oldham of the 1840s gave way to calmer social relations after 1850, as collaborationist, élite workers became supervisors in technically improved factories.

116. For a comprehensive criticism of Victorian social control see N. Abercrombie, S. Hill and B. S. Turner, *The dominant ideology thesis* (1980). G. Crossick, *An artisan elite in Victorian society: Kentish London 1840–1880* (1978), argues that skilled workers pursued such values of self-help and respectability autonomously, not at the behest of the bourgeoisie. See also F. M. L. Thompson, Social control in Victorian Britain, *Economic History Review*, 34:2 (May 1981), which is keen to stress the distinction between socialization and social control.

117. G. Gerbner, Mass media and human communication theory, *in* D. McQuail (ed.), *The sociology of mass communication* (1972), p. 39.

118. Ibid., p. 42, defines propaganda as 'the management of collective attitudes by the manipulation of significant symbols'.

119. In the *German ideology* Marx wrote that: 'The ideas of the ruling classes are in every epoch the ruling ideas ... the class that is the ruling material force of society is at the same time its ruling intellectual force. The class which has the means of material production at its disposal has control at the same time over the means of mental production, so that ... the ideas of those who lack the means of mental production are subject to it.' Quoted in A. Donagan and B. Donagan (eds), *Philosophy of history* (New York, 1965), p. 69.

120. P. Joyce, *Work, society and politics: the culture of the factory in later Victorian England* (1980), shows how a deferential and malleable working class was fashioned by the social infrastructure of paternalist factory owners. Joyce is less concerned with a labour aristocracy than with control over labour as a whole.

121. P. Bailey, *Leisure and class in Victorian England* (1978), p. 79. In early-nineteenth-century Manchester the major fight was, arguably, not between working class and bourgeoisie, but between the liberal Nonconformist business élite and the town's Tory Anglican leaders; V. A. C. Gatrell, Incorporation and the pursuit of liberal hegemony in Manchester 1790–1839, *in* D. Fraser (ed.), *Municipal reform and the industrial city* (1982).

122. G. Ingham, *Capitalism divided? The city and industry in British social development* (1984). G. Crossick (ed.), *The lower middle class in Britain 1870–1914* (1977).

123. Bailey, Leisure and class, op. cit., p. 177, writes of the bourgeois concern of maintaining social distance.

124. F. M. L. Thompson, Social control in modern Britain, *Recent Findings of Research in Economic and Social History*, 5 (Autumn 1987).

125. P. Gardner, *The lost elementary schools of Victorian England: the people's education* (1984). T. W. Laqueur, *Religion and respectability: Sunday schools and working class culture 1780–1850* (1976), p. 239, argues that Sunday schools were not simple control efforts, in that values taught were congruent with certain lower-class values.

126. P. Bailey, Will the real Bill Banks please stand up? Towards a role analysis of mid-Victorian working class respectability, *Journal of Social History*, 12 (1978–9).

127. G. S. Jones, Class expression vs. social control? A critique of recent trends in the social history of leisure, *History Workshop*, 4 (1977).

128. Thompson, Social control in Victorian Britain, op. cit., p. 193.

129. K. Jones, J. Brown and J. Bradshaw, *Issues in social policy* (1983), p. 145.

130. P. Stansky (ed.), *The Victorian revolution: government and society in Victoria's Britain* (New York, 1973), p. xii.

131. See, for example, Chapter 9 of R. G. Kirby and A. E. Musson, *The voice of the people. John Doherty 1789–1854: trade unionist, radical and factory reformer* (1975).

132. S. Simsova (ed.), *Lenin, Krupskaia and libraries* (1968), p. 19.

133. R. J. Morris, *Class and class consciousness in the Industrial Revolution 1780–1850* (1979), p. 61. A. Kadish, University extension and the working classes: the case of the Northumberland miners, *Bulletin of the Institute of Historical Research*, 60 (June 1987), shows that miners willingly participated in adult education (in political economy) organized to build a less volatile workforce.

However, this was not simply a case of control: miners saw it to their advantage to learn the rules of the game.

134. E. Davidson, *Whitehall and the labour problem in late Victorian and Edwardian Britain: a study in official statistics and social control* (Sydney, 1985), p. 11. P. Thane, The working class and state 'welfare': 1880-1914, *Society for the Study of Labour History, Bulletin* 31 (1975) argues that the Social Democratic Federation, whilst rejecting capitalism, supported social reforms which specifically resulted in economic redistribution.

135. E. Royal, Mechanics' institutes and the working classes 1840-1860, *Historical Journal*, 14:2 (1971). Also see the analysis of working men's clubs in Bailey, Leisure and class, op. cit.

136. The social negotiation thesis is explored by R. Gray, *The labour aristocracy in Victorian Edinburgh* (1976).

137. J. Joll, *Gramsci* (1977), p. 100.

138. Gramsci quoted by R. Williams, *Marxism and literature* (1977), p. 110.

139. G. Turner, *British cultural studies: an introduction* (1990), p. 212.

140. The idea of public libraries as instruments of social control has been supported by J. Noyce, *Libraries and the working classes in the nineteenth century* (1974), and P. Corrigan and V. Gillespie, *Class struggle, social literacy and idle time: the provision of public libraries in England as a case study in the organisation of leisure with direct educational results* (1978).

141. Altick, *The English common reader* (Chicago, 1957), pp. 82, 225.

142. Manchester Public Free Library, *Report of the proceedings at the public meeting ... to the effect of the establishment of a free public library and museum ...* (1851), p. 8.

143. L. Barlow, *Independent spirits: spiritualism and English plebeians 1850-1910* (1986). For examples of socialist literature being excluded see A. W. Ball, *The public libraries of Greater London: a pictorial history 1856–1914* (1977).

144. Newscutting, source unknown (1874), Lambeth Public Library Cuttings, Box IV/63/1/23(1). Some libraries provided non-literacy activities as methods of counter-attraction: the public libraries in Hindley and Preston had billiard and chess rooms, respectively; Greenwood, *Free public libraries* (1886), pp. 105, 199.

145. Reading and readers, *Sunday Magazine* (1893), p. 193.

146. A. H. Thompson, *Censorship in public libraries in the United Kingdom during the twentieth century* (1975), pp. 1-4.

147. *Hampshire Post* (11 June 1886).

148. W. A. Munford, *Penny rate: aspects of British public library history 1850-1950* (1951), p. 141.

149. W. Johnman and H. Kendal, *Report of a commission appointed [by Darlington Public Libraries] to enquire into the condition and workings of free libraries of various towns in England* (c.1879), Darlington Public Library.

150. L. S. Jast, *The library and the community* (1939), pp. 45-6.

151. D. Wardle, *Education and society in nineteenth century Nottingham* (1971), pp. 183-5. Numerous autonomous Welsh miners' libraries were formed around the turn of the century; H. Francis, The origins of the South Wales Miners' Library, *History Workshop*, 2 (Autumn 1976).

152. Cohen, op. cit., p. 6.

153. W. J. Hahn, *Camberwell libraries* (c.1955), typescript, Southwark Local Studies Library.

154. P. J. Waller, *Town, city and nation: England 1850-1914*, p. 313.
155. For oral reminiscences of 'larking about' see S. Humphries, *Hooligans or rebels: an oral history of working class childhood and youth 1889-1939* (1981).
156. Manuscript letter (c.1900) to the librarian - signed 'J. W. R.' - recalling the 1870s, Norwich Local Studies Library.
157. *Disorderly conduct in a Leeds library*, unidentified newscutting (19 January 1895) in Sparke collection of documents relating to Leeds public libraries, Vol. 2, p. 1.
158. *Darlington and Stockton Times* (7 November 1885).
159. Exeter Library Committee, *Minutes* (27 February 1871).
160. Q. Hoare and G. N. Smith (eds), *Selections from the prison notes of Antonio Gramsci* (1971), p. 12.
161. Quoted by J. H. Nodal, What is literature?, *Papers of the Manchester Literary Club*, 3 (1877), p. 182.
162. P. Sturges and A. Barr, The Fiction nuisance in nineteenth century British public libraries, *Journal of Librarianship and Information Science*, 24:1 (1992).
163. *Library World*, 7 (1904-5), p. 102.
164. Newscutting, source unknown (1885), Woolwich Public Library Cuttings, p. 1.
165. J. Urie, *Reminiscences of eighty years* (1908).
166. *Report* on the opening of the Salford Museum and Library, *Manchester Guardian* (4 July 1849).
167. Quoted in P. Gordon and J. White, *Philosophers as educational reformers: the influence of idealism on British educational thought and practice* (1979).
168. An article signed 'Bibliophilist' in the *Bermondsey Liberal Monthly* (March 1912), p. 5, praised the local public libraries because 'they show an impartiality which is to be commended, and enables all of us to judge views and form opinions'. The public library allowed considerations of a variety of opinions, but only those which did not threaten the essence of the existing political system.

9   Librarians: their social engagement and controlling discourse

1. M. Tinks, Thomas Carlyle and Victorian culture, *in* P. Scott and P. Fletcher (eds), *Culture and education in Victorian England* (1990).
2. B. Morris, Library and information studies education, in B. White (ed.), *Information for all: access and availability* (1987), p. 125.
3. M. Slater (ed.), *Career patterns and occupational image: a study of the library and information field* (1979), p. 18.
4. L. McColvin, *The public library system of Great Britain* (1942), p. 63.
5. N. Roberts and T. Wilson, Public sector business libraries and research, *Library Association Record*, 89 (1987).
6. Letter from R. Shepherd MP to the *Sunday Times* (25 October 1987).
7. Library Association questionnaire to public libraries (1904), British Library Information Science Service, uncatalogued.
8. Technical college libraries: a symposium, *Library Review*, 15 (1955-6), p. 314. Words of E. A. Savage.
9. M. Dewey, An American view of English librarianship, *Library Assistant*, 1 (1898-9).

10. Quoted in N. Webber, A library historian's thoughts on management, *in* B. Redfern (ed.), *Studies in library management*, Vol. 1 (1972), p. 20.

11. *Library Review*, 15 (1955-6), p. 499. E. A. Savage speaking about libraries in technical schools.

12. Dewey, op. cit.

13. *Dartford Chronicle* (3 March 1915).

14. Newscutting, source unknown (1905), Woolwich Public Library Cuttings, Vol. 1, p. 99.

15. Oldham Public Library and Museum Committee, *Minutes* (26 October 1882).

16. See the first two chapters of R. J. Edwards, *In-service training in British libraries: its development and practice* (1977). Also see the introduction and first three chapters of G. Bramley, *Apprentice to graduate: a history of library education in the United Kingdom* (1981).

17. W. J. Reader, *Professional men: the rise of the professional classes in nineteenth century England* (1966) describes the move away from the 'professional apprenticed' approach which had previously dominated.

18. Edwards, In-service training, op. cit., pp. 1, 11, 25. Bramley, op. cit., p. 26, lists the six sectional certificates leading to full professional status. These were all of immediate, practical use in the library: 'literary history', 'practical bibliography', 'classification', 'cataloguing', 'library history and organization', and 'practical library administration'. Bramley also shows (pp. 54, 58, 65) that occasionally public libraries themselves provided education designed to improve an assistant's general intelligence, as opposed to practical ability. At Newcastle Public Library, early this century, Latin and French were taught. But such classes were rare. Education geared specifically to job requirements was the overriding objective, as at the London School of Economics, where part-time classes in librarianship began in 1902. By 1914 these classes were unpopular and on the point of abandonment.

19. T. Kelly, *A history of public libraries in Great Britain 1845–1975* (1977), p. 99.

20. L. Baldwin, *Northampton public library from its origin to 1910* (1971), typescript held by Northampton Local Studies Library. Tweed Jewers was the Portsmouth librarian 1883-1914. He was a former Royal Marine Artillery non-commissioned officer. It should be noted that many second-generation public librarians had received their training in earlier years in libraries. J. P. Briscoe was appointed librarian at Nottingham in 1869 having spent many years training at Bolton; T. Dunne, *Bolton Public Libraries 1853–1978* (Bolton, 1978), p. 19.

21. Letter from Ernest Axon to Walter Powell (15 March 1909), Collection of letters to the librarian Walter Powell, British Library Information Science Service, uncatalogued.

22. H. Barnett, *Canon Barnett: his life, work and friends*, Vol. 2 (1918), p. 7.

23. W. Pollitt, Staff training and organisation, *Library Association Record*, 27 (1925), p. 83.

24. *North Star* (19 October 1886).

25. *Islington Gazette* (20 November 1905).

26. Eastbourne Technical Instruction Committee, *Minutes* (18 May 1896). J. V. Redhead, *Darlington Public Libraries: a centenary history 1885–1985* (Darlington, 1985), p. 24.

27. J. D. Brown's starting pay at Islington was recorded in Islington Council,

Minutes (16 December 1904). But low salaries were occasionally compensated by 'payment in kind'. The librarian of Fulham was paid a £275 salary in 1889, plus his rent, gas, coal, rates and taxes; S. Holland, *Fulham Public Libraries 1886–1939*, typescript, Fulham Local Studies Library. None the less, pay was certainly low compared with the United States where in 1886 W. F. Poole took charge of the Chicago Public Library on 4000 dollars per annum; D. Garrison, *Apostles of culture: the public librarian and American society 1876–1920* (New York, 1979), p. 6.

28.   *Bournemouth Guardian* (3 January 1920). For an analysis of women workers see N. Webber, Prospects and prejudice: women and librarianship 1880–1914, *Library History*, 6:5 (1984), p. 160, which makes the point that women were less likely to be employed in closed access libraries because their form of dress (i.e. long skirts) was not suitable for fetching books and climbing ladders.

29.   *Croydon Advertiser* (17 December 1910).

30.   Newscutting, source unknown, Library Association Cuttings 1897–8, compiled by B.Matthews, p. 13, British Library Information Science Service. Garrison, op. cit., describes how in the United States similar images of women's suitability for library work were produced. The 'library hostess', displaying virtues of self-denial, passivity, gentility, and spiritual and moral rectitude, was a strong theme of pre-1914 United States librarianship.

31.   Newscutting, source unknown (c.1905), Islington Public Library.

32.   Quoted in S. Bailey, An Edwardian academic library, *Full view: newsletter of the friends of the University of London*, 1 (Autumn 1988), p. 7.

33.   See the Collection of letters to the librarian Walter Powell, British Library Information Science Service, uncatalogued.

34.   Eastbourne Technical Institute Committee, *Minutes* (28 August 1896).

35.   Letter from Edward Edwards to Manchester Council General Purposes Committee, recorded in the Committee's *Minutes* (11 December 1851).

36.   Edwards, In-service training, op. cit., pp. 14–15. Delegation of responsibility was difficult despite the multi-levelled hierarchy. At Croydon it was the custom to call junior assistants by their surnames; senior assistants' surnames were prefixed with 'Mr'; the chief was called 'Sir'; and surnames of female staff were prefixed with 'Miss'; as related by the *Croydon Crank: Magazine of the Croydon Public Library Staff Guild* (January–March 1908).

37.   W. C. B. Sayers, Children's libraries as I saw them, *Library World*, 60 (1958), p. 22.

38.   See the discussion of the entrepreneurial ideal in H. Perkin, *The origins of modern English society* (1969).

39.   T. R. Gourvish, The rise of the professions, *in* T. R. Gourvish and A. O'Day (eds), *Later Victorian Britain 1867–1900* (1988), p. 17.

40.   K. Manley, *E. W. B. Nicholson (1849–1912) and his importance to librarianship*, unpublished DPhil, University of Oxford (1977), p. 15. Manley points out (p. 13) that just 28 public libraries out of 72 sent representatives to the first national conference of librarians.

41.   W. A. Munford, *The history of the Library Association 1877–1977* (1976).

42.   *Daily News* (13 September 1892).

43.   See Manley, op. cit.

44.   P. Sturges, British librarianship and the First World War: a commentary, *Journal of Library History*, 22 (1987), p. 286.

45. D. Ring, Some speculations on why the British public librarianship profession didn't go to war, *Journal of Library History*, 22 (1987), p. 257.
46. M. Dewey, The profession, *Library Journal*, 1 (1876-7), p. 5.
47. Ibid., p. 6.
48. See the discussion on Dewey in Garrison, op. cit.
49. S. S. Green, Personal relations between librarians and readers, *Library Journal*, 1 (1876-7), pp. 74-81.
50. Ring, op. cit., p. 257.
51. P. S. Bagwell and G. E. Mingay, *Britain and America 1850-1939: a study of economic change* (1970), p. 10.
52. D. A. Hounsell, *From the 'American System' to mass production 1800-1932* (Baltimore, 1984). P. A. David, *Technical choice, innovation and growth: essays in American and British experience in the nineteenth century* (1975).
53. G. B. Hotchkiss, Business reading and success, *in What to read on business* (New York, 1912), pp. 7-9 (a book prepared for the Business Book Bureau).
54. P. K. Mutchler, *Public library co-operation with business and industry* unpublished MA dissertation, University College, University of London (1969), p. 5.
55. Library Association questionnaire, op. cit.
56. Ibid., return for Finsbury.
57. Ibid., return for Finsbury.
58. M. R. Marshall, *The history of industrial libraries in Britain to 1960*, unpublished Fellowship of the Library Association thesis (1968).
59. W. G. Fry and W. A. Munford, *Louis Stanley Jast: a biographical sketch* (1966).
60. Ibid., pp. 28-9.
61. L. S. Jast, Some hindrances to progress in public library work, *Library Association Record*, 2 (1900). A paper first read to the 1898 Library Association Conference.
62. Croydon Public Libraries, *Handbook of information and readers' companion* (1907), pp. 47, 57, 61, 113, 115. This handbook was an innovation in itself, for according to the *Surrey Daily Argos* (28 June 1907): 'nothing so complete has ever been issued by a public library, this side of the Atlantic at all events'. Fry and Munford, op. cit., pp. 12-32 discuss these innovations. Jast emphasized the importance of these innovations in the Croydon return to the Library Association questionnaire, op. cit.
63. *Croydon: the story of a hundred years* (1977).
64. *The (Croydon) Readers' Index* (1899), p. 82.
65. Reference work, *Croydon Crank: Magazine of the Croydon Public Library Staff Guild* (January-March 1908).
66. Ibid., see article entitled: A chat with the chief.
67. *Croydon Guardian* (10 September 1910).
68. Ibid.
69. S. Gobalt and W. A. Munford, *The incomparable Mac: a biographical study of Sir John Young Walker MacAlister 1856-1925* (1983), p. 27.
70. Ibid., p. 27.
71. W. H. Fraser, *The coming of the mass market 1850-1914* (1981), p. 132.
72. A. Adburgham, *Shopping in style: London from the Restoration to Edwardian elegance* (1976), p. 168.

73. Ibid., p. 181.
74. Library Association, *The establishment of public libraries* (1909), p. 8.
75. *Library Review*, 15 (1955-6), p. 499. E. A. Savage speaking about technical libraries in technical schools.
76. Technical college libraries: a symposium, op. cit., p. 314. Words of E. A. Savage.
77. Manley, op. cit., pp. 16-17.
78. E. A. Savage, The representation of science in public libraries, *Library World*, 12 (1909), pp. 1-4.
79. Ibid., pp. 11-14, 46-8.
80. A. Mole, The development of library management concerns 1870-1914, *in* A. Vaughan (ed.), *Studies in library management*, Vol. 6 (1980), pp. 73-9.
81. T. W. Heyck, *The transformation of intellectual life in Victorian England* (1982). See, in particular, Chapters 1, 4, 7.
82. P. M. Heimann, The scientific revolutions, in P. Burke (ed.), *The new Cambridge modern history*, Vol. 13 (companion volume, 1979).
83. J. A. V. Chapple, *Science and literature in the nineteenth century* (1986), p. 3.
84. Ibid.
85. W. J. Reader, At the head of all the new professions: the engineer in Victorian society, *in* N. McKendrick and R. B. Outhwaite, *Business life and public policy: essays in honour of D. C. Coleman* (1986), p. 184.
86. E. A. Parsons, *The Alexandrian Library* (1952), p. 70.
87. J. Boardman, J. Griffin and O. Murray (eds), *The Oxford history of the classical world* (1986), p. 350.
88. Sayers, Children's libraries, op. cit., p. 71.
89. Fulham Public Library Committee, *Minutes* (11 December 1905).
90. Director's report on the School of Librarianship 1919-20, cited in University College, University of London, *Annual report* (1920-1921), p. 99.
91. Heyck, op. cit., pp. 24-5.
92. Reader, Professional men, op. cit., p. 1.
93. M. Van de Weyer's evidence to the Select Committee on Public Libraries (1849), cited in the *Athenaeum* (1 September 1849).
94. L. S. Jast, *Libraries and living* (1932), pp. 91-2.
95. Letter from Thomas Carlyle to William Christie (April 1840), *in* F. Harrison (ed.), *Carlyle and the London Library* (1906), pp. 28-9.
96. D. Cuthbertson, *Revelations of a library life 1876-1922* (1923), p. 198.
97. *Hampshire Post* (11 June 1886).
98. Sayers, Children's libraries, op. cit., p. 72.
99. Library Association, The establishment of public libraries, op. cit., p. 10.
100. Library Association questionnaire, op. cit., return for Southwark.
101. *Hampshire Post* (11 June 1886).
102. A. C. Shaw, *What shall I read?* (1909).
103. G. Radford, *The faculty of reading: the coming of the National Home Reading Union* (1910), p. 46.
104. Adburgham, op. cit., p. 178.
105. J. D. Brown and H. W. Fincham, *Report on the Clerkenwell open lending library* (1894).
106. *Croydon Advertiser* (13 June 1896).
107. J. Minto, *A history of the public library movement in Great Britain and Ireland* (1932), p. 307. Clerkenwell Public Libraries, *Librarian's report to the Commissioners on his visit to American libraries* (1893).

108. Library Association questionnaire, op. cit., return for King's Lynn.
109. A. Williams, *Thirty-six Stewart Street, Bolton: an exercise in nostalgia 1901–1914* (1983), p. 22.
110. B. Wiltshire, *The Public library in autobiography*, unpublished MPhil, CNAA (Polytechnic of North London) (1982) shows that there existed a popular enthusiasm for open access.
111. The progress of open access, *Library World*, 8 (1905-6), p. 179.
112. Newscutting, source unknown, reporting on a paper by W. H. Brett (librarian of the Cleveland Public Library, USA) to the Second International Conference of Librarians, 1897, included in Library Association Cuttings (1897-8), compiled by B. Matthews, p. 4, British Library Information Science Service.
113. John Ballinger quoted in M. B. Adams, Public libraries, their buildings and equipment: a plea for state aid, *Library Association Record*, 7 (1905), p. 221.
114. A. L. Champneys, *Public libraries* (1907), p. 133.
115. C. Soule, *How to plan a library building* (1912), p. 112.
116. Select Committee on Public Libraries, *Report* (1849), Q. 1331.
117. Libraries for the people, *Chambers Edinburgh Journal*, 15 (January-June 1815), p. 200.
118. J. D. Brown, *Report on the safeguarded open access system* (1893-8). There was a degree of systematic organized theft. When police inspected the home of one Camberwell reader they discovered over 200 stolen public library books; *Kentish Mercury* (26 March 1909).
119. W. Bailey speaking at the Second International Conference of Librarians, 1897, quoted in a newscutting, source unknown, Library Association Cuttings, op. cit., p. 4.
120. Library Association questionnaire, op. cit., return for Portsmouth.
121. *Islington Daily Gazette* (1 August 1905).
122. *Leeds Mercury* (12 May 1893), letter to the editor by Bell Smith.
123. Select Committee on Public Libraries, op. cit., Q. 2841, called for closed access at the library of the Society if the public were admitted; it was felt that the stock needed to be protected from passionate book collectors.
124. W. Jolliffe, *Public library extension activities* (1962), p. 1.
125. Kelly, op. cit., p. 200.
126. J. P. Briscoe, Libraries and reading circles, *Library Association Record*, 5 (1903), p. 219.
127. Ibid., p. 220.
128. J. P. Briscoe, Half-hour talks about books with library readers, *The Library*, 7 (1895). Briscoe began these in Nottingham in the 1890s.
129. J. P. Briscoe, Libraries for the blind, *Library Chronicle*, 4 (1887). There existed only 11 libraries for the blind by 1887.
130. J. P. Briscoe, Libraries for the young, *Library Chronicle*, 3 (1886). Nottingham was the first library to provided separate premises for a children's library, in 1882.
131. J. P. Briscoe, Public libraries and emigration, *Library Association Record*, 1 (1899).
132. See Chapter 2 of J. Sims, *John Potter Briscoe: Nottingham city librarian 1869–1916*, unpublished MA dissertation, Loughborough University (1983). Briscoe edited the *Midland Temperance Record*.
133. Briscoe, Public libraries and emigration, op. cit., p. 294.

134. J. P. Briscoe, How to extend the library movement, *The Library*, 8 (1896), p. 73.
135. J. P. Briscoe, Subscription libraries in connection with free libraries, *Transactions and proceedings of the first annual meeting of the Library Association of the United Kingdom, 1878* (1879) made a vitriolic attack on the three-class subscription system run by Bolton Public Library.
136. Briscoe, Libraries and reading circles, op. cit., p. 221.
137. Briscoe, How to extend the library movement, op. cit., p. 74.
138. W. Briscoe, Library publicity methods, *Library World*, 16 (1913-14).
139. T. Greenwood, *Free public libraries* (1886), p. 382.
140. Personalities of the past 5: John Potter Briscoe, *Librarian and Book World*, 30 (1940-1), p. 164.
141. H. Franks, Geist, *Papers of the Manchester Literary Club*, 4 (1878), p. 96 wrote of 'our love of German culture and the awareness of the singular transfer of power from the French to the Germans, which has visibly taken place within the last twenty-five years'.
142. W. E. A. Axon, Professorships of bibliography, *Transactions and proceedings of the first annual meeting of the Library Association of the United Kingdom, 1878* (1879), p. 104.
143. Quoted in T. Greenwood, *Edward Edwards* (1902), p. 124.
144. W. E. A. Axon, Bolton and its free library, *Papers of the Manchester Literary Club*, 5 (1879), pp. 28-9.
145. Ibid., p. 29.
146. W. E. A. Axon, The library in relation to knowledge and life, *Library Journal*, 29 (1904), p. 16.
147. W. E. A. Axon, The Thomas Greenwood library for librarians at Manchester, *Library Association Record*, 9 (1907).
148. Axon, The library in relation to knowledge, op. cit., pp. 20, 22.
149. W. E. A. Axon, John Ruskin: a bibliographical bibliography, *Papers of the Manchester Literary Club*, 5 (1879), pp. 173-4.
150. W. E. A. Axon, Thomas Taylor the Platonist, *The Library*, 2 (1890), p. 300.
151. In 1887 Barnett delivered a sermon entitled The work of righteousness, printed *in* S. A. Barnett and H. Barnett, *Practicable socialism* (1894).
152. W. E. A. Axon, Library lectures, *Library Journal*, 3:2 (1878), p. 48.
153. Axon, Libraries in relation to knowledge, op. cit., p. 22.
154. Axon's obituary, *Library Association Record*, 16 (1914), p. 134.
155. Annual report of the Royal Society of Literature for 1914, quoted in R. Walmsley, Dr Axon: Manchester bookman, *Manchester Review*, 10 (Summer-Autumn 1964), p. 140.
156. M. Harrison, T. C. Horsfall and the Manchester Art Museum, *in* A. J. Kidd and K. W. Roberts (eds), *City, class and culture: studies of social and cultural production in Victorian Manchester* (1985), p. 126.
157. H. Barnett, Canon Barnett, op. cit., p. 7.
158. Ibid., p. 10.
159. Letter from T. Aldred to W. Powell (26 February 1906), Collection of letters to the librarian Walter Powell, British Library Information Science Service, uncatalogued.
160. L. Moore, Special provision for women in public libraries: the first hundred years, *Library History*, 9 (1993).
161. *Croydon Guardian* (13 September 1913). W. C. B. Sayers addressing the Library Association Conference, 1913.

162. A. Lancaster, The provision of technical books, *Library Association Record*, 2 (1900), p. 13.
163. E. J. Hunter, *The role of the public library in the development of technical education in Great Britain and Ireland during the nineteenth century*, unpublished MA, University of Sheffield (1973), pp. 155-6.
164. B. Anderton, *Report of the annual meeting of the Library Association* (1894), p. 2.
165. L. S. Jast, *Technical libraries* (1903), p. 3.
166. Foucault's analysis of discourse and/or summaries of his other ideas can be found in S. Hall, The West and the rest: discourse and power, in S. Hall and B. Gieben (eds), *Formations of modernity* (1992); S. J. Ball (ed.), *Foucault and education: disciplines and knowledge* (1990); and C. Ramazanoglu (ed.), *Up against Foucault: explorations of some tensions between Foucault and feminism* (1993), especially introduction by the editor.
167. Chapter 5 of C. K. Watkins, *Social control* (1975), offers a clear discussion of the key characteristics of professionalism.
168. A. Giddens, *The consequences of modernity* (1990), Chapter 1.
169. J. H. Shera, On the value of library history, *Library Quarterly*, 22 (July 1952), p. 240.
170. J. D. Brown, *Manual of library classification and shelf arrangement* (1898), pp. 11-12.
171. R. Garnett, *Essays on librarianship and bibliography* (1899), p. 211.
172. G. A. Stephenson, Read, *City of Norwich School Magazine*, 3:9 (1919).
173. J. Thornton, *Library power: a new philosophy of librarianship* (1974), p. 13.
174. J. Wellard, *The public library comes of age* (1940), p. 3.
175. W. B. Rayward, Restructuring and mobilising information in documents: a historical perspective, in P. Vakkari and B. Cronin, *Conceptions of library and information science* (1992).
176. C. Harris and P. Taylor, *Prospects for information service* (1985), p. 97.
177. C. Dandeker, *Surveillance, power and modernity: bureaucracy and discipline from 1700 to the present day* (1990).

10   Architecture: the social causes of design

1. R. J. B. Morris, *Parliament and the public libraries* (1977), p. 27.
2. *West London Advertiser* (14 October 1905).
3. D. Keeling, British public library buildings 1850-1870, *Library History*, 1:4 (1968). R. G. C. Desmond, Some unquiet thoughts on public library architecture, *Library Association Record*, 59 (1957). A. Ball, *Public libraries of Greater London: a pictorial history 1856–1914* (1977), see the chapter on buildings.
4. A. J. Smith, *Carnegie library buildings in Great Britain*, unpublished Fellowship of the Library Association thesis (1974). M. Dewe, *Henry Thomas Hare 1860–1921*, unpublished MA, University of Strathclyde (1981).
5. See, for example, D. E. B. Weiner, *The institution of popular education: architectural form and social policy in the London Board Schools 1870–1904*, unpublished PhD, Princeton University (1984).
6. R. Gutman, Library architect and people, *in* E. R. De Prospo, *The library building consultant: role and responsibility* (New Brunswick, NJ, 1969), p. 13.

7. A. D. King, *Buildings and society: essays on the social development of the built environment* (1980), p. 1. In the same genre see T. A. Markus, *Buildings and power: freedom and control in the origin of modern building types* (1993).

8. M. Swenarton, *Homes fit for heroes* (1981), pp. 2–3. This study examines how government ideology was reflected in the nature of early state housing in the immediate post-First World War era.

9. See, for example, N. Pevsner, *Pioneers of the modern movement* (1936).

10. See, for example, M. Girouard, Life in the English country house: a social and architectural history (1978). The sub-title is indicative of the new genre. Girouard shows how the power aspirations of country house owners were transmitted into physical form. For a social historian's view, see P. Thompson, Mark Girouard and architectural history, *History Workshop*, 2 (Autumn 1976). For a discussion of the intersection of ideology and design see R. Macleod, *Style and society: architectural ideology in Britain 1914–1935* (1971).

11. T. Kelly, *A history of public libraries in Great Britain 1845–1975* (1977), pp. 73, 170. Ball, op. cit., p. 57 describes buildings as 'obstinately individualistic'.

12. B. M. Headicar, *A manual of library organisation* (1935), p. 69.

13. L. R. McColvin, *The public library system of Great Britain; a report on its present condition with proposals for post-war reorganisation* (1942), p. 81.

14. Desmond, op. cit., p. 79.

15. Ibid., p. 79.

16. John Betjeman's introduction to P. Ferriday, *Victorian architecture* (1963), p. 16.

17. Macleod, op. cit., p. 123.

18. F. J. Burgoyne, *Library construction: architecture, fittings and furniture* (1987). A. L. Champneys, *Public libraries: a treatise on their design, construction and fittings* (1907). B. Pite, Library architecture from the architect's viewpoint, *Proceedings of the second international conference of librarians* (1897). J. M. Brydon and F. J. Burgoyne, Public libraries, *Journal of the Royal Institute of British Architects*, 6 (1899). M. B. Adams, Public libraries, their buildings and equipment: a plea for state aid, *Journal of the Royal Institute of British Architects*, 12 (1905); also in the *Library Association Record*, 7 (1905). H. T. Hare and J. D. Brown, Public libraries, *Journal of the Royal Institute of British Architects*, 14 (1907). A very early commentary was that by J. W. Papworth and W. Papworth, *Museum, libraries and picture galleries, public and private* (1853) which was mostly concerned with library administration.

19. C. Soule, *How to plan a building for library work* (1912), p. 35.

20. Ibid., p. 31.

21. Ibid., p. 22, quoting the eleventh edition of the *Encyclopedia Britannica*.

22. See R. M. Holt, Trends in public library buildings, *Library Trends*, 36:2 (Fall 1987), which argues that architects are still attracted to monumental styles – the glass block, for example – which become the 'wearisome and redundant cliches of tomorrow' (p. 274). Holt doubts if today's styles are more satisfactory than those of yesterday: since efficiency is nowadays used to describe *all* styles, it is unlikely that all styles have attained their goal equally (p. 270). Further, it can be argued that a 'library building is obsolete from the moment it is occupied'; M. C. Jarrett, *Libraries*, unpublished dissertation, Royal Institute of British Architects final examination (1943), held in the Institute's library.

23. Gutman, op. cit., p. 28, has identified the major challenge in his field as

being 'to develop an approach to library buildings which will produce buildings that are successful in performing the variety of social purposes which men and groups require and cherish'.

24. A. Ellis, *Library services for young people in England and Wales 1830–1870* (1971), p. 13.
25. Jarrett, op. cit.
26. C. Norberg-Schulz, *Meaning in western architecture* (1975), p. 428.
27. P. F. Smith, *Architecture in the human dimension* (1979), p. 115.
28. Quoted in R. Porter and M. Teich, *The Enlightenment in national context* (1981), p. 13.
29. J. Ruskin, *The seven lamps of architecture* (1897, first published 1849). Ruskin wrote of 'the distinctly political art of Architecture'.(p. 49) He asserted that 'All architecture proposes an effect upon the human mind' (p. 13)
30. R. Scruton, *The aesthetics of architecture* (1979), p. 15.
31. *The North Star* (11 September 1885).
32. Macleod, op. cit., pp. 87-9.
33. The *details* of Greek architecture were first recorded by James Stuart and Nicholas Revett. Their *Antiquities of Athens* (1762) made an instant impact and generated a mania for Greek architecture. It has been described as a 'landmark in the history of taste'; R. Jenkyns, *The Victorians and ancient Greece* (1980), see Chapter 1.
34. Smith, Carnegie library buildings, op. cit., p. 164. Few Carnegie libraries were fashioned in the Gothic style which, by the time of Carnegie's benefaction, had receded in popularity.
35. Macleod, op. cit., p. 76. The phrase 'iconographic implication', as used by Macleod, is defined as 'meaning' attached to pictorial representation.
36. Ibid., p. 85.
37. Society for the Diffusion of Useful Knowledge, *Manual for mechanics' institutions* (1839), p. 103 (written by B. F. Duppa).
38. T. Greenwood, *Free public libraries* (1886), p. 70.
39. H. Rowlatt, *Description of the new public library at Poplar* (1894), typescript of the original manuscript held by Tower Hamlets Local Studies Library.
40. *Northampton Daily Echo* (9 June 1910).
41. Letter from Andrew Carnegie's secretary to the town clerk of Luton (18 January 1909), Scottish Records Office, Records of the Carnegie United Kingdom Trust, GD281/3/213.
42. Fulham Public Library Committee, *Minutes* (20 January 1908).
43. *West London Advertiser* (28 July 1905).
44. J. D. Brown, Library planning as affected by modern public library policy and interior arrangements, *Journal of the Royal Institute of British Architects*, 14 (1907), pp. 347-8.
45. *Portsmouth Times* (6 June 1908).
46. W. Crane, *Of the decoration of public buildings* (1896). Crane defined organic architecture as that which treated decoration as 'an essential and integral part of the structure to which it gives final expression'.
47. C. Cunningham, *Victorian and Edwardian town halls* (1981).
48. J. W. Clark, *The care of books* (Cambridge, 1902), pp. 11-12.
49. E. A. Parsons, *The Alexandrian Library* (1952), see map opposite p. 74 for location. J. Thompson, *A history of the principles of librarianship*, (1977), p. 88, comments on its political function.

50. There are exceptions, such as Hadrian's Library in Athens; J. B. Ward-Perkins, *Roman imperial architecture* (New York, 1977), Plate 370.

51. N. Pevsner, *A history of building types* (Princeton, NJ, 1976), p. 102.

52. Ibid., p. 96. The Escorial Library was constructed in 1567-84.

53. J. Harthan, English libraries and their furniture, *Discovering Antiques*, 48 (1971), p. 1131.

54. A. Achilles, Baroque monastic library architecture, *Journal of Library History*, 11:3 (1976), p. 249. Girouard, *Life in the English country house*, op. cit., pp. 234, 292 explains how the private collections of the rich, while frequently read in the early nineteenth century, often merely existed for 'show' by the early twentieth century.

55. G. F. Barwick, *The reading room of the British Museum* (1929), p. 106.

56. W. C. B. Sayers, *The children's library* (1912), p. 110 wrote that: 'It is a false economy to provide shelves, tables or chairs in a public building of cheap or inferior materials or workmanship ... The hard woods – oak, mahogany, or walnut – should be chosen for the bulk of the furniture'.

57. Pevsner, *A history of building types*, op. cit., p. 100.

58. Burgoyne, *Library construction*, op. cit., pp. 4-5.

59. Ibid., pp. 153-8. Archer delivered a paper on the issue to the annual conference of the Library Association, 1881.

60. See W. F. Poole, *Circular of information* (1881), published by the US Bureau of Education; and his *Remarks on library construction* (Chicago, 1884) being originally a paper delivered to the annual conference of the American Library Association.

61. Kelly, op. cit., p. 71.

62. E. J. Hobsbawm, *Industry and empire* (1968), p. 91.

63. E. J. Carter, Contemporary libraries ... , *Building News* (14 January 1939), p. 65.

64. A. Ellis, *Public libraries at the time of the Adams report* (1979), p. 9.

65. J. Seed, Commerce and the liberal arts: the political economy of art in Manchester, *in* J. Wolff and J. Seed (eds), *The culture of capital: art, power and the nineteenth century middle class* (1988), p. 73.

66. M. J. Daunton, Urban Britain, *in* T. R. Gourvish and A. O'Day (eds), *Later Victorian Britain 1867–1900* (1988), p. 44.

67. Champneys, op. cit., p. 5.

68. This especially occurred in northern industrial towns.

69. As did the Oldham Public Library Committee; see the Committee's *Minutes* (12 January 1881).

70. P. Thornton, *Authentic decor* (1984), p. 316. This is supported by C. Wainwright, The library as living room, in R. Myers and M. Harris, *Property of a gentleman: the formation, organisation and dispersal of the private library 1620-1920* (1991), p. 21, which argues that by the nineteenth century most library rooms in the households of the wealthy had become a reception, drawing or living room.

71. I. Webb, Bradford Wool Exchange: industrial capitalism and the popularity of the Gothic, *Victorian Studies*, 20 (1976).

72. J. Betjeman, *Ghastly good taste* (1970, first published 1933), p. 98.

73. Fulham Public Library Committee, *Minutes*, (11 November 1907).

74. H. S. Goodhart-Rendel, Victorian public buildings, *in* Ferriday, op. cit., p. 88.

75. R. H. Harper, *Victorian architectural competitions* (1983), p. xiii, explains that

this was common practice in architectural competitions for all types of public buildings.

76. G. E. Roebuck and W. B. Thorne, *A primer of library practice* (1914), p. 34.
77. Design as the product of friction between professional bodies has been examined in the context of hospital architecture by A. Forty, The modern hospital in England and France: the social and medical uses of architecture, *in* King, op. cit.
78. Used, for example, by Albert Rollit MP at the foundation stone-laying ceremony of the Islington North branch library. *Islington Daily Gazette* (30 October 1905).
79. J. S. Rowntree, *Free libraries: an address delivered in the festival concert room, York* . . . (1881).
80. Greenwood, op. cit. (1890 edn), p. 98.
81. Burgoyne, Library construction, op. cit., pp. 152-3.
82. A. Smith, *The Gilstrap Public Library, Newark: the 50th birthday of a great gift* (1933), pp. 3-4.
83. *West London Advertiser* (28 October 1988).
84. *Lincolnshire Leader and County Advertiser* (28 February 1914).
85. *Illustrated Carpenter and Builder* (22 June 1906).
86. C. Nowell, A famous public library [i.e. Norwich] from Shakespeare's time to today, *Millgate Monthly*, 15 (1919-20), p. 106.
87. *East London Advertiser* (28 April 1906).
88. Smith, Carnegie library buildings, op. cit., p. 164.
89. Crane, op. cit.
90. Roebuck and Thorne, op. cit., p. 32.
91. *Southwark and Bermondsey Recorder and South London Gazette* (29 February 1908). Letter to the editor from 'a journalist'.
92. E. Savage, *The librarian and his committee* (1942), p. 222.
93. For a discussion of the noise issue see F. M. Jones, The aesthetic of the nineteenth century industrial town, *in* H. J. Dyos (ed.), *The study of urban history* (1968), p. 172. Centrality and quietude were two aims – perhaps incompatible – of planners in Nottingham in the 1870s, as discussed in *Report on the proposed educational buildings [for Nottingham] by the borough engineer [M. O. Tarbotton]* (March 1876), Nottingham Record Office.
94. Manchester Public Libraries Committee, *Minutes* (4 April 1877).
95. Keeling, op. cit., pp. 109, 120-1.
96. Kelly, op. cit., p. 72.
97. As advocated by William Archer, *Suggestions as to public library buildings* (1881), p. 9.
98. L. Baldwin, *Northampton Public Library from its origins to 1910*, unpublished, Northampton Local Studies Library.
99. Champneys, op. cit., p. 136.
100. H. T. Hare, Some suggestions for a simple architectural plan, *Journal of the Royal Institute of British Architects*, 14 (1907), p. 344.
101. M. H. Harris, *The history of libraries in the western world* (1984), p. 6.
102. Jenkyns, op. cit., pp. 5-6.
103. Ibid., p. 15.
104. Burgoyne, Library construction, op. cit., p. 6.
105. S. A. Barnett, *The ideal city* (1894), p. 10.
106. Report on the proposed educational buildings [for Nottingham], op. cit., p. 6.

107. *Building News* (25 December 1903), p. 854.
108. Ruskin, op. cit., p. 13.
109. *Islington Daily Gazette* (5 March 1906) commenting on a new library building for the borough.
110. Cunningham, op. cit., p. 34. A middle-class visitor to the annual *converzatione* at the fictional Cooling Senior Library (described previously in this chapter) admired the furniture of the reading room because it 'improves people's minds to see these beautiful things. Poor people's lives are so bare and ugly.'
111. Goodhart-Rendell, op. cit., p. 87, writes: 'In Victorian England educated patronage of the arts was to be found only in a class of society from which mayors and corporations were not recruited.'
112. Girouard, Sweetness and light, op. cit.
113. *The Surveyor* (25 August 1905).
114. T. Greenwood, *Free public libraries* (1886), p. 163.
115. Desmond, op. cit., p. 80.
116. S. Pepper, Department store of learning, *Times Literary Supplement* (9 May 1986) deals with the American public library as a socializer coping with immigration, urbanization and national self-confidence dented by civil war. The first Carnegie library (in Braddock) was accordingly given an internal design evocative of traditional American values - it was oak panelled, comfortable and dominated by a homely marble fireplace.
117. *Woolwich Pioneer* (20 January 1905).
118. D. Cuthbertson, *Revelations of a library life 1876–1922* (1923), pp. 32-5.
119. Ball, op. cit., p. 63.
120. King, op. cit., p. 1.
121. Quoted in Gutman, op. cit., p. 13.
122. A. Lipman, Professional ideology: the architectural notion of user-requirements, *Journal of Architectural Research*, 5:2 (August 1976), p. 21. Markus, op. cit., pp. 172-85, discusses the intersection of library design and power.
123. *Nottingham Express* (8 October 1867).
124. G. C. T. Bartley, *Statistics and suggestions on the present condition of and the requirements for promoting technical education in England* (1878), p. 72.
125. E. R. N. Mathews, *Birmingham and Bristol: a few words about public libraries and museums* (1982), pp. 11-12.
126. Champneys, op. cit., p. 135.
127. *Norwood Review* (18 April 1891).
128. J. D. Mullins, *Free libraries and newsrooms* (1879), p. 6.
129. *New free library and technical institute* (c.1902), newscutting, source unknown, Leamington Spa Public Library Cuttings, Vol. 1.
130. J. Manners, *Encouraging experience of free libraries, reading and recreation rooms* (1886), p. 20.
131. *Builder* (28 June 1903).
132. Champneys, op. cit., p. 133.
133. L. S. Jast, *Whom do ye serve: an address given at the jubilee celebrations of the Gilstrap Public Library, Newark-on-Trent* (1933).
134. See also, in this regard, E. Walford, *Old and new London* (1989, facsimile edn), p. 504, and G. F. Barwick, *The reading room of the British Museum* (1929), p. 106.
135. Fourth edition, p. 385.

136. J. Bentham, *Panopticon; or inspection-house*, in J. Bowring (ed.), *The works of Jeremy Bentham*, Vol. 4 (1843), p. 39.

137. See Chapter 5 of R. Evans, *Fabrication of virtue* (1982).

138. Phrase used by F. Driver, *Power and pauperism: the workhouse system 1834–1884* (1993), p. 11.

139. *Details* (January 1901). Furniture - namely the desk - was also used in London Board Schools to control behaviour. Desks were paired and arranged in long rows to facilitate supervision by teachers and to encourage pupils to move about in an ordered and drilled fashion. R. Betts, The school desk in the nineteenth century, *History of Education Society Bulletin*, 27 (Spring 1981), p. 30.

140. *Journal of the Royal British Institute of Architects*, 14 (1907), p. 353.

141. Rowlatt, op. cit.

142. Hare, Some suggestions, op. cit., p. 344.

143. Select Committee on Public Libraries, *Report*, Q. 2956.

144. *Islington Daily Gazette* (15 September 1906) reporting a speech by M. R. Roberts (Chairman of Bradford Education Committee) to the Library Association's annual conference.

145. R. Altick, *The English common reader: a social history of the mass reading public 1800–1900* (Chicago, 1957), p. 238.

146. As explained by Driver, op. cit., p. 11.

147. Savage, The librarian, op. cit., p. 109.

148. R. E. Ellsworth, Library architecture and buildings, *Library Quarterly*, 25 (1955), p. 66.

149. B. H. Streeter, *The chained library* (1931), p. xiii.

150. Harris, op. cit., p. 94.

151. Library Association, *Yearbook* (1909), p. 62.

152. Manchester Public Libraries Committee, *Report of a visit to libraries in the United States and Canada by representatives of the Committee* (1908). The deputation's architectural findings were featured in the *American Library Municipal Journal* (13 November 1908).

153. Ibid.

154. *North Star* (11 September 1885).

155. J. L. Wheeler and A. M. Githens, *The American public library building* (New York, 1941), pp. 7–8.

156. Kelly, op. cit., p. 171.

157. Smith, Carnegie library buildings, op. cit., p. 173.

158. J. P. Briscoe, A well equipped library, *Library Assistant*, 1 (1898-9), p. 49.

159. Champneys, op. cit., p. 123.

160. The chief assessor of designs for Islington's central library congratulated all the entrants for coping so well with the 'irregular nature of the site'. Islington Borough Council, *Minutes* (23 June 1905).

161. P. Thornton, *Authentic decor: the domestic interior 1620–1920* (1984), p. 218.

162. Ibid., p. 230.

163. See Chapter 1 of Macleod, op. cit.

164. W. Morris, Art, wealth and riches, *in* his *Architecture, Industry and wealth* (1902), pp. 103-4. This lecture was first delivered in 1883.

165. Ibid., p. 102.

166. Macleod, op. cit., p. 33.

167. M. B. Adams, *As to the making of architects* (Chiswick, 1904), p. 5.

168. Ibid., pp. 39–40.
169. Ibid., p. 31.
170. A. Service, *London 1900* (1979), p. 196.
171. D. L. Russell, *Public library architecture 1880–1914*, unpublished M.A. dissertation, University College, University of London (1984).
172. J. M. Richards, *The functional tradition in early industrial buildings* (1958).
173. M. B. Adams, Public libraries, their buildings and equipment: a plea for state aid, *Library Association Record*, 7 (1905), p. 161.
174. Ibid., p. 162.
175. Ibid., p. 162.
176. Ibid., p. 173.
177. Adams, As to the making, op. cit., pp. 4–5.
178. Ibid., p. 1.
179. These were: Shepherd's Bush (1986), Edmonton (1987), St George-in-the-East (1898), Acton (1900) and North Camberwell (1903). He also designed an extension to an existing library building at Haggerston, Shoreditch (1896).
180. John Passmore Edwards speaking at the opening of the Custom House Public Library, West Ham, reported in the *Municipal Journal* (28 June 1905), p. 839.
181. Nottingham Free Public Library and Museum Committee, *Minutes*, (16 June 1875).
182. New Free Library and Technical Institute, Leamington Spa Public Library Cuttings, op. cit.
183. W. C. B. Sayers, Children's libraries as I saw them, *Library World*, 60 (1958), p. 23.
184. A. Davin, Imperialism and motherhood, *History Workshop*, 5 (Spring 1978).

11   Conclusion

1. R. Snape, *Leisure and the rise of the public library* (1995).
2. See the concluding chapter of J. Harris, *Private lives, public spirit: a social history of Britain 1870–1914* for an explanation of the rise of the idea of society.
3. For example, Comedia, *Borrowed time: the future of public libraries in the United Kingdom* (1993), p. 14, emphasizes, mistakenly, a working-class origin.
4. T. S. Eliot, *Notes towards a definition of culture* (1948), p. 21.
5. D. Spadafora, *The idea of progress in eighteenth century Britain* (1990), p. 2. However, Spadafora does note elements of historical pessimism which can be taken and applied to pre-1914 Britain: social lamentation at the shortcomings of the national economy and military might; a perception of the inevitability of the historical cycle; and the complacent decadence (evocative of a declining Rome) of Edwardian society.
6. D. MacKenzie and J. Wajcman (eds), *The social shaping of technology* (1985).
7. W. C. B. Sayers, Edward Edwards: Manchester's first librarian, *Manchester Review* (Autumn 1938), p. 323.
8. On the social origins of information technology see K. Robins and F. Webster, *The technical fix: education, computers and industry* (1989).
9. Ministry of Reconstruction, Adult Education Committee, *Third interim report: libraries and museums* (1919), Cmd 9237. L. R. McColvin, *The public library system of Great Britain* (1942).

10. T. Kelly, *A history of public libraries in Great Britain 1845-1975* (1977), pp. 257, 275.

11. Explorations of community librarianship have been made by R. Astbury, *Putting people first: some perspectives on community librarianship* (1989); J. Vincent, *An introduction to community librarianship* (1986); and W. Martin, *Community librarianship* (1989).

12. P. Summerfield and E. J. Evans, *Technical education and the state: historical and contemporary perspectives* (1990), p. 2.

13. Ibid.

14. R. Williams, *Culture and society 1780–1950* (1957), p. 111.

15. Three of the four biographical studies (a Liberal merchant, a Tory banker, a London Liberal manufacturer) in H. L. Malchow, *Gentlemen capitalists: the social and political world of the Victorian businessman* (1991), pp. 142, 255 (note 259), 339 (note 194) were members of the Public Museums and Free Libraries Association.

16. Sayers, op. cit., p. 322.

17. R. Dawkins, The culture of science, *Sunday Observer* (2 February 1992).

18. For a discussion of rights-based theories see L. Allison (ed.), *The utilitarian response: essays on the contemporary viability of utilitarian political philosophy* (1990).

19. For a discussion of the inductive and natural rights traditions see P. P. Nicholson, *The political philosophy of the British idealists: selected studies* (1990), pp. 4, 181, 190.

20. For a discussion of positive liberalism see the introduction to R. Bellamy (ed.), *Victorian liberalism* (1990).

21. Quoted in D. King, *Privatisation and public libraries* (1989), p. 27.

INDEX